33

# EDWARD ELGAR
## THE WINDFLOWER LETTERS

# EDWARD ELGAR
## The Windflower Letters

*Correspondence with
Alice Caroline Stuart Wortley
and her Family*

BY
JERROLD NORTHROP MOORE

CLARENDON PRESS · OXFORD
1989

*Oxford University Press, Walton Street, Oxford OX2 6DP*
*Oxford New York Toronto*
*Delhi Bombay Calcutta Madras Karachi*
*Petaling Jaya Singapore Hong Kong Tokyo*
*Nairobi Dar es Salaam Cape Town*
*Melbourne Auckland*
*and associated companies in*
*Berlin Ibadan*

*Oxford is a trade mark of Oxford University Press*

*Published in the United States*
*by Oxford University Press, New York*

*British Library Cataloguing in Publication Data*
*Elgar, Edward 1851–1934*
*Edward Elgar, The windflower letters:*
*correspondence with Alice Caroline Stuart*
*Wortley and her family*
*1. English music. Elgar, Edward.*
*Correspondence, diaries, etc.*
*I. Title. II. Stuart Wortley, Alice.*
*Caroline. III. Moore, Jerrold Northrop.*
*780'.92'4*
*ISBN 0–19–315473–0*

*Library of Congress Cataloging in Publication Data*

*Elgar, Edward, 1857–1934.*
*The Windflower letters.*
*Bibliography: Includes index.*
*1. Elgar, Edward, 1857–1934—Correspondence.*
*2. Wortley, Alice Caroline Stuart—Correspondence.*
*3. Composers—England—Correspondence.*
*I. Wortley, Alice Caroline Stuart. II. Moore, Jerrold Northrop.*
*III. Title. IV. Title: Windflower letters.*
*ML410.E41A4 1989 780'.92'4 [B] 88–16168*
*ISBN 0–19–315473–0*

*Printed in Great Britain*
*at the University Printing House, Oxford*
*by David Stanford*
*Printer to the University*

FOR PAUL AND ANGELA

# ACKNOWLEDGEMENTS

M Y gratitude goes first to Charles Stuart of Wortley's grandchildren, Mary Elizabeth Wilkey and Robert Cecil. Their memories generously shared with me, and the photographs they have unearthed, have alone made it possible to enter again in imagination the household at 7 Cheyne Walk. From the Millais side I wish to thank my old friend Geoffroy Millais for his help with family recollections and for consulting his father, Sir Ralph Millais Bt., on my behalf.

Elgar letters are printed by permission of the Elgar Will Trust, and Stuart Wortley letters by permission of the family. For access to letters and manuscripts now at the Elgar Birthplace Museum I wish to thank the Birthplace Trustees and the Curator. For access to letters in the Hereford and Worcester County Record Office I thank the County Archivist and the kindness of helpful staff. Quotations from books appear by permission of the publishers.

It is a pleasure to record special thanks to Professor Brian Trowell, R. G. Emblem, Jonathan Cadman, Martin Haines, John Allison, Pippa Thynne, Robert Anderson, James and Christopher Bennett; and especially to Bruce Phillips and David Blackwell for all their help in bringing to birth this latest volume in the Oxford edition of Elgar Letters.

Grateful thanks for illustrations are due to the Elgar Foundation (Plates I, IX, Figure 2), Mrs Wilkey (Plates II, XIa, XIIa), Sir Ralph Millais Bt. and the Courtauld Institute (Plate III), Robert Cecil (Plates IV, V, VIII, X, XIb, Figure 1), Hereford and Worcester County Record Office (Figure 3). The other plates are taken from the writer's collection.

# PRINTED SOURCES

Boult, Sir Adrian, *My Own Trumpet* (Hamilton, 1973).

Burke's *Peerage and Baronetage* (Burke's Peerage, 1970).

Coward, Henry, *Round the World on Wings of Song* (Sheffield: J. W. Northend, Ltd., 2nd edn., 1933).

Hazelton, George C., Jr., and J. Harry Benrimo, *The Yellow Jacket: A Chinese Play Done in a Chinese Manner*, with an Introduction by Brander Matthews (Indianapolis, USA: Bobbs-Merrill, 1913).

Lehmann, Rudolph C., *Memories of Half a Century* (London, 1908).

Mackenzie, Compton, *My Record of Music* (Hutchinson, 1955).

Maine, Basil, *Elgar: His Life and Works* (Bell, 2 vols., 1933).

Millais, J. G., *The Life and Letters of Sir John Everett Millais* (Methuen, 2 vols., 1899).

Moore, Jerrold Northrop, *Edward Elgar: A Creative Life* (OUP, 1984).

—— *Elgar and his Publishers: Letters of a Creative Life* (OUP, 2 vols., 1987).

—— *Elgar on Record: The Composer and the Gramophone* (OUP, 1974).

Nowell-Smith, Simon, ed., *Edwardian England 1901–1914* (OUP, 1964).

Parkin, Michael, *Wendela Boreel* (Parkin Gallery, 1980).

Reed, W. H., *Elgar as I Knew Him* (Gollancz, 1936).

Sassoon, Siegfried, *Diaries 1920–1922, 1923–25* (Faber, 1981 and 1985).

Stuart of Wortley, Charles Beilby, and Caroline Grosvenor, *The First Lady Wharncliffe and her Family (1779–1856)*, with a Prefatory Memoir by John Buchan (Heinemann, 2 vols., 1927).

Young, Percy M., *Elgar, O. M.* (2nd edn., White Lion, 1973).

# CONTENTS

# LIST OF PLATES

*(between pp. 208 and 209)*

# THE EDITION

THE place of origin and date are printed at the head of each letter, even though occasionally they may have been written elsewhere in the manuscript.

Elgar and his wife often underlined for emphasis. A single underline is denoted by italics; double underlining is represented by small capitals.

Elgar's use of quotation marks was not always consistent. For this reason we have used single quotation marks for all quotations within letters, and double marks only to signify quotation within quotation.

There remain certain difficulties in reducing Elgar's exuberant penmanship to type. Interlineations and marginalia which he added as afterthoughts have been incorporated parenthetically in the text where possible—as they would have been if a letter had been revised before sending. When sense or emphasis demands it, the typography of this book has been made to approximate the physical placing of key words and phrases in the manuscripts.

Elgar often used the end of a line to suggest punctuation, and in his large writing line-endings came often to hand. This feature cannot be reproduced in the longer lines of printing, and so it has been necessary to add a certain amount of punctuation in square brackets.

His paragraphing was idiosyncratic. A new paragraph can be indicated by the very slightest of indentations, a tiny interlinear spacing, or even by a line begun proud of the rest. There is some latitude for editorial judgement here, and all I claim is that my solutions have been carefully considered.

To set off a new subject from preceding paragraphs, Elgar sometimes drew a short line more or less horizontally to the left between paragraphs. This has been indicated in the printed text by an extra half-line spacing.

# A NOTE ON THE DESTRUCTION
# OF LETTERS

THE Elgar–Stuart Wortley letters survive as a one-sided correspondence. Many of Elgar's letters were kept—probably the majority of them. On the Stuart Wortley side, the story is different. After the opening exchanges, nearly all of the letters written by all three Stuart Wortleys—father, mother, and daughter—have disappeared. Although the Elgars were generally careful savers of the letters they received, amongst the thousands of such letters preserved in Worcester those from the Stuart Wortleys number hardly a dozen.

Clearly some systematic destruction has taken place. No one now living can shed any light on it. One of Elgar's letters (22 March 1911) shows that he routinely destroyed some of Alice Stuart Wortley's communications as soon as they were opened and read. But the same letter makes equally clear that other of her letters were not so destroyed. What has happened to those? to the letters she addressed to Alice Elgar? to letters from Charles Stuart Wortley (of which there must have been quite a number)? to all the letters Clare wrote to the Elgars over years and years?

Who was the destroyer? Lady Elgar is an unlikely candidate. Her diaries record warm meetings with the Stuart Wortleys throughout the last fifteen years of her life. She was the soul of generosity when it came to observing her husband's friendships with women outside the family. Moreover, half the missing letters were written after her death.

In those later years would Elgar himself have had a motive for such wholesale destruction? Would their daughter Carice? Here things might not seem so clear. Yet Carice's filial piety was great, as I know from personal experience, and her sentiments were on the side of preservation.

There is the possibility that the Stuart Wortley letters were returned to the family by Carice after her father's death in 1934. (This happened with the letters of several correspondents who survived Elgar.) In that case Alice Stuart Wortley or Clare could have destroyed them. Such a course would seem to run counter to the mother's 'sacred request' that Elgar's side of the correspondence be given to the city of Worcester (see below, p. 254).

Yet it appears that Clare Stuart Wortley destroyed both her parents' diaries after using them to make her own notes on the Elgar letters: for the diaries were not found among her effects by her executors.[1] And her mother's 'sacred request' did not cover her own letters addressed to Elgar. Clare's letters to the Elgars are likewise largely missing. That fact makes her the most

[1] Information from Robert Cecil, whose mother and brother were Clare Stuart Wortley's executors.

likely destroyer among the Stuart Wortleys. Yet she may not have been the only suppressor.

With the Elgar letters and manuscripts, Alice Stuart Wortley left her portrait painted by her father, Sir John Everett Millais (see Plate III). The portrait was duly conveyed to Worcester: but if it ever hung in the Elgar Birthplace Museum (where many of the manuscripts are), it was not for long. All the rooms in the Birthplace are small, the portrait is large, and it may well have proved impossible to hang it there with satisfaction. For some years in the 1940s it hung in Carice's own house close by; then a move consigned it to storage, and late in her life she thankfully returned it to the Millais family. (A small watercolour copy, painted by Sir Philip Burne-Jones, remains at the Birthplace.)

Some letters from the Elgar side of the Stuart Wortley correspondence have also vanished—more particularly early ones. Some of these may simply have fallen victim to the chances that overtake private letters through time— misplacement and casual disposal. Later on, Alice Stuart Wortley saved even the smallest scraps—down to the dried flowers Elgar sent in some letters: fragments of those ancient blooms still scatter from certain envelopes at the Birthplace when the letters sharing the envelopes are pulled out for reading.

Yet the wholesale destruction of the Stuart Wortley letters raises the possibility that there was once distinctly more on the Elgar side as well. After the 'Windflower' name was invented, some of his letters reverted to 'My dear Alice', suggesting that they were meant for more general sight. Many intimate 'Windflower' letters have indeed survived: but perhaps others more intimate still have not. From one box of stationery he purchased in 1915 to use exclusively for her, and used up in eighteen months, no more than six letters survive (see pp. 143–4).

In some of the letters which were saved, short passages have been cut away, scored over, or eradicated. (Sometimes this was demonstrably the work of the recipient—as when a letter fragment with the upper half missing is annotated with the date in her hand. Other mutilations may have been done by Clare.) The eradications have been restored wherever possible, for this edition, with the help of ultra-violet light. Some restored passages criticize a contemporary. Others contain expressions of attachment which, read three quarters of a century later, seem mostly innocuous.

The motive for destruction, where there was a motive, was to preserve secrets. The linking text which I have provided does not seek to adjudicate the precise degree of intimacy attained. There is no way to know this. As that very experienced Elgar scholar Percy Young has written to me: 'What one can never do is what many contemporary biographers try to do, to give finality to everything.'

One must be cautious about reading letters written all those years ago with the assumptions of our own day. All the participants in this two-, three-, four-, five-, or six-sided relationship were devoted members of their respective families. They shared that outlook with the society on whom their own positions in life ultimately depended. At the top of the Edwardian tree may have been a gamesome aristocracy. But the world of nocturnal country-house derring-do is not the world of these letters, for all their affection and occasional extravagance.

The backgrounds of the four people at the centre of this story spread right across the middle class. There was Elgar, whose father had been a tradesman housing his family in rooms over his music shop—but going as a piano-tuner into many 'good' houses in Worcester and the surrounding country, some-times taking his little son with him; and Elgar's mother had constantly encouraged her children to admire ability and strive for it. Alice Stuart Wortley's forebears were considerably more comfortable than the Elgars, but their real rise had come only with the spectacular success of her father, the painter Millais (a rise in many ways comparable to Elgar's own a generation later). Alice Elgar's family history was similar, except that her father's rise had come through the Army, and the family had thereupon become country gentry. Charles Stuart Wortley's family had so distinguished themselves in the affairs of the nation that they moved with the aristocracy: yet his was a cadet branch of his family, where individual success counted heavily. Taken together, the four backgrounds tell much about upward mobility in the later nineteenth century. These were just the people to become great destroyers, as well as great savers, of private letters.

Finally one must bear in mind Elgar's exceptional skill at self-expression of all sorts, especially on paper. Here are some of the most intimate and deeply felt of all his letters. Were they not, in those respects, the partial equivalents of his music? There is in the best of them, as in some other of Elgar's choicest letters, fulfilment in the very expression they achieve. Such expression, after all, defines the creative individuality. In one of his most affectionate letters to Alice Stuart Wortley he wrote: 'Well, I have put it all in my music & also much more that has never happened.'

# THE WINDFLOWER LETTERS

How often have I seen him, on his return, after tea, fling the blue 'Order of the Day' House of Commons papers on to a sitting-room table, & go straight to the piano, to seize a last half-hour before dressing to dine out. It was a standing grievance with me (undutiful daughter!) that he did this instead of telling us about the day's political excitements, such as 'What Ministers had said'. Wherefore he, being both peace-loving & shrewd, used to break into one of the big Wagner scenes he knew I adored—the Verwandlungs scene from Parsifal, or the Prelude to the third act of Tristan; for he knew that I should fall silent, enraptured & grateful.[1]

So wrote Charles Stuart Wortley's younger daughter Clare of the public man whose private love of music brought him—and his wife—the friendship of his country's greatest composer. Up to now the story of Stuart Wortley and his second wife Alice Caroline has survived in fragments—in a brief memoir by his niece's husband, the novelist John Buchan,[2] in notes written by his daughter Clare to accompany the Elgar letters and manuscripts given by the family to the Elgar Birthplace, and in the memories of surviving members of the family who have kindly shared them with me.

Charles Beilby Stuart Wortley (1851–1926) was born in his grandfather's house near York. His father, the Rt. Hon. James Stuart Wortley, QC, MP, Privy Councillor, and Solicitor General (1856–7), was expected to become Speaker of the House of Commons, until a crippling riding accident forced his retirement. The family then moved south to Sheen in Surrey, where his five daughters and two sons grew up in much reduced circumstances.

The elder son, Archibald John, studied painting with Sir John Everett Millais, and became a renowned amateur artist. For the younger son Charles, music was the centre of everything. John Buchan wrote:

They were an exceptionally devoted family, and their interests were wide and varied. Music was one of them, and Charles . . . used to be found in the music shop in Richmond, perched on a high stool which did not permit his small legs to touch the ground, trying over the proprietor's stock of music. As a child he was curiously gentle and self-contained, but occasionally, under the goading of his elder brother, he would make solemn but effective reprisals, which invariably succeeded because of their unexpectedness.

Preparatory school in Wimbledon, then Rugby and Balliol College, Oxford, comprised Charles Stuart Wortley's education. He became a member of the Inner Temple, and was called to the Bar in 1876, going on the North Eastern Circuit. Buchan wrote:

He made himself a sound lawyer, and his manner in court—slow, urbane, perfectly self-collected—was admirably suited for heavy cases. The most notable

---

[1] MS reminiscence by Clare Stuart Wortley (Elgar Birthplace parcel 584(lxii) ). All quotations from Clare are taken from manuscripts now at the Elgar Birthplace unless otherwise specified.
[2] 'Charles Beilby Stuart Wortley', written as a foreword to *The First Lady Wharncliffe and Her Family (1779–1856)*, written by her grandchildren: Caroline Grosvenor and the late Charles Beilby, Lord Stuart of Wortley (Heinemann, 1927), vol. i, pp. ix–xx. The family have always preferred their double surname to appear without hyphen.

of his early cases was the trial of Charles Peace, the murderer, in which he held a junior brief.

During these years of waiting he led the pleasant life of the well-born young man of many aptitudes and tastes. He had a deep love of landscape and places, especially those associated with the wide ramifications of his family. Since he had in him the blood of many famous English and Scottish Houses, and could count among his ancestors people so diverse as the Bluidy Mackenzie, Lady Mary Wortley Montagu, and Lord Bute, the Prime Minister, he had a large field for his genealogical interests. With his eldest sister, Mary, afterwards Countess of Lovelace, he made expeditions into Scotland, moving leisurely in the old manner from one country house to another. . . . In England he spent many happy days at Wortley, Muncaster, Escrick, Clouds, Wildernesse and Moor Park. His chief sport was shooting, and, being a good man on the hill, he was an ardent stalker. . . .

Wherever he was, and whatever he was doing, music must have its place. Lady George Hamilton remembers being at a young party at Wortley for amateur theatricals. 'I was dressed early for the play, and, hearing a lovely Chopin mazurka being beautifully rendered behind a screen, I peeped round, and found to my amazement that the performer was Charlie, dressed as a Red Indian chief, feathers, tomahawk and all.'

At the other end of his life, his granddaughter recalls, he used always to sit down to the Bach *Chromatic Fantasy and Fugue* whenever he was kept waiting for his bath. So invariable was this custom that the music became known in his household as 'the bath tune'.

In 1880 Stuart Wortley became Conservative MP for Sheffield (then undivided; on the redistribution of seats in 1885 he was returned for the Hallam Division—a seat he held for more than thirty years, until he was raised to the Peerage). Also in 1880 he married Beatrice Trollope, a niece of the novelist. 'She was', wrote Buchan, 'a beautiful little creature, with something Italian in air and colouring, and she had the voice of an angel.' They were deeply in love, but she died a few days after the birth of their daughter Beatrice (and also like her mother called 'Bice') in 1881. The effect upon Charles, despite the survival of the baby, was devastating. Buchan wrote:

Her loss made a changed man of him. Something in him perished with his wife's death, something which he never quite recovered. . . . He did his work in the world bravely and sincerely, but that consuming ardour for success, which carries a man through the *longueurs* of a career, was never his.

Something was due also to his passion for music. A man to succeed cannot owe allegiance to too many gods, and his allegiance to music was most constant and devout. It gave him a secret world into which too easily he could retire and be happy with his dreams. . . . Music was beyond doubt the greatest thing in the world to him, after his family affections. All his life he would read a score of music as other people would read a newspaper. Every day, while he dressed, he had a score beside him.

He even became a published composer when Chappell brought out a graceful *Minuet* of his. Many years later, after Stuart Wortley's death, Elgar paid a small tribute to that music when he echoed distinctly its formula of melodic sequence in his own *Minuet*, in the same key of G major, written in 1928 for a play about Beau Brummel: the hero therein was pictured as a man ready to sacrifice everything he possessed to save a lady's honour. Stuart Wortley's *Minuet* was dedicated 'To my Wife'.

That was his second wife, Alice Sophia Caroline Millais (1862–1936), whom he married in 1886. 'Carrie' (as she was known to her family and early friends) was the third daughter of Sir John Everett Millais, one of the original Pre-Raphaelites, later the first artist ever raised to the Baronetcy, and in the last year of his life President of the Royal Academy. Millais was a delightful man, and also deeply musical: he had enjoyed lasting friendships with Sir Charles and Lady Hallé, Joachim, Piatti, the Henschels, Anton Rubinstein, and Arthur Sullivan amongst many others. There was always a piano either in his studio or next door, and Carrie was asked to play it by the hour while her father painted: she would have needed a large repertoire instantly to hand. Again in the evening, she recalled:

> ... he would listen to Scarlatti, Bach, Beethoven, or, according to his mood, Chopin, Schumann, Grieg, Brahms, etc., seeing and enjoying beauty in the individuality of each.
>
> In later days he would listen to *Parsifal, The Meistersinger, Tristan, The Ring,* or at least as much of them as my husband could sketch on the piano for him. He would listen to all he could hear or be told of the Bayreuth world with that keen interest, freshness, and appreciation which belonged to a unique personality.[3]

The fond father recorded his musical affection for Carrie in doggerel verses sent in 1881 to the Lehmann family who were entertaining her in Scotland, to show how much he missed her:

> So send me my bairnie
> My bonnie ane Carrie
> To gratifee my lugues        (lugs)
> Wi' Rubinstein and Auld Lang Syne
> And Bach's immortal fugues.

And so on for fifty lines and more.[4]

Lady Millais was the former Euphemia Gray, who had emerged from a disastrous first marriage to Ruskin emotionally scarred. Her subsequent happiness with Millais found witness in their eight children. Yet Victorian morality did not forgive the annulment of her first marriage: Lady Millais was many times prevented from accompanying her husband in his public appearances, her place taken by one of their daughters. In later life she was said to have become hard and somewhat cynical, looking out on the fashionable Kensington scene through the windows of the overwhelming mansion in which her husband's success had finally housed them. It was a contrast which could not fail to mark an impressionable daughter.

Carrie found an almost complete expression in music. Its deepest emotions were everywhere acceptable because they avoided the specific definitions needed for painting and literature. She developed a great affinity for Schumann: it was as if his *Innigkeit* matched her own. She had the most extraordinarily fine and sensitive touch, as her stepdaughter Bice recalled. And Bice's daughter recalls her Granny's little, plump hands—hands trained in the Clara Schumann tradition to remain on the keyboard, never striking from above but able to caress the keys even in fleet passages.

---

[3] Quoted in J. G. Millais, *The Life and Letters of Sir John Everett Millais* (Methuen, 1899), vol. ii, p. 425.

[4] Quoted in Rudolph C. Lehmann, *Memories of Half a Century* (London, 1908), pp. 261–2.

(Both Carrie's own daughter Clare and her step-granddaughter were to study the piano with Clara Schumann's pupil Mathilde Verne.)

Music was probably her chief bond with her husband. Her special vehicles were the Schumann and Grieg Concertos, with Charles Stuart Wortley taking the orchestral part at the second of the two grand pianos that graced the drawing-room of their Norman Shaw house in Cheyne Walk, Chelsea. Alternatively, husband and wife might play on the pair of uprights placed on either side of the schoolroom fireplace at the top of the house.

Carrie's superlative touch at the piano was inherited by her only child Clare (1889–1945). Clare lacked her mother's virtuosity but inherited her father's deep musicality: one of her abilities was effortless transposition of any music at sight (often employed to accompany the Lieder singing of her half-sister). Mother and daughter were very close, and in later years Clare provided invaluable manuscript notes on her parents' friendship with the Elgars. Her knowledge and insights, thus recorded, have much enriched the pages that follow.

If Carrie was an ideal mother to her own daughter, she was less than that to her step-daughter Bice. The difficult position of a second wife was not lessened by what Stuart Wortley's grandson describes as his grandfather's 'almost mawkish' cult for the memory of his first wife. This could hardly fail to make Carrie feel (in the words of her step-granddaughter) 'that she was always second best'. And when the husband focused his affection for his first wife's memory on the daughter who shared her name and nickname, it brought the second wife to jealousy. To Bice, Carrie appeared as 'an extremely jealous woman and bad-tempered—very much a step-mother'.

Those traits were seemingly confined to the step-mother's role. There is no trace of neurotic behaviour anywhere in the long record of her relations with Edward, Alice, and Carice Elgar. And her step-grandchildren have some warm and happy memories: only their Granny was slightly remote in her beautiful house.

Whenever Bice's children visited 7 Cheyne Walk, it seemed that their Granny was always practising, practising behind closed doors—remote, unapproachable, off limits. Yet the public results were meagre. 'She had a neurotic dislike of playing before people, even for friends,' her step-grandson recalls. She shared her father's social ambitions, and also his liking for the company of musicians: besides Elgar, Paderewski especially was her frequent guest. But her own playing remained private—to be shared with her husband, occasionally with her family, rarely with friends: the chief exception was Edward Elgar. Her nephew Ralph (who lived at Cheyne Walk in 1926–7) recalls her playing two pianos with Elgar on several occasions.

The house was irreproachable in every detail. Each table, chair, book, and even the daily newspaper had its appointed place—kept there by two excellent house parlour-maids dubbed by Charles Stuart Wortley 'the Blest Pair of Sirens'. At the centre of the household was a cook of genius, Mrs Alsop, still recalled with vivid affection by the grandchildren. And there was the rusty-black Aberdeen terrier Nigger. Once when master and mistress went on holiday he boarded with neighbours, who were welcoming enough to let him sleep on their beds: but when master and mistress returned, Nigger repaid the neighbourly hospitality by barking at his holiday hosts. He finds his place in this history as the precursor of all Elgar's own Aberdeens.

The mistress at Cheyne Walk decreed that her windows be heavily curtained, with blinds drawn well down against too much daylight. When holidays came she had everything dust-sheeted, even to the piano legs of the drawing-room grands encased in what Charles Stuart Wortley called 'numbered trousers'. His granddaughter recalls her grandfather's frequent visits to her family's home in Kent—always keenly relished by the children (see Plate XI*b*): but he came alone. Their Granny accompanied him only once—and the anticipatory fuss preceding that visitation was never to be forgotten.

For all their shared love of music and of their own daughter, Carrie and Charles Stuart Wortley each kept a certain loneliness of spirit. As Charles rose in the nation's councils—principal delegate to international conferences, Ecclesiastical Commissioner and committee man for many business and charitable interests, Privy Councillor, and a leading Member of the House of Commons until his elevation to the Peerage in 1917—his being could seem to find its own completeness. Buchan wrote of the man he knew from 1906:

> I do not think I have ever met a man so wholly without personal vanity. He had his own clear-cut beliefs, but he never dogmatised or oraculated; though a distinguished man of affairs, he had no pose of superiority; in Dr. Johnson's phrase, he laid his mind honestly to his companion's, whoever that companion might be.
>
> This was partly due, I think, to his innate gentleness and good breeding; partly to the fact that he had been the friend of many great men and tried himself always by the highest standards. But it was due also to his possession of the secret world [of music] . . .
>
> His sane, central mind was always close to realities, and this attitude was notable in both politics and business. But his temper was in the best sense conservative. History dwelt with him almost like a living memory, and in every fibre of his being he felt his kinship with the past. He showed his Scots descent in his peculiar tenderness for old ways and lost causes. For seventy years he lived in a world which was changing faster than it had ever changed before. He saw the confidences of his youth shaken, new manners installed, new ideas in his own class, and new classes arising of which his childhood had never heard. He did not grumble at change, but he was jealous that the memory of the older world should not be lost. . . .
>
> One felt secure with him, secure in the sanity of his judgment and in the unfailing warmth of his heart.

His second wife of all people must have valued that security. She was undoubtedly a woman who needed it. Yet she also found a special bond in a 'little circle of constant friends' (as her daughter described them) who foregathered at each other's houses. Charles Stuart Wortley was of the party when he could be present. But Carrie's inner circle at the turn of the century consisted of Mina, Lady Charles Beresford (d. 1922), whose husband was a senior Admiral in the British Navy; (Sir) Claude Phillips (1846–1924), first Keeper of the Wallace Collection and art critic of *The Daily Telegraph*; and 'last but not least' Frank Schuster (1852–1927). Schuster's wealth came from the German-Jewish banking family of which he was a member. His greatest interest was in helping artists and gaining their friendships. His young friend Siegfried Sassoon wrote: 'He loved and longed to assist in the creation of music . . . He was something more than a *patron* of music, because he loved music as much as it is humanly possible to do.'[5]

[5] Sassoon, *Diaries 1920–1922* (Faber, 1981), pp. 293–4.

Clare Stuart Wortley recalled their group:

They did not meet unduly often, and none of them was exactly the centre of the circle. Art itself was the centre, I think, in all its different manifestations . . .

Their procedure was to go sometimes together, but more often separately, to concerts, theatres, picture shows, & then to meet afterwards at luncheon or dinner (when permitted by larger engagements, of which they all had plenty). Then in a flood of happy enthusiasm from Frank, delicate disparagement or temperate approval from Claude, ruthless satire or honest commendation from Mina, & very penetrating, & very unchanging & unyielding, praise or dislike from my mother, 'the latest' would be discussed and 'placed'.

My own position, if present at these meals[,] was that of a sort of niece, not really wanted, but tolerated out of kindness by Frank & Claude, & out of grim civility by Mina who loathed 'girls'. They talked freely without regard to me (but never unsuitably, bless them) & I listened contentedly & happily, & grew very fond of them all, even Mina too! The one thing my adolescent mind realised— and liked—was that their common ground was a superlative mental honesty in their search for the really valuable & life-giving (because life-having) aspects of art.

They never for one instant 'posed', or advanced an insincere opinion as a sincere one; though Claude sometimes enjoyed tentatively advancing one so wholly outrageous as to deceive no one, & did it I think for the pleasure of spurring the rest to cry 'Oh *No!* Claude!'

Another echo of this intimate talk of art and artists emerges in an undated letter from Schuster, written probably in 1901—perhaps after Henry Wood's afternoon performance of the *'Enigma' Variations* at Queen's Hall on 4 May, and addressed almost certainly to one of the Stuart Wortleys:

22, Old Queen Street, Westminster.
[n.d.]

Dear friend

I couldn't bear your going away without my bidding you Goodbye *properly*. I wanted so to tell you that I was completely *bowled over* by the 'Variations' in the afternoon—now that I know them *so* well I unhesitatingly place them amongst the *masterpieces* of the Arrht & I want you to get them [in piano score] (if you haven't got them) & let them live near you. Of course they're not piano music. This man is *truly* a great man, & I think one can't repeat it often enough,—for we have been so *starved* in poor England for so long!—

Bless you.

> Yours devotedly
> Frank[6]

---

[6] MS at the Elgar Birthplace with the Stuart Wortley material (parcel 584(ii)). Clare found a piano copy of the *Variations* after her mother's death: 'used & worn to rags', as she wrote to Carice Elgar Blake on 24 April 1936: 'she played *them* for years.' (Elgar Birthplace parcel 584(ix)).

Schuster had been the first of the group to make acquaintance with Elgar's music—and then with the man himself in 1899. That was the year the *Variations* had been produced, and Elgar nationally recognized as an important composer.


# 1902

On 15 March Schuster wrote to congratulate Elgar on plans to perform his Catholic masterpiece *The Dream of Gerontius* at the Three Choirs Festival (Worcester Cathedral) in September, and at the Sheffield Festival in October:

> It seems too good to be true, especially as before leaving England at the New Year I had long talks with [Lord] *Beauchamp* about Worcester, & with *Stuart-Wortley* about Sheffield (for which he is member) and neither seemed very hopeful at the time.—If it be true you are indeed avenged for the scurvy treatment hitherto meted out to your great work . . .[1]

After a bad première (through lack of rehearsal) in October 1900, *Gerontius* had languished. Since then it had received only a partial performance in Worcester and one performance at Düsseldorf, with a second there in May 1902.

In the autumn the two English Festival performances duly took place. In fact at Sheffield on 2 October they had a double dose of Elgar: *Gerontius* in the morning, and in the afternoon the première of the *Coronation Ode*. Both were conducted by their composer, who thus became a central Festival personality.

He was forty-five—by turns jocular, intense, insecure. The critic Ernest Newman was to recall a dinner a few months earlier 'at which Mrs Elgar tactfully steered the conversation away from the topic of suicide that had suddenly arisen; she whispered to me that Edward was always talking of making an end of himself'.[2] His wife was nearly nine years his senior, and far more conventionally sophisticated: he depended upon her as a son upon his mother. Few even of his closest friends knew that she was not his first love. Far in the past lay a deep attachment to a girl of his own age who had broken their engagement.

Stuart Wortley and his wife were both Patrons of the Sheffield Festival, together with his cousin the 2nd Earl of Wharncliffe and the Countess. The Patrons' list also included a prominent Catholic element in Lord and Lady Edmund Talbot: he was the younger brother of the 15th Duke of Norfolk, who was President of the Festival. All were friends of the Stuart Wortleys—Lord Edmund a very old friend. All of them met the Elgars during the three days of the Sheffield Festival. Schuster was there too. They all attended the big private dinner which wound up the Festival on the concluding night, and lamentation was loud and general that *Gerontius* had not yet been heard in London.

London saw the Elgars in November, when they came up from their home in Malvern for a series of concerts by the Duke of Saxe-Meiningen's celebrated orchestra under the conductorship of the Brahms disciple Fritz Steinbach. The

---

[1] Hereford and Worcester County Record Office [hereafter designated HWRO] 705:445:6900.
[2] *The Sunday Times*, 30 Oct. 1955.

programmes were mostly of German music: the sole English work was the *'Enigma'*
*Variations*. The Meiningen Orchestra Concerts drew the whole of London musical
society. It was just the sort of affair to galvanize the Schuster–Stuart Wortley group.

Frank Schuster played host to the Elgars for the first time at his London house.
After the *Variations* performance on 20 November he gave a celebratory dinner. The
guests included several notables and future friends of the Elgars: Lady Maud
Warrender (a daughter of Lord Shaftesbury and a fine contralto singer), Lady Lewis
(wife of an eminent solicitor and sister of Marie Joshua, a close friend of the Elgars in
years to come), John S. Sargent, the Hon. Alec Yorke (a member of the Royal
Household), and the Stuart Wortleys.

Three days later the Elgars and Claude Phillips went to Sunday lunch with the
Stuart Wortleys in Cheyne Walk. Alice Elgar's diary recorded a 'most delightful
time'. A first exchange of letters right afterwards reflected some of the subjects over
which the conversation ranged that day: golf and cooking, Elgar's work-in-progress
on *The Apostles* (of which he had played sketches at Schuster's), his summer retreat at
Birchwood, Alice Elgar's translations from German literature, the *Coronation Ode*
and its similarity in one section to Elgar's first published partsong, 'My love dwelt in a
northern land'.

As the majority of later letters from the Stuart Wortleys were not to survive, it is
especially good to have these opening exchanges between Elgar and Alice Stuart
Wortley (who from the start used her first Christian name to him, and not the more
intimate 'Carrie'). These early letters, written after hardly two months' acquaintance,
show less than intimacy of course—yet something like a dawning recognition. Each of
the writers was married—happily on the whole—to a partner about a decade older
and more secure. Each was the younger, nervous, perhaps neurotic partner in the
marriage. So if they did not complement each other as their spouses complemented
them, they might recognize a bond in similar hopes, fears, and dreams.

Craeg Lea, Wells Road, Malvern.
Nov 26 02

Dear Mrs. Stuart Wortley:

Here is the only Copy I possess of my pt-song ['My love dwelt in a
northern land'] & it has been *used* & marked, but you must forgive that
please: I like this northern-sounding thing (you will see the cadence of
'Daughter of Ancient Kings' in it) more than many of my trials.

We are now home & very quiet & working & eating undisguised rice with
relish & proper feeling: my work goes on rapidly & I played a foursome this
p.m.

My kindest regards to Mr.Stuart Wortley & to you—to your daughter my
respectful homage

> Believe me
> Yours sincerely
> Edward Elgar:

P.S. My wife is sending for a copy of the translation of 'Ritter Gluck' & it
shall follow soon.[3]

                        [3] Elgar Birthplace parcel 583(xxx).

7, Cheyne Walk, Chelsea. S.W.
Nov 30. 1902.
Dear Mr.Elgar,

How very kind of you to remember me, & send me the part-song. How much I value it & your kind letter is difficult for me to convey to you, but they have already joined my most cherished possessions where they will ever be my pride, & I fear the envy of my friends—

I have just come in from the Queen's Hall where we heard 'Cockaigne' [.] It is excitingly interesting [—] full to overflowing of everything one must hear again soon—  I was truly very delighted—  Where oh where do you draw all this from? With yr. water at the wonderful cottage! Rather I believe from worlds above than worlds below!—  But I think of you as one of the happy happy ones to be so possessed.

Give my love to dear Mrs.Elgar & tell her how much I shall treasure any book she sends me, & also what a real pleasure it was to see you both here & our little house so honoured—a pleasure you must please give us again—
  Till then

> Believe me
> Yrs. very sincerely & gratefully
> Alice Stuart Wortley.[4]

A week before Christmas Elgar wrote out the words and music of Gerontius's 'Novissima hora est' and sent it to Cheyne Walk—as if in recognition of some new horizon.[5]

# 1903

During the winter several schemes emerged for a London performance of *Gerontius*. The Hallé Society of Manchester proposed it for Queen's Hall. Then a 'British Musical Festival' was organizing, with a large committee and vague plans for giving *Gerontius* a first London hearing amongst a variety of indigenous music. Seeing Charles Stuart Wortley's name on the committee, Elgar made occasion to have his say about some of his contemporaries.

Craeg Lea, Wells Road, Malvern.
March 10: 1903
*Private*

Dear Mr. Stuart-Wortley:

I was very glad to see your name on the Committee as I feel sure it

[4] Elgar Birthplace parcel 584(iiiL). Such few Stuart Wortley letters as survive seem to have escaped destruction because of their placement in files with miscellaneous headings, and not with the main Stuart Wortley file.

[5] Dated 17 December 1902 (in possession of Robert Cecil).

guarantees that something will be done for Music & not for the usual Clique.

I strongly recommend     Granville Bantock.
                         Percy Pitt.

both these men should be fairly represented.

Amongst the others       W.H.Bell.

Persons like             Charles Wood
                         Arthur Somervell

have been assiduously 'pushed' by their influential friends—have *always* failed in any work except the smallest, invertebrate kind of stuff, and,—as they are not likely to interfere with the imaginary artistic position of their backers—are continually put in to festivals &c. to the exclusion of better men. I don't say that everything written by the first above named three is a masterpiece—but they are strong, individual men. In the London press they are usually treated coldly; but, where music is allowed to make its way naturally you will find that Bantock's name occurs more frequently in programmes—good ones—than—for instance—Stanford's, & this without the influence always working in a quaint way for the latter. [*Elgar has lightly pencilled out the words from 'for instance' onward, and has substituted*] some of the old 'Set'.

My wife joins me in very kind regards to Mrs Stuart Wortley & to you

Believe me
Very truly yours
Edward Elgar[1]

Four days later came news of a third scheme for *Gerontius* in London. The Duke of Norfolk and Lady Edmund Talbot proposed to bring the Sheffield Choir for a performance in the unfinished Catholic Cathedral at Westminster. Lady Edmund had been in touch with the Sheffield Festival Secretary, E. Willoughby Firth, JP; now she communicated with Alice Stuart Wortley, who wrote to Elgar:

7, Cheyne Walk, Chelsea, London, S.W.
March 14. 1903.

My dear Dr. Elgar,

*Private*

I enclose you a letter from Lady Edmund Talbot which explains itself.

She is anxious for a performance of 'Gerontius['] in the 'new Westminster Cathedral' & already moved so far in the matter as to try to get the Sheffield Choir

You will see Mr.Firth's answer—   Although in friendship to her I am anxious to help, my husband's connection with the British Musical Festival makes it impossible I should do so—further than putting you and Lady

[1] Elgar Birthplace parcel 583(vi).

Edmund into communication with each other—and leaving the matter there as far as I am concerned—

I could scarcely refuse to do this seeing that I must confess to having given the idea to Lady Edmund— It was suggested to me as far back as the Sheffield Festival, before there was any idea of the British Musical Festival, but since that has been organized I should have been wiser not at present to pass it on to her—seeing my husband's connection with this enterprize

I have told Lady Edmund that it is possible you may be pledged in a like manner to the British Musical Festival & also that a scratch choir could scarcely produce a satisfactory performance by May or June which is what Lady Edmund seems to desire—

Why couldn't it be done in the winter or next year? It would be a splendid thing to do don't you think?

Will you write me a letter I can send on to her or still better will you write direct to Lady Edmund— In any case I should like to hear from you what you think about it—but you will understand when I ask you to regard my letter as private & the necessity to leave my name out of the matter—

With best & affectionate remembrances to dear Mrs.Elgar—

> Yrs very sincerely
> Alice C.Stuart Wortley[2]

Craeg Lea, Wells Road, Malvern.
March 15:1903

Dear Mrs.Stuart-Wortley:

Very many thanks for your letter: I am quite in sympathy with the plan: the *main* difficulty is the Chorus.

The North Staffs. Choral Society knows the work well—it is a very fine Chorus & sang Gerontius under my direction on Friday last. I fear a London chorus cd. not be got together without great trouble & it wd. require a tremendous amount of training.

As to the British Festival I have heard nothing definite & have no idea how things stand except what I have gathered from the papers about the Sheffield Choir.

If Lady Edmund Talbot can see any way to get a satisfactory chorus—and North Staffs: is not more distant than Sheffield—the rest wd. be easy. Mr [John] Coates however must be the Gerontius.

With our kindest regards & thanks for the kind trouble you have taken

> Believe me
> Yours v sincerely
> Edward Elgar.

Individually I do not see why the work shd. not be done in the Cathedral *and* at the Festival—it is being done all over the country & is not a *new* work[3]

[2] HWRO 705:445:3845.          [3] Elgar Birthplace parcel 583(vi).

7, Cheyne Walk, Chelsea, London, S.W.
[n.d., *c*.16 Mar. 1903]

Dear Dr. Elgar

Thank you so much for your kind letter. I went and saw Lady Edmund Talbot last night & read her your note & doubtless by this you have heard from her— She is very much interested & keen to carry the plan of doing 'Gerontius' in the Cathedral, but will be entirely guided by you

I fear I can do no more in the matter than having placed you in communication with each other[,] but if the idea is carried further I shall be much interested & wish you all success & will do what I can without incurring displeasure from the BMF.

I note all you say about the B.M.F. & I am quite astonished if they were so keen that the *first* performance in London should be given by them that they had not approached you before this, & they can scarcely be surprized if someone should forestall them— Surely this is so?

I am taking the liberty of sending you a copy of my friend Mr. T Dunhill's Theme & Variations for the Piano—I think you must find them interesting[.] He is quite young & one of the young "british music" strugglers— After much difficulty he has got these published[.] I have thought hitherto about the other things of his I have heard that they showed more brain less inspiration, but in these Variations I find both [—] I hope you will! the Finale is Schuman[n]esque but none the worse for that & is fine—at least I hope you will be pleased!

Love to Mrs. Elgar

Yrs v. sincerely
Alice Stuart Wortley[4]

The result of all these efforts was a first London performance of *Gerontius* in Westminster Cathedral with the North Staffordshire Choral Society and an orchestra of London players conducted by the composer on 6 June. For the event the Elgars again stayed with Frank Schuster, who gave a lunch between the morning rehearsal and the afternoon performance. His guests included the Stuart Wortleys, Lady Edmund Talbot, Lords Northampton and Shaftesbury, and the tenor Gervase Elwes and his wife. The performance, with seat prices up to 5 guineas, was sold out; and the work made a deep impression.

After a weekend rest at Schuster's country house The Hut, near Maidenhead, the Elgars returned with their host to Old Queen Street. Elgar was trying prospective soloists for his new oratorio, *The Apostles*. On their last evening in London, the Elgars dined again with the Stuart Wortleys, where the guests included Lady Edmund, the Duke of Norfolk, the Poet Laureate Alfred Austin, the artistic and ethereally beautiful Lady Windsor of Hewell Grange (where the Elgars would spend the weekend preceding the Birmingham Festival in October), and the Stuart

---

[4] HWRO 705:445:3846. Dunhill (1877–1946) was to become Elgar's biographer many years later (*Sir Edward Elgar*, (Blackie, 1938). A final chapter chronicles their few but friendly meetings beginning in 1905, but the Stuart Wortleys are not mentioned.

Wortley's thirteen-year-old daughter. Again Elgar failed to catch her Christian name, but directly on his return home next day he wrote to her:

Craeg Lea, Wells Road, Malvern.
June 10 1903

Dear Miss Stuart Wortley:

That looks terribly grown up,—but what else can I say? no one has ever told me your name; which was dreadfully careless of them and I was too shy to ask.

This letter is to say how sorry I am that 'good-night' was not said last evening: I was whirled off to see a table covered with food & was thinking I should see you again.

Of course I was wrong—I always am—& when we returned to the drawing-room you had wisely gone to bed.

Now please send me your (written) forgiveness for
(A) not saying 'goodnight' prettily
(B) for sending such a long letter
(C) for not knowing your name; it must be a 'nice' one—you can tell me this & I will write it in a scented address book.

This is my quite new fountain pen & it does not 'go' at all well but I want to carry this sentence over on to the next page so that the signature may look very imposing.

I think it dull to send a lot of messages to mere grown up people so you have this all to yourself

>With my love
>Believe me
>Yours very sincerely
>Edward Elgar:

We are just home & I think the rabbits & plovers are glad to see us—but it is *so* wet.[5]

He shared with this girl, as he shared with his own twelve-year-old daughter Carice, his love for birds and animals. And when Clare Stuart Wortley wrote and told him her name, he sent further news:

[*Worcestershire Philharmonic Society stationery*]
Malvern
Sunday [14 June 1903]

My dear Clare:

I must be allowed to thank you for telling me your pretty name. Tomorrow I hope to go down to the marsh & if I see my friend the heron—who stands fishing on one leg—I'll tell it to him—

---

[5] HWRO 705:445:4029.

We are the only two people who know much about the lonely marsh & we both love it—he catches frogs & I don't; that's all.

> Your very sincere friend
> Edward Elgar

The pen is better today but not quite good.[6]

The summer of 1903 was spent finishing and orchestrating *The Apostles* for its première at the Birmingham Festival in October. The weekend of 10–12 October with Lord and Lady Windsor at Hewell Grange was joined by Frank Schuster and the Stuart Wortleys. There Elgar inscribed for her a copy of Canon C. V. Gorton's 'Interpretation' of *The Apostles* libretto. And they were all among what Alice Elgar was already describing in her diary as 'the faithful band' in the audience for the triumphant first performance on 14 October. After the Festival, the Elgars went on to another country-house visit at Wychnor Park. On his return he wrote to Alice Stuart Wortley, enclosing in his note something which has not survived.

[*Worcestershire Philharmonic Society stationery*]
Malvern
Oct 22: 03

Dear Mrs Stuart Wortley

I received the enclosed this a.m & hasten to keep my promise.
We arrived home only on Monday & are very tired
Kindest regards to you all

> Believe me
> Yours v sncly
> Edward Elgar[7]

That winter the Elgars went to Italy. Before settling in Alassio, they thought of Bordighera. Under the impression that they would be there, Charles Stuart Wortley sent an introduction they might find useful. Elgar responded:

Villa San Giovanni   Alassio   Italy
11 xii 03

Dear Mr Stuart Wortley:

It was so very kind of you to send the enclosed introduction (via Frank Schuster) but after searching high & low in Bordighera we could find nothing bearable in the way of houses: we then tried this place & have settled in this small villa for the present.

As we were leaving Bordighera at once we did not make use of your kind letter: all the same please accept our very many thanks.

We are very happy with two Italian servants—my wife talks fairly well & I not at all.

[6] HWRO 705:445:4034.    [7] HWRO 705:445:4032.

Our kindest regards to you all including Clare to whom I shall hope to send a card at Christmas if I am permitted.

> Believe me
> Yours v sincerely
> Edward Elgar[8]

The picture postcard he addressed to Clare, postmarked 19 December, showed an Italian fishing boat and bore the legend 'Un saluto da Alassio'. On the verso Elgar wrote:

This might be anywhere! they take Sardines.
Best wishes for Christmas

> Edward Elgar.[9]

## 1904

The winter was occupied with the composition of *In the South*—written mostly in Italy in January and completed after the Elgars' return in February. The new Overture was to have its première at a three-day Festival of Elgar's works planned for Covent Garden 14–16 March. Schuster was silent guarantor, and the anticipated presence of King Edward VII and Queen Alexandra ensured its success in every respect. On the day before the Elgar Festival began, the Stuart Wortleys gave a Sunday lunch, but only Alice Elgar could attend as her husband was ill at Schuster's house with nervous headache. Clare had prepared her own vocal score of *Gerontius* for him to sign, and Alice Elgar took it back for the precious inscription. Elgar duly inscribed the book, and ventured to enclose a printed card reading:

> D[r] Edward Elgar gives his autograph
> at the request of personal friends only.

Below this he wrote: 'What *shall* I do?   E.E.' and added a separate note:

Westminster
March 13 1904
My dear Clare:

Isn't this really dreadful for me!

I have been sending the enclosed in hundreds & now I have gladly signed your book I feel that I am, most intolerably! presuming on the wording of the

[8]HWRO 705:405:4033.      [9] Elgar Birthplace parcel 583 (vii)

printed notice to call you a 'personal friend'. Please, may I? You will kindly
send me a note very soon because I shall feel worried & very guilty until you
do.

With kindest regards

Believe me
Yours very sincerely
Edward Elgar[1]

That evening the Stuart Wortleys came to Schuster's brilliant dinner in Elgar's
honour—at which the subject himself managed to put in an appearance. Alice Elgar
wrote: '. . . we found the dining room decorated with E.E. (initials) & the names of his
works in flowers on the walls . . .'.[2] This large dinner was followed by an even larger
reception at 10 p.m. 'to meet Dr.Elgar'. The next three nights saw performances of
*Gerontius*, *The Apostles*, and an orchestral concert with the première of *In the South* at
its centre. The King attended the first two, and the Queen all three. The Stuart
Wortleys with Clare and all their friends were there. A series of dinners and receptions
followed, at which Elgar met further Royalties as well as the Prime Minister Arthur
Balfour.

On the following Sunday evening, 20 March, the Stuart Wortleys' dinner party for
the Elgars at Cheyne Walk included Claude Phillips, Balfour's great friend George
Wyndham and his wife Sibell Grosvenor, Mr and Mrs W. S. Gilbert, and the Clara
Schumann pupil Ilona Eibenschütz with her husband Carl Derenburg. Alice Elgar
wrote: 'Most delightful evening. We stayed last & E. played to them a little & wrote
out some notes for them—'. A sheet in his hand, quoting the 'Romans' music from *In
the South*, was dated at Cheyne Walk that evening.

Next day, to commemorate the Elgar Festival *Gerontius*, Alice Stuart Wortley sent
an engraving of her father's portrait of the author of the words, Cardinal Newman.
Elgar telegraphed his thanks, and on returning home to Malvern wrote:

Craeg Lea, Wells Road, Malvern.
March 25. 1904.

Dear Mrs.Stuart-Wortley:

Your lovely present came just as we were in the midst of tearful adieux—
the Duke [of Cambridge]'s funeral & general departure. We managed to send
a telegram which wd. assure you of our joy &, I will now add, gratitude.
Nothing could have given us more real pleasure than the possession of the
portrait & we value it the more as it comes from you. I think I am a very
lucky man to have such friends as you all at 7 Cheyne Walk & that my music
leads you to think kindly of me: I *try*—that's all & am not satisfied.

My wife joins me in kindest regards to Mr Stuart Wortley, *my personal
friend* [Clare] &—well, to you all which is quickest & best after all

Ever yours sincerely
Edward Elgar[3]

[1] MS in possession of Robert Cecil.    [2] HWRO 705:445:4598.
[3] HWRO 705:445:7697. The engraving of Millais's *Cardinal Newman* is at the Elgar
Birthplace.

Such a closing might lead to an expectation of quick advances. They did not come. During the next four years and more Elgar's few surviving letters to her were to begin almost uniformly 'Dear Mrs. Stuart Wortley'. The letters from Alice Elgar during these years advanced the intimacy more quickly.

In Cologne for the German production of *The Apostles* at the Lower Rhine Festival, Elgar sent Clare a picture postcard of the Apostles Church in Cologne:

We wish you were all here to hear the Apostles:          with my love
                                                         Edwd.Elgar.[4]


The Elgars returned on 29 May for a three-day stay at the Langham Hotel, their customary London *pied-à-terre* opposite Queen's Hall. Alice Elgar wrote:

Langham Hotel, London.
Monday [30 May 1904]
My dear Mrs.Stuart-Wortley

We have just arrived from Cologne & all the wonderful event of the Lower Rhine Festival, it was a gorgeous performance of the 'Apostles', & the Enthusiasm & 'Bewunderung' immense.

We are to be here till Wednesday, I fear you are very occupied in this time of rush in London, but it wd. be *such* a pleasure to us if we could meet, shd. you be in tomorrow afternoon perhaps? You must not think of troubling if too busy but I felt I *must* write. With much love

                                                         Yr aft
                                                         C.Alice Elgar[5]


But her husband was in the hands of the dentist in those days, and the diary records no meeting with the Stuart Wortleys.

On 24 June came the announcement that Elgar was to be knighted in the Birthday Honours. A flood of telegrams arrived at their Malvern home (from which they were soon to move). One said: 'Many sincere congratulations to you   Alice and Charles Stuart Wortley'.[6] Next day their daughter wrote:

7, Cheyne Walk, Chelsea, S.W.
June 25th 1904.
Dear Sir Edward,

I just send you a few lines to congratulate you on your new honours. We were all so pleased when we heard the news.

Thank you very much for the pretty post-card you sent me from Köln. It was very kind of you to think to send it me. I did indeed wish that I could have been there to hear the 'Apostles'; everyone says it was such a splendid performance, which makes me wish still harder! I am longing to hear it again.

I went to Köln once, with Mother and Father, but somehow we never

[4] HWRO 705:445:4036.          [5] Elgar Birthplace parcel 584(xxv).          [6] HWRO 705:445:5553.

managed to see the Aposteln Kirche. We 'did' the Dom thoroughly, of course, in the most approved tourist fashion, Baedeker in hand, and that took us all our time, as we only stayed a couple of days.

How is Lady Elgar? Please give her my love.

I am still hoping to make the acquaintance of Carice, someday; I was disappointed that she did not come to London for the Festival.

With hearty congratulations from

Yours sincerely
Clare Stuart Wortley[7]

Early in July the Elgars went into their new home, Plas Gwyn, on the outskirts of Hereford. While their belongings were in the chaos of unpacking, the many congratulators waited some time for answers.

Plas Gwyn, Hereford.
Augt 18:1904

My dear Clare:

When congratulations began to arrive—eleven telegrams at a time in one envelope—I put up an umbrella & went out. I think I stayed for three days & when I arrived at Craeg Lea—(which we have since left) I found the doors & windows blocked with letters & telegrams. Out of these I selected a few—Oh! so few—to answer or acknowledge my very own self—yours was one. I feel rather shy when I find that it is nearly two months ago, but every day makes the crime worse, so I now send very many thanks for your congratulations & shall be grateful if you will kindly convey my wife's & mine also to your father & mother.

You are no doubt away from Chelsea just now & I trust you are enjoying this true summer very much: our new house is very nice & the country lovely so we ought to be happy.

Carice is with us now & we explore a great deal.

We all send much love to you all: I know it is quite wrong to jumble it 'all together' like this but you must please make it clear but keep the largest piece for yourself   from

Your friend
Edward Elgar:[8]

The only other mention of the Stuart Wortleys in Alice Elgar's diary for 1904 occurs on 16 December, when the Elgars dined at Cheyne Walk with Claude Phillips, Mina Beresford, the novelist Mrs Craigie ('John Oliver Hobbes'), and others. There was music, but it was apparently not a success: 'Adela Verne played in the Eveng. at wh. E. retired into a recess.'

<hr />

[7] HWRO 705:445:5181.    [8] HWRO 705:445:7912.

Early in the new year Elgar wrote his *Introduction and Allegro*—to be given its première at his first Queen's Hall concert with the London Symphony Orchestra in March. A second concert was to follow ten days later. Between them, Elgar would give his Inaugural Lecture as Professor of Music at the new University of Birmingham. It was a post to which he was temperamentally unsuited, and he was already feeling ill at the prospect when he arrived in London with his wife on 3 March to stay with Frank Schuster.

The round of dinners, receptions, and music parties began. Elgar was suffering from nervous headache on the 5th, when the Stuart Wortleys came to dine. Next day he rehearsed the *Introduction and Allegro* at Queen's Hall with Mrs Stuart Wortley in attendance. A successful première on the 8th was followed next evening by a dinner in Cheyne Walk, with Schuster, Claude Phillips, and Sir Philip Burne-Jones (the artist-son of the Pre-Raphaelite painter). During the evening Elgar inscribed his hostess's copy of the *'Enigma' Variations* miniature score: on the preliminary page reading 'Dedicated to my friends pictured within' he added:

> and to my friend mentioned below:—
> Mrs.Stuart Wortley
>
> Edward Elgar
> Cheyne Walk      March 1905[1]

He got through the lecture at Birmingham on 16 March, and the second Symphony concert in London three days later. That night, when the Stuart Wortleys and Claude Phillips came to dine at Schuster's, he could not join them—but just came down for an hour after the meal.

In June the Elgars visited the United States for the first time. He disliked it intensely (but agreed to go again to conduct at the Cincinnati May Festival in 1906 for the emolument). When they returned to England, the Elgars planned a house party for the Three Choirs Festival in September. The invitations included Schuster—who had given them a sundial for the garden at Plas Gwyn, and who accepted—and the Stuart Wortleys, who could not come. Elgar wrote:

Plas Gwyn, Hereford.
Augt 16. 1905

Dear Mrs.Stuart-Wortley:

It was (is) very sad that you cannot come to Worcester but you must not think that we are *peevish* over it: true it is that I was awfully angry when I found that fate had altered your plans—angry with fate I mean—& I went out & said rude things to the Sundial—this is the lowest & most abject thing I

---

[1] Elgar Birthplace.

can do, because the Sundial is so quiet & peaceful. Please get quite rested and ready for—*Cincinatti* [*sic*] *Festival!!*

Our best regards & forgiveness with my love to Clare

> Believe me
> Yours most sncly
> Edward Elgar[2]

After the Worcester Festival, Elgar and Schuster accepted Mina Beresford's invitation to cruise with the Fleet in the Mediterranean. After that, in October, the Elgars were at the Norwich Festival. In Norwich he met with John Cousins, a skilled valet able to assist him through an approaching tour of English and Scottish cities with the London Symphony Orchestra. This was the subject of Alice Elgar's next letter to Alice Stuart Wortley:

Carrow Abbey[,] Norwich
27 Oct. 1905. We are to return tomorrow—

My dearest Namesake

*Very* many thanks for your dear letter[:] it was *so* kind of you to write & inquire for us, & fortunately Edward has heard of & seen a very much recommended man here & engaged him so that is a weight off my mind—it was so kind of Mr. Stuart-Wortley to offer to help—& as you may suppose, it has to be exactly the right person to be of real use to E.

I wish you both could have been here yesterday[:] the performance [of *The Apostles*] was most beautiful, one of the most touching & impressive I have ever heard. It was good to see Edward look so serenely happy when not too overcome himself—

Now forgive haste & with dear love & true sympathy & concern for the sad days you have had

> Yr loving
> C. Alice Elgar

Please take care of yr cold.[3]

November brought more professorial lectures at Birmingham. On the day after the second of these, 9 November, the Elgars returned to London to stay with Schuster. The Stuart Wortleys came to dine, and Elgar played them sketches of the continuation of *The Apostles* he was writing for the Birmingham Festival in October 1906: it was to be called *The Kingdom*. Their attention was caught by one superb theme, to appear first at the centre of the Prelude as 'New Faith'. The Stuart Wortleys begged for a copy of this theme, and Elgar promised it.

But the London Symphony tour was upon him, and then more lectures. So it was not until Christmas was past that he could renew the promise—in a card posted on 27 December showing Plas Gwyn with its gate welcomingly open, and addressed to Clare:

---

[2] HWRO 705:445:4030.      [3] Elgar Birthplace parcel 584(xl).

Best wishes for the New Year. I am sending the tune promised for N. Year's
day

Yrs ever
Edw Elgar[4]

# 1906

---

Again the tune did not come. Elgar was depressed. He finished the Prelude and
opening pages of *The Kingdom* in short score and sent them to the publishers. But his
heart was not yet in it. And then came the distracting atmosphere of a general
election—in which the Conservatives suffered stunning defeat. The Prime Minister,
Balfour, actually lost his seat, though Charles Stuart Wortley held his own. At last on
22 January Elgar wrote:

Plas Gwyn, Hereford.
Jany the somethingth, 1906
(Dates quite forgotten in the turmoil of writing execrable Music)
My dear Lady:

I have not forgotten the promise to send you the little theme: *but* I have
been waiting to send you a copy in *print* which is much to be preferred to my
awful writing. I sent back a first proof long ago & am expecting a revise[,] one
of which shall come to you. *Now*: you must not let *anyone* see it! because it is
not published & you must not tell anyone—excepting always your M.P. (Oh!
I am so glad he's in) that you have it but just keep it to yourselves or—better
still in relation to its merits—burn it!

I am so sorry the trifle has been so long about & forgive a long letter about
it—I'm not lazy, or evil, but the printers disappoint me.

Alice sends love & so do I, to you both.

Always sncly yrs
Edward Elgar

P.T.O.

P.S. Frank Schuster is of course always excepted but he will D.V. have his
own copy, but do talk it over with him.[1]

A few days later both Alice Stuart Wortley and Schuster had their proof copies of the
new work's beginning.

Elgar's depression grew at the prospect of all the hard work and inspiration still
required to finish *The Kingdom*, until he was on the verge of a nervous breakdown.
Then it was agreed that the oratorio might cover only half the material at first

---

[4] Elgar Birthplace parcel 583(vii).
[1] HWRO 705:445:7850.

envisioned. Improvement in health was immediate. Besides promising further proofs of *The Kingdom*, he accepted an invitation to come up to London for a few days, and to dine one evening with the Stuart Wortleys.

Plas Gwyn, Hereford.
Tuesday [20 Feb. 1906]
My dear Mrs.Stuart-Wortley:

A thousand thanks for your letter: more of my poor work shall follow as the printers allow.

I have written to Frank telling him I will come to him on Friday: & of course I shall be delighted to accept your beautiful dinner.—if Frank can have me. I am a hollow ghost—I told him so—& he may not care to entertain such a thing: I only hope that, properly clothed, I don't look it.

Alice sends love
Kindest regards to you both

Yours always sncly
Edward Elgar:[2]

He went to London not on the Friday, but the following Tuesday, 27 February. He and Schuster dined that night with the Stuart Wortleys, who then took them to see Granville Barker's *The Voysey Inheritance* at the Court Theatre. This play, about an inheritance of irredeemable fraud, was one of the masterpieces of the Edwardian theatre; and when Elgar returned to Plas Gwyn on 2 March he spent the entire evening talking about the play.

For six weeks in April and May the Elgars were in the United States, to fulfil his engagements to conduct at the Cincinnati May Festival. On 18 May, just before embarking at New York for the homeward passage, Elgar sent Clare a postcard showing the large Ingolls Building in Cincinnati, with the message:

It is not *all* so dreadful as this.

Love to you all
Edward Elgar[3]

By mid-July composition of *The Kingdom* was nearly finished. The Elgars spent a weekend at Schuster's country house near Maidenhead, where they were joined by Claude Phillips and the Stuart Wortleys. On Sunday 15 July Alice Elgar's diary records:

After lunch E. played 'The Kingdom' to Frank, Claude, S.Wortleys, they were *immensely* impressed. Alice sd. she cd. hear nothing after it, all sounded foolish & not worth doing.

Back in Hereford eight days later the oratorio was finished in short score. Elgar decided to take it to London, and to stay another night or two. Meanwhile Alice Stuart Wortley had sent a book, which Alice Elgar acknowledged:

[2] HWRO 705:445:4123.     [3] Elgar Birthplace parcel 583(vii).

Plas Gwyn, Hereford.
27 July 1906.

My dearest Alice

Your lovely book came this morning & I have already enjoyed the
introduction & can see what a fine book it is & a true effort for justice to such
a marvellous & noble heroine— That word has been hackneyed, it does not
seem the right one to use for so great a character. *Very very* many thanks, it is
most dear of you to send it me—it will deeply interest us all.

I am thankful & rejoiced to tell you that Edward has finished all the
composing of his work, & is now away for 2 or 3 days for a break— I hope
he will not get tired over the rest of the Orchestration— The end is most
wonderful [—] so intensely solemn & appealing—

He was looking so well & so lighthearted now such a burden was lifted, I
do wish you could see him in other than over wrought & over worn states—
but I hope you will next time you meet—

I do hope you are both well & have good accounts of your Clare.

It is such lovely weather & the garden is full of doves free & very fairly
tame.

I expect you are both longing for the Country & change, please have a very
nice time & be very well & refreshed—

With much love & so many thanks

Yr very aft.
C.Alice Elgar

I hope the little Anthology will come very soon for you—[4]

The Anthology was noted (by the Elgars' daughter Carice) as 'Brotherhood with
nature[:] Treasury selection by Charles Rowley.'

Afterwards Lady Elgar's diary shows no meeting for two months. At the beginning
of October the Stuart Wortleys came to Birmingham for the first performance of *The
Kingdom*, and Elgar inscribed for her Canon Gorton's 'Interpretation' of the new
libretto. In London the oratorio had its first hearing at the Alexandra Palace on 17
November. Next evening Schuster gave a large dinner party for the Elgars, with
guests including the Stuart Wortleys and many musicians and elegant people. Three
nights later Schuster and the Elgars dined with the Stuart Wortleys and went to the
Court Theatre to see Shaw's *Man and Superman*. 'Extraordinarily clever play', Alice
Elgar concluded, 'Not all pleasant.'

[4] Elgar Birthplace parcel 584(xxvii).

Elgar's creative career was approaching a crisis. He felt unable to drive his oratorio ideas farther; yet the symphony he had been trying for years to write would not come. His health grew worse, and the Elgars went for two winter months to Italy. From Rome on 15 February he sent a postcard of the Cloister of the Church of San Paolo to Clare: 'Love to you & all   Edward Elgar'.[1]

Once again there was an American trip in the spring—to conduct widely and to collect an honorary degree from Andrew Carnegie's new Institute in the steel city of Pittsburgh. This time Elgar was going alone. His wife wrote to Alice Stuart Wortley on the day after their return from Italy:

Plas Gwyn, Hereford.
27 Feb. 1907.

My dearest Namesake

We arrived last Evening & my first lines from home are to you. So many thanks for your dear letter & invitation, it is *horrid* not to be able to come, but what is still more horrid is the reason, that the dear E. has to start on Saturday, 2 March, for U.S.A. in the Carmania, & as I have been away so long, he says I must stay at home now—   He is to conduct 'The Apostles' & 'The Kingdom' in N.York, & an Orch. Concert in Chicago—   I trust he will be home in April & I am thankful to say is taking a good nice man to look after him which is the one consolation to me.

I cannot *tell* you how much better he seems, I only wish you cd. see him— & I wish you cd. have seen him in Rome, he was *utterly* blissful—& we have such a store of beautiful sights in our minds.   & he does not look a bit tired although the wretched train was *12* hrs. late & we had 2 nights instead of one in the train & were turned out into wet streaming streets of Paris at 5.30 a.m. & had to wait for our London train till 9.50!—

I pray & trust he will keep well.

I do hope you both & Clare are all well & with dear love in wh. he wd. join if he knew I was writing

Yr loving
C.A.Elgar[2]

He was away during April and May. Alice Elgar took Carice to stay with friends near London for the Easter holidays, and they lunched with Alice Stuart Wortley and Clare on 15 April. About then Elgar was arriving at Pittsburgh, and from there on the 18th he sent Clare a postcard showing the 'Pittsburgh Bank for Savings Building. Fourth and Smithfield'. The message read: 'My love to you all from an unlovely place   Ed:Elgar'.[3] Ten days later he was back at home in Hereford.

He sent a letter now missing—just before hearing of the death of Alice Stuart Wortley's youngest sister, not yet forty.

[1] Elgar Birthplace parcel 583(vii).          [2] Elgar Birthplace parcel 584(xxiv).
[3] Elgar Birthplace parcel 583(vii).

Plas Gwyn, Hereford.
May 31: 1907

My dear Mrs.Stuart-Wortley:

We are so distressed to hear your sad news: our thoughts & sympathies are
with you & I must add regret also that I should have sent you a frivolous
letter at such a time: forgive me!

Yours ever sncy
Edward Elgar.[4]

Surviving letters and diary entries record no contacts during the summer of 1907.
At the Gloucester Festival in September, Elgar conducted *The Kingdom*, and late in
the month he conducted another performance at Cardiff. There he stayed at St
Fagan's Castle, the Welsh home of Lord Plymouth (the former Lord Windsor,
President of the Birmingham Festival: he had been host to the Elgars at Hewell
Grange just before *The Apostles* première in October 1903). The Plymouths and
Stuart Wortleys were friends, and there was some thought of a general meeting at
Cardiff. But it was not to be, as Alice Elgar wrote:

Plas Gwyn, Hereford.
27 Sept. 1907.

My dearest Alice

It was such a pleasure to have your letter today, how *dear* it wd have been
to have met you at S.Fagan's but alas! I was not there either— 'The dear
one' had [to] go on Monday for a rehearsal & I was to join him on
Wednesday & proceed to S.Fagan's but had a wretched sort of gastric attack
& cd. not go! Edward is just home & had a *delightful* visit & is enchanted with
the house &c— 'The Kingdom' also was very finely performed—I wish you
cd. have heard it in its glorious setting at Gloucester—Frank was with us
there & immensely impressed I think—He was not at Cardiff

Is there any chance of being at Leeds? I *hope* to be there for 'The
Kingdom'.

I had been longing to know where you were & so glad you had a refreshing
time in Scotland. I am thankful to say Edward has been keeping well, he is
still ordered not to use his eyes much[5]

*[a second sheet is missing]*

The Stuart Wortleys did not go to the Leeds Festival that year.

In November the Elgars went to Rome for the winter. From there on 20 December
he sent Alice Stuart Wortley a coloured postcard showing Dante looking from a
distance at Beatrice, who looks back while her two companions walk slowly on. It
bore the printed legend: 'Tutti li miei pensier parlan d'amore'. Elgar's message read:
'Love to you all   Edward Elgar   Roma 1907'.[6]

⁴ HWRO 705:445:4119.          ⁵ HWRO 705:445:7907.
⁶ Elgar Birthplace parcel 583(xxxiii).

This was the year that saw the composition and production of the First Symphony. The Elgars lingered in Rome until May, and most of the Symphony-writing was done over the summer. He visited London several times with his wife, and twice went alone for long weekends at Schuster's country house, The Hut. But there is no mention of the Stuart Wortleys in Alice Elgar's diary until autumn. The *Wand of Youth* Suite No. 2 had its London première on 17 October, and two nights later the Elgars and Claude Phillips dined with the Stuart Wortleys and then went to Shaw's *Arms and the Man*.

The Elgars were in London again a month later, when on 23 November he took the London Symphony Orchestra through the new Symphony for the first time. Next evening they dined with the Stuart Wortleys to meet Lord Howard de Walden. The Stuart Wortleys were surely at the Symphony's London première on 7 December, one of the great triumphs of Elgar's career. Two days later he inscribed a copy of the miniature score for them—probably at the dinner party Schuster gave that night. They all met again at Mina Beresford's dinner on 10 December. Next day the Elgars returned to Hereford.

Alice Stuart Wortley attended the second London performance of the Symphony on 19 December, and she wired: 'Lovely performance of wonderful symphony'.[1] But then the holidays were upon them—always a difficult season for Elgar. Christmas morning found him alone in the house, keen neither on music nor on the amateur chemistry he was carrying on just then in a laboratory converted from the former dovecot, styled 'The Ark':

Plas Gwyn, Hereford.
Dec 25 1908
Dear Mrs Stuart Wortley

This is only to convey thanks & many of them for your telegram—  My best wishes to you all three for the New Year—  I am dulling in the house with a cold which is depressing for me & I *mean to make it so* for all around me—that's a nice Christmas feeling.

Meanwhile the Ark is silent & deserted & Mozart's portrait has curled up & fallen into the Hydrofluoric acid; Woe!

Love to you all
Yrs affectionately
Edward Elgar:

Alice & Carice & a friend have gone off to a far church in a car—I am worshipping several things by the fire—memories mostly of the New world geographically & musically—that Symphony *is* a new world isn't it?
Do say 'yes'.[2]

This was Elgar's only surviving letter to Alice Stuart Wortley in 1908. The next year was to be altogether different.

[1] Alice Elgar's diary, 19 December 1908.     [2] HWRO 705:445:7824.

Partly because they were not in Italy this winter, Elgar was depressed. He went by himself to London on 17 February to dine at Marlborough House and join the Prince of Wales's party to a concert at Queen's Hall. Next day, as he told his wife for her diary, he called on several friends—Beresfords and Stuart Wortleys among them.

When he returned to Hereford he was depressed still—or again—until their American friend Mrs Worthington telegraphed that she had taken a villa near Florence for the spring and would they go out with her? Alice Elgar prepared Plas Gwyn for tenants, while Edward took himself to London on 23 March. That evening he wrote:

Langham Hotel, London.
Tuesday [23 Mar. 1909]

My dear Mrs.Stuart-Wortley:

I address you, rather than the much desired M.P., who is busy.

I know you are *all* doubly, trebly engaged, so don't think of me. I only humbly report (principally in the hope that my *personal friend* [i.e. Clare] may not forget me)

1) that I am here:
2) that I am alive:
3) that I am miserably alone!:
4) that I am (not doubly or trebly) *bassly* (no, BASELY) engaged in business pursuits: meaning publishers.

I do *so* want to see you all: but this must wait until better times I'm sure.

But my love to you all the same: & think kindly of me in the next high tea-drinking—wherever it may be.

> Yours snly
> Edward Elgar[1]

She came to see him. And then he sought to acknowledge an advance of intimacy in the Christian name which her family and old friends like Frank Schuster used:

Langham Hotel, London.
March 25. 1909

My dear Carrie.

(That's what I hear other nice people say & so why should not I?—I *may* be nice someday).

This is only to say I can't retire for the night without sending this to thank you for coming *and* for the flowers.

---

[1] HWRO 705:445:4108.

Alas! I have lost my pen and this illegibility looks vulgar—with my own pen it looks clever & is more irritating

Love to you all
Yrs ever
Edward E.[2]

Despite the 'motto' quotation from the Symphony, the 'Carrie' salutation proved less than welcome. Perhaps she was even now separating him from associations with her family and earlier friends. Whatever her motive, he respected it—and his response to a dinner invitation at Cheyne Walk bore no salutation at all:

Langham Hotel, London.
Friday [26 Mar. 1909]

Most lovely plan!—I will be with you at 8.15—I am with you in spirit now. The play is not a play at all but a good lesson

Yrs ever
E[3]

Was that 'play' a matinée shared or a private notion? Next evening he duly dined at Cheyne Walk. Among the other guests was Lord Charles Beresford, who told them all a 'terrible tale of naval unpreparedness' for the rising menace of Germany.

From early April Elgar hovered in London and Paris, while his wife prepared the Hereford house for their absence in Italy. On the 17th she and Carice joined him, and they went with Mrs Worthington to the villa on the outskirts of Florence. From there Alice Elgar sent a letter:

Villa Silli, Careggi. prezzo Firenze.
4 May 1909.

My dearest Namesake

I have been wanting to send you a few lines from this lovely place, & to tell you Edward is looking so well & rested. . . . E. had a pleasant time in Paris which he enjoyed much, I & Carice joined him for two very pleasant days, & then with our dear & kind hostess, arrived from U.S.A.[,] we proceeded here, & till Sunday have had *glorious* weather, the world bathed in sunshine, the air scented with flowers & resounding with nightingales—. It is a very nice spacious Villa, the hall in Roman days was the Atrium & in later ages, it was one of the Medici Villas; the great Medici Villa where Lorenzo died is close by. I trust you will hear E.'s impressions, tonally, some day, some days we hear them already. We look on Fiesole but are separated by a deep valley, however E. & I walked there yesterday, as it was quite cold . . .[4]

---

[2] HWRO 705:445:7817.     [3] HWRO 705:445:4116.

[4] Partial transcript by Clare Stuart Wortley (Elgar Birthplace). The MS has not been found. In cases where it has been possible to compare one of the transcripts with the manuscript, I have found the transcript accurate in the main.

On the road to Fiesole was a monastery about which the Stuart Wortleys had told them, from prior visits of their own. Elgar's first finished work after months of inactivity was a little *Angelus*, a partsong with words adapted from Tuscan dialect: he sent it to the music publisher Novello on 13 May. He was also working at sketches for a violin concerto. Some days later Alice Elgar sent a picture card of the Ponte Vecchio and Lung'Arno with this message:

Villa Silli, Careggi.
21 May 1909.

You will like to hear we have been having the most *lovely* time here, E. is quite devoted to Careggi & we must come here always we feel! & want a Villa here most of which was designed by M.Angelo! & is for sale! The air is perfect & it is all beautiful, and *beautiful* new tunes have been written. I think we go to Venice. c/o [Thomas] Cook wd. find us. Much love dearest namesake.

Yr affte
C.A.E.[5]

And from Venice, on a picture card of the Rialto:

Hotel Regina. Venice.
5th June, 1909.

We *had* to leave Careggi with much regret, but had a very nice time at Pisa & Bologna wh. impressed E. *immensely*. This is *very* wonderful & interesting; just *at first* too much like living in a postcard! but gondola life in these lovely moonlight nights *is* perfect. Trust you are all well. We are turning home-wards on Monday via Bavaria—& its memories.

Much love fr.
C.A.Elgar[6]

Bavaria had been the scene of repeated summer holidays in the 1890s (whose musical result had been Elgar's *Scenes from the Bavarian Highlands*).

They reached Hereford in June—Alice and Carice on the 18th to air and prepare the house, Edward (after a weekend with Frank Schuster) on the 22nd. He now had proofs of the *Angelus*, and sent one to Cheyne Walk with another new salutation:

Hereford
June 23, 1909

My dear *Alice*;

I wanted to *bring** the enclosed little remembrance of Careggi    *had no time, alas!   & ask if your name may go on it: please look at the title carefully & tell me if I have it right & tell me how to amend it or to remove it

[5] Transcript by Clare Stuart Wortley (Elgar Birthplace); MS not located. She noted also 'Sir Edward Elgar also sent picture postcards from Florence, but they said nothing about music.' I have not found those cards.
[6] Transcript by Clare Stuart Wortley (Elgar Birthplace); MS not located.

altogether—it looks so GASTFULLY formal. Also you may not like the words—so I enclose them & you can censor them—but they are of the place & not far from your own monastery on the Fiesole road of which C.B.S.W. has memories also[.] Anyway it wd. give me the greatest pleasure to put your belovèd name on it if you both allow it.

Please return these rough proofs to me & I will follow your commands. Only arrived here last night & all in confusion

Much love to you all

Yours ever
Edward
PTO

The red ink marks are only the PRINTER'S enquiries &c.[7]

She accepted this salutation, and also the dedication of the *Angelus*—with one alteration. The final version read: '*To Alice/Mrs.Charles Stuart-Wortley.*'

Hereford
June 29: 1909
My dear Alice:

In awful haste [—] I send one word of thanks for your letter accepting my little dedication: it is so sweet of you & your amended version of the formula is so much better than my *modest* & muddy brain could have attained to. I was afraid the simple words might be too papistical for you—or for your family!

Yours ever
EE[8]

A fortnight later a printed revise of the first page with the dedication was ready. He posted it during a cold and rainy weekend at Schuster's country house.

The Hut (by Monkey Island) Bray, Berks.
July 10 1909
My dear Alice:

Here is the amended page: is it *quite* right? please correct it if necessary—it looks lovely & I am so *proud*.

If you can conveniently send it back soon please do as the printers want to publish it—there's no hurry however.

I shall be here until Tuesday a.m. I suppose unless the thermometer goes down too low for my summer frocks. What weather!

Love to you all

Yrs ever
Edward

Pippa [Mrs Worthington] is here![9]

---

[7] HWRO 705:445:7827.      [8] HWRO 705:445:4114.      [9] HWRO 705:445:4107.

An autumn of Festivals and concerts yielded no diary record of meetings with the Stuart Wortleys. But the next letter from Elgar (written during another short tour with the London Symphony Orchestra) implies a further advance of intimacy—and dissatisfaction with the salutation which shared the Christian name of his wife:

Royal Station Hotel, York.
Nov 1: 1909
My dear Alice:

You see how dull my invective powers are in the presence of acute emotion & I have found no name for you yet! Alice & I are resting here for a day or two after my tour with the Lond.Sym.Orch. but we arrive in Hereford next Friday.

I will be in London round about the 11th (Phil: Concert) & shall hope to see you—I dine with Lady Charlie on the 10th & perhaps you may be there.

There is no news—it is cold here which is what affects us most & we are thinking of our annual exile—perhaps Rome again

I wish I could hear Paderewski's Symph: you must tell me about it: please I want *your* opinion.

My love & Alice's to you all: this is a dull note & really only to tell you we are alive & want to hear of you—so please tell us nice things.

> Love
> Yrs affecty
> Edward

P.S. Now do look at this smudge! It *is* too bad—I did not do it—it belongs to York railway station.
P.S. How far is it from York to New York: do *you* know?[10]

'New York' meant Mrs Worthington, who had returned to her home there.

Now suddenly there were many letters saved, and we have for the first time something like a full look at the correspondence from Elgar's side. His next letter was dated six days later, from home. Another reference to 'New York' is touched in; closer-to-home affairs are grim enough. Another general election looms, and Elgar is eager to help the Conservative cause. (In January 1910 he will sign the Hereford MP Arkwright's renomination paper.) Yet he is on the eve of another stay in London—to conduct the opening concert of a new Philharmonic season at Queen's Hall.

ˣPlasˣGwyn, Hereford.
Nov 7: 1909
My dear Alice:

I am turning out my accumulated travel papers, letters, billets-doux &c & among the second-named (not the third!) I find your note of Nov 2. Now ˣP.ˣG. Alice will have replied I think but as she is resting in her room with a

[10] HWRO   705:445:7105.

cold I only sit in the sun in my study looking like Hans Sachs without his beard & stoutness & say I am to be at the Langham on Tuesday & that A. of P.G. joins me on Thursday or Friday & we dine with you when & where you please: it is given to you to command but I doubt if the subscriber will accept orders (save from New York!)

It *is* lovely here—the air so pure & soft after the loathèd North with all its mysteries of commerce—I saw locomotives building & torpedoes & other nasty maleficious things: now it is warm & lovely & feels & looks like an ashamed summer.

You are wrong—I am perfectly good, brainless (after the work of the tour) & tractable. I have given up all idea of writing any more so-called music & am going to wildly politicize for the next month or two—(perhaps)

I do not know what I began to write for—oh! yes[:] to say I am coming—and I stop, not because I have no more to say but because I shall have to cross [*script written at right angles over existing script*] which is feminine & untidy (interchangeable terms) or use another sheet which is also feminine & extravagant (also interchangeable).

> Yrs ever
> Edwd.[11]

He went to London next day, and his own Alice joined him in time for the Philharmonic concert on the 11th. Her diary records 'numbers of friends' there including 'Frank, Claude'; perhaps also the Stuart Wortleys. Elgars and Stuart Wortleys dined together the following evening and went to an American play entitled *Lorrimer Labroton, Dramatist.*

The Athenaeum
Nov 13 1909
My dear Alice:

I *did* really enjoy the play last night—but it made me thoughtful & stupid: I don't mean that the main thought of the play affected me—an impossible position never does & no man could have passed on his work I suggested—but the side issues made me silent, which was good for you after all.

How wide the Atlantic seems some days

> Love,
> Edward[12]

Another playful reference to Mrs Worthington. It found its mark, as he noted in the postscript of his next—a reply to Alice Stuart Wortley's invitation to an evening party in Cheyne Walk when Paderewski was to play for their guests.

---

[11] HWRO 705:445:7669.     [12] HWRO 705:445:4115.

The Athenaeum
Nov 15 1909

My dear Alice:

Many thanks: please keep or destroy (an' it please you better) the calendar.
Yes I will come most amiably on Tuesday.
Just in from Ridgehurst for the day. & what an awful day!

Yrs ever
EE

P.S. I am not going to enunciate at all—bother the Atlantic![13]

He and his own Alice were staying with their friends the Edward Speyers at Ridgehurst in Hertfordshire. The weather was bitter, and Elgar was soon in bed with a heavy cold—which made the Paderewski evening impossible for him:

at Ridgehurst & *still in bed*
[n.d., *c*.17 Nov. 1909]

My dear Alice:

I know you are very angry with me—but I did my best to come— The climate is too much for me & I have succumbed—rather early in the season this time.
I am sorry, *sorry*, SORRY; that I could not come to the dinner.
Oh, the awful dulness of me
Bless you

Yours ever
Edward.[14]

From Ridgehurst the Elgars went to the Langham Hotel in London. Elgar kept in until they attended a big dinner on the 19th at the house of the Ridgehurst Speyer's cousin Edgar, who headed the financial syndicate behind the Queen's Hall concerts. Next day they returned to Hereford, where Elgar took another cold. His wife had it too, but that fact did not enter his next letter to the other Alice.

Hereford
Nov 22 1909

My dear Alice:

It was good of you to write [—] we are (as you see) at home. Alice thought—the wish was mother to the thought—that I was well enough to go to dinner in London on Friday—so I went—Saturday we came here— yesterday I have a fresh cold & am 'in'— We make no plans so I fear we are

---

[13] HWRO 705:445:7111.
[14] HWRO 705:445:4120. Alice Stuart Wortley dated this note November 18 1909, which may be the day of receipt. Alice Elgar's diary shows that Elgar was in bed all day on Wednesday the 17th, the day after the Paderewski party. They left Ridgehurst on the morning of the 18th.

fixed for the winter. Thank you a thousand times for all the good things you say.

Love from us all

Yrs ever
Edward[15]

Elgar was ill for the next three weeks and more. He responded to a telegram from Alice Stuart Wortley:

Plas Gwyn, Hereford.
Saturday [11 Dec. 1909]
My dear Alice

Your telegram is the only ray of light seen for 3 weeks!
P.S. Bless you for it.
Alas! I am not well—& nothing to get better for.

Love
Edwd[16]

She sent a description of the Paderewski evening. But with the general election coming in January, the Stuart Wortleys would have to go to Sheffield to campaign. Elgar wrote his response on blue hand-made paper bought in Italy. But the approach of holidays renewed his depression.

Hereford
Dec 21: 1909
My dear Alice:

It *was* good of you to write & such a beautiful long letter—it was dreary to miss your evening & your Paderewski—but what could I do? I am better thank you & may come to town tomorrow for sundry businesses: I shall telephone & find if you have left for Sheffield but I hope you will be spared that journey until the New Year. I write to you on this lovely Florentine paper: *made* there,—this is what Petrarch and the rest wrote on! I would write a sonnet to you but it would not rhyme & if it did, would not be good enough for you otherwise. Anyhow I can *think* sonnets to you & America which probably had better not be scanned.

Alice is busy amending everyone's conscience to the 25th. which is quarter-day & a variety of disagreeable things also including Noël. Best wishes to you at [*blank space under 'Noël'*] & love irrespective of Xtian continuations of heathen festivals

Yours ever
Edward[17]

---

[15] HWRO  705:445:4105.      [16] HWRO  705:445:4102.      [17] HWRO  705:445:4109.

The next day found him not *en route* to London, but busy at home writing new solo songs. One was *A Child Asleep*, for the first birthday of Anthony Goetz, the son of his favourite contralto Muriel Foster. Others were song cycles of frustrated love. One of these cycles was founded on texts 'from the Russian' (according to the legend) and translated by 'Pietro d'Alba': Peter was in fact Carice's angora rabbit, and 'Pietro d'Alba' was a *nom de plume* Elgar had used more than once. The other cycle of songs was planned on poems from a privately printed collection by Sir Gilbert Parker: Elgar had started three out of a projected six. He sent the three sketches to Cheyne Walk.

He went alone to London on 28 December, and found a telephone invitation to dine at Cheyne Walk next evening.

Langham Hotel, London.
Tuesday night [28 Dec. 1909]

My dear Alice

I have your telephone message &, thanks 10000, I'll dance (if necessary) all the way to dine with you: but I *hope* it's not a party because I am not a 'proper object' yet I think to be seen

I await your orders which will be in the promised note

> Ever yours
> Edwd[18]

His own Alice (who noted Edward's Stuart Wortley engagement in her diary) came up to join him on New Year's Eve for a huge party given by Sir George and Lady Lewis. Alice Elgar finished her diary for 1909:

> God grant 1910 have happiness for E. in store.


# 1910

Elgar's great friend A. J. Jaeger (of the music publishing firm Novello, and the 'Nimrod' of the *'Enigma' Variations*) had died in the previous May. A memorial concert was planned to benefit the widow and children, and an Elgar première was considered an indispensable 'draw'. The only work-in-progress which could be finished in time were the three songs of the incomplete Parker cycle: they were quickly orchestrated for Muriel Foster to sing at the concert on 24 January. (The partial première proved fatal to the rest of the cycle, which was never finished.)

Elgar was tiring of Hereford, where they had lived five-and-a-half years. Many interests—not least the friendship with Alice Stuart Wortley—drew him toward London. There he took a service flat in Queen Anne's Mansions, where he stayed alone to work at the Violin Concerto. His own Alice came up on 24 January for the rehearsal and performance of the new Songs at the Jaeger Memorial Concert. The Stuart Wortleys were present, and kept their programme.

[18] HWRO 705:445:4117.

The Elgars stayed on at Queen Anne's Mansions. They were to attend a matinée concert conducted by Landon Ronald, a younger man who had fallen under the spell of Elgar's music and was planning many performances. The day before the concert Elgar wrote:

Q Anne's Mansions   S W
Jany 26. 1910
My dear Alice:

We are going to hear Landon Ronald 'do' the Tschaikowsky No 4—I forget if you are going.

Frank has just gone & Alice & he have been making the wildest schemes to go to the Alexandra Palace & hear 'The Apostles' on Saturday night[.] But we can talk of this on Friday at dinner.

I am trying to write a piano piece called Violettes—but I do not understand the piano well enough I fear.

Ever yours sncly
Edward[1]

The final sentence was mischievous. All his pianist friends, including Alice Stuart Wortley, constantly urged him to write for the piano, an instrument he generally disliked. *Violets* was the name of a song published by Mrs Ellen Wright as her own work, and subsequently shown to be a near-piracy of Elgar's early *Salut d'amour*.[2]

The Elgars attended the Landon Ronald concert on 27 January, and next evening dined with the Stuart Wortleys; Schuster and Claude Phillips were also there. They were given a rare treat by their hostess: 'Alice pl. ed gently & nice to hear.' Elgar played his new Parker songs, and promised to send the book containing the poems.

[n.p.: Queen Anne's Mansions, London, S.W.]
Saturday [29 Jan. 1910] a m
My dear Alice:

Here are Parker's poems which I shall not require for some days: tell me what you think of them.

The Alexandra Palace party's tea is at *5.30* today not 5 o c.

Ever yours
Edwd.Elgar[3]

Tea before *The Apostles* that day was given by Schuster, who took Alice Elgar to the performance—a poor one.

The whole circle—Stuart Wortleys, Lady Charles Beresford, Schuster, and Claude Phillips, together with Lord Northampton—were to go with the Elgars on the

[1] HWRO 705:445:7860.

[2] See the writer's *Elgar and his Publishers: Letters of a Creative Life* (OUP, 1987), pp. 493–6.

[3] HWRO 705:445:4067. Elgar did not realize that she had already received a copy from the poet himself. Parker's covering letter to her, dated 23 January, is at the Elgar Birthplace (parcel 584(iv) ).

Monday evening to hear the eminent Russian musician Vassily Safonov conduct Elgar's Symphony at Queen's Hall. Elgar had taken to sitting by himself at such concerts. It seems there was some plan for him to sit with Alice Stuart Wortley this evening, but circumstances ruled otherwise. His note on the morning of the concert was taken to Cheyne Walk by messenger:

Queen Anne's Mansions, St.James' Park, London, S.W.
Monday [31 Jan. 1910] a m.

My dear Alice:

I want to go on with my songs so the bearer will bring Parker's book—if you are in & can give it to him—if not do not trouble to send it quickly—any time in reason will do.

I return Sir G[ilbert Parker]'s letter—*and* the ticket. I thought your family was to be away & you had no one—Alice says you are all at home so I will look at you from a distance; I shall sit *alone*, if I go, which is doubtful—I *am* really alone in this music!

Yrs ever
Edwd.E.[4]

He did go, and his wife's diary recorded him as 'much impressed'.

Next day Alice Elgar returned to Hereford, while her husband stayed at Queen Anne's Mansions. On 2 February he sent to Cheyne Walk a large envelope containing seven recent partsongs: *A Christmas Greeting*, Op. 52, the four partsongs of Op. 53 (including *Owls*), the finished printing of the *Angelus*, Op. 56 and *Go, song of mine*, Op. 57. Later that day a card followed them:

The Athenaeum, Pall Mall, S.W.
Feb 2:

I believe I must have sent 'Owls' with the 'Go song of mine': I am so sorry—it was not meant for you but for Mrs Colvin! tear it up! 'Go song' is to be sung by the Sheffield Choir at Queen's Hall [at Richter's concert on 14 Feb.]

E.E.[5]

By now he had a rough copy of the Violin Concerto central slow movement. He had tried it privately for friends on 20 January and again four days later with Leonora von Stosch, an Ysaÿe pupil who was in private life the wife of Sir Edgar Speyer. On 6 February the Stuart Wortleys dined with Elgar at Schuster's house, and Clare joined them later. Lady Speyer again played the Concerto Andante with Elgar at the piano. Charles Stuart Wortley turned over, and he was so much struck with the music that he asked if he might borrow the piano sketch to try over for himself. Elgar sent the sketch next day as a gift—the separate sheets tied together with rough twine.

It was almost as if he wanted to put this second movement Andante away from him. He had been making first-movement sketches for several years, but primary and

[4] Elgar Birthplace parcel 583(xxxii).       [5] HWRO 705:445:4038.

secondary themes there would not come together. On the day after Schuster's party, as he sent the Andante to Charles Stuart Wortley, he wrote despondently to the lady of Cheyne Walk:

The Athenaeum
Feb 7: 1910
My dear Alice:

I promised to tell you of my London visit—I do not think it has been a success: it is too lonely & I cannot see how we are to 'take' a place big enough for us all: you shall hear of any plans but I think a decent obscurity in the country is all I can attain to—there is really no 'place' for me here as I do not conduct or in fact do anything & I am made to feel in many ways I am not wanted. I suppose I shall still pay an occasional visit to conduct a new thing—if any new things are ever finished.

I am not sure about that Andante & shall put it away for a long time before I decide its fate. I am glad you liked it. I hope your husband will not think I imagine the sketches to be worth having—but people ask me for them sometimes & *don't* get them.

Thanks for all your kindness to a pilgrim—after all I don't mind a pilgrimage but sacrifice is awful & I've made a good many lately & my home news (Commercial as usual) means many more

My love to you all
Vy sincerely yrs
Edward Elgar[6]

The references in the last paragraph were to music publishers' reports of falling sales and performances, and to the Stuart Wortleys' encouragement in this dark winter of his 'pilgrimage'. Clare recalled:

I remember Mother saying to me in consternation that Edward was threatening not to go on with the Violin Concerto, how dreadful his leaving it wd be, he MUST go on with it as he wd be bound to write *such* a lovely one.

I remember my own dismay & my replying to her 'Oh yes! he *must* go on with it, it would be so lovely, do make him.' . . .

I am certain that Mother, with the moral support of my father & myself, said to him 'Edward, you MUST go on with it' . . .[7]

Then, on the very evening of the day he sent the letter and Andante manuscript to Cheyne Walk, as Elgar sat alone in the flat at Queen Anne's, there came a sort of answer in the shape of a new musical idea:

and on for several bars more or less as

---

[6] HWRO 705:445:7864.
[7] 16 March 1936 to Carice Elgar Blake (Elgar Birthplace parcel 584).

it now appears in the Concerto first movement beginning at cue 2. He inscribed it 'Feb 7:1910 6.30 p.m.' and added:

This is going to be good!

'Where Love and Faith meet
There will be Light'.[8]

The musical meeting was of first-movement primary and secondary themes: for this new idea was to make a bridge between them. And thus it brought the entire first exposition of the Concerto. It stood for a meeting on the personal side as well, and 7 February—the date of the invention—was to be kept as an anniversary between these two ever afterward. It was as though her presence and concern had given this music to him. Perhaps at his request, Alice Stuart Wortley now gave him a photograph of herself.

Returning to Hereford on 9 February, he wrote next day enclosing the new theme invented at Queen Anne's Mansions:

Plas Gwyn, Hereford.
Feb 10 1910

Dear Alice:

Here I am & find a tangled lash to wind! so much to do & everything disagreeable!

About the Black-bird first—you are quite right to feel aggrieved but the French have quite a different *feeling* about him from ours—you have Larousse & I think there are examples there—quotations or something—but it is not *our* blackbird—who is at this moment singing *and* fighting under this very window.

I am so glad to receive C's letter about the M.S.—please thank him for acknowledging the sketch—it was a pleasure to me to send it: there is poetry in the *string* with wh. it is tied together: I had nothing better at Q Anne's.

Thanks also for the photo: but it is not *you*—you would never make a good photograph. Gott sei dank!

I am putting the enclosed (written in dejection as Shelley says) into the Concerto I think & hope; I made it the other evening & like it myself very much. Please tell me (this is what I began to write to you for) what passage in Puccini I have annexed—I cannot place it—but you must tell me at once so that I can remove it. I only *know* 'La Tosca' altho' I have *heard* 'Butterfly'

I am coming up to Frank about the 21st. for the Repertory opening—how good it all looks: also Ronald's Symphony perfce. on the 24th.

Alice is writing & does want you & C. to come here—but it wd. be so dull for you both—only it wd. be nice for us.

Love to you all
Yr affect
Edward[9]

[8] Sketches presented by the Stuart Wortley family to the Elgar Birthplace.
[9] HWRO 705:445:4043.

Alice Elgar wrote the same day:

Plas Gwyn, Hereford
10. Feb. 1910
My dearest Namesake

Edward tells me that you are to go to Cornwall later in the month, & I cannot lose a minute in writing to say, *do* break the journey & come & see us on the way, you & Mr.Stuart Wortley & Claire [*sic*.]

It wd be impossible to tell you what pleasure it wd give us—  If *only* fine weather the country here is lovely, & I think you will like to see where the musics which I know live in your hearts, were written—& you have never seen a home of ours, only Hotel tea or something like that! Now please a Yes—

I am afraid E. will miss London, how I wish we cd. have a flat there.

> With much love
> Yr aff
> C.Alice Elgar

There are very good trains from here to Bristol—for the South—.[10]

But the Stuart Wortleys could not come to Hereford. Elgar quickly sank into depression again. One clue to his thoughts might be found in the words 'paraphrased' by 'Pietro d'Alba' for a passionate song he wrote on 18–19 February amid gales of wind and rain howling round Plas Gwyn. *The River* is seen as a mother flooding to protect the homeland from enemies, but then receding to leave the singer exposed:

> 'Wounded and alone I stand,
> Tricked, derided, impotent!'

Elgar returned to London alone to stay with Frank Schuster, for the opening of the Repertory season on 21 February with Galsworthy's *Justice*. Three days later his own Alice arrived for Landon Ronald's performance of her husband's Symphony. But again they sat apart: and they slept apart, for Alice went to Maud Warrender's sister Lady Margaret Levett for her accommodation, while Edward remained with Schuster.

On 28 February Alice Elgar saw a flat at 58 New Cavendish Street which might please Edward—who dined that night with the Prince of Wales at Marlborough House. He saw the flat next day with her, and liked it: so Alice shot back to Hereford, making all the arrangements at both ends, while Edward spent the interval with Schuster in London. By 7 March Alice and Carice were unpacking and taking inventory at New Cavendish Street. That night they joined Edward at Schuster's house: Alice Stuart Wortley was there. Even in the new flat, Edward subsided into bed with a chill: Alice Stuart Wortley came to tea, and he was better. On the 17th the Elgars dined at Cheyne Walk.

Again the Violin Concerto made progress. The connecting idea written on

[10] Transcript by Clare Stuart Wortley (Elgar Birthplace).

7 February led to the first movement's second subject. Both were now named 'Windflower' themes—after the little white *anemone nemorosa* of early spring. Elgar later wrote of them:

... when the east wind rasps over the ground in March and April they merely turn their backs and bow before the squall. They are buffeted and blown, as one may think almost to destruction; but their anchors hold, and the slender-looking stems bend but do not break. And when the rain clouds drive up the petals shut tight into a tiny tent, as country folk tell one, to shelter the little person inside.

Our native windflower, *Anemone nemorosa*, is often overlooked by gardeners... Who that has read it can forget Farrer's story of his finding the blue wood-anemone, which, like many another, he had pursued all his life as a will-o'-the-wisp? It was in Cornwall, and doubtingly he had plunged into the wood at twilight in search of the phantom flower.[11]

Cornwall, the Lyonesse of Tristan and Iseult, was also the favoured resort of Alice Stuart Wortley.

Suddenly he had his name for this second Alice. She should be his Windflower. The name had come out of the Concerto music, as Clare recalled: '... he ultimately called her Windflower after the themes—not the themes after her'. And so began the Windflower letters.

The first surviving Windflower letter answered her question about a remark she had seen quoted in *The Spectator* for 12 March. The editor, Charles Graves, had begun a review of Strauss's Elektra: 'Genius—modern musical genius—according to the witty perversion of a well-known composer, may be defined as "an infinite capacity for giving pain"'.[12] Was the well-known composer Edward Elgar?

58, New Cavendish Street, W.
Monday [21 Mar. 1910]
Dear Windflower
      (nemorosa)

I return the Spectator with many thanks: the article is very good—of its kind. I am the person referred to in the first sentence—I said the inverted aphorism to Graves in the Ath[enaeum] one night.

[11] See below p. 282.
[12] *Elektra* was in its first English production. Graves was in no doubt about where he stood, for he followed up the Elgar quotation thus: 'and no better illustration can be found than the work in which Strauss has bedevilled Hofmannsthal's squalid perversion of Sophocles's drama'. But that did not wholly represent Elgar's view when he saw *Elektra* for himself on 15 March. Afterwards his wife reported his reaction: 'Much impressed with E[lektra] but kept on saying The pity of it! the pity of it—going back to murderous horrors'.

I hope you will have a not too cold journey & a serene time at the sea—
which is mine by birth, adoption & heritage.

> Love to you all
> Yrs
> E.[13]

Soon it was decided that Frank Schuster should take Edward alone in his car for a
several days' drive in the south-west. Would they include Tintagel, where the Stuart
Wortleys were? Clare recalled of her family:

> They loved the place, and usually went there at Easter or Whitsuntide—
> sometimes in summer too. Mrs.Stuart Wortley had long wished Sir Edward to
> see it, thinking the majestic cliffs and sea would appeal to him.[14]

Elgar went first by train to Torquay. There Schuster was staying at his sister
Adela's house, awaiting him with motor and chauffeur. Next morning Elgar wrote:

Torquay(!)
March 31.1910 [dated by recipient]
Dear Windflower:

I have not the slightest notion, or hope even, that this will find you: but I
do hope you are happy in your very own way in your very own haven of rest.

I am with Frank & his sister & tomorrow F & I commence a motor tour
'round' Cornwall—avoiding Tintagel it seems but I am not *director* or
dictator or Heaven knows what wd. happen to you or to Tintagel. I hope the
invalid is better & all well.

> Love, Windflower.
> Yours E.[15]

The lady at Tintagel renewed her request with insistence. Her daughter recalled:

> It was Mrs Wortley who after much persuasion induced Sir Edward and their
> mutual great friend Mr Schuster to visit Tintagel, saying that if only Sir Edward
> once saw it, he would write something so wonderful! Sir Edward, highly amused,
> used to say that she would have to be responsible for anything, however
> dreadful, that he might compose as a result of the visit![16]

Sunday 3 April found the motorists beginning their journey—toward Tintagel.
Elgar wrote in a small diary he kept of the tour:

. . . Snowstorm on crossing the moors—arrd. at Tintagel about 3.30[.] Sent in
*wrong* names to the Wortleys—Frank's joke.[17]

Clare recalled:

> The afternoon of their arrival, we all walked down to the sea in the 'Cove', below

[13] HWRO 705:445:4106.     [14] MS reminiscence (Elgar Birthplace).
[15] HWRO 705:445:4121.     [16] MS reminiscence.     [17] Elgar Birthplace.

the Castle ruins; and saw it all in very bad weather, at its most stern and forbidding; we three Wortleys loudly bewailing that Tintagel should so badly greet so great a guest. Sir Edward said very little, but did not complain.[18]

They all dined together that night—a farewell for Charles Stuart Wortley, who had to return to London next day.

Next day Elgar wrote:

Monday Ap 4. Weather seems improving, some sun [—] rose early & breakfast alone. *Awfully* dreary village. Coast fine but not so fine as Llangranog [where Elgar's visit in 1901 ultimately proved an inspiration for the *Introduction and Allegro*.] C[harles] Stuart Wortley left for London. Frank & I lunched with Alice & Clare S.-W. [—] after lunch by car to church beyond Boscastle—we four walked thro' lovely valley to B.—there Tea[,] very nice[,] Boscastle harbour very quaint—by car back to Tintagel[.]

Clare recalled:

On the drive home some evening sunshine was enjoyed; and the party walked (a regular custom with Mrs. Wortley) the steep parts of the road down into, and up out of, the Rocky Valley. It was then . . . that the austere yet lyrical beauty of the Tintagel country really showed itself to Sir Edward at last.

Next morning, on Tuesday the 5th, Sir Edward and Mr. Schuster left to continue their motor-tour, west-wards, along the coast. They later sent us a telegram saying something like 'Lovely journey but we miss you'; and Sir Edward sent picture postcards to Mrs. Wortley and to Clare.

One card, postmarked 6 April and addressed to Clare, showed Land's End: that could make the lightest gesture toward 'America'. His message concluded with two climactic chords from the 'Windflower' theme written in dejection:

I restrained myself from jumping in with great difficulty—a very fine coast.

E.E.[19]

That night they slept at Falmouth, which Elgar recorded as a 'very nice place & the first on this car tour which I really feel I want to see again'. That early reaction is fascinating, in view of the fact that within less than a year he was to inscribe the manuscript full score of his Second Symphony 'Venice—Tintagel'. (He did not revisit

---

[18] MS reminiscence.
[19] Elgar Birthplace parcel 584(vii). These chords appear first in the Concerto (in a slightly altered rhythm) in the fifth bar after cue 3.

either place in the interval.) The inscription a year after Elgar's preliminary dismissal of Tintagel shows the value that retrospection could give to a scene—especially when its memory was peopled with special friends.

The evening of 11 April saw him back at New Cavendish Street. There he found Alice, Carice, and Dora Penny (the 'Dorabella' of the *'Enigma' Variations*). The music he played to them on the piano that evening was to find its place in the Second Symphony slow movement. It disturbed Miss Penny: 'The whole movement seemed to me to tell a tragic story of anxiety and sorrow, fears and hopes.'[20]

On the next Sunday, 17 April, while Alice took Carice to the British Museum, Edward dined with the Stuart Wortleys. They went to an afternoon concert, and apparently Edward returned to Cheyne Walk for the evening. They talked of attending the current revival of Pinero's *Trelawny of the Wells* and Gluck's *Orfeo*.

N. Cav St
Monday [18 Apr. 1910]

My dear Windflower:

Please take care of the cold wind. Your name does not mean that you *like* cold winds. How wisely we talked yester even: Alice I think will prefer *Trelawny* tomorrow so the Opera (Orfeo) can be next week & supper after?

I will send the photo of Richter (but I wd. like you to see it first to know if you *really* want it) on your return to civilization and

Yr
EE.[21]

Next evening Elgar saw *Trelawny of the Wells*, but only with Frank Schuster (according to Alice Elgar's diary). On 20 April the two Elgars attended the first in a series of afternoon violin and piano recitals at Queen's Hall by Eugène Ysaÿe and Raoul Pugno. There remained the question of the Gluck opera. That evening Elgar wrote:

58 N.C.St W
Ap 20

My dear Windflower:

We want to know about Orpheus: Alice & I want to go & it wd. be most 'grateful' to us if we cd carry out the suggested plan to go with you: *do* let us hear by telephone what you can do, or, rather what you want to do. which is not always the same thing.

I saw an acct. of Sheffield & hope you are back safely.

How wisely we talked on Sunday!

Yours always
E.E.

[20] 'Some of Elgar's Greater Works in the Making' (TS lecture, 1951: copy in possession of Claud Powell).
[21] HWRO 705:445:4101.

P.S. I am to give A's love & thanks for your note.

I shall go to Q's Hall next Saturday & Sunday for the Wagner Overtures &c.
We went to hear Ysaye & Pugno & are going to their other recitals: I am now
ablaze with work & *writing hard*; you *should* come & see (& hear it!)[22]

It was becoming clear that Alice Stuart Wortley was the Concerto's Egeria. Some
outlines of progress with the first movement, following her initial encouragement in
February to go on with the music, can be traced in manuscript notes by Elgar on two
undated sketches sent to her. A sketch containing the exquisite variation (now
standing at cue 17) of the secondary 'Windflower' subject was inscribed on the verso
'Anemone nemorosa'. On the verso of the passionate recapitulation variant of the
other 'Windflower' theme (now round cue 34) Elgar copied these lines:

> 'The undelivered tidings in his breast
>    Suffer him not to rest
> He sees afar the <u>immemorable</u> throng'
>
> ˣ   Wm Watson<br>ₓ I do not like this word [E.E.][23]

In later years, after her mother's death, Clare Stuart Wortley explained it thus:

> ... Being the soul of honour, he felt himself under an obligation to her for giving
> him an impulse at a critical moment, & he sought to discharge that obligation by
> giving her what she most liked, themes & MSS—dedicating two of the next
> themes to her, & giving her a share in the final triumph, viz, the signed orchestral
> score. This I propose to write down & put with the MSS; as it is the true
> explanation, & honourable to all parties.[24]

During the composition of the Concerto first movement, he seemed to want Alice
Stuart Wortley's presence at nearly every moment. The Gluck opera date was fixed

---

[22] HWRO 705:445:7816. In the first paragraph the last seven words have been eradicated. The
letter bears the marks of flowers enclosed.

[23] Elgar also marked the entire poem, and sent it to her:

The Sovereign Poet

He sits above the clang and dust of Time,
With the world's secret trembling on his lip.
He asks not converse nor companionship
In the cold starlight where thou canst not climb.

The undelivered tidings in his breast
Suffer him not to rest.
He sees afar the immemorable throng,
And binds the scattered ages with a song.

The glorious riddle of his rhythmic breath,
His might, his spell, we know not what they be:
We only feel, whate'er he uttereth,
This savours not of death,
This hath a relish of eternity.

(Elgar Birthplace parcel 584(i) )

[24] 16 March 1936 to Carice Elgar Blake.

for the two couples to attend on 29 April; and before that was another violin and piano recital. This letter's reverted salutation and formal close suggest that it was intended for more general sight:

58, New Cavendish Street, W.
April 25. 1910
Dear Alice:

Here are the two stalls for Friday 29th and we have supper here after: also I send the ticket for the seat next ours for Ysaye on Wednesday afternoon— we are quite close to the platform for these concerts—a good place.

I missed you yesterday—thanks for the Caractacus programme.

Yours most sncy<br>Edward[25]

On the previous day, Sunday, the Elgars had lunched with the conductor Hans Richter and his wife at the home of their friend Mrs Joshua. The Stuart Wortleys had been expected, but she was ill. In fact she might be unable to attend the Ysaÿe–Pugno recital. But she suggested the Royal Academy Private View. The morning of the recital he wrote:

58, New Cavendish Street, W.
April 27.

My dear Windflower

I fear the cold wind has been too much for you. *Please* come to-day & tea here after—or tea only if you cannot come to the Concert.

You must not send me the enclosed.

I have *no* tickets for Private View R.A. [—] only for the dinner[:] do let me go with you to the P. View if you can manage. I will wear a nice hat. Tell me this afternoon.

You *must* come either to the concert and tea—or the latter only

Frank here yesterday—very radiant & you have written to him about music. I have been working hard at the Windflower themes but all stands still until you come & approve!

Love<br>Edward[26]

Alice Elgar's diary for that day records the afternoon recital, but it makes no mention of Alice Stuart Wortley. That evening Elgar went alone to a large dinner party at Sir Gilbert Parker's house.

The next three mornings were booked for him to listen to player-piano rolls which had just been made of the entire First Symphony, and to mark tempo and rubato throughout to guide the listener who would operate the device. After the first morning's work, he returned to the flat and wrote:

---

[25] HWRO 705:445:4075.        [26] HWRO 705:445:7853.

58, New Cavendish Street, W.
Thursday [28 Apr. 1910] p m

My dear Windflower

I am so tired & there are people here & I am very *sad* indeed—a most interesting dinner last night at the Parkers'—you will see it in the M[ornin]g Post— I *do* like to be amongst brains & my wretched music takes me amongst them so seldom: so *you* must come tomorrow to the Orchestrelle[,] Bond St.—any time 10.30 — to 1.0ˣ[:] ask for me & if they do not know where I am say I am with Mr. [Easthope] Martin. All this I said on the telephone but I repeat it because you may not have heard.

[ˣ]? I cd. give you lunch somewhere if you like & R.A. after

It is so dreary to-day & the tunes stick & are not Windflowerish—at present

Your<br>E[27]

Alice Elgar's diary for the next days reads:

April 29.   E. to Orchestrelle—   E. lunched with S.Wortleys & then to private view at Academy.   A. went too but cd. not find him[:] mis[erable]— ... C[arice] went with Miss Paget's party, E. dined with them. E. & A. to Orpheus[,] met S.Wortleys there. Very lovely. Mr. & Mrs. S.Wortley to supper with us after Orpheus, very pleasant time—
April 30.   E. to Orchestrelle—A. & C. allowed to go & hear....

Next day Alice and Carice went to Sunday lunch again with Mrs Joshua, leaving Edward behind in the flat to nurse a 'dreadful headache'. It seems he met Alice Stuart Wortley that afternoon, for a sketch of the second windflower theme was given to her then (according to her own notation). On the sketch sheet he had pasted a newspaper cutting, pencilling it round with double lines and identifying the writer as Claude Phillips. In later years the cutting was torn off the sketch sheet, but enough of the newspaper verso remained for it to be identified long afterward as a page from *The Daily Telegraph* of 30 April. The portion of page corresponding with that fragmentary verso was the conclusion of Claude Phillips's 'Art Notes', discussing a *Nymph and Piping Shepherd* painted by Titian in extreme old age:

It is twilight, and soon will be night, with him; it is twilight, and soon will be night, with the lovers, who dally still in the sombre air shot with silver. The poetry of the early years has come back, intensified by something of added poignancy, and of foreboding that is tinged, it may be, with remorse. This last passion has something that the earlier passion had not; in one sense it is nearer to earth and earthiness; in another it is infinitely higher and more far-reaching, more typical of the love that in its heights and depths, in its tender light and sombre, fitfully illumined shadow, is truly that which to the end of all things must hold and possess Man.[28]

[27] HWRO 705:445:7862.
[28] Elgar Birthplace. The identification was made by Prof. Brian Trowell, who has generously shared his research with me.

These words, juxtaposed by Elgar with his own windflower music, lead far into his thoughts. They seem to make clear, first of all, that he has told Alice Stuart Wortley about his long-ago first love, the broken engagement, its burden of memory. Then there is the hint that this memory is at the base of his music's nostalgia now—perhaps always. Finally the youthful past has come back, and 'this last passion' has found its fulfilment somewhere, somehow on the verge of night.

The ensuing week brought intense work on the Concerto. On 8 May he wrote to Schuster: 'I have the Concerto well in hand . . . 1st movement finished & the IIIrd well on . . . Alice Wortley came to tea today & had a dose of Concerto which beseemingly she liketh well.'[29]

The Concerto moved forward against a background of national grief. Late on Friday night, 6 May, King Edward had died after a very short illness. There was a suggestion (which seems to have emanated from the Schuster–Stuart Wortley circle) that Elgar be asked to write a funeral march for the royal cortège. But Lord Howe replied that there would not be time enough for the music to be written, instrumental parts produced, and rehearsed by the bands before the state funeral on the 20th.[30] Elgar wrote:

58 N.C. St W
May 11 1910

My dear Windflower:

I know you were interesting yourself in the funeral March—but it is not possible—I have a letter from Ld.Howe wh. you shall see—

I have retired from the Albert Hall—the Concert is to be In Memoriam with all sorts of rubbish, so I refused.

It is so dull in London—Oh! these sad days—

On Saturday I go to Frank (Hut) for the week end—Willie—Ld.N[orthampton]—is to be there

I send this in case we do not get to your tea today

Love<br>
Your<br>
Edward.[31]

Elgar's stay at The Hut, to work at the Concerto, in fact lasted ten days. He went there alone, leaving his own Alice and Carice at the flat. They came down to The Hut for three days, and as they left, Alice Stuart Wortley arrived for the weekend of 21–3 May.[32] Elgar's return to New Cavendish Street did not interrupt his absorption. His wife noted:

[29] HWRO 705:445:7019. The main lines of the first movement were now firm enough to play the music to friends, though the documents show that much work was still to be done on details of the solo part.

[30] HWRO 705:445:1668–9.

[31] HWRO 705:445:7852.

[32] Charles Stuart Wortley's diary, cited by Clare in her letter of 3 March 1936 to Carice Elgar Blake. This diary showed that Charles and Clare were elsewhere that weekend, visiting his elder daughter 'Bice' and her family in Kent. Charles Stuart Wortley's diary has most unfortunately disappeared: we know it only from quotations made by his daughter Clare for her notes on the Elgar letters.

Sunday, May 26 . . . E. very hard at work. E. A. & C. lunched at 7 Cheyne Walk. E. & A. with Alice S.W. to Exhibition. . . .

Two days later, at Elgar's request, the violinist W. H. Reed came to the flat to try over the Concerto first movement: that afternoon Alice Stuart Wortley came to hear the results. On the 30th she and Elgar went for an afternoon drive together and on to dinner with the Beresfords—while his own Alice hunted for a new flat in London (as the three-month lease at New Cavendish Street was approaching its end). She found nothing.

Elgar's letter to the Windflower next day reverted to the 'public' form:

58, New Cavendish Street, W.
May 31: 1910
My dear Alice:

It is very sad tearing up this flat. I find all sorts of accumulations of odd music mostly to be destroyed. I rescued the *sketch m.s.* of the first movement of the Concerto & stupidly sent it to you without the much more interesting notation of Busoni—this comes now—please tear it & the MS up when you have done with it: we really *hate* going away.

Lady M[aud Warrender] came in early this am. to say good bye[:] wont you come tomorrow? Mr. Reed comes for a final revision at 9.30 a.m.! & I have dentist at 12. In at 4–6 teatime[.] The piano goes tomorrow!

Yrs affectly
EE[33]

She took the suggestion and came to share a final hour in the flat where so much had happened.

Conducting engagements took Elgar away over the next two days, while Alice and Carice closed the flat and went back to Hereford to prepare Plas Gwyn for his return there on 4 June. But not for long. He was to leave almost immediately for Lincoln to conduct *Gerontius* in the Cathedral. And although he would travel there alone, he was not to be alone at Lincoln.

Plas Gwyn, Hereford.
Sunday June 5 1910
Dear Windflower:

I arrive at the Deanery, Lincoln, on Tuesday eveng: please let me know at that address *when* & *where* you arrive.

---

[33] Bound with sketches for the Second Symphony (Elgar Birthplace).

You may know my hostess (I do not yet!) but she—Mrs Wickham—was a daughter of Gladstone.

Such wet & dreary weather.

Your affecte<br>Edward

The performance will, I *think*, be wonderful!
Please address The Deanery as I shall have left here[34]

And he sent her a set of fine photographic views of Lincoln Cathedral. On a small piece of paper attached to the view of choir stalls he drew an arrow pointing to a central place in the front row left: 'You are to sit here'.[35] She did: and he inscribed her vocal score with the date of the performance: 'Lincoln  June 9: 1910  Edward Elgar'.[36]

From Lincoln he went alone to The Hut to work again at the Concerto. He had written to his host, Frank Schuster, at the end of May:

. . . on Friday the 10th [June] I wd. like to come to you till Monday or Tuesday (13th or 14th)—if you *can* have me[:] never mind about writing. I want to *end* that Concerto but do not see my way very clearly to the end—so you had best invite its stepmother to the Hut. Do.[37]

She was invited, and she came. Also, on Sunday 12 June, came W. H. Reed to try the projected finale. He wrote of The Hut and the people he found there:

I can see it now as it looked that spring morning when I first arrived. It was a sweet riverside house, raised several feet above the level of the lawn, with wooden steps leading up to the verandah from the gravel path . . . Across the lawn, and almost screened by trees, was the studio, away from the house and approached by stones placed in the grass about a pace apart. . . .

In the course of my visits I met many of the Elgar worshippers who surrounded him in those days: Mrs.Stuart Wortley (afterwards Lady Stuart of Wortley), Lalla Vandervelde (. . . daughter of Mr.Edward Speyer . . .), and many others. They all seemed a very happy party, each going his own way and meeting on the raised verandah for meals. Sir Edward spent most of his time at work in the studio, where the others wisely left him alone unless invited to come and hear some of the concerto . . .[38]

Once again Elgar's visit extended to more than a week. On 15 June the whole party went to London to see 'the Russian dancers' at the Palace Theatre. In this pre-Diaghilev season, Pavlova and Mordkine astonished the West End with their *Bacchanal*.

[34] HWRO 705:445:4073.
[35] Bound with Alice Stuart Wortley's copy of the large English–German vocal score of *Gerontius*, which Elgar sent her a week after the Lincoln performance (see his letter of 16 June 1910). This score, bound to include the views of Lincoln Cathedral, is at the Elgar Birthplace.
[36] This English vocal score, which she had with her at the performance, is in the possession of Robert Cecil.
[37] HWRO 705:445:7055.
[38] W. H. Reed, *Elgar as I Knew Him* (Gollancz, 1936), pp. 26–8.

The Hut, Bray, Berks.
June 16 1910

My dear Windflower:    How lovely it was yesterday—I never saw anything more beautiful.

I am causing a German Gerontius (which is better printed than the English edition) to be sent to you as a memento of Lincoln: it has the English words also. Here is one of your own flowers. I have just been walking round between work: it goes well & I have made the end serious & grand I hope & have brought in the real inspired themes from the 1st.movement[:] Frank approves. I did it this morning. This place is like

[*portion cut away; then on verso*]:

go home on Saturday—Frank motors me part of the way—it is so lovely here today & the music sings of memories & hope.

My love to you all

Bless you<br>E.

My hand is quite tired & this pen—my letter pen—has gone wrong—hence the scribble which is worse than usual. Tell me if you receive the Gerontius.[39]

What seems finally to have brought Elgar's sojourn at The Hut to a close was news from Plas Gwyn that Mrs Worthington had arrived there on 17 June. He returned to Hereford and his own Alice next day. And the day after that he wrote of the central section in the finale:

Plas Gwyn, Hereford.
Sunday [19 June 1910]

My dear W.

Here I am after a very hot & dull journey & have been at work—it took me a long time to 'find myself' here but the work goes on & the pathetic portion is really fixed

Please think no more of the cab fare—the Russians were worth more! I do want to see them again.

My room is lovely & we have heaps of roses & *white pinks* on our tiny domain

Love<br>E

The pianola is really most amusing but I prefer to hear you play so please practise all your pieces.[40]

She telegraphed some bad news about Paderewski's latest proposed visit. He responded:

[39] HWRO 705:445:7851.    [40] HWRO 705:445:4072.

Plas Gwyn, Hereford.
Thursday [23 June 1910]

My dear Windflower:

It was so good of you to send that (very sad) telegram: I am so truly sorry for Paderewski & for you too!

I have no news except that I am appalled at the last movement & cannot get on:—it is growing so large—too large I fear & I have headaches (here); Mr Reed comes to us next *Thursday* to play it through & mark the bowings in the 1st.movement & we shall judge the finale & condemn it, if you like. The weather is for the moment dull: I wish you could have seen the flowers before this last heavy rain.

As I said, I have no news. I go on working & working & making it all as good as I can for the owner[x]

Love<br>from<br>Edward

[x]but it sadly needs inspiration, editing, & a few well-nourished notes added—[41]

He pasted onto the letter two coloured photographs—'Lady Coppice, near Hereford' and 'On the Wye, Hereford'. For he had asked his own Alice to invite the Windflower to Plas Gwyn, and she had accepted. Alice Elgar wrote:

Plas Gwyn, Hereford.
24 June 1910.

My dear Alice

We are delighted that you can suggest a day but much hope you will be able to make a slight modification & come from Saturday to *Monday*, as Edward has to conduct at Bournemouth on Friday evening, the 8th. & cannot reach home till Saturday & the Sunday train is very slow—so please let it be Monday. We so much hope you will be able to do this, it will be a great pleasure to see you here & we hope for a glimpse of Mr.Stuart Wortley & Clare another time.

This is a dripping Midsummer Day but I hope it will be fine & hot again for your visit & you must see one or two of Edward's favourite & beloved old Churches—

The 3rd. Movement is *nearly* finished & sweeps along irresistibly—

With love & looking forward so much to seeing you, & we so much hope the 9th will suit you

Yrs. aftly<br>C. Alice Elgar[42]

    [41] HWRO 705:445:7854. The final words in the body of the letter, 'for the owner[x]', have been eradicated.
    [42] HWRO 705:445:7917.

Before that visit, the Elgars were to spend a few days in Cornwall at the home of the former Lady Mary Lygon, now married to Col. Trefusis. It seemed that the Stuart Wortleys were once more at Tintagel: but a meeting in Cornwall was not to be. Alice Elgar wrote:

Porthgwidden, Devoran, Cornwall.
6 July 1910
My dear Alice

Many thanks for yr. kind card of invitation for this evening wh. E. has just given me—& you see we are too far away—

We are much looking forward to seeing you on Saturday. Your train only stops at Worcester & Malvern, & leaves Paddington 1.40—I do hope it will clear up for you to see the Country looking beautiful.

It is *lovely* here, & E. looks so rested & refreshed—   Perhaps it is as well we have to leave tomorrow, it is so beautiful & soothing one might forget the outer world too soon.

The 3rd movement of the Concerto is beyond words beautiful—

> Much love
> Yr Aft
> C.Alice Elgar

How often I have used the word 'beautiful' you see it permeates the atmosphere & will in.

Elgar added:

P.S. I wrote such a *nice P.S.* on a *wrong sheet of paper*[x]—a real Lyonesse P.S. for you. Bless you

> Love
> EE[43]

[x]destroyed by accident

Then Alice Stuart Wortley's visit to Hereford was put off a fortnight. After his initial disappointment Edward wrote:

Plas Gwyn, Hereford.
July 13 1910
My dear W.

All radiance again—the Concerto-orchestration dances wildly along.
Today I have had my copyist here writing in the Violin part in the score
No new proofs yet but you shall see the last movement—& like it

[43] HWRO 705:445:7918.

Kreisler has seen it—with me—& he likes it better than the first Allegro. I am very happy over it.

The roses will be all gone before you come

Love
Edward

Swallows all gone—but more eggs are being laid! Sweet little things[44]

Again conducting engagements took him away. First came a rehearsal of *King Olaf* for the York Festival.

N.E.Station Hotel[,] York.
Friday [15 July 1910] evening

My dear W.

I have to travel to London (Q Annes Mansns) *tomorrow*—I shall remain at Q.A's until early Tuesday morning—Concerto business—I think you are all away from town—I travel on Tuesday from Kings X to York leaving in time for rehearsal at 2 30

I have just scored

so happy over it now

Yrs ev
E.E.[45]

Queen Anne's Mansions, St.James' Park, London, S.W.
Sunday [17 July 1910]

My dear W.

The rehearsal (Chorus) was fine & promises well

Our Concerto [première] is fixed for Nov 10 (& *30th*) Kreisler—Philharmonic Socy[,] Queen's Hall

I am here from two o'clock onwards and shall remain scoring hard till theatre time. Love to you all

Yours aye
E.[46]

What they saw that night seems nowhere recorded.

Two days later he returned to York, where he was joined by both Alices for the final *King Olaf* rehearsal before the Festival performance. He conducted a concert of his orchestral works on the 20th and *King Olaf* the following night. On 22 July all three travelled together to Plas Gwyn. It was the Windflower's first view of the Elgars' home. Alice Elgar wrote: 'Alice S.W. much excited seeing house, running seeing everythg.'

[44] HWRO 705:445:7855.     [45] HWRO 705:445:4066.     [46] HWRO 705:445:4099.

Elgar's next days were divided between Concerto orchestration in the mornings and walks with Alice Stuart Wortley in the afternoons. On 25 July there was a motor excursion to the tiny early Norman church at Kilpeck. The day after brought W. H. Reed: 'Mr.Reed playing the Concerto thro' & thro'—Cadenza *wonderful*. . . . E. & C. & Alice S.W. & Mr.Reed for Boomerang walk . . .'.

It was the latest fascination. Reed remembered:

When we were tired of our musical jobs we used to go to one of his beloved spots, a meadow down by the Wye River, and practise with the boomerang, watching its peculiar flight and constantly striving to acquire the necessary skill to bring it back to our feet at the end of it. Once, Edward was almost too successful. The wretched thing circled all over the meadow, then, suddenly altering its course for no apparent reason, it made a bee-line for us. We ran like hares and barely escaped with our lives, for it was about eighteen inches in length and fairly heavy. It whizzed round in the air at a terrific speed and looked quite capable of taking off both our heads if it had caught us under the chin.[47]

Whether that was during the Windflower visit history does not relate.

Next day, 27 July, she left to join her family for a holiday at Muncaster Castle near Ravenglass, Cumberland. Apparently she had an eventful journey.

Plas Gwyn[,] Hereford
Friday [29 July 1910] a m

My dear Windflower

I have just posted the full score [of the Concerto first movement], over which we worked, to the publishers

I was so glad your letter reached Alice this a.m.—what adventures and how glad I am you are safe out of all the trials

I cannot get away this week at all & must remain here: tell me if you recd. one letter, on *my* paper & a telegram contradicting it—I *am* so dreadfully sorry—   The weather is now better but I must go on—working.

The Ark is desolate & so is the Wye & so is

Edward[48]

He sent a large envelope of proofs.

She telegraphed an answer, with a request for more proofs. But those would not be available until about the time her holiday entered its next phase, at Strathyre, Perthshire. That evening Elgar sent her a picture card of Bishop Booth's Porch at Hereford Cathedral:

Thanks for telegram: so sorry, no more proofs to send you to-day—they must go to Scotland

This is THE porch[.] The little inside door is not visible but remembered

E[49]

[47] *Elgar as I Knew Him*, p. 38.        [48] HWRO 705:445:4077.        [49] HWRO 705:445:7087.

She wondered whether he was coming to the Leeds Festival (where Stanford was conductor-in-chief) in the autumn. This he answered in the 'public' style designed to meet all eyes:

Plas Gwyn, Hereford.
July 31: 1910
My dear Alice:

About Leeds festival [—] I am not going as I am not asked: my popularity shews, in dismal relief, the unpopularity of someone else!

They propose to ruin the Variations, to travesty (the accompaniments) to the Sea Pictures & conventionalize Go song of mine. The festival has steadily gone down in interest & is now a dull affair of only Kapellmeister interest

Love to you all

Yrs always
Edward[50]

In early August he finished the Concerto orchestration. Then he and his Alice went for a reminiscent visit to Severn Grange—an old house whose owner, in Edward's young days, had a great library of music and used to hold regular chamber music sessions. The teenaged Elgar had there gained much knowledge of musical repertory and also of literature, for there he was given books by such authors as Ruskin. Near the old house was Claines Church, where his mother's parents were buried: it was another site of early memories. Some of these were alluded to in Alice Elgar's next letter to the other Alice (now in Scotland).

Severn Grange, Worcester.
12 Augt.1910.
My dear Alice

It was so nice to have your letter & hear how beautiful your surroundings are, I hope the change & rest will give you (& each of you) a great store of strength— It is very sad not to have you for the [Three Choirs] Fest—but we thought it wd. be very impossible from the North.

Edward has finished all his Orchn. & was quite sad & depressed when the last sheet left the house—Kreisler wrote the *most* deeply & movingly enthusiastic appreciation of it.

E. & I came here yesterday, it is about 2 miles from Worcester & he used to come here & steep himself in art & music from about 20 yrs. old till after we were married & left the neighbourhood. The son of the old music lover now reigns here & they are very nice. The garden is most extraordinary, planted with every rare shrub & tree & so grown up that it seems to me more like a Maeterlinck fantasia than any English place—

E. & I have just been out to a fine old Church & seeing the tomb of '*Helen Leslie*' [—] early last century but E. used to think it a pretty name & used to

[50] HWRO 705:445:7859.

walk out of the town with a Score [—] perhaps Pastoral Symph. [—] & sit on the stone & read it—

Tomorrow we are to go till Monday to the DeNavarros at Broadway[.] Carice is with the Miss Colmans & going today to steam (I suppose steam) on the Norfolk Broads wh. sounds most delightful—

Please enjoy the Hills & views & all come back very radiant.

Thanks *many* for writing about Beaconsfd. I wonder what you will hear— With love dear Alice

> Yr aft
> C.A.Elgar

So difficult to write on such minute paper.[51]

Beaconsfield was one of many places in the Home Counties being considered as a possible new home for the Elgars: for he was restless again, and had decided they must leave Hereford.

After the round of visits they were back at Plas Gwyn until time for the London orchestral rehearsals before the Gloucester Festival. Kreisler was rehearsing for a separate performance at Gloucester, and he planned to go through the Concerto privately with Elgar both in London and again at Gloucester.

Langham Hotel, London.

Sep 1 1910

Dear Windflower

Such a fine rehearsal to-day[:] Symphony & Gerontius

Tomorrow I try the Concerto with K. [—] he is delighted with it—I want *someone* to turn over? Then at Gloucester we do it again—alas!

My visits here [to look at houses] have scarcely been a success. I am a dull visitor now. Pippa is here & I take her to Tree's first night (Henry VIII) this evening.

When do you return to London?

We have looked at more flats with desperate results

> Love
> Yrs
> E.[52]

---

[51] Elgar Birthplace parcel 584(xix).
[52] HWRO 705:445:7103. At the end of the first paragraph '—alas!' has been eradicated.

Langham Hotel, London.
Sep 2

My dear W.

I have played it for 3 hours with Kreisler & it is tremendous

He will play it thro' at Gloucester privately with me to all the dear people.
Prof Terry turned over for me & so worthily took some one else's place

                                                              Yrs
                                                              E

Where were you?[53]

She was still in Scotland, not to return until mid-September.

On 22 September Elgar left Hereford for another week at The Hut. Between trains he went to tea at Cheyne Walk. There a subject of conversation was the inscription on the poet's tomb in Lesage's *Gil Blas*—the inscription which was going atop the Violin Concerto. On a sheet of Cheyne Walk notepaper Elgar wrote it out: 'Aquí está encerrada el alma del. . . . .'.[54] He left Cheyne Walk late, and from Paddington Station sent a wire handed in at 5.58 p.m.: 'Missed train   Esta Encerrada El Alma'.[55]

The Hut, Bray, Berks.
Friday [23 Sept. 1910]

My dear Windflower

I missed the train but took a later one. found Mrs. Howard & Pippa here. P. departed this a.m. but, I think, returns tomorrow.

We have asked Kreisler and [Landon] Ronald for Sunday but at this moment I know nothing—I shall hear tomorrow I hope. I have been round to all the dear, well-remembered bits of the garden: it is very lovely peaceful & quiet now.

I loved every minute of my visit yesterday—I can't tell *when* I come in again but if I can come to see the flat tomorrow a.m I'll wire or telephone

                                                              Love
                                                              yr
                                                              Edwd.[56]

No record has survived of any further meeting during this visit to The Hut, and on 29 September he returned to Plas Gwyn.

A communication from Alice Stuart Wortley, telling of wisdom tooth trouble, arrived in the midst of printing difficulties over the Concerto.

[53] Elgar Birthplace parcel 583(xxiii).      [55] Elgar Birthplace parcel 571.
[54] Elgar Birthplace parcel 583(xii).        [56] HWRO 705:445:4074.

Plas Gwyn, Hereford.
Oct 9 1910

My dear Windflower:

Thanks for the verses—the title is the best part[.]
*I* knew this was your wisest year—hence the tooth which I hope does not hurt
now.

Alice has one coming!

I am coming to London for a week & will let you know where I am. Alas!
there is small enjoyment in the Concerto—the printers are all behind & there
is no peace.

Thanks for your news of the impossible flats—all else when I come

Love
Yr
Edward

Oh! Professor Terry is here & I do want him to see you & he is dying to see
you: he will travel to London with me tomorrow—shall I tell him to call say
on Tuesday—he goes on to Leeds almost at once & then home to Aberdeen.

I have miles of concert news to tell you—only all is deadly uninteresting—
(to you?)[57]

Charles Sanford Terry was at Plas Gwyn for a weekend of work at Concerto
proofs. During a walk Elgar's foot had been stung, and it swelled so that he had to put
off his journey to London on Monday 10 October. Terry left by himself, to stay with
his sister in London. From her flat, he wrote to Alice Stuart Wortley on the 11th,
reluctantly declining her invitation to Cheyne Walk:

Hélas! people are coming here to dine tomorrow night, & this afternoon I am
pledged to meet Sir Edward at Paddington & expound to him some
important details concerning the Concerto. . . .

*The* Concerto grows more & more *Dante*sque! It is bound to create an
enormous sensation on Nov.10, & thereafter to be acclaimed the compeer of
those of Beethoven & Bach. It is a *glorious* work, & *what* a glorious man he is!
When I leave Plas Gwyn I always feel like a schoolboy facing the awful
blackness of a return to school.[58]

Elgar duly arrived that afternoon, but there were as yet no proofs of the Concerto
finale.

---

[57] HWRO 705:445:4064.
[58] HWRO 705:445:7916.

Queen Anne's Mansions, St.James' Park, London, S.W.
Wednesday [12 Oct. 1910]

My dear W.

I am here & Alice joins me tomorrow. I have not yet a last movement to send you & I cannot call as I had hoped as I got a bad *sting* (beast unknown but presumably wasp!) on the instep & my foot has been *very* much swelled & irritated & I must keep it more or less in midair & bandaged. I went to the Theatre with Terry last evening & it was not good for it—so here I am a prisoner.

Love to you all three

Yrs ever
E.E.[59]

Queen Anne's Mansions, St.James' Park, London, S.W.
Wedy [12 Oct. 1910] night 10 0 c

My dear W.

Your letter has just come & I am so *very*, *very* sorry for you: do be quite well.

My foot is better but I am not sure of being able to get out: will you telephone to me in the morning or if you cannot do that can you come to tea here? Alice arrives about 4.30—come as early as you like.

I am writing also to say that Kreisler is going to play thro' the Concerto sometime between 15th & 18th & I wd. like to arrange it to include you—but I have settled nothing & have only told Frank by this post of the possibility—& await your commands.

I *do* hope you are better

Love
Yr
E[60]

Alice Elgar did not in fact travel up to London until the Friday, 14 October. That night they dined at Cheyne Walk, and went to a play—unidentified except that the diary noted: 'Not a good play.'

October 15 ... Kreisler came after his aftn. concert & played thro' the Concerto—Wonderful. quite different from previous time. Most enthusiastic. Alice S.Wortley turned over for E.   A. turned for Kreisler—

They were making many revisions in the solo part. Kreisler was to come again in two days' time for another session. Alice Stuart Wortley suggested that might be at Cheyne Walk. Elgar wrote next day partly to answer this, and partly to convey a

[59] HWRO 705:445:4076.    [60] HWRO 705:445:4062.

request from Ernest Newman. The request remains somewhat obscure: surviving letters from Elgar to Newman show that Newman was planning some sort of history (never completed) for which he needed a loan or gift of books. On 18 October Elgar wrote to him: 'I fear the moneyed amateur is mostly bent on exploiting his own imagined abilities but there are some of lesser means who might be moved.' Elgar's letter to Alice Stuart Wortley is further obscured by the heavy scoring over in a later hand of eight words (of which I have been able to retrieve only four):

Queen Anne's Mansions, St.James' Park, London, S.W.
Oct 16 1910

My dear W.

The writer of the enclosed is Newman who wrote the article you liked about the Concerto in the M[usical] Times

—Do you know [Lord Howard] de Walden really well & couldn't he be persuaded to do this (to him) small thing & be really useful in music, [2 words illegible] in which he himself [2 words illegible]!

Send me the letter back some time & your wise views.

I fear Kreisler must come here tomorrow—he wd. fear society & audience if I propose your beautiful house.

Love
Edwd[61]

Kreisler came again to Elgar's flat, but this time with no mention of Alice Stuart Wortley's presence. Then:

October 18. A. lunched with A.S.Wortley, E. came afterwards & we went to see Flat together—

October 19 . . . Mr.S.Wortley & Alice & Clare dined with us at E.'s Club. Then to Henry VIII. very very fine—E. saw Tree & Bourchier between the Acts. Said he was quite afraid to shake hands or talk to Bourchier he looked so really like Henry VIII.

Next day the Elgars went back to Hereford for more work on Concerto proofs.

The London friends were planning festivities around the Concerto première. Schuster devised a big supper party to follow the performance, and wrote to Alice Stuart Wortley:

[61] HWRO 705:445:4065. Thomas Evelyn Scott-Ellis, 8th Baron Howard de Walden, was a generous patron of the London Symphony Orchestra from its beginning in 1904. Elgar later possessed Lord Howard de Walden's sumptuous books on heraldry, and his copies bear evidence of close study.

22, Old Queen Street, Westminster.
23rd. [Oct. 1910]
Dear Carrie

Will you & Charlie & Clare (if going) sup with me after the concerto—my Elgar supper. Of course you will!

Your affecte.
Frank.[62]

The Stuart Wortleys asked the Elgars for the night following, but Mina Beresford had forestalled them. Alice Elgar wrote:

Plas Gwyn, Hereford.
23 Oct. 1910
My dear Alice

Very many thanks for your letter & kind wish for us to dine with you on 11th Nov. We heard from Frank that he believes we are to dine with the Beresfords that evening—so if he has arranged that, you will see that we shall not be able to come & fulfil *your* lovely plan—  It is dear of you to think of it—

Mr. Austin has just come & begun the playing over of parts wh. will take hours—& leave E. & he exhausted somewhat. Then I hope the labours will be over for this time.

We are so often talking of Henry VIII, & did enjoy it so much—

With love
Yr aft
C. Alice Elgar

Lady Charlie had invited us for *10th* Supper—but Frank had his party.

Edward added in pencil:

Oh! you *ought* to have been here—to help. Please ask Frank about the Beresfords

D.o.m.D. in haste[63]

The Stuart Wortleys changed their invitation to 8 November, two days before the première.

Working hard with his assistant John Austin, Elgar had the Concerto parts checked nearly completely by the end of the following day. But he was tired. A grey autumnal day found him with sketches made over several years for what would become his Second Symphony. As he wrote to Alice Stuart Wortley, he enclosed a cutting from *The Daily Telegraph* of 'Art Notes' by Claude Phillips.

---

[62] HWRO 705:445:7919.
[63] HWRO 705:445:7920. Elgar's closing initials, several times used in later letters, remain obscure.

Plas Gwyn, Hereford.
Oct 25 1910
My dear W.

You do not see the Telegraph so you never see Claude's articles which are splendid. Here is one. You may condescend to return it some day.

I am so glad we are to be with you on the 8th.— I may come to town before that though.

I have been working too hard over this absurd printing muddle & have a slight headache—& I have also been making a little progress with Symphony No.2 & am sitting at my table weaving strange & wonderful memories into very poor music I fear. What a wonderful year this has been! with all the sad things in the great public life—the King's death downwards—the radiance in a poor, little private man's soul has been wonderful & new & the Concerto has come!

Love<br>E[64]

Then Elgar was booked to assist his northern friend Nicholas Kilburn by conducting part of the 50th Anniversary Concert for the Sunderland Philharmonic.

Grand Hotel, Sunderland
Nov 2 1910
My dear W.

Oh! this awful place quite in the atmosphere of the Tivoli

I called at Queen's Hall & *all* tickets [for the Concerto première] are gone except some back 5/- ones. So hold your spare ticket fast. I wish I could use it & you might conduct—but you *will* be conducting the concerto wherever you are.

I think Prof. Terry has a ticket but I am not yet sure.

I hope it is warmer for you than here—very cold & such a fearsome Hotel. Pity me!

I go home Via Manchester tomorrow

I began a diary again & have just torn it up.

Love<br>Edward[65]

[64] HWRO 705:445:7856. The Claude Phillips cutting has not been preserved with the letter, and may have been returned as Elgar requested. Phillips's 'Art Notes' appeared in the *Telegraph* on Saturdays. There were none, however, for 15 Oct. 1910. That makes it nearly certain that the column Elgar sent was from the Saturday immediately before his letter, 22 Oct. (His own Saturday, Sunday, and Monday had been entirely given over to correcting orchestral parts; Tuesday 25 Oct. would thus have afforded his first real chance to send a cutting from Saturday's paper.) The Phillips column on 22 Oct. is headed 'The Wax Bust'. It deals with a *Flora*, then in Berlin, and attributed by some experts to Leonardo da Vinci. Phillips sifts the evidence, but concludes with a plea for trusting one's own responses: if genius such as Leonardo's were there, it would shine clearly through, he says, and there would be no disagreement. As it is, he cannot believe that the *Flora* is Leonardo's work. It lacks the intensity of genius.

[65] HWRO 705:445:7861.

Back at Plas Gwyn, Elgar sent a coloured card showing Della Robbia's *Adoration* and *Choristers* to Clare with her initials worked in:

Plas Gwyn, Hereford.
Nov 5 1910
My dear Clare:

I am foolish enough to send you the enclosed just found amongst my Italian papers;—it was 'inscribed' in rebus festivi to you when we were in Florence—covered up & forgotten—although you were not & never will be by

Yr
Edward Elgar.[66]

Plas Gwyn, Hereford.
Nov 5 1910
My dear W.

Many thanks. I hear Prof Terry *has* a ticket so keep yours for some *understanding* person [—] don't let the seat be empty.

We arrive at Old Queen St on Monday some time & I want to see you.

The piano arrgt was published yesterday—how I detest its' being made public.

I shall see you on Tuesday at dinner anyway

Love
Edwd[67]

Charles Stuart Wortley's diary read:

Tuesday November 8, 1910: Dinner-party at home: Speyers, Elgars, C.Grosvenor, Ld Howe, Owen Seaman, F.Schuster, Cl.Phillips.

Wednesday Nov 9, 1910: To Queen's Hall 10 a.m. for rehearsal Elgar's new Violin Concerto.

Thursday Nov.10 1910: Dined early (at home), & thence to Queen's Hall (we three) for first performance of Elgar's Violin Concerto.[68]

Alice Elgar wrote of the evening:

To concert with Frank in car. Poured in desperate torrents. Crowd *enormous*. Excitement intense—Performance wonderful. Enthusiasm unbounded— *Shouts*—E. walked backwards & forwards bringing Kreisler . . .

Then back & E. changed & Frank had a supper about 40. Table all done with White heather for E.   he took Maudie [Warrender] & sat between her

[66] MS in possession of Robert Cecil.
[67] HWRO 705:445:4071.
[68] Quoted in TS notes by Clare Stuart Wortley (Elgar Birthplace).

& Winifred [*sic*] Elwes with Lord Northampton close by. Frank took A. Then E.'s health [—] Frank & Kreisler[.] Then surprise. E. part Songs from the Greek [Anthology] sung by men from Westminster & S.Paul's—Frank thought of everythg & made all beautiful—

To which should be added the memory of a young guest there, the twenty-one-year-old Adrian Boult:

> We sat at three separate tables, filling the big music room, and the menu at each table was headed with a theme from each of the three movements. I heard Elgar say to Claude Phillips, the great art critic, 'Well, Claude, did you think that was a work of art?'[69]

Charles Stuart Wortley and Clare were placed at the first table, Alice Stuart Wortley at the second—next to Kreisler and opposite to where Elgar sat at the top table. Alice Elgar was near the bottom of that table, opposite Mrs Kreisler, with Schuster himself between them.

The reviews next day recorded the Concerto's triumph. That night Elgars and Stuart Wortleys dined at the Beresfords' house. On 12 November, while Elgar conducted a concert at Eastbourne, Alice looked at Lady Constance Leslie's house with a view to renting it, and then returned to Hereford. Elgar himself came back to London early on the 13th, to go to a concert with Alice Stuart Wortley and dine at Cheyne Walk. It was his last night in London, and next morning before leaving he wrote:

22, Old Queen Street, Westminster.
Monday [14 Nov. 1910] 9.30 a m

My dear Windflower

How nice it wd. be to pay a solemn call 'after dining'—but I must go. It was so lovely yesterday.

Another house has faded into fog. The last (Lady C.Leslie's) seems to be miles from any station & has *no* bathroom! I really cannot go back to savagery even to be near London

The Vineyard is not very interesting[.] Thanks for it.

I love the Pearl.

I wish you were coming down to H'fd [—] it is so fine & lovely this early morning

Love
Yrs
E.E.

The book is (in English) Wagner at Home from the Fr[ench] of Judith Gautier [—] twaddly but you shd. skim it
pub Mills & Boon   49 Rupert St[70]

---

[69] *My Own Trumpet* (Hamilton, 1973), pp. 18–19.
[70] HWRO 705:445:4056. The Gautier book was also mentioned in Elgar's letter of 9 November to Hans Richter (see Basil Main, *Life* (*Elgar: His Life and Works*. (Bell, 1933)). p. 280 for a transcript).

Elgar's next visit to London was to conduct the second performance of the Violin Concerto on 30 November. He was conducting from the set of score proofs he had used at the première, but after the second performance these were promised to the Windflower. Following the morning rehearsal he wrote:

The Athenaeum, Pall Mall, S.W.
Nov 30 1910

My dear W.

The Concerto at 9 a m. in the dark was divine—all the seats empty but a spirit hovering in block A.

I do *not* send the score as it must be kept till next Concert—all the orchestra, Kreisler & myself *sign it* for you—a valuable collection of autographs

All good wishes for the campaign

Your
EE.[71]

For another general election was imminent.

There is no record of a meeting with the Stuart Wortleys then. A week later Elgar wrote to return two tickets which Alice Stuart Wortley had sent them for a Philharmonic Concert at which Landon Ronald was to conduct the Elgar Symphony. The Elgars had to return home to prepare for a pre-Christmas trip to Germany for him to conduct the Symphony:

Q Anne's
Dec 7:1910

My dear W.

Here are the Phil.tickets which you so kindly sent

Alice is just leaving for home & I go tomorrow—I don't know why but it seems to arrange itself so & what I want to do pleases no one!

We went to the Criterion last night—the end is not right I think—do go & see it 'The Liars' [by Henry Arthur Jones.]

Love
EE[72]

They left Hereford on the 13th and arrived in Germany next day. Then came a letter from Alice Stuart Wortley full of praise for Ronald's conducting of the Symphony.

Krefelder Hof[,] Krefeld
Dec 16 1910

My dear Windflower: I was so rejoiced to receive your letter which came as a
ray of light & cheered us up although today Friday everything goes well
except the weather—it rains incessantly. Our arrival was tragic—the sea is
nothing to us & we slept calmly all the way. Gott sei dank! But the Hotel!—
you see we are not at the address I gave you (your letter came safe here)—the
room they shewed us was the old Künstler Zimmer since 1801 I shd. think &
never cleaned since—a huge gas stove full on without *any* ventilation. We
nearly fainted & fled. Here it is a little better but noisy from trains & I get
headache: walking next to impossible on account of rain. Now to more
interesting things—the *first* reading of the Symphony was sad! but now it
goes well & the band is very enthusiastic & charming—some things sound
odd—the Hautboys are so different (& rough)—I longed for dear old Malsch
[principal oboe of the Queen's Hall Orchestra, later of the London Symphony and Philharmonic Society Orchestras]—all else good. We have been to
lunch with the Professor [Theodor Müller-Reuter] who is good & clever as a
writer as well as conductor. He conducts the London Sym Orch in Jany
(14th. I think) so please be there!

All else must wait till our return on Monday—we fly through London
town & I may not see you—if we do stay the night we shd probably be at the
Langham & I will telephone

I am delighted you like Ronald's conducting & that you like the Symphony
better than mine! [i.e., than Elgar's conducting of it.]

I will remember  & many other things.

Alice joins me in love

Ever yours
Edward.[73]

They did not meet during the Elgars' few hours on their way back through London
on 20 December. But it was arranged for Alice Stuart Wortley to come to Plas Gwyn
for what was destined to be their last Christmas there. Alice Elgar was planning a
little house party to drive away her husband's anticipated depression at holiday-time.

Plas Gwyn, Hereford.
20 Dec. 1910

My dear Alice

We are delighted to have your telegram & look forward to seeing you on
Saturday here, & your maid of course—but we much object to your leaving
on Monday, so please do not do it!

[73] HWRO 705:445:7863. Müller-Reuter's concert with the London Symphony Orchestra was
in fact to take place on 16 Jan. 1911.

Edward is feeling rather knocked up today, no wonder, [Krefeld] Concert at 6 to 8—rushed back to change, then the Fest Essen with music & *roar* of voices & speeches till 12.30—& a long day in Düsseldorf next day before starting home, but all *so* beautiful [—] such affection & devotion & enthusiasm for the Symphony as in England—boundless—& generous—

Much love & we shall meet you at 5 on Saturday I hope

Yr aft<br>C.Alice Elgar

Elgar added:

I am tired out: please come & cheer us up. You can*not* leave on Monday

Love<br>E[74]

Plas Gwyn, Hereford.
Dec 21:1910

My dear W.

We were so really delighted to receive your telegram.

You will find the railway journey very 'calm' I think: the train leaves Paddington at *1.40*—you will send the day before & reserve a seat & you will be met here. You pass thro' Worcester at 4 o'c & the guard (at Paddington) would telegraph for *Tea* to meet you at Worcester if you like it:—you arrive here at 4.58

I am better & the weather looks finer but such floods.

Love from us all<br>Edward[75]

From the moment she arrived on Christmas Eve, much of Elgar's attention went to her. His own Alice wrote:

December 25. Lovely sunny day not cold—E. A. C. Troyte [Griffith] & Mad<sup>e</sup> Léry to Belmont [Catholic pro-Cathedral]. Large car. Short détour home—Alice S.W. to [Hereford] Cathedral. Pleasant lunch—E. & A.S.W. for walk ... Very pleasant evg. E. showed his robes &c & then played new *Symphony*. A very dear day—E. so much happier than ever before over Fest.

December 26. Nice fine day. E. & Alice played some music—Alice, E. & Troyte as far as Ross together ...

---

[74] Elgar Birthplace parcel 584(xxx).

[75] HWRO 705:445:4054. Alas for railway amenities: the telegraphed tea remained available, I am told, until the Second World War.

There Alice Stuart Wortley departed by train. She was the first of the little party to leave.

After the others went next day, Elgar subsided into bed. He was too ill the day after to go to London to hear the latest Concerto performance by Kreisler, with Henry Wood conducting.

Plas Gwyn, Hereford.
Dec 28 1910

My dear Windflower

This is too sad for words: I have a chill & may not go out. I *hope* you will have been to the Concert & will tell me all about it. I am very sad & where is the apple blossom & the two fish. Never.

Love<br>Edward

So glad you arrd. safely [—] we heard this a m.
Troyte & I had a lovely cross country walk—cold but bright.
It was a sad parting at Ross.[76]

Plas Gwyn, Hereford.
29 Dec 1910

My dearest Windflower

I send all thanks for your letter. I am better & go to Liverpool tomorrow evening—staying at the L.& NW Railway Hotel for the night: on Saturday I have a rehearsal at eleven & Concert at three—returning here at seven o clock & arrg at 10.25—then I hope peace[.] I wish you were going to be there.

I was so dreadfully disappointed about Wedy[;] thanks for the telegram & for everything.

I have reached out the sheets of the Symphony & am going on or rather— trying to go on

My love to you

Edward[77]

In Liverpool to conduct the Concerto for Kreisler on the last day of the year, Elgar went to the Walker Art Gallery to see the painting by Alice Stuart Wortley's father, *Isabella* (also known as *Lorenzo and Isabella*)—described in Alice Elgar's diary as her husband's 'favourite picture'. Millais's painting is based on a passage from Keats's poem 'Isabella, or the Pot of Basil':

[76] HWRO 705:445:7143.        [77] HWRO 705:445:4055.

Fair Isabel, poor simple Isabel!
  Lorenzo, a young palmer in Love's eye!
They could not in the self-same mansion dwell
  Without some stir of heart, some malady;
They could not sit at meals but feel how well
  It soothèd each to be the other by.

After the concert he returned to Hereford in time to join his own Alice in bidding farewell to this most eventful year.

# 1911

The opening of the new year found Elgar at home, worrying over his Second Symphony. Alice Stuart Wortley was alone at Cheyne Walk, her husband and daughter enjoying winter sports at St Moritz. Elgar's first surviving letter began with a phrase which seems to have been a byword of the moment. It went on to answer her request for his view of her piano playing:

Hereford
Jan 6 1911

My Dear W.

Here is an odd little letter! I was so delighted to receive yours this morning & all you say. I heard from Lady C. & hope that they are better.

I never said anything about you playing—that is in answer to your former letter: I *love* to hear you play—one reason why so many people cordially dislike me is that I cannot stand their music whether written or performed & I pay no compliments & I *never* ask anyone to play unless it gives me pleasure[.] I do not like piano solo players' playing but I love yours—you will understand the difference[.] I am not going to praise you now because you are quite vain enough! but you *must* play when I ask & I would not think of asking you to play to ordinary people who wd. not understand what poetical playing really is.

I love Lorenzo & Isabella—wonderful

                                                    Love
                                                    EE

When do your snow birds return?[1]

Charles Stuart Wortley had come back on 4 January, but Clare was to stay another three weeks.

The Elgars had in prospect another London visit—for him to conduct the Violin Concerto on the afternoon of Monday 16 January, and that evening to attend

[1] HWRO 705:445:7865.

Theodor Müller-Reuter's concert with the London Symphony Orchestra: for this Alice Stuart Wortley was getting tickets. But Elgar also wanted the change of scene for his composing, if he could secure a service flat at Queen Anne's Mansions.

Hereford
Tuesday [10 January 1911]
My dear Windflower

I have been rather ill & am now somewhat better.

Have you tickets for Monday *night*? Alice is coming up & will probably sleep at her Club—I am trying for Q. Anne's for a week. I *must* be in town on Monday early for rehearsal & shall travel up on Saty or Sunday.

The Müller-Reuters may come down here & so our plans are vague until we hear from them.

I do not get on with my work at all & want helping a great deal: Have your truants returned yet? I hope they have had a good time in the snow.

I told Alice you were getting me a ticket for Monday night & she wants one too but is writing: quite a white frost this a m.

Love    pitifully<br>E

Another odd little letter[2]

Three days later Alice Elgar wrote:

Plas Gwyn
13 Jany 1911
My dear Alice

Very many thanks for your letter & very many for all the trouble about the tickets—very good of you. I am rejoiced to be able to say E. is much better today & the music is the most radiant, exulting strain you can imagine.—

We have just been another motor drive in his beloved country wh. seems to do him so much good—He is going to Queen Anne's Mansions tomorrow, & hopes to telephone to you, we are making some scheme for the Müller-Reuters.

Much love & hoping to meet on Monday

Yr very aft<br>C.A.Elgar[3]

A separate envelope, dated '15.i.11' by Alice Stuart Wortley, was addressed to her in Elgar's hand. Round the address he wrote:

---

[2] HWRO 705:445:4166.
[3] Transcript by Clare Stuart Wortley (Elgar Birthplace parcel 584).

I arrive at Q A's about 4.30
Please call me on Telephone or *come to tea*! anytime
    The new Symphony is glorious!

Inside, on a sheet of Plas Gwyn stationery, he wrote:

'Musicians thinke our Soules are harmonies.'

(Sir John Davies (15–  )[ )]

Violin

Elgar's first day in London was chronicled (from his reports) by his wife, still in Hereford:

January 15    E. at Queen Anne's—    Went to Queen's Hall in aftn. & then with Alice S.W. to tea with the Colvins. E. played a little of the Symphony there.. . .

January 16    E. at Queen Anne's—    To his rehearsal at 10—in Small [Queen's] Hall. A. & C. to Paddington . . . 9.53 train. A. to Queen's Hall & heard some [Violin Concerto] rehearsal & some of Müller-Reuter[.] Then to Queen Anne's & back & to Concert.

Kriesler played the Beethoven and Elgar Concertos side by side. Both the Stuart Wortleys attended. Afterwards Charles Stuart Wortley left to dine with his elder daughter Bice, while his wife joined the Elgars for the Müller-Reuter concert in the evening. After that, Alice Elgar noted, 'Alice S.W. went back with us & heard a little of the Symphony.'
    Two days later Alice Elgar moved from Queen Anne's mansions to her Club, so as to leave the flat clear for her husband's composing. Meanwhile she and Carice looked at houses in the Chilterns, Farnham, Weybridge, Reigate, and the outside of No. 24 Church Row in Hampstead. On 19 January Charles Stuart Wortley's diary recorded: 'Dinner-party at home: Lady Constance Leslie, Elgars, Colvins, C.Phillips.' Then Alice Elgar took Carice to Petersfield to visit her friend Mrs Winifred Murray for the weekend.
    Each day found Elgar working on the Symphony at Queen Anne's Mansions. One day he and Alice Stuart Wortley went to Hampstead to look at the Church Row house from the outside. What they also discovered was a large property a few streets away called 'Kelston': it was, like 7 Cheyne Walk, a Norman Shaw house: this one had been designed for the late Edwin Long, RA, and it was on the market. Its appearance attracted Elgar.
    His eyes were tired by the concentration of close work on the Symphony in the January murk of that era in London. By Sunday evening he was ready to go back to Hereford as soon as Alice and Carice returned from Petersfield. He wrote to Alice Stuart Wortley, enclosing money for his Müller-Reuter concert ticket:

⁴ HWRO 705:445:7829.

Queen Anne's Mansions, St.James' Park, London, S.W.
Sunday [22 Jan. 1911] night

My dear W.

I am so sorry I forgot the ticket: here it is with many thanks for the concert it provided.

I have no further news of the family so I conclude they will return here for a moment tomorrow (Monday) & fly home

Yours
Edward

 I have no room
(on paper) for the
all powerful chord[5]

Next day, by the time Alice and Carice had arrived from Petersfield, Alice Stuart Wortley had some information about 'Kelston' but not yet about Church Row.

Queen Anne's Mansions, St.James' Park, London, S.W.
Monday [23 Jan. 1911]

My dear Windflower

Thank you so very much for all the information about the Hampstead House. I hope Alice, who is having tea here[,] will be able to speak to you on the telephone but I send this in case we do not hear your voice.

We think it best to go home now as we know nothing of rent or rooms at No.24 [Church Row] & you will hear of this from L.Cust: when you do perhaps you cd. see the House if not too troublesome or at any rate let us know the extent of it

Bless you

This is the only remaining pen—all my music pens are packed [—] Alas! Alas! alas!

Love
Edward

We are leaving now [—] 4.45 train[6]

Back at Hereford Elgar remained engrossed in the first movement of his new Symphony. In London Alice Stuart Wortley went to see 'Kelston' and wrote of it. Alice Elgar replied:

<hr>

[5] HWRO 705:445:7665.        [6] HWRO 705:445:7819.

Plas Gwyn.
26 Jany. 1911

One line dear Alice to thank you for going to see the house when especially
you had a cold—& much for your clear & exact description ...   Dear Alice,
the Symphony is wonderful. One is led away to regions beyond worlds—
He is working *very* hard & I trust will not get knocked up—. I have
persuaded him into a motor drive 2 or 3 times & it is such a refreshment to
him & today & yesterday have been beautiful & scenery, earth & sky—
transporting.
   Do take care of your cold. Much love & thanks

                                                      Yr aff
                                                      C.A.Elgar

Surely with what he does for the world, I wish you could see some letters
about the Concerto, he must have a house he wd like.[7]

   On 28 January Elgar finished the new Symphony's first movement, and next day
made a few revisions and wrote:


[*postmarked* Hereford]
Sunday Jany 29. 1911

My dear W.

   Forgive the paper & hurry—
I have recorded last year in the first movement to which I put the last note
in the score a moment ago & I must tell you this: I have worked at fever heat
& the thing is tremendous in energy. *Thank you for your note* which came this
a.m.—   I am sorrowful I am missing—the Concerto [played by Kreisler at a
Sunday Concert in the Palladium conducted by Enrique Fernandez Arbos] &
nearly ran up last night on purpose to hear it but the distance is too great & I
must not give time to anything but my work
   I have written the *most extraordinary* passage I have ever heard—a sort of
malign influence wandering thro' the summer night in the garden—

                                                      Bless you
                                                      Yrs
                                                      E.[8]


   Kreisler was to play the Concerto again hardly a week later with Henry Wood
conducting.


[7] Partial transcript by Clare Stuart Wortley (Elgar Birthplace parcel 584).
[8] HWRO 705:445:7809.

Hereford
Jan 31.

My dear Alice-W.

Are you going to the Kreisler–Wood Concerto Concert? if so please let me know if you have a ticket for me. I want to come—I think it[']s the 7th Feb—but am not sure & the advt. has been missed

The work goes well

Your
Edward E

I can only scrawl on this flimsy paper now between scoring times—[9]

He was already at work on the Symphony slow movement.

His own Alice prepared to go to London to see houses in Hampstead and the Home Counties. She wrote the same day:

Plas Gwyn, Hereford.
31 Jany. 1911.

My dear Alice

So many thanks for your letter. We are still waiting for letters from the two Agents who are considering the amendment of the houses (Hampstead)— Meanwhile we have heard of others & Edward thinks I had better come up & see them & more, so I am to come tomorrow, early, & expect to stay till Saturday. If there is any moment to meet, I shd. *love* it, but I expect to be out all day.   E. was so glad to hear about the Concerto at the Palladium—   The 1st Movement of the Symphony is *gone* to the publishers & he is deep in the 2nd wh. is inexpressibly beautiful—

Much love & I must see my dear Namesake

Yrs.
Alice.[10]

So Alice started for London next morning, leaving Edward to work on the Symphony slow movement at Plas Gwyn. She spent four days looking at houses in Kingston, Tenterden Hill, Farnham, and Oxted, besides two houses in Church Row, Hampstead and 'Kelston', which she liked best. She visited her cousin William Raikes, the trustee of her mother's will, at his chambers in the Temple, to see if she could break the trust and have the capital for purchasing a house. On Friday evening 3 February she dined with Alice Stuart Wortley at Cheyne Walk and they talked over the houses. She returned to Hereford late the next evening.

[9] HWRO 705:445:7101.
[10] Elgar Birthplace parcel 574.

Plas Gwyn, Hereford.
5 Feb.1911

My dear Alice

I must send a line & tell you I was much refreshed by my pleasant little evening with you—. Thank you—. I had a long day seeing failures & reached home late but found Edward all well & making wonderful progress. I hope he will be able to see the house I like so much soon—I still dream of it.

> With love
> yr aft
> C.A.Elgar[11]

Next day Elgar finished the Symphony slow movement—'wrote it all from his sketches in one week', Alice recorded. She wrote:

Plas Gwyn, Hereford.
6 Feb. 1911.

My dear Alice

Edward asks me to send a line to tell you he is to come up tomorrow, (Tuesday) (bringing the whole 2nd movement of the Symphony) & wd. like to hear where he shd. find the ticket for the Concert.

Will you be very kind & let him hear this. He expects to arrive about 4.30 at the Langham.

> With love
> yr affte.
> C.Alice Elgar[12]

He went up next day, 7 February. He saw 'Kelston', and that evening he and Alice Stuart Wortley went to hear the Concerto at Queen's Hall. He stayed at the Langham only one night, and returned home the next afternoon. He was quickly at work on the Symphony Rondo. There was news of this when his wife wrote to settle her own debt over the Müller–Reuter concert three weeks earlier:

[*postmarked* Hereford]
11 Feb. 1911

My dear Alice

I am so distressed to think I entirely forgot my ticket debts to you. You so very kindly took one for the one concert & the Queen's Hall people sent us some after all, were you able to send it back? if not I am in debt for the two, & will send directly I hear from you whether it is one or two which I owe— So *very* many thanks for having troubled about them—My head has been so full of things! please forgive me.

[11] Transcript by Clare Stuart Wortley (Elgar Birthplace parcel 584).
[12] Transcript by Clare Stuart Wortley (Elgar Birthplace parcel 584).

Edward loved the house, the perfectly beautiful one, I mean—He came home rather sad, as there are many difficulties in the way but *if* he really likes it, wh. he does, I feel he must have it, & have a proper room to dream dreams of loveliness in. So we are going on more or less about it.

The larger house in Church Row [No. 24] is impossible. Landlord will do nothing. I think the other is too small—.

How vivifying to have this sunshine today. The Symphony progresses splendidly & I am thankful to say E. is keeping well—.

> Much love
> Yr aft.
> C.Alice Elgar[13]

The envelope may have been shared by a note of Elgar's in 'formal' style:

Hereford
Feb 11: 1911
My dear Alice:

I quite forgot the tickets! Here is the amount & so many thanks for getting them sent for me. I have been wondering whether you have seen the Hampstead House! Please tell me.

> Love from
> Yr
> Edward

I am *so* hard at work but it does not go well now—since my journey—it has gone cold.[14]

Soon it was hot again.

Hereford
Monday [13 Feb. 1911]
My dear W:

I am moving heaven & earth to finish the 3rd movemt by Thursday & if I can write the last note I shall bring it up—so perhaps the Langham at 5 o'c or a little before will see me.

I was very much depressed last week on my return & could not work well—however yesterday [ — ] no Saturday [ — ] I had a cheering letter & all goes on very furiously & gloriously—   I have just played over the 1st. movemt & *love* it

---

[13] Transcript by Clare Stuart Wortley (Elgar Birthplace parcel 584).
[14] HWRO 705:445:4103.

I hope you are practising your piano & getting a large repertoire ready for me when I've finished this work.

> Yrs ever
> E.

Do go & see 'Kelston'—at Hampstead. We are again thinking of it[15]

But when Thursday morning came he could not leave. Shortly after mid-day he telegraphed: 'Music not quite finished   coming tomorrow same train'.[16] Later that afternoon he wrote:

[n.p.]
Thursday [16 Feb. 1911]

My dear Windflower:

I have just put the last little dot to the IIIrd movement & very wild & headstrong it is with soothing pastoral strains in between & very, very brilliant[.] I bring it tomorrow, & then for the great serene movement

I am so sorry I could not finish in time for the train & I am conducting, here, the little piece for Bassoon & orchestra

> Love yr
> E.[17]

The *Romance*, Op. 62 was dedicated to Edwin James, principal bassoonist and chairman of the London Symphony Orchestra. He played it in the Hereford Philharmonic concert, and next morning came up to Plas Gwyn with colleagues to breakfast: it had just been settled that Elgar should become the Orchestra's chief conductor in succession to Richter, who was retiring. So the Elgars were practically committed to living in London.

That afternoon, 17 February, Elgar took the Symphony Rondo to the publishers in London. That night he attended a concert which included a rare chance to hear Wagner's early Symphony. He returned home next day and settled to his own Symphony's Finale. His wife wrote:

[n.p. *postmarked* Hereford]
23 Feb. 1911.

My dear Alice

I must send a few lines, you will be wondering what we are all doing.

E. is far on into the 4th movement. I think *you* have heard some fragments so will not try to describe it, save to say it is one of his greatest things, & sums up all human life—the ending is really overwhelming in its appeal & then finishes in gorgeous triumph. He has been keeping so well I am thankful to

---

[15] HWRO 705:445:7670. A letter of 14 February 1911 from Alice Elgar is mentioned by Clare Stuart Wortley but not transcribed 'because it deals entirely with house-hunting, and does not mention the Symphony'. (Elgar Birthplace parcel 584.) The MS has not been found.

[16] Elgar Birthplace.

[17] HWRO 705:445:7818.

say—in all this tremendous work. Houses must wait, I was hoping to come up this week but Carice has been & still is laid up with tonsilitis, & has suffered very much. The Dr. promises speedy amendment. She is such a wonderfully good patient   so stoical & content.

I cannot leave till she is down again & I have had a wretched cold & must wait also for that.

I *do* want to see Heath Brow so much though I fear it is impossible.

> With our love
> Yr aft
> C.A.Elgar.[18]

The Stuart Wortleys sent Carice a present of books.

Plas Gwyn, Hereford.
26 Feb.1911

My dear Alice

I must send a line to tell you Carice is so pleased with her books, it was really too dear of you to send them—I am glad to say she is considerably better today but not allowed to get up yet, but now I hope will soon improve fast.

These winds & gales are so trying.

You will love to hear the Symphony is nearly finished—   All being well, that happy moment will not be far off. E. has loved writing it, but really needs some rest.

He hopes to be up next week, & I *hope* to be so too so shall hope to meet.

> Much love
> Yr aft
> C.A.Elgar[19]

Two days later Elgar finished his Second Symphony. After revising the Finale score, he took it to London on 3 March. He dined with Schuster and all three Stuart Wortleys at the Savoy Grill.[20] Then the whole party went to the Coliseum to see Max

---

[18] Transcript by Clare Stuart Wortley (Elgar Birthplace parcel 584).

[19] Transcript by Clare Stuart Wortley (Elgar Birthplace parcel 584).

[20] Clare Stuart Wortley wrote: '. . . I think it must have been during this dinner that Sir Edward made a remark which I have always remembered; certainly it was made in company at table somewhere, and this is the date at which it is most likely to have been made: "I shall dedicate the [Second] Symphony to Edward the Seventh, so that dear kind man will have my best music." I remember wanting to ask questions "When was he so kind?" and "Can it be better than the 1st Symphony?" but as always happened in our most talkative circle, someone else began to speak first, and I never did ask either question.' (TS notes, Elgar Birthplace parcel 584.) The tone of Elgar's remark, however, suggests that it was made during the King's lifetime. The Second Symphony had been projected from at least Apr. 1910, when its première was planned for May 1911. (See *Edward Elgar: A Creative Life* (OUP, 1984), pp. 573–4.)

Reinhardt's production of *Sumurun*, 'a mimed Arabian Night which in movement and colour rivalled the art of the Russians'.[21]

Next day the Elgars returned to Hereford. From there, in an envelope postmarked 6 March, he sent Alice Stuart Wortley another musical quotation of the Second Symphony opening.[22] At home the Elgars were preparing for two journeys. The longer, which he was to undertake alone, would be to America for several weeks to conduct his works with the Sheffield Choir as part of their world tour. But first came a four-day visit to Brussels to conduct the First Symphony with the great violinist Eugène Ysaÿe's orchestra. From Brussels, after the performance, Elgar wrote:

Hotel Metropole[,] Bruxelles
Saturday [11 Mar. 1911] p m.

My dear Windflower

We have had a most triumphant performance to-day[.] Ysaye created a sensation by leading the orchestra *himself* in my honour. I wish you had been here.

We arrive at the Langham in the early hours of Monday morning. Alice stays till Tuesday & I remain until Wedy or perhaps Alice goes at 1.40 on Tuesday & I may go at 6.10 but we must—I must—see you before America— I hope all goes well with the politics &c

Love to you all<br>Edwd[23]

The last reference was to the constitutional crisis over the House of Lords: no doubt they discussed it on their way back through London two days later, when they dined with Frank Schuster, and Alice Stuart Wortley came in for the evening.

The Elgars returned to Hereford next day, to pack for his American trip. But a heavy cold delayed his departure until 25 March. A few days before that, Alice Stuart Wortley had sent separate letters to the two Elgars, with roses for his going. Elgar's reply contained a little lifting of the veil which usually covered their epistolary arrangements.

Hereford
Mar 22

My dear Windflower:

I am back in my own blue room. I am really better & have had a short walk: also I have booked my passage on Saturday by the Mauretania!

Thanks a many many for your *ship* letter & the one recd. this a.m. Unfortunately I destroyed it & as you referred to it in Alice's letter you must write all your Concert news over again!

---

[21] W. Bridges-Adams, 'Theatre', in S. Nowell-Smith, ed., *Edwardian England 1901–1914*, (OUP, 1964), p. 404.
[22] Now bound with Second Symphony sketches (Elgar Birthplace).
[23] HWRO 705:445:7810.

Carice has been down to-day for an hour or two & is better but must be carried up stairs

The flowers are still lovely

Love to you<br>E[24]

And on the eve of sailing:

Plas Gwyn, Hereford.
March 24.1911
My dear Windflower

This is the last! I sail tomorrow as arranged.

I have asked Alice to send you (—only a loan!) the sketches of the (your) Symphony—they may amuse you & you can let me have them again when I return—if you have a piano at Tintagel you can play them there &—well, *and*—

My love to you all

& now goodbye

Your<br>E.E.

Your roses are still lovely
Telegraphic address   c/o Pippa   New York
*Code*   American Express Coy's travellers' code[25]

His voyage, beginning on 25 March, was to take a week. Alice Elgar got through the early part of her husband's absence by spending several days in London to go over 'Kelston' again, interviewing Heal's experts about furnishings, and consulting further with lawyers. She met the Stuart Wortleys several times—notably at an enormous party given by Theodore Byard, a Society baritone with a big house in Mayfair.

Elgar meanwhile had arrived in America. He conducted *Gerontius* at Toronto, where they all endured bitter weather. From there he went via Buffalo to New York, where he subsided into Mrs Worthington's apartment until his next engagement with the Sheffield Choir in Cincinnati—the only city on the tour offering much familiarity, as he had conducted there at the May Festival in 1906.

On the morning of his Cincinnati concert he received a letter from Alice Stuart Wortley, written at Tintagel. He replied within the hour:

Hotel Sinton, Cincinnati.
April 18 9.15 a m
My dear W.

How *very clever* of you! your letter was handed to me at Breakfast & was most dearly welcome—more than ever really as I have friends here & was

---

[24] HWRO 705:445:7107.
[25] MS bound with Second Symphony sketches (Elgar Birthplace).

looking forward to an oasis here in this awful desert: now some are ill & the rest away in N.Y. &c.&c. so I am most lonely. It is sweet to hear of Tintagel & our own land—I hope you had good weather after the snow & cold—just at that time it was drearily cold in Toronto & I nearly died of it. *Now* it is summer—not spring—but summer without any leaves or flowers. I rushed from Buffalo to N Y. where Pippa & nice Mr.Gray [the music publisher Novello's American representative] took care of me. Trains full this way so I had to leave on Easter Sunday [16 Apr.] morng 11 o c & travelled until 7.30 the *next* morning: I loathe & detest every moment of my life here! but I have lovely things to think of & shall soon be back & hope to see you. All I can do is to count the days—I despise myself for not bearing it better but I cannot help it & want to talk to you & perhaps other '*educated*' people—it is all so raw & silly out here.

I was interested in all your news & if Byards was a sample of what you go through in town I am sure you are better in Tintagel—I am selfish enough to be thankful that you can think of me there & you will not forget Frank's car taking us to Boscastle & you will not forget the road home—how lovely it was—a year ago! Easter joys—& *now*: My love to you. I long to be back & forget this worse than nightmare

Yrs<br>Edward[26]

His communications with his own Alice said much the same.

She went to London for another week to look at flats. 'Kelston' was beset with problems, and Edward felt he had to have a base in London. She found a furnished house at 75 Gloucester Place to let on a short lease, cabled her husband, and he cabled her to take it.

He had meanwhile moved on from Cincinnati. At Indianapolis the entire party was received with a civic parade before their first concert there. In Chicago the weather weather turned frigid again. There they encountered the raw contrasts of the American mid-west to the full: opulent wealth and (as the regular Sheffield Choir conductor Henry Coward observed) 'countless motors rush along and keep up a constant buzz, hum and hoot, which is almost bewildering. At one point we counted thirty in as many seconds . . .'.[27] Yet a recent street murder confined the party largely to their hotel.

At Milwaukee they met another civic reception. Elgar, again with a heavy cold, spent as much time as possible barricaded in the Choir's special train. He seemed to take his cue from the one titled lady among the tour soloists, the soprano Lady Norah Noel. But he had written to his sister Pollie Grafton at Stoke Prior and asked her to send a windflower from the garden there to Cheyne Walk.

[26] HWRO 705:445:7805.
[27] H. Coward, *Round the World on Wings of Song* (Sheffield, 1933), p. 65.

Hotel Pfister, Milwaukee, Wis.
Ap 26 1911
My dear W.

Do you not know that the postage to U.S. has been 1*d* for years! However it is just like you—(& I like you the better for it!) not to know anything so sordid—only I smiled when I recd your Tintagel letter with its 2½d.

Oh! what an *awful* place Chicago is—I have been having (only don't tell Alice) an awful cold & am only now slightly better so I am *living* in the special train—the winds are bitterly cold off this lake—but it will soon be over [ — ] *soon! soon! soon!*

And when shall I see you or any friends? If I understand Alice's code cable she has secured a furnished house for us in town for May & June—but at this moment I do not know if I land at Fishguard or go to London or Hereford & I have seen no English paper since I left—my mind is a blank on which these people scrawl, or try to, their offensive ideas. (Perhaps!) Pippa is the only bearable one! & I have seen only too little of her.

I loved having your letter from Tintagel & all the sea was in it—I wonder how long I shall live in London—not many months—& I am so old now I really have no desire to live—I feel so. Yes! I 'commanded' the windflower—I was afraid I might be forgotten altogether unless you had a reminder: there is really nothing to tell you—How we are met with flags & banners & 'processed' — all without a smile, entirely *well meant*, ludicrous to the last degree but *dead serious*.

Lady Norah & her brother are extremely nice & have cut the rest in silence—and we will hope, dollars!

Now, if for *myself*, I would never degrade myself for all the wealth of America to go thro' this awful depth of infamy! They asked me what I wd. take to settle in the States & conduct one of the big orchestras—I said nothing in the world wd. induce me to spend 6 months here—not $10,000,000—this they do not understand—  Well—all the rest I reserve until we can talk & then 'I guess' we will not talk of U.S.A. but of Sea pictures and Clean things like the Symphony

My love to you all

Yrs
Edward[28]

After his last concert at St Paul on 28 April, Elgar went back to New York, and soon embarked for home. During the voyage he wrote an undated note for posting as soon as the ship should dock at Liverpool late on Monday 8 May:

[28] Elgar Birthplace parcel 583(xxv).

On board the R.M.S.'Mauretania'
at sea—really, not metaphorically

My dear W.

It seems unbelievable that I can be home at Hereford on Tuesday [9
May]—such joy to me & then real life once more after this dreary nightmare.
The ship rolls & so does the writing
Love to you all

Yours
Edward[29]

He reached home to find the garden full of spring sunshine and flowers. Next day
came the miniature score of the Second Symphony prepared in advance for sale at the
première on 24 May. He sent two windflowers in a note:

Plas Gwyn, Hereford.
May 10 1911

My dear Windflower

These two of you were growing *close* to the Ark door!

It is lovely to be back, & all the world is more lovely than ever—my
swallows are here & the garden full of birds & nests & buds & blossoms & the
air full of divine scents—after U.S. it is heavenly beyond words. Thank you
for your letter: I am so grieved to hear of your sorrows.

Please keep the MS for the present—the small score has just come—
advance copy—it looks lovely. We come to London next week
Till then

love to you all
Edward[30]

Mid-May found the Elgars ensconced at the furnished house in Gloucester Place,
preparing for the Second Symphony première. On 16 May he inscribed and sent to
her a copy of the miniature score, which she acknowledged instantly.

75, Gloucester Place, Portman Square, W.
May 17: 1911

My dear Windflower:

Many thanks for your note—no thanks were due or needed. I have been
working at the separate [orchestral] parts & it is *wonderful*!

You *must* come to rehearsal on Friday at 2–4—Q's *Small* Hall right at the

---

[29] HWRO 705:445:4052.
[30] Elgar Birthplace. Alice Elgar's diary mentions the miniature score on 11 May, but she
occasionally was a day out through making up her diary in arrears. The short score manuscript
and sketches remained with Alice Stuart Wortley—ultimately to be given to the Elgar
Birthplace.

top of the building[:] you enter by a door *between* the chief entrance & door
15— We shall have the full orch: & the strings have been *increased* & it
sounds fine.

> Our love
> Yr
> Edward[31]

The afternoon rehearsal on Friday 19 May was followed by another next morning.
That evening Alice Elgar noted: 'Alice W. to dine & E. & she to see [Delibes's ballet]
"Sylvia"'.

The Windflower asked him to inscribe her copy of the large English-German vocal
score of *Gerontius*. He returned it with information about the final rehearsal on the
morning of the Symphony's première:

75, Gloucester Place, Portman Square, W.
Sunday [21 May 1911]

My dear W.

I have signed your book & put in a bit of the symphony extra—
The rehearsal is in the large [Queen's] Hall 10 – 11.30 on Wedy
I enclose a card

> Yours ever sin
> Edward

His visiting card enclosed was inscribed:

Admit Mrs.C Stuart Wortley May 24 (Wednesday) rehearsal Q's Hall
10 – 11.30[32]

On the Tuesday Elgars and Stuart Wortleys attended another performance of the
Violin Concerto by Kreisler. Next evening came the Second Symphony première. It
proved nowhere near the brilliant success anticipated. But the Elgars had planned a
supper afterward at Gloucester Place: it included all three Stuart Wortleys as well as
Frank Schuster and Claude Phillips.

Several performances of the new Symphony had been booked before the première,
and these now had to be got through. On 1 June Elgar conducted it with the London
Symphony Orchestra: the audience was small. Alice Elgar had another supper after,
and Alice Stuart Wortley came again.

They went to Edward Speyer's home, Ridgehurst, for the weekend, and Elgar
found distraction in billiards. On Tuesday 6 June Alice Stuart Wortley arrived to
motor him back to London, after his own Alice and Carice had left by train.

The next Second Symphony performance was to take place two days later, and
more than half the tickets were unsold. The mood in the Elgar household on the
morning of the concert was conveyed in a note from Alice Elgar:

[31] HWRO 705:445:7832.
[32] HWRO 705:445:4118. This vocal score of *Gerontius* had been given to her in June 1910 (see
above, p. 51).

75, Gloucester Place, Portman Square, W.
Thursday [8 June 1911]

My dear Alice

If you can come on after Concert, I hope you will—So far we have only the Landon Ronalds coming.

The rehearsal was splendid & the playing of the Symphony quite a different thing but E. is dreadfully depressed over business matters & it grieves me dreadfully that he is losing the joy of his wonderful work—& his depression makes it impossible to progress with plans.

> Much love
> Yrs.
> C.A.E.[33]

Queen's Hall that night was hardly a quarter full. The little party afterwards consisted of Alice Stuart Wortley (her husband and daughter were resting for a long journey to Scotland next day), the de Navarros and their friend the novelist Robert Hichens, Landon Ronald and his wife. On the 12th Elgar and Alice Stuart Wortley attended part of a Nikisch concert to hear Paderewski play the Chopin F minor Concerto. On the 16th Elgar dined at Cheyne Walk with Paderewski and other guests. Nine days after that he joined Alice Stuart Wortley and Paderewski for a Sunday at The Hut.

In the Coronation Honours Elgar was given the Order of Merit. Among the many telegrams on 20 June came this: 'Many warm and affectionate congratulations. Stuart Wortley family'.[34] Another, from Charles Stuart Wortley to Alice Elgar, read: 'Please express my delight at very distinguished honour'.[35]

Yet he was gloomy—at least partly owing to a report from his publisher Novello that few performances of the new Symphony had been booked. The frantic popularity of the First Symphony had also run its course, and the novelty of the Violin Concerto seemed to be wearing off. Fearing his financial prospects, Elgar broke the long-standing agreement by which Novello published virtually all of his music. He would not attend the Coronation of King George V to which he had been invited, and whose Coronation March he had written.

He was booked to conduct the *Coronation March* at a commemorative service in St Paul's Cathedral on 29 June. The day before it he was in bed with a headache. His wife wrote:

28 June 1911 . . . E. thought he cd. not go to Rehearsal at S.Paul's but Alice S.W. came & drove him in Car—& back—Alice delighted to hear the March—  E. not the worse for it—

The car was hired and chauffer-driven, as always with the Stuart Wortleys (who never kept a car of their own).

Next day Alice Elgar wrote of the service and lunch afterwards at the house of the Cathedral organist, Sir George Martin:

---

[33] Elgar Birthplace parcel 584(xxii).    [34] HWRO 705:445:4954.    [35] HWRO 705:445:4961.

29 June ... A. & C. went on first to St.Paul's & were fortunate taking very good places.   E. soon followed & sat in Choir with Sir H.Parry robed in Cambridge Mus.D. [ — ] robe over his Levée [Court] dress—  Saw the Procession very well. Loved the Fanfare of trumpets. E.'s March sounded splendid & he looked most beautiful conducting. Then all 3 to lunch with Martins—large party very pleasant ...

75, Gloucester Place, Portman Square, W.
Thursday [29 June 1911]

My dear Alice

I must send a line & tell you Edward was better this morning & able to go—& thank you once again for your dear kind help driving him down there yesterday—  It would have been *such* a pity if he cd. not have gone—

It was all really *very* fine, a beautiful sight & his March gorgeous. & so nice to see him conduct in that splendid setting in his gaudy things all flaming in colour. I think he really enjoyed it all—

We were not back till 3.30, left before 10, having had a very festive time at the Martins—  Lady Martin admired you so much—

Much love dear Alice

Yr aft
C.A.Elgar

E. is still not quite recovered—[36]

On Saturday evening 1 July they shared a box at Covent Garden with Alice Stuart Wortley to see Melba in Puccini's *La Bohème*. On 11 July Elgar went with the Windflower and 'Lady Charlie' Beresford to Martin-Harvey's production of the Maeterlinck play *Pelleas and Melisande*. On the 15th the Windflower dined at Gloucester Place—now nearing the end of its lease. Next day she drove Edward down to Wimbledon for a weekend at Adela Schuster's house there.

All this while Alice Elgar was toiling in the background. She supervised the packing up at Gloucester Place. She was assiduous in moving forward plans to decorate the big house in Hampstead—which Elgar was now calling 'Severn House' to their friends,[37] even though it was far from certain that his wife could get the money in her trust fund or that the vendors would compromise over the price.

Elgar remained at loose ends. On 19 July he met the writer Maurice Baring over the possibility of an opera libretto—which came to nothing. The chief happiness now seemed to lie in older associations, as he sent a programme for the Three Choirs Festival at Worcester in September:

---

[36] Elgar Birthplace parcel 584(xxix).
[37] See his letter of 17 July 1911 to Adela Schuster (HWRO 705:445:6845).

75, Gloucester Place, Portman Square, W.
July 20 1911

My dear W.

I was glad to see M.Baring yesterday but *how* nervous he is.

Here is the Worcester programme—we are very busy packing up—alas! I hope for 3.30 tomorrow

Yrs sny
E[38]

Alice Elgar's diary for the following day—their last at Gloucester Place—gives quite a full account but says nothing about a visit from the Windflower.

On Saturday 22 July Alice Elgar left for Hereford to reopen Plas Gwyn—where her husband had little interest now. He lingered in London, lunching with the Stuart Wortleys on the Sunday before returning to Hereford on Wednesday 26 July. There the Worcester Cathedral organist Ivor Atkins came with his new edition of Bach's *St Matthew Passion* for use at the Worcester Festival: Atkins had wanted Elgar's collaboration, as had the publisher Novello, even though Elgar did minimal work on it.

After the single day's effort with Atkins, he was restless again. The weather was hot. The mood at Plas Gwyn was clearly conveyed in a plea from Alice Elgar to the Windflower to change her plans for Tintagel and come to Hereford—before the Stuart Wortleys went to Germany for a visit to Bayreuth:

Plas Gwyn, Hereford.
30 July 1911

My dearest Alice

It is sad not to have you here today—but I send a line to say if you could come tomorrow for a few days instead of going to the Sea, we should be delighted & love to see you—   Just a telegram wd. be enough—   Your room wd. be ready directly & for yr. maid—   I quite fear yr. plans are made long ago, & all arranged so you may not be able in the least to change them, but cd. not resist writing, on the chance.

It is very quiet here, a car is more wanted then ever, in this lovely weather—we have not emerged from the garden, at least I have not once, & E. *very* little.

Ivor Atkins was here one day for a long day's work with E. over their new Edition of the S.Matthew Passion Music—

Shall you all be back in England by the Worcester Fest.   if so you will have to come, as we have a house there—at least a friend & we have taken it between us—as E. has so much to conduct there—

[38] HWRO 705:445:7106.

Dear love & take care of yr.self [ — ] so *many* thanks for my fan, so pleased it is found

Yr loving
C.A.E.[39]

Elgar added his own note:

[n.p.]
Sunday [30 July 1911]
My dear W.

It is cooler: any day wd. do for us if you found it possible. I am trying to compose 'The Soul'—I will send you the words some day

Love
Edward[40]

His setting of 'The Soul' (by the Herefordshire poet Sir John Davies) remained unrealized. When she could not come, his next surviving note was silent as to disappointment.

Hfd.
Augt 4   1.30 p m
My dear Windflower

Your letter has just come—I posted the programme to you at 11 o c.
For the letter my love & thanks
Here is the poem

Your
E[41]

He went for a week to Frank Schuster at The Hut, returning on 15 August. At Plas Gwyn he found a postcard from Clare Stuart Wortley at Bayreuth. It may have been the postcard snapshot reproduced in plate X. He sent a card in return, enclosing a printed notice: 'Sir Edward Elgar is away from home; your communication shall be laid before him on his return.'

Hereford
Augt.16.1911

So many thanks for your p.c.—   You nearly recd. this in return without any added word of mine as I have only just returned from the Hut where we have been burnt very much. Enjoy all you can & tell me on your return. My love to you

Edward Elgar[42]

---

[39] Elgar Birthplace parcel 584(xxi).
[40] HWRO 705:445:4051.
[41] HWRO 705: 445:4104. The enclosures are missing.
[42] HWRO 705:445:4048.

Three weeks later came a card showing the Stuart Wortleys' accommodation in the Tirol. Elgar wrote a card to the Windflower from London, where he was for orchestral rehearsals before the Worcester Festival:

Langham Hotel, Portland Place, London, W.
[*postmarked* 7 Sept. 1911]

My love to you: I love your cottage but this is the sort of cottage I am condemned to—it is quite airless here; I came up yesterday for rehearsal & am now, this moment, commencing the [Second] Symphy, the Concerto & the Coronation March—it sounds hot doesn't it—& I am *so* lonely—no one in London.

Yr. EE

I am delighted to learn you are all having such a lovely rest.[43]

The Worcester Festival also included the new Elgar–Atkins edition of the *St Matthew Passion*. As a special 'draw' Elgar arranged two of the Chorales for brass instruments, and the players sounded them from the top of the Cathedral tower. After the Festival, Elgar sent Alice Stuart Wortley a picture card of the Edgar Tower near the Cathedral:

[*postmarked* Hereford
21 Sept. 1911]

The festival was wonderful[.] The Chorales from the tower were marvellous. No news. We hope you are all well

EE[44]

A week later Elgar took himself up to the Langham for two nights, and dined at Cheyne Walk. Ten days after that he went again, meeting the young violinist May Harrison for tea at the Stuart Wortleys' house to go over the Violin Concerto for her performance.

Throughout this time delays and frustrations about the Hampstead house accumulated. Alice Elgar was tireless in coping with them, going to London by herself on 22–23 September to try to settle questions and even attend to some of her husband's continuing business with Novello. It was he who fell victim to the strain. The day after the May Harrison tea, he felt giddy and ill at the Langham, and the day after that—10 October—telegraphed for his wife to come to him. She came, summoned Dr Maurice Abbot Anderson to visit him, and herself doctored and comforted him with such success that they were able to travel to Italy four days later to fulfil a conducting engagement in Turin. From there they both sent messages to Cheyne Walk:

[43] HWRO 705:445:4050.    [44] HWRO 705:445:4047.

Hôtel Ligure[,] Turin
Sunday [15 Oct. 1911] 2.30

Arrived all safely: met by deputation (secy) & conducted in state to this shelter—rehearsal tonight at nine o'c—I have the talisman safe & feel quite well & Alice is well also. Very bright & sunny & I think the orchestra is going to be good [—] it *is* very large.

Love
EE

E. kept wonderfully well [—] rather tired now. *Lovely* Sun & country & tints. All looks nice.

Love
A.[45]

After their return from Italy came the Norwich Festival. Elgar travelled from London with his faithful valet in Norwich, John Cousins. Alice and Carice went later that day. Two days later Alice Stuart Wortley arrived. Elgar sent Cousins to meet her train with this note:

Carrow Abbey, Norwich
Thursday [26 Oct. 1911] 4 p m

My dear W.

Hopeless weather! the *party* is on & I cannot get out
I send my John [—] he may help you with luggage at the station & if he misses you he will take this to the Hotel. *Do* telephone *here*
Stuart
Carrow Abbey
& tell me what you do this evening—if concert or what

Love
Edward[46]

The ensuing days are blank in Alice Elgar's diary. But on 28 October *The Norwich Mercury* printed a photo of Elgar and Alice Stuart Wortley with the caption: 'Sir Edward and Lady Elgar . . . ' (Plate I). They were all to return to London on Monday 30 October. That may have been the date of an unsigned scrap from Elgar which Alice Stuart Wortley preserved:

[n.p.]
Monday 8 a m.

I am so afraid your head may be aching as you may find the room stuffy so I put up the 'headache eau de Cologne' for you in my old cycling bottle[47]

---

[45] HWRO 705:445:4049.      [46] HWRO 705:445:4046.      [47] HWRO 705:445:4059.

In London they took a service flat at Hyde Park Mansions—as there was no progress at Hampstead, and Elgar was shortly to conduct his first regular concerts with the London Symphony Orchestra. On 4 November Alice Stuart Wortley, Frank Schuster, Claude Phillips, and the contralto Muriel Foster came to the flat for tea. Then at the first London Symphony concert two days later Elgar conducted the Beethoven Seventh Symphony and Brahms's B flat Piano Concerto with Donald Tovey as soloist. Alice Stuart Wortley almost certainly attended. She joined Alice Elgar in the stalls when Elgar conducted a concert for Landon Ronald on 9 November. The next London Symphony concert brought the young Pablo Casals to play the Saint-Saëns A minor Cello Concerto and Bruch's *Kol Nidrei*. After the rehearsal on 19 November Alice Stuart Wortley carried Edward off to tea.

When the Elgars' time at Hyde Park Mansions ended they stayed briefly at the Langham, and then went in different directions. Alice returned to Hereford to pack up their furniture: 'It seemed very cold & dreary at Plas Gwyn,' she confided to her diary. Alice Stuart Wortley went on a journey of her own. Elgar went to Manchester to conduct a concert with the Hallé Orchestra. He was feeling better, perhaps at the prospect of returning to London afterwards.

Midland Hotel, Manchester.
Nov 22 1911.
My dear W.

*So* sad about your headache on Monday & the lonely journey—if you had only called at the Hotel we were staying in.

I have had a good rehearsal & have really eaten some lunch today.

Frank has telegraphed about theatre *with you* on Friday & I have wired *yes*.

This hotel is full to overflowing—racing men *and* women of the most extraordy type: I was lucky that I got my rooms which in a provident mood I ordered long ago.

The music sounds *lonely* here—I have no one at all.

Love
Yrs siny
Edwd. E

I am glad the Bach [*St Matthew Passion* vocal score] is liked.[48]

For the rest of the year the Elgars were homeless—Plas Gwyn returned to its owner, no completed contract for the Hampstead house, and their furniture in storage. Alice Elgar's 1911 diary may have gone with the furniture, for her entries ceased after 29 November. That evening had found her still at Hereford, her husband staying with Schuster in London. Yet still in hope, coal had been ordered for Hampstead. Elgar wrote:

[48] HWRO 705:445:7104.

22, Old Queen Street, Westminster.
Wedy [29 Nov. 1911] eveng

My dear Windflower

I have heard nothing more from Alice about the trustees! neither has the coal arrived!

Frank *is* thinking of the ballet & *may* be going with friends so you might telephone to him— *What* a lovely day!

Yrs sincy<br>Edward[49]

A fortnight later the fate of the Hampstead house was still unsettled.

The Athenaeum, Pall Mall, S.W.
Dec 12 1911

My dear Windflower

You did not tell us yr address [for the holidays]: I fear you will feel this cold—it *is* cold.

We had a satisfactory interview about the house—i.e. more or less & our fate trembles in the balance today but there is a great chance of the thing being settled very soon. In the meantime all music, pictures & books are quite unenjoyable & we are dreadfully lonely. Alice is at Q. Anne's Mansions zur Zeit [—] do send her a cheery line & me too

Yrs<br>Ed E.[50]

At last on 22 December 'Severn House' became theirs. Furniture could begin going in after Christmas—which the Elgars spent in the Beresfords' house at Brighton.

# 1912

One of Elgar's first letters from Hampstead was written amid the packing cases.

Severn House, 42,Netherhall Gardens, Hampstead, N.W.
Jany 2 1912

My dear Windflower

I send the first sheet of the new note paper to bring you all good wishes for the New Year.

Yours<br>Siromoris[1]

[49] HWRO 705:445:4044.     [50] HWRO 705:445:7672.     [1] HWRO 705:445:4177.

That was the new telegraphic address (as there was yet no telephone installed)—a palindrome composed of 'Sir' and 'O M'.

Severn House, 42,Netherhall Gardens, Hampstead, N.W.
Jany 3 1912

My dear Windflower:

We have been violently busy & entertained by our settling. Köln I have given up but I am much better & have eaten breakfast *two* mornings! & our Danish cook does things *so* thoroughly & nicely but *not at all* picturesquely.

The house is divine—so quiet—quieter than Hereford even where we heard trains: the heating apparatus we can't manage well & get too hot (I think, entre nous, it was designed for the comfort of [the original owner the artist Edwin] Long's nude ladies!)

Now *do* come up tomorrow afternoon & see the chaos & have wild tea—*do*. If you came early we cd. walk you on the heath—

I may be in town tomorrow looking for my writing desk & table: I've found some *round* ones—sublime [—] at Maples & must measure them[.] I hope to be in the 2nd.hand Maple dept at *11.30*.

I hope your wanderer has retd. safely & refreshed—how lovely it was with you & Claude

> Love
> Yr
> Edwd

The house *is* perfect[2]

Details of the first days at Severn House are scanty because Alice Elgar did not begin making regular entries in her 1912 diary until February. Elgar sent Alice Stuart Wortley a printed programme with details of his next London Symphony concert:

Severn House, 42,Netherhall Gardens, Hampstead, N.W.
Saturday [13 Jan. 1912]

My dear W.

So busy!

Please look at the enclosed programme—I do not conduct until Jany 29

I hope you are much better—

We are having worries—John [Cousins] is quite ill with gout & instead of being a help the poor lad requires a nurse so the house stands still somewhat

> Yrs ever
> EE[3]

---

[2] HWRO 705:445:7807. The round table purchased for Severn House is now at the Elgar Birthplace.
[3] HWRO 705:445:4141.

Four days later Alice Elgar sent an invitation:

Severn House, 42, Netherhall Gardens, Hampstead, N.W.
17 Jany. 1912

My dear Alice

We so much hope you will be able to come tomorrow & that you are home all the better for the change—but what weather—

We long for you to see the music room now with its beautiful table wh. makes it really perfect.

You will like to see E.'s delight in it all—

Will you come early in afternoon & have a walk if weather shd. be possible?

There are lovely tunes going on—

> Much love
> Yr aft
> C.A.Elgar[4]

The new music was for an 'Imperial Masque', *The Crown of India*, to celebrate the Indian Coronation of King George V and Queen Mary. The Masque was to figure as the major item in a music-hall bill to play twice daily at the Coliseum. It would be produced in March, and Elgar had contracted to conduct the first fortnight. The fees would go far toward paying the expenses of the move to Severn House.

Yet he was ill with giddiness. A week later an eminent specialist pronounced, as Elgar wrote:

Severn House, 42,Netherhall Gardens, Hampstead, N.W.
Jany 24 1912

My dear Windflower

Victor Horsley has been here & 'it' is *gout*—I shall have to rest as soon as the pressure of work is over: but it is not serious & curable with massage.

In greatest haste

> D o m D
> Love
> Yrs afftly
> Edward.[5]

His London Symphony concert on 29 January included Tchaikovsky's *Romeo and Juliet*, Mozart's Symphony No. 40, three of the *Sea Pictures* with Clara Butt, as well as Hamilton Harty's *With the Wild Geese* conducted by its composer. Two days later Elgar sent a note of further progress at Hampstead:

---

⁴ Elgar Birthplace parcel 583(xv).          ⁵ HWRO 705:445:4200.

Severn House, 42,Netherhall Gardens, Hampstead, N.W.
[31 Jan. 1912]

Telephone:– 4771   P.O.Hampstead
Telephone fixed today

*dolcissimo*

I have been not quite well yesterday [—] Cambridge Tomorrow[.][6]

That was a provincial engagement with the London Symphony Orchestra—to
include, of all things, a Stanford Symphony: 'made the Orch. play it splendidly', Alice
Elgar recorded from her husband's account.

It would appear that Alice Stuart Wortley came to Hampstead for a walk on the
Heath on 5 February, as Elgar wrote next day (before leaving to conduct another
provincial concert):

Severn House, 42,Netherhall Gardens, Hampstead, N.W.
[6 Feb. 1912]

My dear Windflower

I am just off to Queen's Hotel, Leeds—it is thawing & warmer than it was
on the heath yesterday about four o'clock.

I am rehearsing Queen's Hall (Phil[harmonic] ) on Thursday eleven till one
if it is fit for you to come out

I *am* glad the house is approved of.

Yrs ever
EE[7]

Arrived at Leeds, he remembered the second anniversary next day of the first
'Windflower' theme from the Violin Concerto—though again the music he wrote was
the second 'Windflower' theme:

Queen's Hotel, Leeds.
Feb 6. 1912

My dear W.

This is only one line for the anniversary.[x]
I am quite well but a dismal thaw. All good wishes & love

Yrs ever
EE

He returned for the Philharmonic rehearsal and concert (including the *'Enigma'*
*Variations* and Beethoven's 'Emperor' Concerto with Alfred Cortot) on 8 February.
It is not clear whether the Stuart Wortleys attended. But next evening the Elgars dined
with them and the party went to see Max Reinhardt's hugely successful production of
*The Miracle*.

[6] HWRO 705:445:4207.        [7] HWRO 705:445:4175.        [8] HWRO 705:445:7117.

On 11 February came the rehearsal for his last London Symphony concert that season. The main items were Brahms's *Tragic Overture*, the Saint-Saëns Piano Concerto No. 2 with the young Polish pianist Jules Wertheim, Schumann's Second Symphony—and Holbrooke's *The Raven* conducted by its composer. Alice Stuart Wortley probably attended the rehearsal, for she came up to tea afterwards with Wertheim. On Saturday 13 February, the day after the concert, she came up again.

On Sunday 3 March Alice Stuart Wortley came to tea with Hans Richter and his wife. Later in that week Elgar went to conduct the Second Symphony at Bournemouth: there he found a souvenir of the Cornish coast to send to her. He returned to London in time for final rehearsals of *The Crown of India* on the Sunday:

Severn House, 42,Netherhall Gardens, Hampstead, N.W.
Sunday [10 Mar. 1912]

My dear Windflower:

I am so very sorry you were not with us—it *is* so nice now.

I managed Bournemouth very well & at an old print shop I found some of Daniel's sweet little engravings so I sent Boscastle to you (1814) with a piece of the old wrapping paper with the watermark. You may not like the little picture but if you should care about it sufficiently to want it framed please let me have that done for you.

I am very well & wish you were also

Love
EE[9]

Next day commenced *The Crown of India* run. Elgar was booked to conduct two performances a day for a fortnight. She came several times, as did most of his London friends.

Severn House, 42,Netherhall Gardens, Hampstead, N.W.
Thursday [14 Mar. 1912] night

My dear W:

I fear your Windflowers are faded.

About tomorrow I hope you can come to the Coliseum. Do not get tickets as they will give me a *box*—only in the morning (if you have not yet written) telephone your plans—you cd. dine here or I with you or anything

Love
EE[10]

Next day she drove him to the rehearsal and back. On Sunday 17 March the Elgars entertained the great Brahms conductor Fritz Steinbach to tea: he was conducting a London Symphony concert the following day. But Elgar would not be able to go to the Stuart Wortleys' musical party on the Tuesday because of his conducting at the Coliseum.

[9] HWRO 705:445:4211. Clare Stuart Wortley noted: 'The print by Daniell of Boscastle here mentioned is in Mrs.Stuart Wortley's collection of Elgar souvenirs and has been duly inscribed on the back of the framing.   Clare Stuart Wortley.   1936.'
[10] HWRO 705:445:4150.

Severn House, 42,Netherhall Gardens, Hampstead, N.W.
March 18 1912

My dear W—

I am so sorry to miss your evening tomorrow & send all good wishes—my term of slavery will soon be over: I had the P[iano] F[orte] *duet* arrgt of the IInd Symphy here & had to send it away without consulting you—that was the first movemt—but the others will come.

The weather is awful & dreariness looks all around.

I nearly telephoned asking you to come to meet Steinbach yesterday— When shall we see you. I am at the Theatre all this week.

I hear nothing of Windflowers from my sister [Pollie Grafton, who lived at Stoke Prior, Worcestershire] yet but she comes up for one night this week

I was horrified at your Gloucester Place taxi affair—bless you I am so rejoiced you are safe

Love
EE[11]

Pollie Grafton duly arrived on 21 March, together with their eldest sister Lucy (Mrs Pipe) from Worcester. They were shown the wonders of Severn House, and taken to *The Crown of India*.

Elgar's 'slavery' at the Coliseum ended on Saturday 23 March (though the *Crown of India* bill went on). The effort had taxed him heavily. Within a few days he was suffering again from noises in his ear and giddiness. A rest cure of several weeks was prescribed—baths and manipulations at home, no writing, no excursions, no visitors: 'cold storage' Elgar called it.

After a fortnight Alice Stuart Wortley, just back from Tintagel, sent flowers. Elgar's reply was written the day after the worst fears were confirmed about the sinking of the *Titanic*.

Severn House, 42,Netherhall Gardens, Hampstead, N.W.
Wednesday [17 Apr. 1912]

My dear W.  I must send you (quite against the rest cure rules) a thousand thanks for the flowers—they are lovely.

I am allowed out & can walk or drive between 3 & 5: do come if you can or at least to tea—tomorrow

I have been very, very dreary & have felt this terrible Titanic disaster acutely [—] & I have been lonely—I have a prose poem for you too! So we shall see you soon.

Welcome home

Yr
EE[12]

She came up for a little visit on Monday 22 April. Next day his wife and daughter lunched at Cheyne Walk and went with Alice Stuart Wortley to see Yeats's play *The Hourglass*. Elgar was still allowed only small walks as far as Hampstead Heath. That afternoon he sent a copy of his early *Spanish Serenade* ('Stars of the Summer Night') inscribed 'with love to C.A.S.W.   Ap.23 1912.' with a note:

My dear W.   Alice promised to convey this to you with my love—She evidently forgot it as I find it here on my return.
So lovely yesterday.

E.E.[13]

Two days later Alice Stuart Wortley and Frank Schuster took him for a drive to Hampstead Garden Suburb and Edgware. On 28 April she was one of several guests entertained to tea by Elgar (as his wife was in her room with a cold). Gradually life assumed something like a normal shape at Severn House.

The beginning of May found Elgar busy with sketches for the large choral and orchestral setting of O'Shaughnessy's Ode 'The Music Makers' promised for the Birmingham Festival in five months' time. This work was once again to be associated with Alice Stuart Wortley. Yet now another attractive woman entered the picture— Muriel Foster, for whom he was writing a big solo contralto part in *The Music Makers*.

He found the beginning of formal composition heavy work, and on Sunday 5 May his own Alice arranged a car to drive them as far as Totteridge. When they returned to Severn House, Alice Stuart Wortley came up to tea. The Elgars were planning their first large tea party in the new house. Alice Stuart Wortley was coming, perhaps by omnibus. Two days before it Elgar wrote:

Severn House, 42,Netherhall Gardens, Hampstead, N.W.
May 8 1912

My dear Windflower:

You see that is written in full as becomes the season when they are at their best.

I find the omnibus goes to West End Lane which is very far from here I fear but I am going to find out.

You are coming here on Friday I believe & I want to know when I may come to tea as I am free—or free-er   from my rest cure than during these last few weeks & can begin to be civilised again —I do want you to see *Totteridge now* while it is full of beauty—it will be like too many things all over very soon—too soon

Yrs ever<br>EE[14]

The tea party at Severn House on 10 May included Alice Stuart Wortley and about a dozen friends.

Five days later Elgar sent her a piano version of the introduction to the new work. Clearly he had promised it to her, for it came with this note:

---

[13] Elgar Birthplace.                    [14] HWRO 705:445:4149.

Here is your piece of M.S. my dear Windflower: you can fit in the top line in 8ves. the second time through.

Ever yours
EE

[15] Elgar Birthplace parcel 583(xviii).

The remainder of May 1912 was devoted to composition of *The Music Makers*. On 8 June he sent her a piano version of the music which was to set the poem's final words:

> Yea, in spite of a dreamer who slumbers,
> And a singer who sings no more.[16]

With this went a cutting about the new work and a note:

My dear W.

You may not see this in the Musical Times so I send it with all good wishes

Yrs
EE.[17]

Three days later he was able to send the first eight pages of the vocal score in printed proofs, stamped 'Proof   private' and inscribed 'for you! (W)', with this note:

Severn House, 42,Netherhall Gardens, Hampstead, N.W.
Tuesday [11 June 1912]

My dear Windflower

These sheets have just come—you may keep this set & some day tell me of any mistakes you find.

I have marked it Proof Private which is the official way of saying it is not published—do not make it public therefore

I *hope* you will like it.

Love
EE[18]

On 13 June Elgar went to tea at Cheyne Walk. A week later Alice Stuart Wortley dined at Hampstead, and he played her portions of *The Music Makers* on the piano. The Elgars dined at Cheyne Walk on the 21st and again on the 27th, with the Paderewskis and Philip Burne-Jones. On Sunday 30 June Alice Stuart Wortley brought the Paderewskis to tea at Severn House.

The first ten days of July found Elgar engrossed in the final stages of composition. His wife noted:

July 10 1912. E. very hard at work—A. to pay call & tea with A.S.Wortley who taxied her back. Found E. very tired & gone 'mis', 'very lonely' with all that great music. Alice motored them up to Heath. Nice rest there & E. soon better—

That evening he gave another *Music Makers* sketch to the Windflower.

On 14 July he motored her to Totteridge. Four days later the vocal score of *The Music Makers* was finished. It brought only disillusion.

---

[16] Elgar Birthplace.     [17] HWRO 705:445:4148.     [18] Elgar Birthplace.

Severn House, 42,Netherhall Gardens, Hampstead, N.W.
July 19.1912

My dear Windflower:

Yesterday was the usual *awful* day which inevitably occurs when I have completed a work: it has *always* been so: but this time I promised myself 'a day!'—I should be crowned,—it wd. be lovely weather,—I should have open air & sympathy & everything to mark the end of the work—to get away from the *labour* part & dream over it happily. Yes: I was to be crowned—for the first time in my life— But—I sent the last page to the printer. Alice & Carice were away for the day & I wandered alone on to the heath—it was bitterly cold—I wrapped myself in a thick overcoat & sat for two minutes, tears streaming out of my cold eyes and loathed the world,—came back to the house—empty & cold—how I hated having written anything: so I wandered out again & shivered & longed to destroy the work of my hands— all wasted.—& this was to have been the one real day in my artistic life— sympathy at the end of work.

　　　　　'World losers & world-forsakers for ever & ever'
How true it is.

　　Please read the enclosed and arrange anything you like
　　I go to the Hut this evening & must return on Sunday night

　　　　　　　　　　　　　　　　　　　　　Love
　　　　　　　　　　　　　　　　　　　　　Yr
　　　　　　　　　　　　　　　　　　　　　Edward[19]


He went out to Maidenhead by train, and on the Sunday evening Alice Stuart Wortley motored him back. He was still depressed, and therefore ill.


Severn House, 42,Netherhall Gardens, Hampstead, N.W.
Monday [22 July 1912]

My dear W.

I am not well enough to leave home but I shall take the air a little as usual. It was lovely yesterday but very short.

I send you the poem & the first sketch of your chords: it is one of the cardinal virtues to 'visit the sick' remember

　　　　　　　　　　　　　　　　　　　　　Yrs ever
　　　　　　　　　　　　　　　　　　　　　Ed E[20]


Three days later he went to tea again at Cheyne Walk. On 27 July they went once more to Totteridge, and next day she came up to Sunday lunch and a walk on the Heath (when they were caught in heavy rain). On the next Sunday—a wet and stormy day—Alice Stuart Wortley motored the Elgars to St Jude's-on-the-Hill, and went on with Edward as far as St Albans. It was farewell for a time, as she was about to go

---

[19] HWRO 705:445:7676.　　[20] Elgar Birthplace parcel 583(xxi).

again for several weeks to Bayreuth (where Hans Richter was still conducting), and then to Venice.

The letters that followed her were fuller expressions than the mostly short notes of preceding months: and thus perhaps they capture more of the flavour of conversation passing between them when they met. Elgar's spirits were much affected by the weather, and 1912 was one of the worst summers of the century. The first items of news were the orchestration of *The Music Makers*, a renewed attack of gout and proposed cure at Harrogate, an expedition with Carice to see aeroplanes flying at Hendon—whence they could see Judge's Walk as they walked back to Hampstead, the installation of new central heating at Severn House and a planned escape from the disruption by visiting Alice's friend Winifred Murray in Hampshire:

Severn House, 42,Netherhall Gardens, Hampstead, N.W.
Monday [12 Aug. 1912]

My dear Windflower:

Oh! I hope you are well & able to enjoy Bayreuth: my thoughts are there all the hours & minutes—I *did* long to go this year as Richter wished it—but nothing goes right. I have brought my writing into the Library where it is quite silent & full of books & memories. Silent now 6.30 as the workmen have gone but all day we have various noises. I have been ill & am rather a poor-poor (Carice's baby word) still—everyone has gone & it seems very lonely in London. The rain has been worse than ever & spoils walking almost entirely. We can get no lodging or Hotel in Harrogate until the end of the month so all "cure" plans are in abeyance & I do *not* think my cure will be undertaken—my gout has quieted down but I am suffering from my ear noises &c &c—enough of this.

I have just finished the orchestration of 'the multitudes &c' & so nothing complicated remains and on Thursday Alice & I go down to Mrs Murray's for a week or so—it's the only thing possible[:] *very* dull for me but there's nothing nice left in the world for me to do.

I *must* take you to Hendon to see the flying some *Sunday* afternoon[:] it is quite easy & most interesting[.] Carice & I did it yesterday & *walked* all the way back. There is no news except jubilation over Manchester's 1,202.

We saw Judge's Walk transfigured by the evening sun from miles away thro' my field glasses—but it looks *fearfully* desolate—desolate.

All the carpets are now gone! & the heating apparatus men have fine technique with the pick axe &c. so it is time to fly—but it is so very, very *cold* & dark & drear: was there ever such a season

Bless you: I think of you in the music & hope you have not become disappointed with the Ode now you have it.

Love
EE.[21]

[21] HWRO 705:445:7828.

For he had sent the completion of vocal score proofs to her at Bayreuth. There they were examined with interest by Richter, who later posted them back to her.

Before the Elgars left for Hampshire, he had a first letter from Alice Stuart Wortley at Bayreuth, and replied:

Severn House, 42,Netherhall Gardens, Hampstead, N.W.
Thursday Augt 15.1912

My dear Windflower:

I was delighted to receive your letter & to hear that you were well—I began to fear you might have been prostrated by the journey—combined with the awful weather—here it is worse than ever if possible: we have large fires every evening & do what we can to keep warm: today we go to
Little Langleys<br>Steep, nr.Petersfield
till (at least) Monday but you can address *here* always: if the weather should improve we *may* go to the Lakes—I can get no room at Harrogate so I am doing the best I can here which is not saying much: it is really a *desperate* summer & the heating apparatus—which we badly need!—is hors de combat[:] the men have it all to pieces.

It was joy to hear that you had heard the Meistersinger & that my dear old friend conducted.

You must see the enclosed Note—tell me how it will do & if it sounds too—anything—it is an outpouring of the soul—Shelley's poem I have not been able to copy: let me have the sheets back with your notes on the margin—please [—] and tell me what you want altered. It has been too wet to think of going out for days so I have had no sight of the Heath & only little town walks. Write soon

Love<br>EE[22]

The Note (despite his reference to the Shelley poem which might suggest the Second Symphony) was for *The Music Makers*: he had sent this on 14 August to Ernest Newman for use in writing programme notes for the first performance.

Little Langleys, Steep, Petersfield, Hants.
Tuesday [20 Aug. 1912]

My dear W.

Your letter just come to see the last note written of the Score of the Ode. I hope the orchestration is worthy of you. I *long* for someone to see it—the end of my work is as dreary as that awful day when I finished the composition & perished with cold on the Heath.

I cannot live much longer in this weather & loneliness.

[22] HWRO 705:445:4147.

Nice p.c. from Percy Anderson [designer of sets and costumes for *The Crown of India*] from *Munich*

Love
EE

So glad to hear of dear Hans Richter[.] You *are* so good
It is *lovely* here when the rain ceases & I take long lonely walks in the dense woods[23]

Two days later the Elgars returned to London.

Severn House, 42,Netherhall Gardens, Hampstead, N.W.
Sunday Augt 25.

My dear W.

I was rejoiced by your letter: thanks for all you tell me: please open the Ode parcel if you wd. like to play it.

Alice & I are here alone—& it is impossible to get out: we came up from Hants on Wedy & it has rained ever since: so we remain & I am ill—better now—I wd. not have told you only I promised: everything is sad, & dull, & unhappy & miserable

I am sorry—but it is worse, worse than when I finished the composition that bitter day. I try to go to Harrogate for the wretched Concert on Wedy. I do hope you will have it fine & warm at the Lido—I hear good accts of weather in Italy. Let me know when you return. I ~~cannot~~ may be able to write again & am unhappy.

Yrs
E.E.[24]

He went to Harrogate, and from the train through eastern counties saw the result of the sodden summer: 'undreamt of desolation—square miles of corn floating or beaten down into brown mass'.[25] At Harrogate, however, he met Lady Charles Beresford, and they had an amusing time. From there he was on his way to Hereford to rehearse the Festival Chorus:

In train Harrogate to Hereford
Thursday Aug 29 1912

My dear Windflower

You will understand the joggling of the train makes this illegible.

My Harrogate visit (Concert) is over—so dull & lonely—& what it might have been. I wept during the Variations[:] my friends seemed so far away.

---

[23] HWRO 705:445:7673. In the first paragraph at the end of the second sentence the words 'of you.' have been eradicated; also the underlining of 'long' in the third sentence.
[24] HWRO 705:445:4143.
[25] Alice Elgar's diary, 27 Aug. 1912, reporting a letter from Elgar.

Now I am travelling to Hfd for a rehearsal & shall go home tomorrow as the weather is hopeless, altho' there have been five hours sunshine yesterday— but today again all gloom.

Lady C. sent her car to the station to meet me & I dined with her last night—very amusing—she looks much better & ate a *great* dinner! much more than double my effort. She telephoned that I was not to dress—but I *did* put on something. I found her loathing the whole place & *people*. Of course Harrogate thinks itself very fashionable & more than chic—& the ladies dress up terribly. Lady C. shews her contempt for the whole thing by wearing a hat at dinner & a curious sac-like robe something like a waterproof—the Majestic Hotel visitors are very much hurt I think. She informed me genially & generally for the edification of all round that everything was horrible &c &c. She is really bored to death & apparently only speaks to one gentleman, a Belgian [—] I forget the name. We left the dining room nearly last & went into one of the salons—somebody began to sing. Whereupon Lady C. uttered a shriek & we fled! it was all very amusing.

I am brokenhearted over the weather & the corresponding gloom. I feel as if I should never see you again—tell me I shall. The train is really beyond words awful—but I am going over the very ground you travelled over from York to Hereford—two years ago.

There is no news to tell you of us—you will have seen the dreadful plight of Norwich—inconceivable. Carice is at Brighton. Alice remains at home— there is really nothing to be done. I have a choral rehearsal today—next week orch—the week after the Hereford fest: week of the 19th. Birmingham [Festival] rehearsals [of *The Music Makers*] begin—now I have lost *all* interest in it. I have written out my soul in the Concerto, Sym II & the Ode & you know it & my vitality seems in them now—& I am happy it is so—in these three works I have *shewn* myself.

Now there is a gleam of sun & we are nearing Stockport. You will not forget that Birmingham is on Oct 1st–4th. & from then till end of November I am going to rest as much as I can & I trust the weather will be fine enough for something. Claude I hear is bored at Wiesbaden but going to Munich, &c

So you are the only person who is well placed. I do hope the sun & warmth are with you & that it is all beautiful for you & that you will come back very much refreshed

> Adieu
> Yrs ever
> Edward[26]

At Hereford, before the rehearsal, he walked up to look at Plas Gwyn. Next day he returned to London.

---

[26] HWRO 705:445:7806.

Severn House, 42,Netherhall Gardens, Hampstead, N.W.
Sunday September 1: 1912

My dear Windflower:

Here we are in September & really no improvement: yesterday was lovely only cold. Carice came back & we had an afternoon out: today rain & clouds as bad as ever. I recd. yr letter & card & rejoiced to know that you, bless you, are warm & in sun.

Since I wrote (in the train, Crewe) I arrd. at Hereford thro' most awful floods caused by the lovely river you walked by in the days that seem (now) to be kinder than these: I immediately on arriving walked up to Plas Gwyn, now occupied, to see if the swallows are still cared for. Alas! the new tenants are 'tidy' people—the loft is repainted—(as I saw from the lane) & the windows closed tight—so my companions of eight years found no welcome this year & have had to seek new homes—we had seen & known them & I resented their disturbance very much. I do not know who lives at P.G. so walked down to Hereford: had a good rehearsal of Gerontius, stayed the night & came here on Friday—the weather was too depressing to allow of staying in Hereford for pleasure.

Next week the orchl. rehearsals [in London for the Hereford Festival] are going on & on Saturday we go to Castle Pool House[,] Hereford for the week from 7th.Saturday to 14th.Saturday[.] I am sorry you will miss it all—Gerontius will be lovely in the Cathedral & I had such a seat for you—remote like Lincoln. Please let me hear when you are to arrive. I have to go to Birmingham on the *16th*. for *chorus* rehearsal at 7.45 p.m. [—] after that I shall be in London & the *first* orchestral rehearsal of the Ode is on the *19th*. 10.30–1.0   *you must* come

Love
EE[27]

The London rehearsals for Hereford anticipated two song premières—*The Torch* (with its fortissimo beginning refrain 'Come, O my love!') and *The River*, both orchestrated for Muriel Foster (Mrs Goetz).

Severn House, 42,Netherhall Gardens, Hampstead, N.W.
Friday [6 Sept. 1912] 11.30

My dear Windflower:

All in confusion of starting to Hereford: thank you for your letter just received: I was rejoiced to get it & to know you are leaving soon &c. I shall *not* write again to Venice as you will have left &, I hope, on your way home very soon

This week has not been so bad either meteorologically or socially. Frank is

---

[27] HWRO 705:445:7803. In the first sentence of the second paragraph, the 'y' of 'you' has been eradicated.

back & came up here one evening: we had good rehearsals for Hereford &
Muriel Goetz sings splendidly—the two songs make a terrific effect with
orch—'Come o my love' &c. You have the Hereford address but Hereford
*Festival* will be enough. On Monday week I go to Birmingham for 1st.
Chorus [rehearsal of *The Music Makers*]—but you should be in England by
then. Bless you!

Love
EE

It is still cold but there is a gleam of sun[28]

He sent a book to Cheyne Waik for her return with a note: 'Just to greet
you [14] Sep 1912'.[29] A week later he sent his first letter to Cheyne Walk in many
weeks, with details of rehearsals for *The Music Makers* première:


Severn House, 42,Netherhall Gardens, Hampstead, N.W.
Saturday Sep 21st. 1912

My dear Windflower:

I have just addressed the envelope & it seems so strange to write the
familiar words, although I did write them last week in sending the little book
to welcome you. I am so glad you have had such a delightful rest & change in
such lovely places but you were wanted back[:] you have been away a long
time.

Alas! the rehearsal you dreamed of never came off—with this I send you
the revised list: those in London are in the *Small* Q's Hall—Tuesday a.m. is
for Wind only so you will not come to that even if you are awake—which I
doubt—Tuesday afternoon I am free & evening also.

On Wedy. there is a rehearsal from 2 – 3 & I go on to Birmingham at
4 o'c—returning the next day for the rehearsal from 3 – 5.

On Friday morning I go to Birmingham as you see on the list: I conclude
my rehearsal on Saturday night & shall return to London on Sunday &
remain here until Tuesday morning when we all go to the Grand Hotel[,]
Birmingham for the week.

What a weary lot of detail! Let me hear of you very soon indeed

Love
EE

I am very weary & want a change badly[30]

Four days later he sent another letter. But she cut away the top half of the sheet,
noting the date 'Sept 25. 1912.' on the remainder:


[28] HWRO 705:445:7825.
[29] HWRO 705:445:4179. Day supplied by recipient.
[30] HWRO 705:445:4174.

I enclose the column from the D.Telegraph—I want you to see what dear Richter says about Parsifal—very fine: you can also see a word about the
*Edward Elgar*
of very long ago. Let me have the scrap back sometime[31]

Near the end of the month he inscribed a copy of *The Music Makers* vocal score 'to C. Stuart Wortley with kind regards from a Music Maker   E.E. Sept. 1912'.
On 1 October the Elgars travelled to Birmingham with Alice Stuart Wortley for *The Music Makers* première that evening. Alice Elgar wrote afterward:

E. conducted magnificently. Had a great reception—Dear Kilburns there & many friends. Frank much impressed. Stuart Wortleys gave a supper for E.[:] Mr. & Mrs. S.W.[,] Kilburns, Prof.Terry, Frank, Mr.Cobb

2 October. Fine rather cold—E. took Alice S. Wortley to Stratford-on-Avon & Kenilworth &c—Enjoyed the day . . .

3 October. Frank motored E. & Sir E.Evans Gordon & Alice S.W. & Mr.Cobb to Kenilworth & Warwick & Stratford on A. Very nice expedition . . .

The Festival concluded the next night with *The Apostles* and a big supper party given by Mr and Mrs Goetz: Alice Stuart Wortley almost certainly went with the Elgars.
Next day all three Elgars carried out their plan of a visit to the Lakes, despite Alice's heavy cold.

Prince of Wales Lake Hotel, Grasmere.
Monday [7 Oct. 1912]
My dear W.

I hope you are quite safe after your sad looking journey, & that you are rested & quiet after that hideous Birmingham.
I wish you were here [—] *so* lovely & quiet[.] Alice is better & out today. Yesterday in the sun Carice & I wandered up high—the tints are marvellous & no leaves gone yet. Then we have a boat & are on the lake all day—no one here or nearly no one—I go to sleep in the boat! & float about—so restful & good for nerves.
Please tell me how you are—we are here for the week & Alice wants to go to Ullswater but that will depend on the weather. I was really ill all last week & you must forgive much to a sick man. I want to stay here always if I could only find a cot.
I send a few cards but I think you will already know the look of the dear place

Love
Yrs ever
Edward[32]

[31] HWRO 705:445:4172.        [32] HWRO 705:445:7109.

A week later they returned to Hampstead. Elgar had to prepare his first London Symphony Orchestra concert of the new season. It was to include the Franck Symphony, a work he had never conducted. To study it he asked Alice Stuart Wortley to get an arrangement for piano duet. She asked which Franck Symphony: that such a music-lover should not have known the answer is some measure of the musical education which has since been accomplished by records and broadcasting. He answered:

Severn House, 42,Netherhall Gardens, Hampstead, N.W.
Thursday [17 Oct. 1912] 6 p.m.

My dear W.

There is only one Symphony by C.Franck & I think it is sure to be published for piano—tell me if you have any difficulty in getting it.

Just in from a long & lonely walk on the Heath—I went out early this morning & went straight on! Doctor's orders—all fresh air possible so I go again tomorrow afternoon—

I fear it will be tiring for you to come & dine here [in advance of an evening out] unless you come very early & rest a little—this you can do in the library. I will telephone in the a.m. when I see what time the Winter's Tale begins.

Love<br>E.E.

The Heath was lovely this afternoon—even after the lakes[33]

Next morning he sent her a picture book: it was recalled by Clare as *Shakespeare's Country*.

Severn House, 42,Netherhall Gardens, Hampstead, N.W.
Oct 18 1912

My dear W:

I have found (at last) the book of views—it is old & has some markings begun yesterday & discontinued—you can mark the rest if you cannot remember the places without!

Love<br>EE[34]

That evening she went with the Elgars to see Granville Barker's production of *The Winter's Tale* at the Savoy. Its run was epoch-making in the post-Edwardian theatre because Granville Barker put the play first: sets were semi-abstract, every word of Shakespeare's text was included, and there was no 'star' favouritism. One witness wrote:

---

[33] HWRO 705:445:4167.
[34] Elgar Birthplace parcel 583(i). The book may have been *The Shakespeare Country Illustrated* by John Leyland (Country Life, n.d. [c.1900]).

His hygienically white staging and his egalitarian lighting, which shone alike on principals and supers, were not, as someone wickedly suggested, a sop to Fabian planners; they were part of his attempt to recapture in the London of 1912 the daylight and open air of the Globe. [There was a] sense of freshness, alertness, enfranchisement to many who felt they were seeing Shakespeare for the first time. It was, as a leading critic observed, post-impressionist Shakespeare.  ...
As for the moments—and more than moments—of dramatically significant beauty, they linger in the recollection of all who were there to hear and see. Leontes (Henry Ainley) pacing up and down beside the flaming brazier; Perdita (Cathleen Nesbitt) footing it with her lover [Dennis Neilson-Terry] in the sheepshearers' dance; the golden voice of Paulina (Esmé Beringer) bidding Hermione come down, and the grace of the descent as Lillah McCarthy made it ... these are ineffaceable memories.[35]

Alice Elgar wrote: 'E. & A. much delighted & thoroughly admired & enjoyed it.'

On Sunday 20 October Elgar and Alice Stuart Wortley went for a short drive. On the following Saturday the two went again to *The Winter's Tale*—'again very much pleased'. The day after that she came up for a Sunday tea with numerous guests, including E. F. Benson and Philip Burne-Jones. Alice Elgar wrote: 'Part of the time E. sat upon his corner shelf in Libry—& almost all there talking. P.B. Jones wants to paint him—'. Arrangements were made, and during the next month there were many sittings at the artist's studio.[36]

On 31 October, when Landon Ronald conducted the Second Symphony at Queen's Hall, Elgar sat with Alice Stuart Wortley—leaving his own Alice to deal with their other guests elsewhere in the Hall. Two nights later the Elgars dined at Cheyne Walk. The guests included Claude Phillips, the Sidney Colvins, Lord and Lady Edmund Talbot, and Sir Arthur and Lady Colefax (he the MP for Manchester SW, she a formidable hostess to the upper crust).

On 4 November Alice Stuart Wortley came to Severn House to play through the Franck Symphony with Elgar in piano duet, to prepare his conducting. On the 8th they played it again, and once more on the 22nd. The concert on 25 November also included *In the South*, the *Introduction and Allegro*, and the Dvořák Cello Concerto with Serge Barjansky. Alice Stuart Wortley was there, and showed Elgar a letter from Philip Burne-Jones. But she did not go to supper afterwards with the Elgars (whose guests were Mrs Murray and Muriel Foster's accompanist Katherine Eadie). Next morning he wrote:

Severn House, 42,Netherhall Gardens, Hampstead, N.W.
Tuesday [26 Nov. 1912]

My dear W.

Many thanks for the sight of P B-J's letter—I fear he is very flattering—not to you, that could not be—but to me.

[35] W. Bridges-Adams (writing in the early 1960s) in *Edwardian England*, pp. 406–7. In the 1920s Bridges-Adams became a friend of Elgar's.
[36] Elgar disliked the result, and when the Worcester City Council proposed to buy it for the Guildhall, Elgar wrote to Troyte Griffith: 'I *wish* you cd. persuade the Worcr. people *not* to buy that weak-kneed portrait! *do*. Phil is a good creature but is feeble & makes me stand like himself...' (12 December 1922. HWRO 705:445:7376).

I am *so* glad you liked it last night

I am very depressed about many things & wanted a different end to the evening—it all 'fizzled' out: but I did my duty at supper. I have proposed to go to Burne-Jones tomorrow at eleven—but he's away to-day so only a telephone message could be got to him & he does not return until late—if I do hear I will let you know. His letter is very nice. I am not sure about going to the country—the weather is so awful. I am anxious to hear your news & the nice things you have

Yrs always
EE[37]

On Sunday 1 December she came to tea, and he gave her the short score manuscript of a piece first drafted as long ago as 1879. He called its revival *Cantique*, and orchestrated it.

Severn House, 42,Netherhall Gardens, Hampstead, N.W.
Wednesday [4 Dec. 1912]

My dear W.

This is only to say that Landon Ronald is going to play (full orchestra) the little Cantique on Sunday afternoon the *15th* (not next Sunday) at the Albert Hall—perhaps you can go to the Concert—it will not be announced as *new* or *first time*—only to see how the public like it. I did not go in to the Colvins' [afternoon party the day before] after all—I wandered off into the dark & walked a long way quite alone & kept my memories undistributed and unbroken

Ever
EE[38]

His own Alice was confined to the house with a bad cold, so did not record her husband's movements that afternoon other than to note that he did not get to the party.

At the afternoon concert on 15 December Elgar found himself disappointed by *Cantique*. But Alice Stuart Wortley came up to tea afterwards. A week later she came again, and yet again on Christmas afternoon—when Elgar was depressed as usual on such days. On Boxing Day the Elgars lunched with her, and they all went to a revival of *John Bull's Other Island* by Bernard Shaw. Alice Elgar wrote:

Most delightful. The noble & ideal left in instead of the poison of other B.Shaw. Alice motored us back (& sent for us) to tea & stayed. E. Better   D[eo] G[ratias].

---

[37] HWRO 705:445:4173.

[38] Both this letter and the *Cantique* short score are at the Elgar Birthplace. The letter is in parcel 583(xiv).

During the winter months Elgar entered a deep depression from which no person or experience seemed able to rouse him. It was as if, having produced his reminiscent *Music Makers*, the future held nothing. On 16 January, while his wife was confined to the house with a bad cold, he and Alice Stuart Wortley went to a recital of Paganini Studies by the violinist Alexander Sebald. Five days later the Windflower came to tea.

In an effort to raise his spirits, Alice Elgar consented to having a dog in the household. (Edward had always been fond of animals, but it was one area where they differed.) The first dog was tried and sent back as not being sufficiently reliable on the new Severn House carpets. On 22 January Edward and Carice chose an Aberdeen (the same breed as the Stuart Wortleys' Nigger). But perhaps the small arrival sensed something less than hospitality in his grand new home: for after two hours he ran away and was never seen again. Next day Elgar went to the Dogs' Home in Battersea without success, before going to an afternoon party at Schuster's house. On the way home he stopped to write:

The Athenaeum, Pall Mall, S.W.
Thursday [23 Jan. 1913] 6.30
My dear W.

I missed you at Frank's & hope nothing worrying kept you away? I thought you were sure to be there.

I have been looking for our dog—Home for Lost dogs—so sad—we lost him last night.

I went for a short walk yesterday [in Hampstead] & it was beautiful [—] sun with us in the morning—but alas! dreadful fog I fear in town. Write soon[.] Alice is bettering slowly & we hope your invalid is improving also.

Love
Yrs
EE[1]

Another trip to Battersea next day produced no result, as Alice Stuart Wortley learned when she came to tea.

There was some thought of Elgar's going alone to San Remo on the Italian Riviera to try to raise his spirits. (Having conducted only two concerts with the London Symphony Orchestra, he told them he could do no more just then.) But when the day came he could not face the journey, and gave up his ticket. His wife wrote:

30 January 1913 . . . E. very depressed at going to Riviera, said in car: 'If only we cd. go to Naples.' A. said: 'Why not?' Naples then—& E. brightened from *terrible* depression & took passage for Naples next day.  . . .

---

[1] HWRO 705:445:4195.

Alice Stuart Wortley came to Severn House to set up a liaison with Carice, who was being left to tend the grand property that a year earlier had seemed the embodiment of her parents' dreams for success and happiness. That night Elgar wrote:

Severn House, 42, Netherhall Gardens, Hampstead, N.W.
Jan 30 1913 10 p m

My dear Windflower

The exile begins tomorrow & will end—?
I send all thanks for your sweet kindness to Carice & for coming up here. Bless you.
We sail tomorrow 12.30 from Tilbury & call at Gibraltar[,] *Toulon* and arrive Naples in about a week's time.
Do send a p.c. to    S.S.*Osterley*
                      Orient Line
                      Toulon.
We shall go to Parker's Hotel[,] Naples if only for a day.

Love<br>EE.

Bless you
S.S Osterley (Orient Line)
   Gibraltar Feb 4
   Toulon Feb 6
   arr Naples Feb 8.[2]

Next morning he sent a picture card of the Osterley:

Friday [31 Jan. 1913] 10.30 a m

just off

The trip produced no surviving correspondence with Alice Stuart Wortley. As the Elgars were starting the return journey from Rome by train on 22 February, news reached them that their dear friend Mrs Worthington was fatally ill in New York: she had at most a few months to live. 'E. & A. dreadful shock & mourned & wept all the way along.' They arrived home next evening in no very good spirits.

On 28 February he sent Alice Stuart Wortley a picture card of Guy's Cliff Mill, near Warwick—one of the places visited on the little excursion from Birmingham with Schuster in October.[4] Elgar was not well enough to attend a performance of *The Music Makers* on 3 March. He was to go next day to Llandrindod Wells to try a cure. The morning of his departure brought a letter from Alice Stuart Wortley. His answer was such that she cut away the upper half of the sheet, leaving only:

[2] HWRO 705:445:4140.
[3] Elgar Birthplace parcel 583(xxii).
[4] HWRO 705:445:7796.

I am not well & did not go to the Music Makers but I leave in hope for
The Gwalia Hotel
Llandrindod Wells
& cheered by your missive

Love
EE[5]

On 11 March Alice Elgar lunched at Cheyne Walk before Edward's return that afternoon: he said the week away had done no good. Two days later he went to the West End for errands, met Alice Stuart Wortley, and she motored him home. 18 March brought his last portrait sitting at Philip Burne-Jones's studio; afterwards he lunched with Alice Stuart Wortley at Cheyne Walk and again she drove him back to Hampstead. The following evening she came to dine. His own Alice remained 'much troubled about E.'.

The morning of 22 March found him working a little on *Falstaff*, his commission for the Leeds Festival in October. That afternoon the Windflower took him for a drive to Totteridge. Two days later he was as wretched as ever. On the 25th she came up for a little visit while his own Alice went to consult doctors about him. Five days after that Alice Stuart Wortley got him out for another drive, this time to Chorley Wood: her chauffeur lost the way, and Elgar returned home tired and late.

He spent the first half of April at his sister's house in the Worcestershire countryside. Before his return on the 16th, his own Alice lunched with Alice Stuart Wortley and Clare, and they attended a concert of modern French orchestral music: Alice Elgar was not much impressed, and they came away before the end. On 17 April, the day after his return, Alice Stuart Wortley came to tea. Elgar gave her a sketch dated that day of a descending phrase (now at cue 103) to show Falstaff resting in Shallow's Gloucestershire orchard:[6] it might mirror his own visit to the country.

On 2 May the Elgars went to the Royal Academy Private View to see the finished Burne-Jones portrait. Next day he and Alice Stuart Wortley went to a matinée of a play which was to become a great favourite of his, an oriental fantasy called *The Yellow Jacket*:

> The story of the play is often beautiful in its several episodes, now poetic, now pathetic and again fantastic. It sets before us the everlasting appeal of maternal self-sacrifice; and it presents the always-sympathetic figure of the rightful heir recovering his place by his own powers. It is a story as old as the hills and as young as the spring-time ... [7]

During the next month Elgar was to go to this play half a dozen times, taking all sorts of friends to see it.

After the first *Yellow Jacket* matinée Alice Stuart Wortley drove him down to the Royal Academy for the annual dinner. But it was not to be, as he wrote that evening:

[5] HWRO 705:445:4222. Dated by receipt 'Mar 4 1913'.
[6] Elgar Birthplace MS 66.
[7] Brander Matthews, Introduction to *The Yellow Jacket: A Chinese Play Done in a Chinese Manner*, by George C. Hazelton Jr and J. Harry Benrimo (Indianapolis, USA; Bobbs-Merrill Co., 1913). Elgar's copy is now at the Elgar Birthplace.

The Athenaeum
Saturday [3 May 1913] 8 p m
My dear W:

   After all I did not dine at the R.A.—I went in, found they had *omitted* my
O M & put me with a crowd of nobodies in the lowest place of all—the
bottom table—I see no reason why I should *endure* insults—I can understand
their being offered! to me. Love & thanks for all your kind troubles: all
wasted.

   I left at once and came here & had a herring

Yrs ever<br>EE.[8]

   The following week brought contrasts. First came two of his sister's daughters from
Worcestershire to be shown the sights of the great city by their famous uncle. Then on
7 May the Elgars went to lunch with Henry Harris (who had been one of the
Beresfords' party cruising with the Mediterranean Fleet in 1905). Harris's guests
included one of the late King Edward's favourites, Mrs Cornwallis-West, as well as
Lady Speyer, a beautiful woman in her own right and Elgar's erstwhile helper over the
Violin Concerto.

Severn House, 42, Netherhall Gardens, Hampstead, N.W.
May 9 1913
My dear W.

   I have heard nothing of P.Burne-Jones & there is no news & nothing to
tell. I went (for Alice's sake) to an awful lunch with Bogey Harris & sat
between Jenny West! & Lady Speyer!! too awful for words.

   My two dear little nieces are here & I have been taking them out to all the
old shows—N.Gally[,] B.Museum &c.&c. & The Yellow Jacket—today Zoo
& then I have done. I hope the weather is better with you than here—it is
truly awful & very cold.

   I am not well & all sorts of difficulties accumulate—but of these I do not
write

Yours ever<br>E.E.

We enquired about E.F.Benson & he is somewhat better. Adela Schuster
writes that Frank is home looking 'very well, brown & prosperous.' curious
adjective.[9]

   A vaguely dated letter may belong to the latter half of May, when Alice Stuart
Wortley was largely absent from Lady Elgar's diary, probably because of a
Whitsuntide holiday.

---

[8] HWRO 705:445:7685. Misdated by recipient 'May 3, 1914'.
[9] HWRO 705:445:4223.

Severn House, 42,Netherhall Gardens, Hampstead, N.W.
Thursday [?22 May 1913].

My dear Windflower

It is really ages since I have heard a word of you—I *do* hope the visit is doing you good & that the weather is kind

I was in a mood to think all sorts of things, then your wild flowers came & Alice & I knew you are at least alive, Bless you! & presumably well.

Yesterday was quite warm & fine—today bright but cold winds—really cold. I am just the same & really ought to get better—I do want some country—real country: not too much London Lavender. When do you return?

Love
EE.

I hope the car is a success & that you have seen much: & what read you?[10]

On 27 May he sent 'A scrap of Falstaff for the Windflower's return': the broad melody introducing Prince Hal (at cue 5).[11] Next day Alice Elgar noted:

28 May 1913. Very hot—Alice S.W. drove E. into town to try new clothes after hearing some Falstaff music to her joy

On Sunday 1 June the Elgars lunched with her at Cheyne Walk. The other guests were Henry James and Sidney Colvin: 'interesting talk', noted Alice Elgar, without a clue to its subject. On 9 June came Elgar's last appearance of the season with the London Symphony Orchestra—to conduct the first London performance of *The Music Makers*. Alice Stuart Wortley was there, and she drove the Elgars back to Hampstead. But the day was cast in shadow by a cable from New York announcing the death of Mrs Worthington. Next day Elgar sent Alice Stuart Wortley a leaf from his sketchbook. One side contained a two-bar sketch for *Falstaff*. The other side bore a fragment of *The Music Makers* setting the words:

In spite of a dreamer, a dreamer who slumbers
And a singer who sings no more!
The end.

this original sketch—the very first thought—for *you*.[12]

An extra unhappiness was the termination of his chief conductorship of the London Symphony Orchestra. The Orchestra regretted that they must look for a man with a bigger public following as a conductor, and with better health.

Depressed again, Elgar went for a few days to The Hut. He returned to Hampstead on 17 May, and next day they joined Alice Stuart Wortley to tea at the Colvins': among the other guests were Henry James and the influential Unionist editor of *The*

[10] HWRO 705:445:4024.
[11] Elgar Birthplace MS 114. The sketch was dated the previous day.
[12] Elgar Birthplace MS 114.

*Observer*, J. L. Garvin. On 21 May Elgar sent his own Alice and Carice to the Irish Players' production of Synge's *Riders to the Sea*, while Alice Stuart Wortley drove him to Hendon to see the flying—and back to tea.

June 26 1913. E. very hard at work . . . E. to French play with Alice S.W.— she came back & had tea & heard Falstaff.

June 27 . . . E. very absorbed in Falstaff, orchestrating all the morning. Beautiful things he was writing. E. & A. to tea Cheyne Walk[:] Ranee [of Sarawak], Lady Northcliffe, Claude &c—Tiresome lady sang. Most boring. E. tell[ing] Charles S.W. all kinds of journey advice &c&c . . .

On 8 July he wrote out another *Falstaff* fragment for her: the jollity in the tavern (at cue 66)[13] and posted it next day. The last half of July found him keen on his music now it was coming together at last. On the 17th Alice Stuart Wortley took him an afternoon drive to Barnet and Hadley Green. Next day there was lunch at Severn House and another drive; and still another drive on Sunday the 20th—before the Russian conductor Emil Cooper brought Chaliapin for tea at Severn House.

Severn House[,] Hampstead, N.W.
Monday [21 July 1913]
My dearest Windflower

All goes well: I have just sent off 80 pages of *your* score to the printers— Was it not nice yesterday? & isn't he a great Man?

> Dear love to you
> EE.[14]

The following weekend the Elgars were Schuster's guests at The Hut with Alice Stuart Wortley. Elgar worked at *Falstaff* in the Garden Room. The Windflower left on Monday. Next morning, before he and his own Alice took their leave, he sent the short score of the second Interlude, inscribed:

> With Justice Shallow [—] Pastorale
>
> (Farewell to the Hut) July 1913
> written on Tuesday after you left
> and now Good night
>
> EE[15]

The Elgars had engaged a holiday house in North Wales, and were to go to it on Tuesday 5 August. He bent every effort to finish his full score before leaving. Another fragment of the music went to Cheyne Walk with a note:

[13] Elgar Birthplace MS 66.
[14] HWRO 705:445:4226. The letter has been mutilated in three ways. In the first sentence the word *'your'* has had its 'y', 'r', and the underline erased. In the closing, 'Dear' is erased. And the lower part of the sheet has been cut away.
[15] Elgar Birthplace MS 66.

Sunday Aug 3 1913

I have no minute to copy all this out—I hope you can make out this sketch which I have inked over[16]

He finished *Falstaff* by starting work at 4 a.m. on the morning of their departure.

The holiday house was at Penmaenmawr—a once-romantic site of ancient British fortification, but gradually eaten away over more than half a century as its granite was quarried for setts and macadam to pave the cities and towns of the Industrial Revolution. In the shadow of those excavations Elgar worked on proofs of *Falstaff*, and on the programme note which only he could write for this most complex of programmatic works. He wrote to the Windflower's holiday address in Switzerland:

Penmaenmawr
Augt 12 1913

My dear W.

It was good of you to write & we loved to hear of your safe arrival & that the place is nice for you: I hope you are settled in the little house with the piano & everything as you wish.

Here we go on as usual. I am busy with my proofs & spend much time in the garden room where I have all my own writing things spread out & I work a great deal more than I should do—the weather is generally cold but we do have sun occasionally & the country—one side at least—is beautiful—even the Bergwerk on the other side is imposing in the enormity of the excavations & the stuff they throw aside—granite works.

I have sent you a little book which seemed good to me to take up for a few minutes at a time & you will accept it on H.James's recommendation (see preface) if not on mine—monotonous of course but the descriptions bring back so many particular days. We have no news of the outer world: the extra rooms here are not adapted for visitors, so we shall have no one but ourselves—I tried to fly the golden-hued kite but the wind was too strong for such a delicately constructed thing & it refused to be buffeted by sea gales.

Love
Yrs ever
EE[17]

Penmaenmawr
Sunday [17 August 1913]

My dear W:

This is a heavenly day [—] a successor to a real hot summer day—but this is really 'Sweet day so cool—the bridal of the earth & sky'

[16] Elgar Birthplace MS 66.
[17] HWRO 705:445:4139. In his letter of 29 July 1926 Elgar referred to 'the book I made when you were there [in Switzerland] 13 years (is it possible?) ago'.

We have been expeditions & have fought our way through cold & mist to this beneficient weather; would 'twould last.

I am working on my Falstaff notes, but want your assistance badly! So you see we have no news & very much wish to hear of your doings & surroundings. —I hope the weather is kind to you & that the Châlet is still a joy. I should like to hear the woolley piano. We hear (via Percy A[nderson]) that [Frank Schuster's chauffeur] Barry is better & out—that was early in this last week—the tour was postponed until Saturday (yesterday) & I hope Frank & P. have really started: we warned them against coming here, although it is very beautiful in good weather: yesterday we had an exciting afternoon—in very scanty costumes—on the sands fishing with a huge professional net—I cannot bear to see anything caught tho' & long to put them back. We have seen Carnarvon Castle which is beautiful.

I have been busy arranging rehearsals & am tired! I hope you have good news of your Wanderer.

Love
EE[18]

Penmaenmawr
Friday Augt 22 1913
My dear W:—

Pouring rain now, after the promise of a fine day: so many thanks for your letter & the news of the chalet: I am so delighted to know you are happily placed & in surroundings so much more congenial & suitable than the hotel. I have been more than busy; as the score is behindhand I undertook to furnish the notes (analysis) *myself* for the *October* number of the Musical Times;— no outsider cd. write about Falstaff without the score. After my offer was accepted they said it was *September* they wanted the analysis for! so for two days I have done nothing else—two lovely fine days—& today I am stranded with no very particular work & it is pouring a deluge down on this resonant garden room.

I have no news; we work hard & make little excursions but the weather has been evil for many days. I think I may leave this on Wednesday & go to Gloucester to take a [Three Choirs Festival] *chorus* rehearsal in the Cathedral; in that case I should not return here but go on to London to be in time for the orchestral rehearsals—think of Gerontius &c. on Thursday the 4th of September: I shall be rehearsing the orchestra & the Sym II from 2 till 4 o'c.

Our house is very *cold* and peculiarly built so as to avoid any sunshine! most extraordinary—but I go & sit on the wall the other side the road to get

[18] HWRO 705:445:7826.

warm; the garden is small but 'diversified' & I have this garden room to write & work in & have learned to love it

All good wishes

Ever yrs
Edward[19]

He did not go to Gloucester, but stayed on at Penmaenmawr for the remainder of the month. On 27 August he had proofs of his Falstaff notes, and sent a first galley to the Windflower inscribed: 'This is the Introduction to the musical notes.'[20] The Elgars returned to London on 1 September.

She came to the Gloucester Festival, where he gave her inscribed copies of the *Messiah* and *St Matthew Passion*. After the Festival Elgar went to stay with the organist of Hereford Cathedral, G. R. Sinclair.

Hereford
Sep 14 1913
Dearest Windflower

Thanks for your sweet letter & all your news. I was *bound* to send a telegram [—] it seemed such years. I regret your awful journey but hope you are quite rested

My morning's letters leave me rather vague—but I think I go home tomorrow—probably to a club for a night [as his wife was away from home]: but the Falstaff proofs are in a wild state.

Anyway I send my love & your ticket for rehearsals [at Leeds]. You will know that dull Hall by this time.

Good news of A. & C.

My love. I mark all you say of Gloucester & of the future.

Yours ever
E

I shall of course go to the Hut in the middle of the week[21]

He was at The Hut between 16 and 21 September; whether Alice Stuart Wortley joined him there seems nowhere recorded.

He was sharing chief conductorship of the Leeds Festival with Arthur Nikisch and Hugh Allen. Elgar was to conduct a wide repertory of music in addition to *Gerontius* and the *Falstaff* première. He sent Alice Stuart Wortley a note of rehearsal times:

[19] HWRO 705:445:7830.    [20] HWRO 705:445:7831.    [21] HWRO 705:445:4169.

*Leeds* rehearsals.

### Town Hall

Monday Septr.29th.

|        | |
|--------|---|
| E.E. | 10 a.m.     Gerontius<br>Ode to Music [Parry]<br>[Alto] Rhapsody Brahms<br>Song [actually 'O don fatale' from Verdi's *Don<br>Carlos*, sung by Muriel Foster] &c<br>end at one o'clock |
| Nikisch | 2 o.c.     Selections    Wagner<br>end at five oc<br>7.30     Verdi [Requiem] |

I end at one o'clock

There seems a good train [from] King's Cross at *1.30*. arriving at 5.12—the next is too late.

Tuesday at *10.30* I do *Falstaff* [rehearsal] & will get you an admission.[22]

Elgar himself went to Leeds on 26 September for a preliminary rehearsal next day.


Hotel Metropole, Leeds.
Saturday [27 Sept. 1913]

My dear W.

Very *hot* here[:] rehearsals going well—I was overjoyed to get your letter this morning & wanted a word since. I hope for news tomorrow

I have a pass for you for Tuesday's rehearsal.

Love<br>EE[23]

Alice Stuart Wortley, with her daughter Clare, arrived on the Monday afternoon— missing Elgar's morning rehearsal, but in time for the *Falstaff* rehearsal next day. Elgar sent a note to meet her:


Hotel Metropole, Leeds.
Monday [29 Sept. 1913]

My dear W.

I hope you & Clare are all safe & well & perhaps rested but this is a weary town.

---

[22] HWRO 705:445:4220. MS dated by the recipient 'Sept:25 1913'.
[23] HWRO 705:445:4184.

I am sorry that I cannot get another pass for tomorrow—I will of course send one round to the Hotel for Clare if I can secure one: my love to her.

I send also a [*Falstaff* miniature] score for you

Yrs ever
E.E.

Carice & Alice have arrived—dusty.[24]

Next day Alice Elgar wrote in her diary:

30 September 1913. E.'s rehearsal was to be at 11—but Nikisch had a cold & E. let him finish first. So E. had only a short time & tired Orchestra for *Falstaff*[.] A. dreadful nerves about it—

It seems that Elgar dined with the Windflower, for he wrote next morning:

Hotel Metropole, Leeds.
Wedy [1 Oct. 1913] a.m.

My dear W:

I was *so* early for my dinner last night—I hope your tickets are all right? I feel a great responsibility over you two.

Yrs ever sncy
Edwd.Elgar[25]

That day he conducted an enormous programme: *God Save the King*, Beethoven's *Leonora* Overture No. 3, *Gerontius*; and after the interval, Parry's *Ode to Music*, Brahms's *Alto Rhapsody* and Symphony No. 3.

The following evening was to see the *Falstaff* première. There was no rehearsal (as Nikisch was conducting the Verdi Requiem—to which Alice Elgar went). Alice Stuart Wortley proposed an expedition to Fountains Abbey—to include her daughter, and she asked Edward to follow the example. He answered:

Hotel Metropole, Leeds.
Thursday [2 Oct. 1913]

My dear W.

So many thanks[.] I am quite refreshed by my evening & will gladly come at 10.30. May I bring Carice? As you so kindly suggest one of the family she wd. like to come so much

In greatest haste

Yrs ever
Edward[26]

---

[24] HWRO 705:445:4219. Misdated by the recipient 'Oct 2 1913'. The inscribed score is at the Elgar Birthplace.

[25] HWRO 705:445:4221. Misdated by the recipient 'Oct 4 1913'.

[26] HWRO 705:445:4196. An undated note on Hotel Metropole stationery possibly followed the outing: 'My dear W. I am so sorry we forgot these[.] Love[,] EE[.] It was lovely today'. (HWRO 705:445:4170.)

So the two parents were accompanied by their daughters. He inscribed a guide
booklet to Fountains Abbey 'A memento of a lovely day  Oct 2 1913  to the
Windflower from E E.'[27]

Elgar's portion of the concert that night comprised Bantock's *Dante and Beatrice*,
the Prologue to Boito's *Mefistofele*, 'O don fatale', and *Falstaff*. His wife wrote:

E. conducted the Bantock splendidly but it seemed long & dreary. A. had
dreadful fits of nerves—Then Falstaff. E. rather hurried it & some of the
lovely melodies were a little smothered but it made its mark & place.

E. changed [—] very depressed after—then to pleasant supper [given by]
Muriel [Foster].

The following day was their last in Leeds. Elgar took Muriel Foster to Fountains
Abbey, while Alice Elgar and Carice went to tea with Alice Stuart Wortley. Then in
the evening the Windflower came to the Elgars' hotel to share the final evening before
they all scattered next day. Elgar remained depressed. Despite the protests of the
faithful coterie, *Falstaff* had not touched the public as he hoped. Back in London, he
got out sketches for a setting of Callicles's Song from Matthew Arnold's *Empedocles
on Etna*. It was intended for Muriel Foster. Yet a typescript of the verses survives
among the Stuart Wortley papers. Two lines of this pastorale were later to become
well known in a setting by Arthur Bliss (and dedicated to Elgar):

On the sward, and the cliff-top,
Lie strewn the white flocks . . .

Elgar's setting was never finished.

On 9 October the Elgars lunched at Cheyne Walk. Then Alice Elgar went to a
concert while Edward and Alice Stuart Wortley saw two plays by J. M. Barrie—*The
Adored One* and *The Will* (originally entitled *The Accursed One*). The thesis of the
latter was that the good individual was always beset by some deep flaw. Elgar found it
'most touching'.

On 18 October he and Alice Stuart Wortley spent another afternoon round Hadley,
just beyond the northern fringes of London. Next evening the Elgars dined at Cheyne
Walk. Three days later Edward lunched there, and went with his hostess to
Harlequinade and Shaw's *Androcles and the Lion*—another Granville Barker production backed by Lord Howard de Walden. On 28 October they went to a rehearsal of a
*Joan of Arc* pageant for which Percy Anderson had designed the costumes. But
nothing could rouse Elgar from depression.

On 3 November London heard *Falstaff* for the first time, in an all-Elgar concert
conducted by the new work's dedicatee, Landon Ronald. Ronald and his wife gave a
supper afterwards with the Elgars as guests of honour and Alice Stuart Wortley
present. But the audience had been sparse. Next day Edward wrote—not of *Falstaff*,
but of the Second Symphony which had shared the programme:

Severn House[,] Hampstead, N.W.
Tuesday [4 Nov. 1913] afternoon

My dear W.

I have spent a desolate day thinking over the tragedy of last night's concert
& I wanted to say much about you & it—your symphony—which I heard for

[27] Bound with her copy of the *Falstaff* miniature score (Elgar Birthplace).

the first time last night (I have always conducted it) is I believe a fine thing—
not

*[bottom of sheet cut away; then overleaf:]*

in the morning. It is rather cold & Troyte has gone [after a visit] & the world
is emptier than ever it has been.

I am reading old plays & find divine things.

Love from
Edward Elgar[28]

Ronald's own response was to programme the Elgar concert all over again in three
weeks' time. He wrote to urge Alice Stuart Wortley to 'help me by telling everybody
you know about it & making them take tickets. If by any chance there should be a
profit, I should hand it to Elgar ... '.[29]

By then Elgars and Stuart Wortleys were in different parts of the country—the
Elgars at Madresfield Court near Malvern, he to go on to his sister Pollie's house.


Madresfield Court[,] Malvern Link
Sunday [9 Nov. 1913]
My dear W.

We have had a most heavenly day—
I go to Stoke tomorrow

The Elms
Stoke Prior
Bromsgrove
Worcestershire

I like to think of you having rest in the old world surroundings—we have
much formal clipped yew here & all charming & delightful—except politics

I hope to hear in the morning

Love
EE[30]

Following a general return to London, the Windflower came to Severn House to
tea on 20 November. Next day she brought E. F. Benson to read his play *The Friend
in the Garden* as a possible opera libretto. Alice Elgar wrote: 'E. much taken with the
idea at first—but later saw it wd. not do.'

On 1 December Henry Embleton, treasurer of the Leeds Choral Union, told the
Elgars that he was arranging a performance of *The Apostles* in Canterbury Cathedral
for the following June. The prospect brightened Edward more than anything in these
weeks:

[28] HWRO 705:445:4171. Misdated by recipient 'Feb 27 1912'.
[29] 8 November 1913 (Elgar Birthplace parcel 584(x) ).
[30] HWRO 705:445:4194.

[n.p.]
Dec 2 1913
My dear W:

Only to ask you to reserve June 20.1914 Friday for a great performance of
The Apostles in *Canterbury Cathedral*! Leeds chorus, London orchestra &
the best Soloists available. I conduct & it begins at 3 o'c.
There's news—but it will not be announced yet

Yours ever sncrly<br>
Edward Elgar[31]

On 4 December Elgar went with Alice Stuart Wortley and Frank Schuster to see the
new opera *Westward Ho!* with libretto by E. F. Benson and music by Philip Napier
Miles. The composer, a member of the landed gentry of Gloucestershire and a well-
known patron, had studied in Dresden and could not be ranked quite as an amateur.
But they could not sit through it, and left in the second act.

The Windflower offered company during the holidays. On 20 December she and
Elgar went again to Hadley. On Boxing Day she gave the Elgars dinner, and took him
with Claude Phillips to a revival of *The Doctor's Dilemma* by Shaw. Two days after
that she came to tea at Severn House and stayed the evening. But the last day of the
year found Elgar in low spirits. He went with the Windflower to see *The Great
Adventure*. He himself had nothing in prospect.

# 1914

This was to be the emptiest year of Elgar's mature creative life so far. The best of what
there was came in January with the Choral Songs, Opp. 71–3, settings of two poems
by the seventeenth-century writer Henry Vaughan, and three poems translated from
the Russian. None were dedicated to Alice Stuart Wortley, but three bore place
names—Mill Hill, Totteridge, Hadley Green—associated with their excursions north
of Hampstead.

On 6 and 8 January she came to tea, though Elgar was depressed. On the 10th she
came and played to him a fragment of a piano concerto he had written out for her. It
was a project he toyed with during the next years—always with her playing in mind.
She came again on 19 January, and after tea drove Elgar down to the offices of his
latest publisher, Elkin, with the orchestral parts of *Carissima*, a new little piece which
was next day to inaugurate his conducting career for the gramophone.

The three mornings 20–22 January saw the composition of the biggest Choral
Song, *Death on the Hills*. On the afternoon of the 22nd perhaps they met, for that
evening he wrote:

[31] HWRO 705:445:7108. The performance in fact took place on 19 June.

Severn House, 42,Netherhall Gardens, Hampstead, N.W.
Thursday [22 Jan. 1914] evening

My dear Windflower

I am better & had a *divine* hour

I send you my sketches [—] the partsong made on that very sad Russian
poem—I will shew it to you—the transcribed clear copy for the printer. It is
one of the biggest things I have done. This is only the first sketch—a slight
pencil *record* for me to read—& you.

Love
EE.[1]

At the top of this letter Elgar pasted a cutting quoting an American report of their
friend Paderewski's latest tour:

The following curious criticism appeared in the St.Louis (U.S.A.) 'Post-
Dispatch' on the morning after the recital recently given in that city by
Paderewski:—

'Jan Ignace Paderewski, of Poland, revived an old art in St.Louis last night,
when he played the piano by hand before a local audience. Everybody was very
much interested, and the performer was frequently urged to do it again.

'Most of those present had heard their parents and grandchildren [sic] tell of
the time when pianos were played by hand, but few of the younger generation
had seen it done, and it interested them as much as it would interest anyone now
to see a spinning wheel run or a rag carpet made. M.Paderewski, who is known
as the last of the piano players, is making a farewell tour of the country.'

The last day of January found all three Elgars with Alice Stuart Wortley at Covent
Garden for a rehearsal of *Parsifal*. This was to be its first production there, since the
expiration of copyright had at last voided Wagner's prohibition of its staging outside
Bayreuth (a prohibition the Americans had contravened several years earlier).

On 1 February Novello's choral expert W. G. McNaught came to Sunday lunch at
Severn House to hear the newly completed 'Choral Songs' (the title devised by
McNaught). Alice Stuart Wortley was among the guests that afternoon when (as
Alice Elgar wrote) 'E. played his new part songs, most stood round him, very
beautiful interesting group.'

After dinner at Cheyne Walk on 13 February, the Stuart Wortleys took the Elgars
and their other guests to Granville Barker's latest production at the Savoy, *A
Midsummer Night's Dream*. But Elgar was again depressed—too unwell to attend the
public première of *Carissima* at the Albert Hall on the 15th—when 'Alice S.W. came
to ask after E.'.   Nine days later he was well enough to drive with her to Hadley:
after walking there they returned to Severn House to tea, and the Windflower played
on a new Bechstein piano recently arrived. Next day he answered a letter from her:

---

[1] Elgar Birthplace parcel 583 (in an envelope postmarked '12.15 AM JY 9 13').

Severn House, 42,Netherhall Gardens, Hampstead, N.W.
Wedy [25 Feb. 1914] night

My dear Windflower

Yes: it was a day of days—weather & *all* divine.

I am awfully busy but much better for the fresh air. I send one of the
Canterbury [Cathedral *Apostles* announcement] notices with love

EE[2]

With this note he enclosed the piano arrangement of two Interludes from *Falstaff*.
The following weeks were filled with 'busy-ness' that added up to little. He seems to
have visited Cheyne Walk around 11 March, for that day he wrote to Clare:

Severn House, 42,Netherhall Gardens, Hampstead, N.W.
March 11: 1914

My dear Clare:

I have the photograph quite safely—it travelled, apparently happily, in the
midst of my own & I cherished it all the way home. I write this because I do
not think I thanked you half enough; I know I did not but it leaves me
something to say when next we meet.

With Love
Your grateful friend
Edward Elgar[3]

He was never at a loss as to what to say to her mother, as witness this note dated the
same day and enclosing a copy of the first of the Vaughan Choral Songs, *The Shower*:

Union of Graduates in Music, Incorporated.
Mar 11 1914

I send you this very simple little thing for voices [—] only at the end I put *Mill
Hill* to remind us of our afternoon when it was so cloudy & nice & lovely in
the Church yard looking over the vale.

Love
EE[4]

March 22 1914. Dined at Cheyne Walk. E. & A.—3 Wortleys—Lord & Lady
[Edmund] Talbot, Lady Montague & Lady J Lindsay. Claude—H[enry]
Ainley—No-shows. E. not pleased! & did not like the evening at all. There
really was no *lift* in it.[5]

[2] HWRO 705:445:4214.
[3] HWRO 705:445:7911.
[4] Elgar Birthplace parcel 583(xvii).
[5] A letter of 'Monday eveng', 23 March, acknowledges the evening (HWRO 705:445:4130).

It was the season for windflowers. Elgar's sister Pollie would send them up to him from Worcestershire for presentation to Cheyne Walk. Pollie, his favourite sister, was a wise and happy spirit: she knew all about her brother's 'Windflower' and was later to correspond with her.

Severn House[,] Hampstead, N.W.
Saturday [28 Mar. 1914]
My dear W:

No flowers—windflowers [—] have come. Your letter came for wh. thanks—it is now after ten o'clock so I send these proofs [of Psalm 29 'Give unto the Lord'] to amuse you,—we leave tomorrow [for the Isle of Man, where he was to adjudicate.]

> Bless you
> Yrs
> EE

It was too dreary a prospect last night to think of going to your 'Mollie' [Lady Northcliffe]!!⁶

On 29 March the Elgars took the evening train to Liverpool, and before sailing next morning at eleven, Elgar went to the Walker Art Gallery for another sight of Millais's *Lorenzo and Isabella*. At Douglas they found a warm welcome from Lord and Lady Raglan at Government House. Next day Alice Elgar wrote:

Government House[,] Isle of Man
31 March 1914
My dear Alice

A line to tell you we are here all well & it is most delightful here—high up, with lovely views of the sea & woods all around—Our hosts are perfectly dear & delightful & E. liked everything the first minute & made them laugh so much at tea on arriving that E asked Lady Raglan if she had really expected a *serious* musician & it seems she had! E.had some adjudicating this morning & we go in again this evening—it is very interesting—& he is looking so well I am thankful to say—

The journey was, well, *weary* & Douglas looked most depressing but that was soon forgotten—

I do hope you will not be too tired, I am sure you will have a delightful dance.

> My love
> Yr aft
> C.A.Elgar

Letters go out at 7.30 A.M. & do not arrive till eveng—⁷

---

⁶ Elgar Birthplace parcel 583(xxxiv).    ⁷ Elgar Birthplace parcel 584(xxviii).

That evening there was a letter from the Windflower. He answered:

Government House, Isle of Man
Tuesday [31 Mar. 1914] eveng
My dear W.

Your note just come & most welcome. I *do* hope your dinner & dance will not tire you: so good of you to think of my dear Carice.

I am working hard & wish you were here—our host & hostess & family most kind & all goes well: the crossing was the *most ghastly* experience—beyond the pen[.] I did not know such things cd. be in these days

At Liverpool I ran in to see the dear, dear Lorenzo & thought of you—it is hidden away for fear of Suffragettes—but I got in by persuasion & a card: bless you for having such a father & bless him doubly for having such a daughter.

We leave here early on Saturday morng & *shd* be in London at night.

Love<br>Yrs<br>EE

If windflowers flourish my sister will send them straight to you[8]

They reached home as planned, and on 7 April he sent printed copies of the recent *Choral Songs* to the Windflower. On 7 May she came to tea.

A week later came an event rare in these days—a performance of the Violin Concerto—which London had not been able to hear enough only three years ago. Elgar conducted, Kreisler played, and the big audience (including Alice Stuart Wortley) applauded to the echo. Her letter of thanks caught Elgar leaving for Canterbury to arrange details of *The Apostles* performance. His rushed note of acknowledgement still found time and space for a windflower-theme quotation.[9]

Early June found him on a reminiscent journey—to speak in the Worcester Guildhall at a ceremony presenting the Freedom of the City to another native son, the distinguished old landscape painter Benjamin Leader. From there Elgar went to his sister Pollie at Stoke, just after his birthday.

The Elms
Friday [5 June 1914]
My dear Windflower

The home of the Windflowers is rather cold & rainy today—but your present came—how could you? & the *old* one quite good enough for me for years yet. Bless you for it.

I am rested in this quiet old world place & am really at rest. I did not send you my *nice* speeches because all the *nice* clever things I said are, of course, left out by the reporters.

I do not know *when* I shall return—I go to Leeds on Tuesday [to rehearse

---

[8] HWRO 705:445:4126.          [9] HWRO 705:445:4188.

the Choral Union for *The Apostles*] & may do that from here. Anyway I shall be home on Wedy—

Frank has asked Alice & me to the Hut for the week end—next week [—] & we are going

Love & thanks
Yrs ever
EE[10]

He stayed at Stoke until the morning of the Leeds rehearsal, went across to it, and went home on Wednesday morning. The weekend was spent at The Hut, and the day after they returned to Severn House Elgar wrote out a series of two-stave *incipits* for the *'Enigma' Variations*, Violin Concerto (the opening and the two 'Windflower' themes), and Second Symphony (last movement opening and last retrospect of the Symphony's opening music). The sheet was inscribed 'for my Windflower   June 16. 1914'.

Alice Elgar chronicled *The Apostles* performance at Canterbury:

19 June 1914. Lovely day & of good augury . . . the most perfect perform-ance—Vast audience, beautiful surroundings & beyond the world's music—Audience most visibly deeply impressed—Everyone thought it the greatest performance[.] Many friends there Frank M. Crawshay Alice S.W. Gainsboro &c—All thrilled. Frank said it was the greatest musical experience he had ever had . . .

The performance was the precursor of a request from the promoter, Henry Embleton, that Elgar should at last complete *The Apostles* trilogy with the final oratorio. On the final day of June 1914 he agreed. But they were now barely a month away from the event which was to put paid to further oratorio writing and much besides.

Alice Stuart Wortley had written a new hymn-tune for 'O Perfect Love' for the wedding of a niece. The music was copied out by Elgar on 22 June with some revisions of harmony.[11] He had just returned from another visit to Worcestershire when he wrote:

Severn House, 42,Netherhall Gardens, Hampstead, N.W.
Friday [10 July 1914] 7.30

My dear W.

I arrived home at 4.15 all safe but very hot. I hope you are all well after your expedition & that the Hymn Tune was well done & that you were happy over it—I also hope your foot is better.

I am hoping to hear from you in the morng—but you will ring up as *early* as you can

Love
EE[12]

[10] HWRO 705:445:4208.
[11] Elgar's manuscript of the hymn-tune is at the Elgar Birthplace (MS 85).
[12] HWRO 705:445:4213.

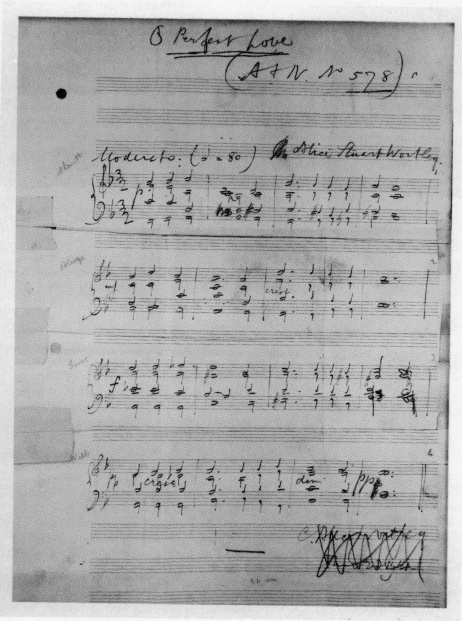

'O Perfect Love': Elgar's manuscript of Alice Stuart Wortleys' hymn-tune.

He arranged for the music to be stereotyped for other performances:

Severn House, 42,Netherhall Gardens, Hampstead, N.W.
July 14 1914
My dear W.

I am sending you the *Stereo* of your beautiful tune: any printer could print you copies from this block & it will save the trouble of setting up the type again: I hope it will be used many many times

Ever yours
EE.

Will you ring up early tomorrow Wednesday—between 10 & 10.30[13]

When she said people loved the hymn-tune, he twitted her:

Severn House, 42,Netherhall Gardens, Hampstead, N.W.
July 16 1914
My dear W
Many thanks for the enclosed papers &c
I am so glad the Hymn tune went well—I am sure no one could help loving it—perhaps not so much as I do

Yrs ever
EE.[14]

On 19 July the Elgars left for a holiday in Scotland. Their days passed peacefully. It was almost a fortnight before Alice Elgar's diary suddenly noticed world events:

1 August 1914. Rainy, wired for news to Novello—Most anxious—Feared the government wd. not take action & feared betrayal of Belgium & treaty &c. Most lovely evening. Sat out till 10 or later[:] sky, clouds, sea, perfectly beautiful—Wonderful light—

The Gairloch Hotel, Ross-shire.
Sunday [2 Aug. 1914]
My dear W.

Many many thanks for your letter: I cannot tell you how sorry I am for all your worries about travelling & upset arrgts. I do hope you will be able to do something sweet & restful—I need not tell you of this—it is *heaven*

How truly awful all the news is—I cannot think of anything else—yes there's one other thing—we get very little news & I have been wiring to London as trains are *hours* late—posts very vague and newspapers scarce & old: thanks for those you sent—we shall remain here until the 9th. & longer if

13 HWRO 705:445:4178.     14 HWRO 705:445:4202.

we can so please write as often as you can & tell me news, not only of the war, for which I hunger

Love
Yrs
EE[15]

By the time Elgar wrote his next letter four days later, the war was fact.

The Gairloch Hotel, Ross-shire.
Thursday [6 Aug. 1914]

My dear W:

I hope you did not mind our telegraphing to you—we were really *despairing* for news—*anything*—posts are all anyhow: the omnibuses required for the territorials & no sort of communication anyhow—we had a word from the Goetz's [Muriel Foster and her husband] but it took $3\frac{1}{2}$ hours to get thro' & said nothing & you were the only other person whose address we knew, or thought we knew.

I am quite ill with the awful business—but that is nothing—the confusion is terrible & reduces me to a sort of comic despair—when you find that [English] five pound notes are of no use, where are you? there is no change here! We were to return by steamer to Lochalsh—today we are told the steamers have no crews & are stopped—we shall see. The weather is too awful: I want to be assured that you are quite well

Forgive a dreadfully silly note but it is not possible to write in this scramble—all the people who have their cars are just starting—some with little petrol hoping to get some on the way

Bless you
Yrs ever
EE

Alice & Carice send love.[16]

The Gairloch Hotel, Ross-shire.
Sunday [9 Aug. 1914]

My dear Alice:

I do not know how to thank you for your telegrams: we were nearly mad to get any news & our friends seemed to fail us thinking, no doubt that we had moved on. We had intended to do so but we are thirty miles from a station; the means of communication, I mean transport, were the motor-charabanc— the hotel motors [—] two [—] to Achnasheen & the steamship to Lochalsh.

---

[15] HWRO 705:445:4197. In the last sentence words 'not only', the 'no', 'o', and 'y' have been eradicated.

[16] HWRO 705:445:7811.

The public vehicles were all commandeered to carry the territorials & were so occupied for two days—gradually all the guests left & we are now the only people left except an elderly gentleman & his wife. We decided to leave by the steamer—but this was also commandeered to pick up reservists &c. from the islands—since that voyage it has ceased to run. In the meantime *both* the hotel motors are hopelessly broken down & the necessary parts must come from Glasgow & now only the road is usable so the repairs may not be completed for a month. The last charabanc informed me on Friday that he wd. not return—    So we felt that all was over but to our delight he arrived here last night & we hope & trust that tomorrow (Monday) will see us on our way south. We have great difficulty over money as English 5£ notes will not be accepted anywhere.

It has been a weird & affecting time: seeing these dear people bidding good bye but the spirit of the men is splendid—the Seaforths went first—later in the week the mounted Lovat's Scouts rode through—were given a sort of tea meal here by the manageress & rode off in the moonlight by the side of the loch & disappeared into the mountains.

I purposely refrained from any rush or excitement but I am returning to London as soon as possible to offer myself for any service that may be possible—I *wish* I could go to the front but they may find some menial occupation for a worthless person.

I will not say anything of the loveliness of this place—it is divine: the strange wild birds feed their young within 30 yards of this window [—] gannets, oyster catchers & divers & a dozen others.

You must forgive me for worrying you about the telegrams: there were such muddles in spelling &c. '*Chairman* ambassadors says so-and-so'[:] from this we imagined there was a meeting as suggested by Sir E.Grey—later we found the Chairman shd. be *German*. Another day a visitor stuck up a telegram 'Germans advance on Liege we do not move yet'—on this we subsisted two days thinking the latter part referred to England's attitude & were puzzled to tears—later he found out that it referred to his friend's wife & two children at Felixstowe: so[17]

[*portion of perhaps 10 words cut away*]

We hope to get to Inverness tomorrow evening where we may get change & shall work our way south via Perth which I must see: but the family's money amounts to four pounds in gold & one in silver—I have notes which, as I said before, are waste paper here.    I am having letters sent to *P.O.Edinburgh* so if you have written here we may find it there. Posts have been so vague that we gave up all hope—although some letters were brought to our room after eleven at night: as I write the whole world may be at an end for all we know as our latest news is Saturday morning's Scotsman.

Now as to yourselves[:] I hope you have had a haven of rest at Harrogate & am anxious to know what you will do? You will write & tell us: I shall let you

---

[17] HWRO 705:445:7808.

know what we really take up—Carice is burning to get to work—if not nursing some sort of help with her whole soul. Among

[*verso of portion cut away, losing perhaps 30 words*]

to be amongst it

Our love
Yrs ever
Ed.Elgar[18]

Next day the Elgars began a slow homeward journey through Inverness and Edinburgh. On 13 August Edward parted from Alice and Carice at Carlisle; they to continue south to London, while he went across to see Henry Embleton at Leeds and spend a final night before returning. From Leeds he telephoned to Alice Stuart Wortley who, together with her unmarried sister Mary Hunt Millais (1860–1944), was spending her holiday with family connections at Muncaster Castle in Cumberland. When Elgar reached home he wrote:

Severn House, 42,Netherhall Gardens, Hampstead, N.W.
Friday [14 Aug. 1914]

My dear Windflower

We are all here safely & trying to be calm & be prepared for anything. I had a most lovely day yesterday & again today the weather is heavenly— everything here *looks* normal & at St.Pancras & on the way—just as usual.

I hope you are having a real rest in good air & being refreshed after the London toils—when do you return? The air here is not so bad as I expected after the pure & 'culler' air of Scotland.

There is really no news: you will have seen the papers & we hear nothing else.

It seemed odd being so close as Leeds to you yesterday & I could not deny myself the pleasure of telephoning[x] to you—I hope I did not disturb your sister?

All good wishes

Bless you
Yrs
EE

[x]Alice was so glad to hear of you[19]

By the time he answered the Windflower's next letter three days later, Carice was working at first aid for the Navy League, and he himself was attending organization meetings for a Special Constabulary of citizens to replace policemen called up: he was to be sworn in later that afternoon. Their correspondence, however, kept its secrets.

---

[18] This sheet has been given a separate number: HWRO 705:445:7823.
[19] HWRO 705:445:4145.

Severn House, 42,Netherhall Gardens, Hampstead, N.W.
Monday [17 Aug. 1914] 3 p m.

My dear Windflower

Thanks for your letter & all it says: I am so glad the air & [*sic*] are doing you good

No news but what you know & s.o.m.s is scarcely new altho' not old. Alice has a bad cold—Carice is plunged in work—I have been hard at it & go to anr. meeting this afternoon.

London seems almost normal & no inconveniences:

Love
E.E.[20]

Severn House, 42,Netherhall Gardens, Hampstead, N.W.
Monday [24 Aug. 1914] night

My dear Windflower:

It is so dreadful in these heartbreaking times to have no word—so your Sunday letter—which you say is not a letter—came very sweetly this afternoon. I fret & fret at my inaction—I am not well enough to exert myself yet—& I am Staff Inspector to the whole corps & dying to do a man's part in the work—on the top of it came this awful cold.

Financially Alice & I and Carice are absolutely ruined—we can see daylight for a year & are quite happy—I envy the lazy fat Beasts opposite— whose property I have to guard!

[*two lines entirely eradicated and the beginning of a third*]
let me know about Muncaster & you[x]

Love
EE

[x]return-dates &c.&c.   [*Another line eradicated*][21]

She sent him a letter from Lady Charles Beresford. Lady Charles was deeply apprehensive about the Navy, ever since her husband's pre-war quarrel with Sir John Fisher over Naval policy: in the end they both had resigned, but it was Fisher's policy which prevailed.

Severn House, 42,Netherhall Gardens, Hampstead, N.W.
Thursday [27 Aug. 1914] a.m.

My dear Windflower:

I have just recd. from you Mina B's letter which is destroyed as you said. Her view is too gloomy & distorted

I shall not write again to you until I hear as I am not certain of your

[20] HWRO 705:445:4146.        [21] HWRO 705:445:7674.

journeys: I have heard from Frank (I wrote to him) he is at the Hut & wants me but I shall not go *yet*. He has given his car & man & also the Westminster house to the Belgian minister for his wounded.

My cold is trying but I am just going out on my rounds & to Headquarters to look after my men. I am a fool & look a fool but I am doing what I can!

Your letters have been very _____ —no word of yourself & how you are— if better & if the massage has done you good—in fact nothing I really wanted to know: my heart is heavy & will remain so until—we shall see.

> Love
> EE[22]

The war was making itself felt everywhere. The Germans destroyed much of Belgium; soon Reims Cathedral was in ruins and they were advancing on Paris. British ships were sunk every day and British lives lost. At home the losses were as yet less physical. On Sunday 5 September Alice Elgar noted that they would have been staying at Madresfield Court for the Worcester Festival now. Three days later she wrote: 'It wd. have been "Gerontius" tonight at Worcester Fest—but for Hun Kaiser.' On 9 September her husband wistfully inscribed a copy of the new *Gerontius* miniature full score: 'Alice Stuart Wortley (Windflower) with love from Edward Elgar.'

Elgar was restless. He wrote a Soldier's Song, *The Roll Call*, for performance at the Albert Hall in October: later he withdrew it. He went to his sister Pollie on 22 September: 'E. to The Elms after visit to his Station. Travelled with wounded Soldiers (Mons) & gave them tea . . .'. Even at The Elms he was restless.

Stoke
Thursday [24 Sept. 1914] evng

My dear W.

I recd. a telegram all right & so many thanks. I shall return tomorrow Friday to Euston—[*word or two heavily eradicated*] if at all possible.

It is too lovely in the country but it is lonely also—so I come back—I want news, news.

Neither of the papers will print my letters—very polite & thankful but *too terrible*—for the present.

The Naval news is dreadful & I cannot *rest*

> Bless you.
> Yrs ever
> EE

I proposed myself to Frank for the week end but he is full up & cannot have me: says 'another time' [—] I must propose[23]

On 11 October the Stuart Wortleys were among the guests to Sunday tea at Severn House. The following weekend Elgar went to The Hut, and Alice Stuart Wortley motored him home late on the Monday. In November he went again to Stoke.

[22] HWRO 705:445:4168.          [23] HWRO 705:445:4192.

Stoke
Friday [13 Nov. 1914]

My dear Windflower

I recd. your note with joy & sorrow this morning—it is too terribly sad, all this.

Today is warm but much rain—& I write early as I may be able to go out later.

Yesterday I went to Worcester & had the joy of sitting in the old Library in the Cathedral amongst the M.S.S. I have often told you of—the view down the river across to the hills just as the monks saw it & as I have seen it for so many years—it seems so curious, dear, to feel that I played about among the tombs & in the Cloisters when I cd scarcely walk & now the Deans & Canons are so polite & shew me everything new—alterations[,] discoveries &c.&c. It is a sweet old place [—] especially, to me, the library into which so few go. I will take you in one day.

I return on Monday & I hope to bring the little palefaced niece [Pollie's second daughter, Madeline Grafton] for a change: unless I hear to the contrary I shall try [*illegible*] at *4.30*—I hope you will continue to be brave & strong through all these inevitable troubles—it is too dreadful to dwell upon but we must go on—on—on.

I shall hear no news till 12.30 & I wait as calmly as I can.

Bless you.
Yrs
EE

Your sweet letter came this a m. with the cutting — I had the Times[24]

A few days later Elgar completed a recitation with orchestra to Emile Cammaerts's poem 'Carillon', commemorating the destroyed bells and towers of Flanders. On 18 November he wrote to Frank Schuster: 'Alice Wortley heard it in its complete form & was good & kind enough to give approval.'[25] Eight days later he sent her a printed proof of the music. And she was almost certainly present on 7 December when he conducted the tumultuous première in Queen's Hall.

Four days later she came to Severn House for a private concert in the big music-room in aid of Belgian charities. The guest artists were largely Belgian refugees— among them the composer Joseph Jongen and the violinist and conductor Désiré Defauw. The afternoon was a success in every way, and £36.10.0 was raised. Afterwards Elgar escaped to walk in Hampstead streets darkened against air raids.

[24] HWRO 705:445:7668. In the last paragraph the words 'as calmly as I can' have been eradicated. Madeline Grafton (1883–1972), known in the family as Madge, was the frailest of Pollie's children; but as sometimes happens in such cases, she outlived all her brothers and sisters.

[25] HWRO 705:445:6912.

Severn House, 42,Netherhall Gardens, Hampstead, N.W.
Dec 11: 1914

My dear Windflower:

I am sorry I saw so little of you today at our music but I was torn in many pieces: I hope you liked some of it. I rushed out & had a very refreshing walk after it all as I wanted air & refreshment—both of which I had & am now better for the rest from crowds & police work. How beautiful it is in the still quiet streets without the trying brilliant lights: all seems so muffled—a muted life to me and so sweet & pure; I do not like the idea of garishly lit roads & streets again—I love them so much, so much as they are.

This is only to ask you how you liked the Belgian folk-songs. I thought they were good & well done

> Love
> Yrs always
> E E.[26]

Just before Christmas he sent to Charles Stuart Wortley the words of one old carol he had discovered with a mention of 'Master Wortley'.

Severn House, 42,Netherhall Gardens, Hampstead, N.W.
Dec 23 1914

My dear Wortley:

I send the enclosed not very respectable performance with all good Christmas wishes to the house.

The suggestion in the second stanza will one day encourage me, in these non-alcoholic days, to come to tea.

> Yours very sincerely
> Edward Elgar

### A CAROL IN PRAISE OF ALE.

(Carols relating to drinking are somewhat numerous, and the following specimen is copied from a manuscript of the XVIth century in the British Museum, and is there entitled 'A Christmas Carol'.)

> A bone, god wot! sticks in my throat—
>   Without I have a draught
> Of cornie ale, nappy and stale,
>   My life lies in great waste.
> Some ale or beer, gentle butler,
>   Some liquor thou us show,
> Such as you mash, our throats to wash,
>   The best were that you brew.

---

[26] HWRO 705:445:4193. Alice Elgar's diary chronicles the concert as having taken place on 10 Dec.

Saint, master, and knight, that Saint Malt hight,
   Were pressed between two stones;
The sweet humour of this liquor
   Would make us sing at once.
Master Wortley, I dare well say,
   I tell you as I think,
Would not, I say, bid us this day,
   But that we should have drink.

His men so tall walk up his hall,
   With many a comely dish;
Of his good meat I cannot eat,
   Without I drink, I wis.
Now give us drink, and let cat wink,
   I tell you all [a]t once,
It sticks so sore, I may sing no more,
   Till I have drunken once.[27]

Christmas Day 1914 'seemed a strange blank', wrote Alice Elgar. Then 'Alice S.W. came to tea, brought flowers & E.'s lovely lavender water.' On New Year's Eve she took them to a play: instead of the elegant productions of Granville Barker and Barrie, this was 'a German Spy play [—] most exciting & seemingly a great success'.

---

[27] Elgar Birthplace parcel 583(vi).

# 1915

---

The year began with an enquiry over a book of poems sent to Elgar.

Severn House, 42,Netherhall Gardens, Hampstead, N.W.
Jan 1 1915
My dear Wortley:

You have had our good wishes over the telephone already.

Here is the little book—whence it came I cannot tell; I receive so very many verses & books of verses[,] with requests to set them that it is impossible to trace the givers.

Please keep the book

Yours very sincly
Edward Elgar:[1]

Two days later Elgar conducted the latest performance of *Carillon* with the actress Constance Collier. After a morning rehearsal at the Albert Hall, Elgar lunched at Cheyne Walk with the Stuart Wortleys, the Colvins, Claude Phillips, and Henry Ainley (who was shortly to record *Carillon* for the gramophone with Elgar conducting). Alice Elgar and Carice came to the afternoon performance, but it was Alice Stuart Wortley who brought Elgar back to Hampstead to tea.

Ten days later she came again, and Alice Elgar noted one strand of conversation that day: the subject was the Liberal war minister R. B. Haldane (who had reorganized the British Army before his resignation in 1912) and his supposed 'German tendencies'. The last day of January brought both Stuart Wortleys to tea at Severn House. The conversation this time centred on the happier subject of Elgar's boyhood sketchbooks, which were open before them.

On 21 February Alice Stuart Wortley, Philip Burne-Jones, and the novelist Robert Hichens shared the Elgars' box at a Landon Ronald Sunday Concert. The programme included Dvořák's 'New World' Symphony, which Elgar was particularly keen to hear as he himself was to conduct it (side by side with *Carillon* and other popular fare) on a short tour of northern cities with the London Symphony Orchestra. Before the tour, and because of ill health, Elgar resigned on 22 February from the Hampstead Special Constabulary.

The tour began on 1 March. After an opening concert in Birmingham, the tour went to Liverpool. There Elgar bought a box of blue stationery decorated in one corner with the circular device of a buckled belt: inside the circle was to be engraved an initial. He ordered an 'E' engraved inside the belt, and kept the stationery exclusively for letters to Alice Stuart Wortley. In her last letter to him, she had subscribed herself his 'faithful' Windflower. That adjective made a special appeal to him because royalist Worcester, during and ever after the civil war, had been known as 'the faithful city'.

[1] HWRO 705:445:7913.

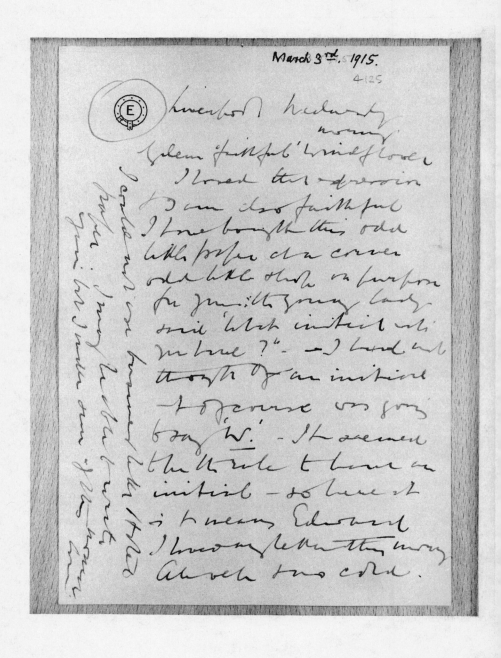

*March 3rd. 1915.*

*4.125*

Liverpool
Wednesday [3 Mar. 1915] morning
My dear 'faithful' Windflower

I loved that expression & I am also faithful

I have bought this odd little paper at a corner odd little shop on purpose for you: the young lady said 'What initial will you have?'—I had not thought of an initial—& of course was going to say '*W*.'—It seemed to be the rule to have an initial—so here it is & means Edward

I loved my letter this morng[.] All well & no cold.

I could not use business letter Hotel paper. I may be able to write you but I make sure of this moment

Love[2]

He was to use this stationery for some of his letters to her—by no means all—until it was exhausted in September 1916. Six only of the letters on this paper survive. The box will have contained certainly twelve sheets, and more probably twenty-four, thirty-six, or even forty-eight. So it provides some clue to the survival rate of his letters to her during these eighteen months.

[*belted monogram* E]
Grand Hotel[,] Sheffield
Thursday [4 Mar. 1915]
My dear W.

Once more I turn to this paper after business notes: It is quite warm & fine & I have wandered about these depressing streets *trying* to find something to look at—it is early closing day which adds to the dulness. No letter since Liverpool. I am not sure if this is *your* hotel [when staying in Sheffield for her husband's political appearances] but it is *clean*. Carillon is encored every night.

Love<br>EE

A longer journey [to Glasgow] tomorrow & then after Edinburgh I shall feel I am coming home. *pinting* [*sic*] for home.[3]

He reached home on 10 March. During the next days and weeks he was much in the old bookshops again, and viewing book sales. In one sale to come he saw an old sketchbook of her father's, and told her about it when she came to tea on 16 March.

[2] HWRO 705:445:4125. The reproduction shows Clare Stuart Wortley's notation of the date (superimposed on her mother's notation), and the HWRO number.
[3] HWRO 705:445:7815.

Severn House, 42,Netherhall Gardens, Hampstead, N.W.
Monday [22 Mar. 1915]

My dear W.

I knew you wd. forget the address of the Saleroom where the Sketchbook is to be sold—it is Hollyson[,] 115 Chancery Lane
I do not think the book is in good enough condition.

>Love
>EE[4]

Severn House, 42,Netherhall Gardens, Hampstead, N.W.
Tuesday [23 Mar. 1915]

My dear W.

I could not go [to Stoke] to-day but have arranged to leave at 1.15 tomorrow *Wedy* p m. so you see I must tell you this as I cannot be at the sale when the sketchbook is sold.

>Yrs ever
>EE[5]

Elgar was facing a difficult decision. He had begun to make choral settings of Laurence Binyon's 'For the Fallen' and other poems from a collection entitled *The Winnowing-Fan: Poems on the Great War*. Then it was pointed out that the Cambridge composer Cyril Rootham had already submitted a setting to Novello: the publisher begged Elgar to desist. He was turning it over in his mind during the visit to Stoke—from which he made a reminiscent excursion to Worcester on 25 March.

Back at Stoke that night, he found a letter from the Windflower asking whether they were going to F. R. Benson's Shakespeare Festival at Stratford in April. He wrote his answer on a sheet of twelve-stave music paper whose margin was imprinted 'M. L. Perosi—Vaticano': Perosi was director of music there, and had met the Elgars often during their visits to Rome.

Stoke Prior
Thursday [25 Mar. 1915]

My dear Windflower:

This is the paper easiest to find at this moment & scribble a hurried note to catch the post

Thank you a thousand times for yr. dear letter—*No* Stratford for us.

I have been walking far today round Worcester & had to leave early to get trains right.

I fear I must give up 'The Winnowing Fan' alas! The figure of the disappointed composer who set it before me comes between me & my work & I cannot go on—after all nobody *wants* any real music.

>Bless you & love
>EE

[4] HWRO 705:445:4122.        [5] HWRO 705:445:4156.

Be sure get todays D.Telegraph & see Paderewski's manifesto—*and* the notice of the Nelson autograph (Red Cross Auction Sale[)][6]

A manuscript letter from Lord Nelson had been the Elgars' contribution to a war charity sale to be held at Christie's.

After Elgar's return to London at the beginning of April, Sidney Colvin and other friends persuaded him to continue his Binyon music by convincing Novello to publish both settings of 'For the Fallen'. One of the persuaders was the poet's colleague at the British Museum, R. A. Streatfeild. Streatfeild also persuaded Elgar to join the Hampstead Volunteer Reserve—which was to involve him in shooting and rifle practice for the only time in his life.

The Elgars decided after all to go to the Shakespeare plays at Stratford for a week, despite the fact that Carice had been accepted for a post in the Censorship of the War Office. Before that, Elgar was to conduct *Carillon* and other items in a Royal Concert at the Albert Hall. Alice Stuart Wortley would sit in the Elgars' box, but Edward almost always found himself overheated by the exertion of conducting. On the eve of the concert he wrote:

Severn House, 42,Netherhall Gardens, Hampstead, N.W.
Friday [23 Apr. 1915] evening
My dear Windflower:

I was so happy over your letter this morning amongst all the dull begging letters & the usual worries: I went out this morning for necy things & remained at home all the afternoon *sad*: now I am off to drill. It is so disappointing about Ainley [not appearing] at S. on A. I shall go & I think A. also but we do not know *when* C. will take up her Govt. work.

Tomorrow I will try to get to our box but I shall probably go straight away home as I may be hot. On Sunday we have people to tea: Cammaerts has a new little *scena* to read to me—if you are free come but I know it's next to impossible—Monday we leave alas alas

Yrs ever
EE

My hand is shaky: I have just been doing *rifle* exercise[7]

She did come to tea on the Sunday, when Cammaerts read 'Une voix dans le désert'—another picture of devastation in Belgium. It was to become a new Elgar recitation with orchestra.

At Stratford the Elgars had a full week of plays—*The Merchant of Venice* and *The Merry Wives of Windsor* with Oscar Asche; *Romeo and Juliet; Twelfth Night; Richard III* starring Benson himself, with the fine old actress Genevieve Ward as Queen Margaret: she appeared again as Volumnia in *Coriolanus*.

Back at Severn House, Elgar cut out a newspaper photograph of Paderewski in New York, his shock of hair incongruously surmounted by a bowler:

[6] HWRO 705:445:7666.      [7] HWRO 705:445:4157.

Severn House, 42,Netherhall Gardens, Hampstead, N.W.
May 5. 1915

My dear W.

You *must* see this: how shocking [—] these newspapers shd. be suppressed: poor dear P.—& he always looks so fine—surely he has some other person's Hat.

Ever
EE[8]

Then followed a letter of slightly uncertain date, addressed to the Windflower at Stratford:

Severn House, 42,Netherhall Gardens, Hampstead, N.W.
Thursday [?27 May 1915] eveng

My dear W:

I am so glad the weather is so lovely [—] how heavenly S. on A must be.

First: here is a prescription, which is Carice's property, made 'against' gas fumes by the official chemist: *do* get it made up—soak your handkerchief & inhale—if necy—Please let me have it again. The chemist says it is the best antidote & it is issued to all the staff.

We go to Ridgehurst on Sunday morning until Monday a.m. [—] home by mid-day I hope. There is much news—or rather no news—small things.

I have worked hard at the Polish piece & to-day do not like it. I want help.

Yrs ever
E.E.[9]

Elgar's Polish piece was *Polonia*, a 'symphonic prelude' incorporating Polish themes. One of these, from Paderewski's *Fantasie polonaise*, Op. 19, had been chosen by Alice Stuart Wortley. Elgar's music had been requested for a concert in aid of the Polish Victims Relief Fund, to take place in early July. The Executive Committee, headed by Paderewski, included Cardinal Bourne and Charles Stuart Wortley. Among the Patrons were Alice Stuart Wortley, the Beresfords, the Duke of Norfolk, Thomas Hardy, John S. Sargent, the most eminent British statesmen from the Prime Minister downward, and ultimately the Elgars. He finished the score on 1 June. Next day, his birthday, he sent the 'short' working score to the Windflower.[10]

He went again to Stoke, and on 8 June travelled up to Birmingham to see a group of Worcestershire prints for sale. He hoped they might rival the collection assembled by his old friend Hubert Leicester, now in his third term as Mayor of Worcester; but in this he was disappointed. Back at Stoke that evening, he wrote:

The Elms
Tuesday [8 June 1915]

My dear W.

Such a tremendous thunderstorm last night & to-day hotter than ever. I had a lovely day yesterday in my own land & today had an arid & lonely time

⁸ HWRO 705:445:4111.        ⁹ HWRO 705:445:7814.        ¹⁰ Elgar Birthplace.

in Birmingham: the prints of Worcestershire which I went to examine are worthless almost & I had a wasted journey: I rode in the train with Ld.Plymouth—very grave & sad, alas! I found a telegram here with joy:

I think I shall return on Thursday having seen wonders here & on Monday[:] it seems lonely & dull—if the country ever can be dull.

I shall go to tea on Thursday I hope

Love
Yrs
EE[11]

Alice Elgar's diary for the Thursday only shows Edward attending a London sale in the afternoon to buy some aquatints: tea with Alice Stuart Wortley could have been combined with that.

On 16 June he went for another reminiscent visit to Stoke and Worcester. It was as if in these wartime days of living in London, the associations of his youth in Worcestershire held some restoring power. The Windflower understood, and sent him a letter written by her mother as a girl of thirteen in 1841 from Worcester, where she had stayed at Mr Parker's house. Elgar replied from the home Hubert Leicester had built for his family far up the main street of Worcester. With his reply he enclosed one of the Mayor's cards, on which he noted:

I must use one of the Mayoral cards: you will recognise the Arms [of the City of Worcester] from seeing my own attempt in the Billiard room [at Severn House].[12]

The Whitstones, Worcester.
Friday [18 June 1915] morng

My dear W.

Your dear letter came this morning at Stoke & I have travelled here since[.] Here I remain until tomorrow [—] Saturday [—] afternoon & I get back to Severn House in the evening. It is lovely here—flowers[,] sun & everything except good news, alas!

I return the treasured letter—the picture *is* the same. The wood so prettily referred to in the letter *is* the one which Frank Parker told us little children was private.

I hope to see you very soon now.

The little dog is a dear although Juno is not 'my soul's Joy'!

Yrs
EE[13]

Those were the dogs at Stoke: the canine experiments at Severn House had all ended in failure.

Back in London, he answered her enquiry about meeting. On the Friday he was to go to Bournemouth to conduct, and before that there were preparations for *Polonia*.

---

[11] HWRO 705:445:4134. Robert George Windsor Clive (1857–1923), 14th Baron Windsor (see above, pp. 14,25), and from 1905 1st Earl of Plymouth.
[12] HWRO 705:445:4135.     [13] HWRO 705:445:4136.

Severn House, 42,Netherhall Gardens, Hampstead, N.W.
Sunday [20 June 1915]

My dear W:

Next week looks very unpromising—tomorrow you will come here.

I enclose a programm[e] of Bournemouth—I leave Waterloo at 4.50 o c. Friday & it is doubtful if I can get back on Saturday at all. I have promised to be 'on hand' to hurriedly correct proofs & I must be interviewed I believe— all unfixed.

Bless you
Yrs
E[14]

Two nights later the Elgars joined a large party in the Stuart Wortleys' box at the Albert Hall for Landon Ronald's performance of the *'Enigma' Variations*. Then Elgar went to Bournemouth, conducted the concert on Saturday afternoon, and was able to return to Hampstead that night. Next day Alice Stuart Wortley took him for a drive in the rain. On 1 July Elgar took the corrected orchestral parts and score of *Polonia* to the publisher, and joined the two Alices for a Henry Ainley matinée—a piece entitled *Quinney*. Alice Elgar wrote: 'All 3 much disappointed—such a common touch about it all—Lower Middle Class English domestic drama—& sad for Ainley not to have a part in higher work—A.W.S. [*sic*] drove E. & A. up home to tea ... '.

*Polonia* was rehearsed at Queen's Hall with the two Alices in attendance. And the Stuart Wortleys would have been amongst the audience for the première the following evening. On Sunday 11 July Alice Stuart Wortley and Lady Colvin came to Severn House in advance of other guests to tea: 'E. played all his Binyon music to them, Frances quite white with excitement ... '. (She had been one of the chief persuaders responsible for bringing this finest of all Elgar's war music to its slow birth.) Even now it was not complete. He also finished the second Cammaerts recitation with orchestra, *Une voix dans le désert*.

On their way to a dinner at the Automobile Club four days later, Elgar wrote to thank Alice Stuart Wortley for finding a sought-after book.

The Athenaeum, Pall Mall, S.W.
Thursday [15 July 1915] 8 p m.

My dear W:

We are a little early for our dinner party so I stepped in here to wait

I send you all thanks for your very very clever capture—Streatfeild thought it was out of print—I am so delighted[.] Thank you

Oh! you *must* hear the new piece *finished* & done

I *love* it

and you:

Yr
EE[15]

On the following Sunday she came to tea to hear Elgar play it.

He made another visit to Stoke (during which his own Alice lunched at Cheyne Walk on 22 July). He went on to The Hut, and returned keener for work. On the 29th he looked at a book sale in London and brought Alice Stuart Wortley back to tea. He wanted her to come again on Sunday afternoon, when W. H. Reed would be at Severn

---

[14] HWRO 705:445:4144.

[15] HWRO 705:445:7821. In the closing sentence the 'and' and the colon have been eradicated.

House to play through the string parts of *Une voix dans le désert*. The poem would then be recited to Reed's and Elgar's accompaniment by the Belgian actor Carlo Liten (who was shortly to appear at the Coliseum in a fortnight of *Carillon* performances under Elgar's conductorship). But for *Une voix dans le désert* there was yet no prospect for an orchestral or stage production. Elgar wrote on the special stationery:

[*belted monogram* E]
[n.p.]
Friday [30 July 1915]
My dear Windflower:

I remind you that this Ⓔ stands for Edward: I told you this when the young lady forced me to buy it in Liverpool.

Now Sunday is impossible [for another plan] as many people are coming & Mr. Reed comes at *3 o'c* to play thro' the 'Voix dans le désert'—so you will please come here *then*—it will be amusing to hear it with the Violin—*later* Litens etc are coming so if you elect to come at all come quite early—A[lice] expects you, I told her of the proposed country drive.

I had a varied day yesterday & today have a headache

Yrs
EE[16]

She was not mentioned in Alice Elgar's diary account of the afternoon. She did come to the first of the Liten *Carillon* performances at the Coliseum on Monday afternoon, and took Elgar for a drive before the evening performance. The following Sunday she motored him to The Hut for the day, while his own Alice remained in London.

Another week of *Carillon*, and then the Elgars went to a country house set deep in Sussex woods which they had taken for a fortnight.

Hookland, Midhurst.
Friday [20 Aug. 1915]
My dear W.

*What has* become of you? We are in distress & despair at not hearing & fear you are ill or that the bombardment was too near to you & a thousand other things.

Post is just in & I must race this off now—or the messenger will be gone—I will only say it is lovely here but so *lonely*—lonely in many senses—I will describe it in another letter—I sent you a long one *days* ago.

I have a large dog friend 'Schiff' who has adopted me & takes me for walks in the wildest places [—] he knows them all & I tell him everything!

Love
E[17]

Back in London at the end of August, 'E. restless & wanting to go away again.' Within two days it was decided that they would join the Stuart Wortleys for their holidays at Walls, near Ravenglass in Cumberland, a house lent to them by Charles Stuart Wortley's cousin Lord Muncaster. Elgar left by himself on 6 September,

[16] HWRO 705:445:7671.
[17] HWRO 705:445:4165. Miss Ann Caulfeild, whose parents owned Hookland, tells me that the dog's name was Ship—much beloved by all the family despite his incessant barking.

wandering about Ullswater and Grasmere while his own Alice prepared to leave Severn House again. (Two of her nights there produced Zeppelin raids over London, clearly visible from Hampstead.) On 10 September she came up in a nine-hour railway journey to join Edward at Ravenglass:

... Alice [Stuart Wortley] met us. Such a warm kind welcome. Very nice house & lovely looking grounds—Nice evening. C.S.W. such a kind nice host & Alice made the house &c all so nice.

During the next ten days the Elgars explored the surrounding country with the Stuart Wortleys and Clare:

September 11 1915. To Drigg in morning. Lovely on the sands—  Most beautiful day—  To [Muncaster] Castle after lunch—  Wonderful view from front door[:] group of the beautiful Lake mountains—Delightful Garden—  The old Lord Muncaster, rather ill & so lonely in that large house—the last of the direct race of *centuries*—  Walked back—  Rough road & thin shoes rather bad for Braut's [i.e., Alice Elgar's] feet—

September 12. Lovely day—  After lunch all but Alice [Stuart Wortley] who was laid up with headache to Wastwater—Lovely drive—E. & I had longed to see this—Very fine & sinister, along the 'Screes'—Nice walk on Moor beyond Inn where we had tea, Lovely looking up the Pass ...

Next day Charles Stuart Wortley went shooting—rabbits with a rook rifle in the morning, partridges in the afternoon. That was one pursuit which Elgar, despite his interest in upper class life, never joined. While Stuart Wortley shot, Elgar accompanied the ladies through Upper Eskdale, with tea at the Woolpack Inn.

They drove what Charles Stuart Wortley called 'curly roads' to Furness, Calder Abbey, the Tarns—all the sights within reach. Other days were spent close to Walls, taking a wasp nest and making bonfires. Clare recalled:

The bonfire was a source of great delight to Sir Edward and Mr Wortley, who enjoyed themselves like boys over it, being nevertheless very scientific as to the lighting and management of it! Clare helped, under their instructions. Mrs Wortley and Lady Elgar viewed it from afar, beseeching them not to set themselves on fire!

The taking of the wasps' nest was for long a legend in the family. Sir Edward and Mr Wortley did it together, while Mrs Wortley who was seriously afraid of wasps, remained indoors in a state of great nervousness, thinking that Sir Edward ought not to be encouraged to do dangerous things while he was our guest![18]

On the Elgars' last day, the Beresfords arrived. Alice Elgar wrote:

19 September 1915 ... Lord Charles ... told us Germans had lost numbers of submarines & some captured & used by us ...

[18] Elgar Birthplace parcel 584(xvi).

20 September ... E. & A. left Walls—Alice, C.S.W. & Clare all at the station with us very early—I saw miniature Ry. & stroked the infant engine. They nearly wept to part with us. Then along looping 'curly' journey on Furness Ry. . . .

The rest of the journey was described by Elgar in his letter next day:

Prince of Wales Lake Hotel, Grasmere.
Sep 21: 1915
My dear Windflower

The memories of Walls are too strong to be dimmed by even the beauty of this place: we arrived at five having had a good journey—passed the Abbey— & took the steamer up Windermere—sent our things on & *walked* the rest— tomorrow we walk over the pass to Ullswater & so home but I *may* go to Hereford & Stoke.

I shall say nothing of our visit to you which was a pleasure the whole time[.] I am sending a line to C.—it was good of you to have invented our visit. It has done A. a world of good.

There is no news but what you know—I shall be interested to hear of the Beresfords' adventures. Write to me please to Hampstead & it will be forwarded.

I go over all the days with interest & some of the minutes with joy—[*one or two words cut out*.]

Bless you
Yrs ever
E[19]

The walk over the Kirkstone Pass did not materialize (doubtless much to Alice's relief) because they could not find a coach to take only their luggage.

They left Grasmere on 23 September—Alice to return to Hampstead, Edward to go to Hereford to stay a night with Sinclair.

The Close, Hereford.
Friday [24 Sept. 1915]
My dear W:

We left the Lakes yesterday m[ornin]g. Alice went home & I left her at Crewe & came here.

I saw your little note to her &, if you have sent to me via Hampstead I shall receive it in due course[.] I go to Stoke tomorrow & home on Monday & then a steady grind for the Winter

Frank writes that he is returning to the Hut on Oct 9 & asks A. & I to go sometime so he may ask you also sometime

[19] HWRO 705:445:4112.

We had a nice time at Grasmere & it softened the departure from Walls & made it easier to bear than if we had gone straight from Windflowers to work.

Thank you dear W for the lovely time you gave us.

Love
E[20]

Three days later he was back at home.

On 2 October he rehearsed *Polonia* with a new orchestra in the morning, and that afternoon began another run of *Carillon* performances at the Coliseum (this time with the recitation spoken by Edward Speyer's daughter Lalla Vandervelde, who was the wife of the Belgian minister-in-exile). That night he wrote:

Severn House, 42,Netherhall Gardens, Hampstead, N.W.
Saturday [2 Oct. 1915] night

My dear W:

I cannot tell you how glad I was to receive your letter & to know that you are safe & well—not hearing for so long I was getting anxious—very much [ — ] & thought of illness or accident & was worrying very much, very much: however all is well now that you are well.

I want further news of you & hope the waiting will not be long. Alas! I got a really bad chill & have been quite ill—better now & able to go to rehearsal of Polonia at 10 & then on to the Coliseum for the Carillon—I missed you at Q's Hall but I thought of you & my eyes wandered to empty Block A: When I wrote to Paderewski I told him our friend—*you*—had chosen a piece to be quoted from his works [ — ] bless you! it sounded well but the orch: is largely new — '*wild*'

I hope you may choose Bournemouth round about the 23rd as I have a concert on that day—I should not be tied up with the children even if they spend their holiday there—which is not yet certain. Let me know directly you decide & also tell me if you come to London first even for one day. We are in darkness now & I cannot say it is lively in the evenings but I want to see you & when I say that all is included. I treasure the remembrance of Walls & all your dear kindness to us—so long ago—so *unreal* & so remote—but so blessed.

Percy Anderson was here & I asked him about their names [Anderson's and Frank Schuster's, which the Elgars and Alice Stuart Wortley had seen] in the visitors' book at Wastdale Head [the recipient has corrected this to read 'Woolpack Inn—Eskdale.']—they did sleep there & must have driven over the bridge & under the Castle which they never saw & also they went thro' Gosforth & never saw the cross: Oh! these motorists[.] His house [in Church Row, Hampstead, recently taken] is a dear little place [—] I called yesterday.

[20] HWRO 705:445:4113.

You are here at every turn: our grapes are quite good this year & I long for you to taste them but they will not last. I note all you say about the future of the house & wonder—I hope as ever—the best for you. [*Eradication*]

[?] I kiss your hands

                                                    EE[21]

At the end of the latest fortnight of *Carillon* Elgar took his daughter for her holiday to Stratford. There they met the Stuart Wortleys, saw *Troilus and Cressida* with them, and they all shared a drive to visit Mary Anderson and her husband Tony de Navarro at Broadway. On the last day Edward took Carice to Warwick and Leamington—where he found an old print of Calder Abbey, which they had visited from Walls. Next morning he wrote:

Shakespeare Hotel, Stratford-on-Avon.
Tuesday [19 Oct. 1915]

My dear W.

I am so sorry the visit is over. I felt I *ought* to take C. to see something & so—& so—& so—

We went into Leamington & I sent you the very soiled & bedraggled print of Calder—burn it—it is of no value but I wrote a word on it's[sic] very smoky back—

We leave for Stoke at Midday & I look for letters there—no news; our loves to you & your party

It is cold, dark, and grey—the table in the dining room [at the Shakespeare Hotel] empty—the sitting room dark & Troilus & Cressida as a spent star.

                                                    Bless you
                                                    Yrs ever
                                                    E.[22]

He returned to London with a cold; but well enough to go to Bournemouth to conduct the Violin Concerto with Albert Sammons, *Carillon*, and *The Wand of Youth* Suite No. 2. Before the Elgars left for Bournemouth on 22 October, Alice Stuart Wortley came to tea; but she could not go to Bournemouth. Afterwards he wrote:

Severn House, Hampstead, N.W.
Sunday [24 Oct 1915]

My dear W.

The concert went off very well—rain—Sammons played very beautifully & you were desired—missed but scarcely expected—it seemed too difficult

---

[21] HWRO 705:445:7798. In the first paragraph, the second 'very much' has been eradicated. In the closing, heavy eradication leaves legible only the word 'your': the rest is conjecture based on word lengths approximating this formula often repeated in other letters, and sometimes eradicated less completely.

[22] HWRO 705:445:4190.

The journey was horrid—crowded & very hot train down which made me ill.

To-day I have been nursing & cannot go out tomorrow unless the weather is quite fine & warmer which seems impossible. I feel very dreary & not well but my cough is better—I had to take so many jujubes etc etc that my head aches from the sheer force of numbers of remedies.

We returned in the rain & the dark last night & I am desolate

Love
Yrs
EE[23]

His own Alice could not fail to be aware of this affection turning toward obsession. That awareness gave several shades of meaning to her diary entry for 11 November, when the Elgars shared a Kingsway Theatre box with the Windflower for a matinée performance of Lena Ashwell's latest production, *Iris intervenes*:

. . . Alice S.W. with us. Enjoyed 'Iris intervenes' extremely. Lena wonderfully clever in it. The only play or novel in which a woman has the sense to say 'Nothing wd. make me believe it' (tale about her Husband). 'Even if it were absolutely proved I'd not believe it'   A. [i.e., Alice Elgar] clapped & was joined by someone . . .

Lena Ashwell had come closely into the Elgar circle just then because she wanted Elgar to write incidental music to a fantasy play she was to produce at Christmas entitled *The Starlight Express*. Its theme was the special insight of childhood: that appealed deeply to Elgar particularly in these war years, when his life in London appeared more and more as an exile from his beloved Worcestershire. He resolved to adapt some of the *Wand of Youth* music—which he had first written down in his own childhood during the later 1860s—for this London production half a century later.

On 12 November (the day after *Iris intervenes*), while Alice Elgar was attending the performance of a Quartet by young Arthur Bliss, Edward entertained Alice Stuart Wortley to tea at Severn House to show her the words of *The Starlight Express*. Two days later Lena Ashwell brought the play's author, Algernon Blackwood, to Severn House. He proved a sympathetic spirit: 'Told E. about rearing a horse to run in the Derby on dried milk'. At the end of the morning Edward left his own Alice at Severn House and went with his guests to the West End, with the idea of talking to the music publisher Novello. But when he got into town, he found his thoughts elsewhere (as he wrote that evening):

Severn House, Hampstead, N.W.
Monday [15 Nov. 1915] night

My dear W.

Alas! I tried to telephone. no use. wrong numbers

I had a 'meeting' author producer & composer this a m & decided to do the music—consider the amount of help I shall want & the responsibility!

<hr />

[23] HWRO 705:445:7822.

I went to Willis' rooms—found Claude—he lightened a dull afternoon by speaking of his day with you yesterday—then I went to Novellos & then to tea in the Strand & wasted long—then to Coliseum & then home very cold

Tomorrow we go to Leeds—home on Thursday so it must be till then farewell—but *do* ring up in the morning

I brought a unique little ring today.

> Ever yours
> EE.[24]

The tone suggests a long farewell. In fact the Elgars were to be away two nights—just long enough to rehearse and conduct the Leeds Choral Union in what turned out to be the 'best Caractacus ever done' (as Edward was to tell his own Alice after the concert). But on the morning of the performance, his own thoughts were in London—arranging the earliest possible meeting:

Queen's Hotel, Leeds.
Wednesday [17 Nov. 1915] a m

My dear W.

So many thanks for your letter: I am better & we hope to return by two o'clock tomorrow so I shall go to Willis' [sale *noted by recipient*] at *3* & failing that tea at four.

It is very cold but it *is* nice to feel a little more alive—I only hope it will last. I have much to talk over about the play

> Yrs ever
> EE

I had a nice long letter from C. about names—Mul & Mun etc. I *did* want to be in the house the other night

The figure was from *The Wand of Youth*: in *The Starlight Express* it was to become the motive representing Sleep and Starlight (the medium of childhood inspiration in the play). And indeed, as soon as the Elgars reached London next day, 'E. stayed in town for the afternoon'.

On the evening of 23 November the Elgars were invited to Cheyne Walk to meet Charles Stuart Wortley's cousin Lord Montagu of Beaulieu. Lord Montagu was Colonel of the Hampshires: he was shortly to sail to the Mediterranean in the P. & O. Line ship *SS Persia*. Alice Elgar wrote:

[24] HWRO 705:445:4137.    [25] HWRO 705:445:7813.

... Lalla [Vandervelde] said Zeppelins were expected—S[pecial] Constables called out. Cd. not get any information about them & E. & A. went to dine at Cheyne Walk. Very pleasant evg. Only Lord Montagu there who was very interesting & devoted to '*my* Frontier' as he called it & told us many Rudyard Kiplingish things—

As Elgar's work on *The Starlight Express* intensified, his wife's diary remained blank for days at a time. One of these days was Sunday 28 November. That afternoon Charles Stuart Wortley noted: 'Tea with Clare at the Elgars'. The conversation turned on a famous description of Leonardo da Vinci's *Mona Lisa* (*La Gioconda*) in Walter Pater's book *The Renaissance*. Clare wrote afterwards: 'My recollection is ... that as Sir Edward said he could not properly recall it, I sent the paragraph copied out to him next day.' It was nearly a fortnight before Elgar was able to reply.

Severn House, 42,Netherhall Gardens, Hampstead, N.W.
Dec 10 1915
My dear Clare:

I have been so *sumptuously* busy over the play—slow copyists—inferior & rejected singers etc etc that all the nicest things in the world, & you the best of all, have had to be neglected, but not forgotten.

Thank you so much for the quotation—a real riot of language—I have the essay somewhere & you lead me to look at it again

Bless you
Your affectionate friend
Edward Elgar[26]

*The Starlight Express* score was finished on 15 December—against a stage production date only a fortnight away. For most of those days of concentrated effort in making and checking parts and rehearsing the orchestra, the diary is blank. The last days of the year were written in by Alice Elgar later—after recovering a little from a concussion she suffered in a taxi accident two days after Christmas in streets darkened against air raids. Elgar was very upset, and that did not help his hopes for *The Starlight Express*—which were so dashed by the costumes and sets that he refused to conduct the first night or even at first to enter the theatre.[27] On top of all this, near the end of the year came the news that the *Persia* had been sunk off Malta by German torpedos, and Lord Montagu was presumed lost.

[26] HWRO 705:445:7910, accompanied by the recollection of Clare Stuart Wortley quoted above.

[27] With the Stuart Wortley material presented to the Elgar Birthplace was a programme for the first performance, 29 Dec. 1915, suggesting that at least one of the family attended it. Clare Stuart Wortley noted specifically that she went to see it during its run.

Severn House[,] Hampstead, N.W.
Jany 2. 1916

My dear Windflower:

What an awful New Year: I had hoped & now the crowning horror of the P. & O. —

All else seems nothing—our invalid is going on all well but more *fidgetty* at which we are not surprised—the tedium must be very great.

I am sorry to hear that your C. is laid up with chill & hope he will soon be all right again.

I am very sad and nothing goes right—I *may* go down to Stoke on Tuesday for a day or two but all our plans will be decided by Sir Maurice [Abbot Anderson, the doctor]'s report tomorrow.

We have had people here—but I *was not here*—I am somewhere else always & am not happy

I hope you are well.

> Love as ever
> Yrs
> EE[1]

Then came news that Lord Montagu had been picked up from the wreckage and landed at Malta.

Royal Societies Club, St.James's Street, S.W.
Tuesday [4 Jan. 1916]

My dear W.

In case I do not see you—I cd. not leave today but go tomorrow. 2.25 to Stoke for a few—very few—days

> Yrs ever
> EE

A. is still going on well
I cannot tell you how glad I am about Ld.M.—it wd have been too terrible had anything happened to him fatally: but Heaven knows he must have been through a great deal.[2]

---

[1] HWRO 705:445:4163.     [2] HWRO 705:445:4133.

Severn House, Hampstead, N.W.
Tuesday [4 Jan. 1916] eveng

My dear W.

I find that after all it is best for me to go from Padd[ingto]n at eleven; I then arrive in daylight.

I tried to get to the theatre [for *The Starlight Express*, to whose production he was becoming reconciled] to-day but could not; I heard a good solid report of a cannon about four o'clock & the people called out Zeppelins.

I shall be at Stoke *I think* until Monday

Love
EE

We are more glad than we can say to hear of Ld.M's escape.[3]

For several weeks at the beginning of 1916 Alice Elgar was not well enough to make regular entries in her diary. On 29 January Elgar conducted the première of *Une voix dans le désert* (with the recitation spoken by Carlo Liten) at the Shaftesbury Theatre. At least one Stuart Wortley may have been there, for among the Elgar souvenirs was a first-night programme. (The same evening saw the close of *The Starlight Express*.)

Elgar's third and final Cammaerts recitation, *Le drapeau belge*, was being published by Elkin & Co. with a cover reproduction of Frank Dicksee's *Resurgam*—St George raising his cross above the flames of war. Dicksee was a friend of the Stuart Wortleys, and the suggestion for the cover may have come from her. Dicksee wrote:

Greville House, 3,Greville Place, Maida Vale
Feb. 1st 1916

My dear Mrs Wortley—

It was so very pleasant to see your handwriting again—I wish I had had your letter sooner—I have already given permission to the Publishers—Elkin & Co—to reproduce my drawing that appeared in King Albert's book [a commemorative anthology also containing Elgar's *Carillon*]—for the very purpose about which you write—but I made the condition that they should pay £5 to a Belgian Charity in my name—had the request come from *you* of course there would have been no conditions—but the money will go to some good cause I hope—

Very many Thanks for your kind invitation for next Sunday—I shall be delighted to come—    I am very hard at work on a big picture that I think the Germans would shoot me for if they caught me—but I cannot resist coming to see you—for it seems to me too long since I have—so I shall look forward to Sunday.

Yrs. always
Frank Dicksee

The bottom of this letter contains a brief (and unique) note from Alice Stuart Wortley to Elgar:

[3] HWRO 705:445:4138.

This explain [*sic*] itself—It is a pity Mr.Elkin did not wait[.] Dicksee is coming (I had to ask him to lunch Sunday[ ) ] if you & Alice care to come & meet him we shall be very pleased [—] you or both.

I thought of asking Liten as he has asked to call! & I shall have to do so sometime!

Yr.<br>W.[4]

On Sunday 6 February Alice Elgar noted:

E. to lunch at Cheyne Walk. A. not quite up to going. Pleasant time. Frank Dicksee there & Dosia & Liten—E. travelled back [toward Hampstead] with F. Dicksee.

Elkin was also publishing *Une voix dans le désert*. It bore a dedication 'To my friend, Sir Claude Phillips.' The dedication would have formed a natural topic for discussion—perhaps on the following Saturday, when Elgar may have shared his walk with the Windflower.

[n.p.]
Sunday [13 Feb. 1916]
My dear W.

I had a lovely walk yesterday. I hope *you* had a happy time.
I found a lovely letter from Claude which I will shew you sometime—he is very happy & pleased with the dedication

Love<br>Yrs<br>EE[5]

The end of February found Elgar orchestrating the second and third of his Binyon settings, which were to be collectively entitled *The Spirit of England*. The first was still incomplete. Alice Elgar had by now fully resumed her diary:

27 February 1916 ... Delightful afternoon—Percy [Anderson], Laurence Binyons, Alice S.W. & A[nthony] Bernard [who had acted as musical assistant for *The Starlight Express* production]—E. played his wonderful Binyon music—all immensely impressed—

Next day Elgar was to begin a short northern tour with the London Symphony Orchestra. Before starting, he wrote on the special stationery:

[4] Elgar Birthplace parcel 584(xxii).        [5] HWRO 705:445:4127.

[*belted monogram* E] this stands for Edward
[n.p.]
Feb 28 1916

My dear Windflower

All my pens* are packed & I am just off. A year since I bought this silly paper—to write to you! Bless you.

*Farewell*

*I cannot write with this stick—I shall go to see Lorenzo [by Millais] at Liverpool but I fear it is hidden away in these troublous times

Love.
Yrs ever
EE[6]

While he was away, on 1 March his own Alice lunched at Cheyne Walk. Five days later he was back.

During March Alice Stuart Wortley visited Severn House at least twice—on the 14th and the 30th. The latter day found Elgar practising 'wild flights' on a new typewriter with smaller type. He began a letter next day with the old machine:

Severn House,
March 31: 1916

My dear Mrs Stuart-Wortley, (!!!!)

How is that for a beginning? This machine is beyond praise & knows exactly what to say and how and when to say it! How frightful it looks printed like this; it is not to be borne.

——: :——: :——: :——: :——: :——

[*then with the new machine*]

My dear Windflower, —— this is much smaller type and more befitting, —— you said I must never use type in writing to you, but I m u s t practise this new machine which gives all the foreign accents and is a great amusement, —— as you see. I am quite laid up and am not so well to-day, but I hope things may be better soon. Cold and general chill.

I hear from my sister [Pollie] that the third boy [Roland] is called up so the dear little house will indeed be lonely for my poor women folk: they are very brave but it is a great upheaval.

More windflowers will soon lift their lovely little heads looking for their chief, —— that is you, —— and they shall find you if I can shew them the way.

Love,
E.[7]

Both the Elgars were ill with influenza. In a cold springtime, war shortages meant that there was not enough fuel to run the big central heating system at Severn House.

[6] HWRO 705:445:4160.      [7] HWRO 705:445:7118.

8 April 1916. E. ready to start for Stoke. Said he felt giddy & was not sure he wd. go. A. in bed & afraid of the cold house, no coke, for him so did not persuade him to give it up hoping change wd. do good. A. dismayed to hear by telephone from Capt.Dillon that E. was ill in the train & Capt.D. took him out at Oxford & motored him to the Acland Nursing Home . . .

It was the old illness, and Elgar spent two days in the nursing home before he was able to return. On the night of his arrival back at Severn House, he wrote:

Severn House, Hampstead, N.W.
Tuesday [11 Apr. 1916] eveng
My dear W.

   I have just found your Stoke letter here—Alas! I was taken ill in the train & removed from it to a *Nursing Home* at *Oxford*—so strange[:] so instead of Stoke I have been taken by some unknown good person to the Acland Home where I have been lying till today when Carice escorted me home. I am of course better but not well—I went out too soon after Influenza & collapsed in the train
   Bless you [—] I loved your letter

                                                                        EE.
I was brought home in a car all the way from Oxford[8]

   Two days later she came to tea, and the day after that she collected and brought up the results of a successful bid he had made with auctioneers in London. The objects were reputed fragments from King John's tomb: the tomb was in Worcester Cathedral, and Elgar had bought them on the chance of their being genuine, to present to the Cathedral. During her visit that day, he gave her a vocal score proof of the new Binyon settings.[9]
   Four days later he sent her the proof of an article on the Binyon settings which Ernest Newman had written for the forthcoming issue of *The Musical Times*. It was a skilled description, and it also explored wider implications, concluding: 'Here in truth is the very voice of England, moved to the centre of her being in this War as she has probably never been moved before in all her history.'

[n.p.]
Tuesday [18 Apr. 1916]
My dear W.

   Thanks for your telegram: I am not well & do not improve as I cd. wish.
   Let me have the enclosed back sometime—read the end—I think you will like E N.'s description. No one else has this proof

                                                                     Love
                                                                     EE[10]

---

[8] HWRO 705:445:4128.     [9] Now at the Elgar Birthplace.     [10] HWRO 705:445:4210.

About a week later (the diary was again blank for nearly a fortnight) there was a private trial of the Binyon music in the Severn House music-room: no chorus, but W. H. Reed brought several players from the London Symphony Orchestra. Alice Stuart Wortley had been invited, but was unable to be there.

[n.p.]
Thursday [27 Apr. 1916]

My dear Windflower:

Thanks very many for your letters: I had a bad turn on Saturday but have steadily or unsteadily improved since

Our music—which was meant for *you*—went beautifully & the men played like angels—we had only Mary Crawshay, Percy & the Landon Ronalds: he played piano [filling in missing parts] when I conducted & conducted when I played—the things sounded lovely & the room is divine for a small orchestra—only the goddess of the feast was not there & it was all, all wasted. It was nice to hear Reed's eager voice asking, disappointedly, '*Where* is Mrs.W.?' & later Landon '*Where on earth* is Mrs W in all this music?' I said *to myself* 'Everywhere—and alas! nowhere' But you see they all thought it was nothing without you. & so did I.

We have been drives—Hadley—Epping Forest & I am stronger & am really going to try a walk to-day.

I lie & think of the wide open views, and a gate, and a church (many) and a brake, woody & flowery by the distant Wye but the end of every vista [*three or four words eradicated*]

Bless you
EE[11]

Dreaming of past times in Herefordshire, he was booked for Leeds and Bradford to conduct initial performances of *The Spirit of England*. On 1 May he sent her the printed vocal scores inscribed. Next day, far from well, he went with his wife to Leeds for an evening rehearsal. But then his thoughts were all back in London, as he wrote a card:

Queen's Hotel, Leeds.
May 2 1916

To remind you that the full rehearsal [of the Binyon settings] is at *Queen's Hall* on *Sunday* next at *10 o'c*[.] I will send particulars as to admission—but do reserve the time. I am fairly well

Yrs ever
EE[12]

The northern performances made a deep impression. Back in London, he rehearsed the two settings on Sunday morning 7 May. His own Alice noted: 'The faithful band

[11] HWRO 705:445:7667.     [12] HWRO 705:445:7119.

there to hear.' That day the Windflower's scores were signed by the poet, Laurence Binyon. There followed an entire week of performances in which Elgar conducted the Binyon settings followed by *Gerontius*: the Angel was sung by Clara Butt (the scheme's organizer), Royalty was present at most of the concerts, and the whole net receipts of £2700 went to the Red Cross.

Afterwards the Elgars spent a few days on the south coast trying to repair his health. After his return he was worse than ever. The doctors seemed powerless to help. He waited day after day hoping to feel well enough to go to Stoke. At last on 2 June, his fifty-ninth birthday, he went.

Stoke
Saturday [3 June 1916]

My dear W.

I am here & *much* better—so far: it is lovely and—lonely. I rest & play with the dog & cut down thistles. Your telegram came—love & thanks

I will write again soon—but this *awful* navy news! it's killing to the spirit

Love
Edward[13]

That day the first news had come of what at first appeared to be a shattering defeat at Jutland: three major British ships were sunk.

He returned to London on 15 June, but could settle to nothing. A week later the Windflower arrived with a present: 'Alice S.W. brought him Hardy's books, those he did not already possess.' By 6 July even the Hampstead air was hot and steamy, and Elgar did not feel well enough to go to the matinée of *Disraeli* which Alice Stuart Wortley had planned: she came instead to tea. He went with his own Alice to The Hut for a weekend—the last time that summer, as Schuster was letting it. Back at Severn House, depression crept even into the box of special stationery.

[*belted monogram* E]
[n.p.]
Tuesday July 11: 1916

My dear Windflower

This E stands for Edward—almost the last sheet of the old Liverpool paper, do you remember it? We got back from the Hut yesterday afternoon: I spent my time like [Dickens's] Old Mortality renovating old inscriptions. It was lovely to *see* (between the rain-storms) but not restful with *four* soldiers in the house & only A. & myself as other guests—so I did not feel rested, rather worried than otherwise.

I *may* hear of you by telephone but I write this in case I do not. I hope you are well & have nice plans—we have none! Frank leaves on Wedy for

13 HWRO 705:445:7677.

Bournemouth having let the Hut for *two months*: I *may* go to my sister any day but all is vague, uncertain & unprofitable.

> Bless you
> Yrs
> EE[14]

That afternoon, while his own Alice went to Penshurst in search of a holiday house, Edward entertained the Windflower to tea.

On 15 July he was off to Stoke for another fortnight and more. Soon he had a letter from the Windflower elaborately sealed in wax stamped with a floral design.

Stoke.
Tuesday [18 July 1916]
My dear W:

So glad to receive your letter—the seal! is it a Windflower, it's not quite distinct.

I sent you a note on Sunday by my 'flying' nephew who was leaving for London—I tell you this in case the post mark puzzled you. I am better to-day & am writing early as I think the sun is coming out & I shall go off by train to the Severn Valley. The pony is the prettiest dearest little thing—so *willing* & trotty & plays with the girls like a kitten! My dog is well but alas! this dreadful year for woods & lanes—too wet & horribly dreary—it has rained practically for a month—but, as I said, better today. I am glad you thought of St.Pauls & (I am sure) of Cripplegate.

I will write again soon & tell you things of the country & I wait for more news of you

> Love
> EE[15]

The next letter from the Windflower hinted that she might visit Stratford. She conveyed an invitation from the Beresfords to share their holiday at a house with a windmill in the grounds. (Lord Charles had recently been created Baron Beresford; and Clare Stuart Wortley recalled: 'Mina—characteristically—said the peerage was such a blessing, because people always *would* call her Lady Beresford, (in ignorance & error) instead of Lady Charles; so now at last they really could call her Lady Beresford & be done with it!').

---

[14] HWRO 705:445:4159. The 'old inscriptions' Elgar renovated at The Hut probably included the gnomic initials 'D.o.m.D.' carved by him during an earlier summer visit.
[15] HWRO 705:445:4164.

Stoke
Wedy [19 July 1916]

My dear W.

Many thanks for your letter & enclosure which I return—answd

I went out to *Bridgnorth* yesterday [—] such a lovely place so curiously placed on a hill with my beloved windflowerish Severn winding round it: but I am not well today, alas! The heat seems too much—

I am anxious to hear your plans—I fear Lady Ch.—(I mean Lady B but she will always be Lady C.) must work her windmill without me.

The weather is lovely now but it *has* brought out millions of FLIES!

Love
EE[16]

The Windflower was to be in Stratford at the weekend. Could she come over to Stoke? Edward began to make plans for meeting her.

Stoke Prior
Saturday [22 July 1916]

My dear W.

I am so glad you are having at least a week-end in the country. Here it is divine again after a very stormy day. Do send a telegram saying if anything possible on Monday: by road it is 20 miles to this: it wd. be perfect if you could 'car' to *Droitwich* in the morning[.] I cd. meet you & lunch there & shew you (four miles) our bit of forest but the trains to London *from Droitwich* are very bad—i.e. if you *must* go back to London on Monday. I see there's a train from Drtwch at 5.19 arrg Paddington at 9.2. If that wd. do why not come to Droitwich either by car (or by train—a train leaves S-on-A at 11.35 arrg at Drtwch at 1.14)—I wd. be at the station but driving wd. be difficult*—but not impossible. I think it wd. be simplest if I plan to be at Drtwch station at *one* o'c—but if you wire anything let it be early as must leave this house soon after eleven.

If you spend the night at Stratford there is a train back from Dtwch at 6.22 arrg S-on-A at 8.17.

Love
Yrs
EE

* I mean if you come by train we shd have to take an old *cab horse* round here to the forest—but still it *has been done*![17]

She came on the Monday, and the afternoon was described for his own Alice back in London. She noted: 'E. lunched with A.S.W. at Droitwich & then drove round by the Elms & to the Common.' But the Windflower's return journey was as tedious as they feared.

[16] HWRO 705:445:4161.          [17] HWRO 705:445:4189.

Stoke Prior
Friday [28 July 1916]
My dear W.

I am so glad to have your letter & to know that you are safe after the terribly tiring journey. I need not say how heavenly the day was & so satisfying that you like this place & the forest.

I am leaving here today & am going to try to find hotels for Alice to join me on Tuesday—?Bridgnorth etc [—] so I can give you no address to write to; for the present. *do not write* here as I am GONE—the Common is too lovely now. Goodbye. I kiss your hands

Yrs<br>EE

I am no better[18]

On 1 August he met his own Alice at Bridgnorth, and two days later went for their holiday to the Lakes. On the 16th they were in a passenger boat on Ullswater when a sudden storm came up. Alice Elgar wrote in her diary:

... E. & A. sat at end of bench on boat very close together & very happy under one umbrella, & a man who had been standing by talking to another suddenly said, putting his face close to theirs, 'You are l*u*vers still like me & my wife.' A. rather speechless with surprise, E. said in a sweet way 'I hope so.' it was quite sincere & very touching.

That day he wrote to the Windflower:

Ullswater Hotel, Patterdale.
Wedy [16 Aug. 1916]
My dear Windflower.

I hope you are well & that the lower temperature is good for you.
We leave on Friday for
P. of Wales Hotel[,] Grasmere
it is quite time you wrote to me please: I wish you could come to us for a week-end visit—we want you so much.
We have rain storms but lovely times in between.
I want to know all the news of you. [*Four words heavily eradicated.*]
Alice is much rested & this has done her any amount of good—she thinks it is good for me but I stay on for her sake. I do not know when we shall arrive in town:—next week I think

Love<br>Yrs<br>EE[19]

---

[18] HWRO 705:445:4209.  [19] HWRO 705:445:4131.

Two days later, walking over the Kirkstone Pass, Elgar was overtaken by torrential rain and soaked to the skin. A sore throat quickly developed. Alice got him back to London, where the doctor took so serious a view that on 29 August the throat was cauterized by electricity. Elgar was just able to go to Cheyne Walk to lunch, and Alice Stuart Wortley brought him back to Severn House to tea. Next day he started with his own Alice to a luncheon date with Lalla Vandervelde, but had to give it up and return home. Was another rest cure in 'cold storage' looming? He wrote to the Windflower next day—beginning with a response to her news that the Stuart Wortleys were helping another concert scheme of Landon Ronald's:

Hampstead
Augt 31. 1916

My dear W.:

Many thanks for the letter which I return: I am so much obliged to you for interesting yrself & C. in L.R.—I have a *personal* feeling in this you know.

I was so sorry about yesterday—I started out but had to return—not well—today—the same feeling & I write this, in case I cannot see or otherwise communicate with you, to wish you a happy, restful & peaceful time at the beloved sea.

I feel that everything has come to an end & am very unhappy—
Bless you & good-bye

EE.[20]

He tried a weekend at Ridgehurst—thus missing a Zeppelin raid over London. Returning home, he found a letter from the Windflower, now at Tintagel, and replied on a last sheet of the special stationery:

[*belted monogram* E]
[n.p.]
Wedy [6 Sept. 1916]

My dear W.          This 'E' stands for Edward.

I was so glad to receive your letter & can picture the sea & all: also the road [to Boscastle *supplied by Clare Stuart Wortley*] & the gate—which must all be forgotten now.

I am better but not happy: I missed the raid here but all is safe. I am not sure if I am going to Stoke but, as the weather is quite bright this morning, I may go at any moment; so I will not expect anr. letter until I send an address. Make the most of the sea & the Arthurian land—this is a dreary matter-of-fact world I am in now—& not worth living in.

Good bye
Love
EE[21]

[20] HWRO 705:445:4162.          [21] HWRO 705:445:4191.

Later in the month the Elgars visited the Berkeley family at Spetchley Park near Worcester. On the way home he stopped a night at The Elms.

Stoke
Friday [15 Sept. 1916]
My dear Windflower:

I am just passing on my way home from Spetchley.

Alice & I paid a week end visit to the Berkeleys—a visit which was prolonged day by day—lovely place where I played as a child, 3½ miles from Worcester—  Deer park, fish ponds etc etc—I caught 70 good fish! But I am very sad—& cannot *rest* even here, so after *one* night I restlessly go home

I kiss your hands
Yr
EE[22]

In London there were more Zeppelin raids.

Severn House, Hampstead, N.W.
Tuesday [3 Oct. 1916]
My dear W.

I have been hoping to hear from you. I did *not* go away & see no chance of going for a long time. I hope you are well & that the 'romantic sea' is still a joy.

When do you return? I feel you are all safer on that coast than here but it is good to know that we can capture the Zeppelins sometimes.

I have been

*[remainder torn away]*[23]

Next in the correspondence comes its greatest rarity—a surviving letter from Alice Stuart Wortley, now returned from Tintagel. Although written to Alice and not to Edward Elgar, here for once we can catch her own accents—and with them some sense of what those accents meant to the man who seemed to have lost his way in life.

7, Cheyne Walk, Chelsea. S.W.
Oct 20 1916
My dear Alice

Just come in & hurrying to catch the earlier post to let you get this tomorrow morning—  I have seats for tomorrow Ambassadors [Theatre], West Street Shaftesbury Av. & will meet you at 2-30 tomorrow.

It will be very nice our going together, it is so long since we had an afternoon play—

I have had a real thrill this evening

²² HWRO 705:445:4132.        ²³ HWRO 705:445:4100.

Coming along Cheyne Walk, I saw two lads about 10 & 12 walking along singing at the top of their voices & very correctly too, 'My old tunes are rather broken' & they come from far away etc. [from *The Starlight Express*] their fresh young voices rising above the wind

I caught them up & stopped them & said What's that yr. singing & where did you learn it—oh that's 'My old tunes' they answered—& we learnt it at the 'Oratory Schools'[.] Miss Weston teaches us & we sing lots more! I said well done, go on sing it all the way home & tell Miss Weston how much pleasure you have given!

Isn't that a pretty story—& is that not Fame?

Are we down hearted?

N O !

Love to the Master!

Yrs. affect
Alice.[24]

Thus she turned a current question-and-answer byword of the war to homely use.

Alice Elgar's diary for the following day says merely: 'E. lunched with A.S.W.'. It was the diary entry of just a week later that showed them all at the theatre:

28 October 1916. E. & A. after lunch to the Ambassador's Theatre, Alice S.W. taking us to see Pell-Mell—A. hated it, degrading spectacle—Martin, the Frenchman, *very* clever & amusing—   Tea together at a Lyons—

Meanwhile in the week intervening the Windflower had been up to Severn House to tea, and had played them the old fragment of the piano concerto—hoping to tempt Edward's music. Nothing came of it. On Sunday 28 October Alice Elgar joined the Stuart Wortleys for a Queen's Hall afternoon concert in which Henry Wood conducted the *Introduction and Allegro*: afterwards she brought them back to tea—to find Edward playing billiards with Percy Anderson. Several other tea guests turned up, including Clara Butt—who sang portions of the still unfinished first part of *The Spirit of England* to Edward's accompaniment: 'It sounded gorgeous.'

He was more or less ill for the rest of the year. On 21 November the Elgars were able to lunch at Clara Butt's house: Alice Stuart Wortley was among the guests. She came to Severn House to tea on 4 December. A week later he wrote:

Severn House, Hampstead, N.W.
Monday [11 Dec. 1916]

My dear W.

Many thanks for yr. message etc. I will see to the return of the book, which C. so kindly left out for me [,] to the London Liby.

I am very unwell indeed and do not know what to make of it—I suppose it

---

[24] Elgar Birthplace parcel 584(vii).

is the old thing but I can make no plans at all. I *have* to go to the Gramophone Co[mpan]y on Saturday but I am waiting for further information as to time & mode of conveyance

> Love
> E.E.

I hope you are really better.[25]

The date at Hayes was to conduct an abridged recording of the Violin Concerto with Marie Hall. A morning session was fixed, and the Gramophone Company sent a car. But thick fog imperilled the journey: they had a slight accident on the way out, and a near miss coming back. Afterwards Elgar was ill again.

A week before Christmas came the news that Charles Stuart Wortley was to be raised to the Peerage. The Elgars telegraphed congratulations, but it was two days before Edward could write. His letter could not resist contrasting their fortunes with his own:

[*postmarked* Hampstead]
Wedy [20 Dec. 1916]

My dear Windflower:

I am out of bed for the first time since Saturday & I use the first minute to send you love & congratulation on the event,—I gave you a coronet long ago—the best I had but you may have forgotten it—now you will have a real one, bless you!

I cannot tell you how glad I am—I expected it—wanted it for you long ago & now its come I feel afraid of you & wonder in a vague sort of way what will be the difference? But you are still the Windflower I think & hope.

I may try to get out today but I am very shaky still.

Everything pleasant & promising in my life is dead—I have the happiness of my friends to console me as I had fifty years ago. I feel that life has gone back so far when I was alone & there was no one to stand between me & disaster—health or finance—now that has come back & I am more alone & the prey of circumstances than ever before.

> Bless you,
> Your
> EE

I wonder what the new name will be—this may be the last time I address you in the old, familiar way.[26]

Thus the news of his friends' preferment started a contrast which threatened to strip him naked, as this terrible year of war and private illness went toward its end.

December 23 1916 ... Alice S.W. came in afternoon—Brought E. his Lavender water present & A. dear pottery bowl of White hyacinths—& C. a nice umbrella—E. & A. walked with her to Finchley Rd. omnibus— ...

[25] HWRO 705:445:4129.     [26] HWRO 705:445:7689.

December 26. E. & A. to lunch with Alice S.W. Went by train. Then she motored us to S.James's Theatre for 'Charley's Aunt'—*very* poor & silly—coming out *dense* fog & darkness—Eventually we drove to S.Kenn.Station & Alice drove on home. We had to wait quite 15 mins. for train in the fog & cold—Of course it gave E. bad cold . . .

On the last day of the year he just crept down when the Windflower came to Sunday tea with other guests.

## 1917

A note to accompany the letters of 1917 was written by Clare Stuart Wortley:

It is important to remember that the constant indisposition, & depression, & the occasional giddiness of which Sir Edward Elgar complains in these letters were due to the fact that he suffered from Menière's disease of the ear. He was, & he felt, ill. Consequently the past, in which he had been himself & been well, seems to him infinitely brighter by contrast. His biographers [up to 1945] appear to ignore or suppress this ear-trouble; though it was perfectly well known to his family & friends. The doctors were a long time finding it out.[1]

5 January 1917. E. to see Sir Maurice [Abbot Anderson]. A. with him. Throat again burnt with electric cautery . . .

10 January. E. (A. with him) to Sir Maurice. More painting of throat—A.S.W. to tea—A. saw her to omnibus late—not so very dark—  E. feeling throat uncomfortably.

Severn House, Hampstead, N.W.
Thursday Jany 11: 1917
My dear W.

I wonder how you are: I went to the doctor yesterday & am no better today; I am trying the dentist this afternoon but I do not see beyond to-day!

I have heard nothing from Lady B. (Mina.) in response to my letter. I fear she's ill—*do* find out: and come on Sunday afternoon & tell me all about it. Troyte is 'coming' for a day or two

Love<br>EE[2]

---

[1] HWRO 705:445:7710. Of Elgar's distress there could be no question. But the possibility remains that the doctors never did 'find it out'. On the question of diagnosis and the possible relation of Elgar's ear trouble to what is now called alienation (and hence his nostalgia), see *Edward Elgar: A Creative Life*, p 715.
[2] HWRO 705:445:4155.

The diary does not record that she came that Sunday. The next Sunday he wrote to her on the investiture:

Severn House[,] Hampstead, N.W.
Jany 21: 1917
'Dear Lady Stuart of Wortley:'

I do hope I am the first to put this beautiful title; bless you in it & may you wear it and (as you do to everything you touch or look upon) beautify it & decorate it for long & many happy years.

Still, the Windflower can never become wholly a 'conservatory plant', can it? It will sometimes remember its woods.

Yours ever sincerely
Edward Elgar:[3]

That afternoon found them all together attending a party at Lalla Vandervelde's flat to meet Yeats. Four days later:

25 January. E. & A. to 'Lord & Lady Stuart of Wortley of the City of Sheffield' to lunch & to meet Claude [Phillips]. Claude wd. talk nothing but war—of course it is the subject filling our beings, but not to be talked about *always*—A.S.W. brought E. back . . .

He seemed better. One day he visited Mary Anderson de Navarro in her suite at the Savoy Hotel. There he played the piano concerto fragment over and over—as if the presence of another beautiful woman might strike the spark. Early in February he began another cold.

Severn House, 42,Netherhall Gardens, Hampstead, N.W.
In my room
Tuesday [6 Feb. 1917]
My dear Windflower

Alas! I am not up & cd. not possibly telephone
I have a most terrible cold & do not know when I shall be out[.] I must go to the Gramophone on Friday
Tomorrow Feb 7th I kept for you—us—alas! I shall remember everything

Love
EE[4]

The recording session was postponed. The anniversary of the Violin Concerto's windflower theme was kept in their memories.

Alice Stuart of Wortley was on the executive committee for a project to stage a 'Chelsea Matinée' (in aid of Lena Ashwell's 'Concerts at the Front'). It was to consist of a 'Review of Modern Chelsea': 'All the great figures in modern Chelsea life, from Carlyle and Whistler to Augustus John and McEvoy, will be seen.' The last two were

---

[3] HWRO 705:445:7698.    [4] HWRO 705:445:4158.

in fact also members of the executive committee—along with Sir Philip Burne-Jones and one or two other acquaintances of the Elgars. One proposal was to include a short ballet founded on the 'Fan in Sanguine' drawn by Charles Conder (and owned by another of the executive committee, the wife of the publisher John Lane). And although the Elgars knew Chelsea only as visitors, it was Alice Stuart of Wortley's hope to persuade him to write the ballet music.

The ballet's deviser was an old friend of the Elgars from Malvern days—the daughter of Canon Raymond Pelly, now Mrs Christopher Lowther. She was an amateur dancer of skill and experience, and a figure well known and well liked in West End artistic and political circles. Her aim, moreover, was to interest several eminent actors and actresses to dance with her.

7 February. E. in bed & his room all day but rather better—just came down in fur coat to see I.Lowther[, who] came to lay the Chelsea Ballet idea before E.

Conder's 'Fan in Sanguine' showed a forest glade with Pan and Echo on one side; from the other side eighteenth-century beaux and belles wandered far toward an open prospect near the centre. From this Ina Lowther had made her scenario. Near 'a somewhat disfigured statue of Eros', Pan enters, and falls asleep. A young man appears with young ladies, and their amorousness leads to a quarrel as they wander away. Echo approaches, wakes Pan, and tempts him to love. The young man and his quarrelling ladies reappear: he curses Eros. Thereupon Echo steals Pan's pipes to seduce the young man. Pan's jealousy is aroused: he creates a storm whose lightning strikes the young man senseless. Pan turns to punish Echo, is stayed by her beauty, and ends by carrying her off with sardonic laughter—leaving the prostrate lover mourned by his mortal mistress on her knees in the glade as the curtain falls.

Alice Stuart of Wortley was to have come to Severn House with Mrs Lowther, but was away. Still the shifting patterns of attraction among the four principal dancers could cast their shadows between Severn House and Cheyne Walk. Elgar was tempted to this sizeable but not very practical project.

(n.p.)
Thursday [8 Feb. 1917]

My dear Windflower:

It is so dreadful your not coming—I am better & am doing the Ballet—or *think* of doing it—but where are you? I wanted to tell you the theme & *every note* must be approved by you (bless you!) before anything can be done. Oh! why are you so far away & so difficult to get at??

Love
EE

I thought of using up *your Piano Concerto*! (Labour exchange!) but you would not allow that would you?

*Ballet*!!⁵

He enclosed sketches for the music already shaping in his mind: not the concerto fragment (which was never to be used in any finished work), but an opening theme as it was to appear in the ballet—in G major rather than the ultimate F major.⁶

10 February 1917. E. better & out for short walk with A.S.W. who came to tea. She was very anxious & grieved about the Duke of Norfolk's illness...

The Duke died next day. It followed closely on the death of Elgar's great friend G. R. Sinclair of Hereford Cathedral—a loss deeply felt. Yet work on *The Sanguine Fan* continued.

17 February. Quite a nice day, mild with feeling of Spring. E. busy with Fan music. Alice S. of W. came & had a walk with E. Immensely excited over E.'s new music. Described 'Charlie's' taking his Seat in House of Lords [four days earlier.]

At the end of the month the hundred-page score of *The Sanguine Fan* was nearly complete.
     Early in March Elgar was booked to conduct a Choral Union concert in Leeds. It put him in mind of other expeditions in Yorkshire, in other days, in other company. The weather had turned arctic again.

Severn House, Hampstead[,] N.W.
March 5. 1917
My dear Windflower:

Oh! this weather! & I was dreaming yesterday of woods & fields &, perhaps, a little drive round Harrogate—or a little play journey to Fountains or some lovely remembrance of long ago idylls, & now deep snow.
     Well, I have put it all in my music & also much more that has never happened.
     A. & I are just starting but I must send a line to say how glad I was you came yesterday.

---

⁵ HWRO 705:445:7804. Several undated sketches for the piano concerto, listed by Clare Stuart Wortley as given to her mother in 1918, are at the Elgar Birthplace (MS 61).
⁶ Elgar Birthplace MS 114.

I *hope* you will find a conductor but I fear the time is too short to do much good.

> I kiss your hands
> Love
> EE[7]

For the 'Chelsea Matinée' scenes other than *The Sanguine Fan* (which Elgar himself was to conduct), they secured the young theatre conductor Howard Carr—and promptly put him on the music committee just below 'Sir Edward Elgar, O.M.'. She telegraphed the news to Leeds.

Queen's Hotel, Leeds.
Tuesday [6 Mar. 1917]
My dear W:

Your welcome telegram came last night: I *am* so glad your troubles are over concerning a conductor. Get him to submit to the musical Committee *all* things he (or others) suggest for *Overture, entr'actes* etc[:] *don't* have any rubbish [—] anything as amusing & lively as you please but draw the line somewhere.

I think of the old days here—how happy we were before the war! The *service* here is beyond belief—e.g. I ordered breakfast at 8.40 [—] sole & porridge—at 9 o'c the young lady came back to say they had no sole: I sd. What have you? She didn't know: then she went away for ½ an hour to find out: of course, I had said that anything wd. do.   eventually she (& anr. handmaiden worse than herself) produced from the lower regions coffee (for A) & tea for me & the eatables, *two* pint jugs of *cream*, no serviettes[.] I thought perhaps the chef wd. be hankering after his cream so I gently drew attention to it: the young lady declined to recognise it as cream, pitied me & left. Alice had just finished her porridge so sd. 'please take away this plate'—handing it to her[.] The young lady solemnly took it &, instead of placing it on the sideboard, slowly stalked out of the room and down the corridor! It's like being in a nightmare.

Chorus excellent & best soloists—I fear the orchestra may be poor tomorrow but who cares?

I sent a little note to a little Windflower before I left because I felt I could not go without [*eradication*] so far away

> Love
> EE.

Alice sends love & so glad you have a conductor[8]

By the morning of the Leeds concert Elgar was thinking of home and the Windflower:

---

[7] HWRO 705:445:7678. In the closing, 'I kiss' and 'hands' have been eradicated.
[8] HWRO 705:445:4182. In the body of the letter's final paragraph, the words 'a little Windflower' have been eradicated.

Queen's Hotel, Leeds.
Wedy [7 Mar. 1917]

My dear W.

All well.

Do come to tea at Severn Ho: *tomorrow* Thursday if you can & tell us news[.]
Alice expects you & sends love. We arrive at Kings X at 2.40 & shall not go
out at all

Love
EE

I want to hear all your news of vocalist etc etc[9]

After a fine concert, the Elgars returned next day; and Alice Stuart of Wortley came
to Hampstead with latest news of the 'Chelsea Matinée'. To begin the programme,
they had secured the services of a Madame Rosovskaya—who came at least with the
recommendation of her accompanist, the celebrated Vladimir Rosing.

Then Elgar began another cold.

12 March. E. better. Sir Maurice came & said he might go out & to Worcester
[to conduct a performance of *For the Fallen* on 15 March]—E. to rehearsal of
Fan—much amused although tried by inefficient pianiste. G[erald] Du
Maurier [as Pan] very good & delightful. Alice S.W. brought E. back & we
took her down to omnibus after tea. She was going to hear Lan do E.'s
Variations [—] Philc. Concert. ...

The first orchestral rehearsal of *The Sanguine Fan* was to take place right after the
Worcester visit, on Saturday 17 March, and it was arranged for Elgar to go direct
from the returning train at Paddington to Cheyne Walk to correct the manuscript
parts.

[n.p.]
Tuesday [13 Mar. 1917]

My dear W.

Thank you so much for allowing me to come on Friday to correct the
orchl. parts etc

We leave tomorrow mid-day [for Worcester] & I send something so that
you shall not forget me

Bless you.
Yrs ever
EE

He enclosed a sketch of the music which was to close *The Sanguine Fan*, inscribed at
the bottom: 'The End [—] should have been the beginning'.[10]

Her letter of thanks went to Worcester—whence he replied on the day of the
performance there:

⁹ HWRO 705:445:4180.    ¹⁰ Elgar Birthplace parcel 583.

Star Hotel, Worcester.
Thursday [15 Mar. 1917]

My dear W.

Thanks one thousand times for your letter.

All goes well but frightfully crowded days. I hope to arrive at Paddn. at
12.40 & will gladly come down to you

Love<br>EE

Greatest haste
*Cathedral heavenly*[11]

Again the performance was impressive, again the return was quick. The ballet parts
were corrected for the first rehearsal next day. That rehearsal was also to include
other turns in the 'Chelsea Matinée', as Alice Elgar found to her cost:

17 March 1917. First rehearsal of Conder Ballet—Supposed to begin at 3?
Kept E. waiting nearly an hour, doing stupid vulgar things—    Then a *very*
poor unworthy orchestra—Made A. start from her seat at some of the noises
they made—Everyth. very confused—    G. DuMaurier & [Ernest] Thesiger
[as the Young Man] delightful of course—

18 March . . . E. & A. to lunch at Cheyne Walk—C[lara] Butt, M. & Mad^e
Hoch—Leslie [Henson, who was to sing 'My friend John' as a reference to
Augustus John in the Matinée] there—not very interesting. Then to dress
rehearsal. Watteau dresses lovely. Shepherds *very* trying! Ballet promised to
be lovely.

19 March. To rehearsal at Wyndham's Theatre— Orch. more bearable—
Ballet lovely, other scenes vulgar, in bad taste & wretched—

20 March. To lunch at Cheyne Walk. Frank arrived so pleased to see us
again as we were to see him—& [the painter (also on the Matinée executive
committee) Glyn] Philpot, nice— Very pleasant lunch— Then to
Theatre—Stupid music first & some stupid things[:] Rossetti scene disgust-
ing—& degrading great men— Ballet perfectly beautiful. Music exquisite &
enchanting actors delightful. Ina Lowther *very* good [—] just filling the part
with gaiety & spontaneity. Much applause.   . . .

26 March . . . Alice S. of W. to tea longing to hear the Fan Ballet again.

A second performance was soon arranged for 22 May.
    Late March and early April found Elgar finishing two long-standing projects—four
sea songs topical to the war, setting Kipling's verses from 'The Fringes of the Fleet';
and at last the setting of Binyon's 'The Fourth of August', to complete *The Spirit of
England*. Would she come and hear? But she was unwell.

[11] HWRO 705:445:4183.

[n.p.]
Easter Monday [9 Apr.] 1917
Dear Lady Windflower:

Your message has just come & I am so sorry about your headache & *so* disappointed. I had so much to shew you & the Binyon Big thing is in full blast—for the moment. I fear tomorrow may be impossible & on Wedy you go [to Stratford]. I am sending a trifle [a book] to meet you at the Hotel.

Then on Monday I go to Stoke so I fear it's a long farewell—

Anyhow Bless you. I will of course let you hear what happens & expect you to telephone in the morning.

Love
EE[12]

On 13 April Elgar rehearsed his portion of a Belgian Concert to celebrate the birthday of their brave King Albert. The Elgar works were to be *Une voix dans le désert* and the orchestral première of *Le drapeau belge*, both with Carlo Liten. After the rehearsal Elgar wrote:

[*postmarked* Hampstead]
Friday [13 Apr. 1917]
My dear W.

I fear there are none of your namesakes with their faces above the snow—earth I was going to say—perhaps you *can* see earth & green things to-day.

I am just in from rehearsal—Q's Hall was empty—I only *saw* a vacant chair.

The *Drapeau Belge* makes a fine noise. I am tired because I finished the remaining Binyon thing & *The Spirit of England* is at the printer's—it went yesterday. Tea with Frances [Colvin] yesterday & much talk, interesting all round. My plans are vague, depending mostly on weather as it is still too cold for Stoke, alas!

It is nice to know that you love *my* Stratford: I wanted to take you a walk beyond the mill by the river: if fine enough walk past the Church & straight on (the road dwindles to a foot-path past the mill) [—] you come to the railway & it looks rather 'messy' sometimes, but go straight on *under* the railway bridge and you come to a lovely field path by the Avon[:] you can go for miles—    It's really lovely there & quiet

Bless you
Yr
EE

I hope you like the tiny little book—I fear you may have had it already[13]

---

[12] HWRO 705:445:4224.        [13] HWRO 705:445:7682.

The Belgian Concert next day attracted a small audience. The Windflower was not present, but she was back from Stratford in time to come on Monday to tea at Severn House. Elgar was still postponing his visit to Stoke from day to day because of the weather.

21 April 1917. E. & A. after lunch to Theatre, A.S. of W. took tickets for the 'Triple Bill'[.] The 1st Barrie piece *very* touching[,] 2nd rather amusing & the other piece amusing but needed a better ending. E. & A. enjoyed the little change—

22 April . . . To Albert [Hall] Concert with E. after lunch. Delightful Concert & E.'s Serenade from String work [*sic*] *most* beautiful. Quite a demonstration of enthusiasm after it. Very unusual for that audience.   A.S. of W. returned with E. & A. for tea—

23 April. Sunny still cold wind. E. not very well but thought he wd. like to start for Stoke.   A. with him to Paddington 1.40 train [—] he just went into Station but felt he cd. not go on so we returned— Poor Ducksie so disappointed.   . . .

[n.p.]
Monday [23 Apr. 1917] eveng

Alas! My dear W—we packed & got to Paddn. & then I was not well enough to go—so we drove home & here I am with a splitting head & a broken feeling of disappointment. I am *hoping* to go tomorrow Tuesday but can't tell.

>                                    Bless you
>                                    Yrs ever
>                                    E[14]

Two days later he was able to make the journey.

[The Elms, Stoke Prior, Worcestershire]
Thursday [26 Apr. 1917]

My dear W.

Here are a few of your prototypes—I am quite well & arrived in good order; a cuckoo yesterday & a swallow to-day! Juno has not forgotten me & the meeting was more exciting than ever

Write & tell me how *everything* is. I am just off to Worcester: having made a huge bonfire first

>                                    Love
>                                    EE

I want you to help as at Walls[15]

[14] HWRO 705:445:4151.        [15] HWRO 705:445:4026.

The journey to Worcester was to help settle the affairs of his bachelor Uncle Henry, his father's last surviving brother who had died in his rooms in the shadow of the Cathedral in late February.

He returned to Hampstead on 4 May and settled to orchestrating 'The Fourth of August'.

[*postmarked* Hampstead]
Thursday [10 May 1917]
My dear W.

We have thought much of you & your very busy days & hope now that the time of hard work is drawing to a close [—] that you are not too tired & are quite well. I am very busy with my work

Love
EE

Frank has commanded me to the Hut for the week-end, 25th.[16]

But that plan did not materialize. For his own Alice had found what was to become the best of all his country retreats during those years—an isolated cottage with the slightly sinister name 'Brinkwells', together with a disused studio, set in a remote corner of the Stopham Estate in west Sussex near Fittleworth. After rehearsals and the second performance of *The Sanguine Fan* on 22 May, Elgar wrote on the morning of starting to Brinkwells (and as Alice Stuart of Wortley was about to visit Malvern before going once again to Stratford):

[*postmarked* Hampstead]
Thursday [24 May 1917]
My dear W:

I am so glad you saw the ballet—there were *many* shortcomings
We are just starting & this is a temporary farewell[.] We shall be back in ten days or so.
I hope Malvern will be nice.
The Coliseum affair begins on June 11th.

Love
EE[17]

That was a première series of performances of *The Fringes of the Fleet*, with Elgar conducting and the lead baritone part sung by Charles Mott (who had played the Organ Grinder in *The Starlight Express*). But Mott was under threat of imminent conscription. The first letter from Brinkwells was written by Alice Elgar on the second morning there:

[16] HWRO 705:445:4152.          [17] HWRO 705:445:7833.

Brinkwell [*sic*,] Fittleworth[,] Sussex
26 May 1917
My dear Alice

I know you will be thinking of us & I want you to have a few lines before
you start on Monday. I am delighted to tell you that Edward's first
exclamation was 'It is too lovely for words' & he was quite pleased with the
house & has loved every minute since we came—   So you may think how
relieved & pleased I felt. I am in the garden & before my eyes lies a wonderful
deep wood & low hills beyond & then the Downs, larks are singing as there
are some fields as well, & a nightingale is heard sometimes, & in the evening
the nightjars go whirring around on the fringe of the wood—   It is a most
extraordinarily lovely spot. Endless walks & paths in the woods—   There is
also a Carpenter's bench & tools &c & E. has already made me 2 rustic
footstools—   Today Carice is to arrive & I am going in to meet her,—

Here post came, about 10.30! & we are feeling very *damped* hearing Mott
has to join & cannot sing those wonderful songs—

Much love & do love our very own Malverns & if you drive along the Wells
Road give my love to *Craeg Lea* just above the Golf Links.

Yr.aft.
C.Alice Elgar[18]

Back in London on 4 June, Elgar immediately began rehearsing the four baritones
in *The Fringes of the Fleet*. Mott was singing, but was having to drill between times.
Elgar wrote on the morning of the première:

Severn House, 42,Netherhall Gardens, Hampstead, N.W.3
Monday [11 June 1917]
My dear W.

Thanks for your S on A letter, oh! how I wish I could have been there.

To-night at *nine* o'clock the turn comes off—of course this afternoon also
but I am not sure of the time. We did want you yesterday as I had the quartet
to luncheon here. I wanted you but we had Mary Crawshay & Mrs.Ark-
wright [the wife of the Hereford MP] to balance things.

Love
EE[19]

Then she returned to Cheyne Walk unwell.

---

[18] Elgar Birthplace parcel 584 (xx).          [19] HWRO 705:445:4153.

Severn House, 42,Netherhall Gardens, Hampstead, N.W.3
Wedy [13 June 1917]

My dear Windflower:

I was so very, very sorry to hear you were not well—the sun has been too hot: I hope you will soon be all right again. Do send a line to the Theatre (or home) if I may come to you anyday: the Songs go well but I have a continual fear that the drilling will kill Mott! Do let me know *when* you can come: I missed you at the rehearsals and the first performance & always.

Please be well very very quickly

Love
EE[20]

She was able to come to a matinée on 16 June. Afterwards, when she had gone home under thundery skies and he was waiting for the evening performance, he wrote:

The Athenaeum
Saturday [16 June 1917] eveng.

My dear W.

I hope you are home safely[.] I am sitting here with the storm crashing round wildly

How lovely it was this afternoon [—] Like old times & I hope you were amused.

Love
EE[21]

Late in the month a more general attendance was arranged:

28 June 1917. E. to Coliseum in aftn. & then to Cheyne Walk.   A. went by train & E. & she arrived almost at same moment—   Claude there—   Very pleasant dinner & then all to Coliseum. All delighted with Songs, Claude much touched by them, then to E.'s dressing room & heard the part Song [*Inside the Bar*, recently completed to add to *The Fringes of the Fleet*, but not yet published]—*Very* fine & stirring. *Very* nice evening.   ...

5 July ... In evening Alice S. of W. took a box, & Admiral Charles (Beresford) came & Mary Crawshay. All quite delighted.   E. took Lord C. on to the stage & he talked to the Singers & delighted them & then came round & heard the part song—Most pleasant evening.   ...

Elgar wanted to meet the Windflower the following Saturday, but she could not. His next letter enclosed a note of thanks from Lord Beresford (who was now over seventy).

[20] HWRO 705:445:7812. At the end of the main paragraph, the concluding words '& always.' have been eradicated.
[21] HWRO 705:445:4154.

Hampstead
Monday [9 July 1917]
My dear W.

What weather: you threw away your one chance on Saturday—it was fine
& lovely & we might have (for once) dined together. but no!

I send the enclosed letter because you did all the nicest things & made it
possible: you *are* good—  He seems to have been quite happy—alas! the
writing is rather shaky.

Alice wd. like it back.

Again all thanks & love

Yrs ever
EE.[22]

They met on 12 July, and arranged to listen to gramophone records recently made
of *The Fringes of the Fleet*, test copies of which were at Severn House. But it was
not to be.

The Athenaeum, Pall Mall, S.W.1.
Friday [13 July 1917]
My dear W.

This is a sad note to say our party on Sunday is *'off'*[.] We shall have the
records some other day

Frank rang up very pathetically (he is *really* ill I believe) begging me to go,
so I shall go to luncheon on Sunday

Love
it was lovely yesterday
Yrs ever
EE[23]

He stayed the Sunday night at The Hut, and wrote afterwards to send some
snapshots taken at Stoke:

Severn House, 42,Netherhall Gardens, Hampstead, N.W.
July 17: 1917

My dear Windflower:

It seems impossible to meet & I have so much to do: these poor little
pictures came this morng—it all seems so far away. The little pony seems to
be *overfed*—it *is* a sweet place.

The Hut was somewhat sad: Claude, Lionel Holland[,] Mad: V[ander-
velde], myself & Frank: much rain & consequent shutting up in small rooms:
I found sundry pencil records & came home on Monday very tired as I had

[22] HWRO 705:445:4204.        [23] HWRO 705:445:4181.

not slept much—Holland's valet in the next, communicating, room to mine seemed to sneeze or cough all night.

Frank was very dear & kind, but he has really aged a good deal during the last three months or so. Claude & I got off for an hour (or two) while the others were walking & I played(?) much to him of the dear old things. He was most amiable & good.

Mott is free till the end of next week—after that I know not what will happen. I am more distressed than I can say about Sammons—but it is inevitable I fear, unless one has much money.

Let me have my beloved pictures back sometime
                  [*perhaps three words eradicated*]

Yrs
EE[24]

(The violinist Albert Sammons was only the latest distinguished musician to be conscripted.) Alice Elgar's diary states that the Elgars did after all lunch at Cheyne Walk that day.

At the Coliseum, the orchestra of ladies (as men had been called up) gave Elgar a silver inkstand at an onstage tea party after the matinée on 27 July. Both Alices were there. The following night was the last for Mott: his replacement was to be George Parker.

Severn House[,] Hampstead, N.W.
Monday [30 July 1917]

My dear W.

I was so glad to receive your letter: I knew you were puzzled over that silly speech—the point, or want of point of the 'joke' was that the extracts were not about me at all, but few understood this.

Yes, Mott has gone with the rest of the heroes, while those who can afford to pay are let off. Why does not someone, *not* a musician, interfere?

I am glad it is cooler & I stil! feel the effects of the sun

The Songs go to Manchester on the 13th
                  Leicester on the 20th
but I do not think I shall go with them

Love
Yrs ever
EE[25]

(Afterwards he decided to conduct both the provincial weeks.) Later that day, waiting between performances, he found a new book.

[24] HWRO 705:445:4201.          [25] HWRO 705:445:4205.

The Athenaeum
Monday [30 July 1917]
My dear Windflower:

'*The joyful years*' novel by S.T.Warren pubd. Andrew Melrose Ltd[.] I have just picked up this—I cannot tell what the whole thing is about but the early chapters are *all* Tintagel & I loved it in consequence: the book may be drivel for aught I know but the mention of the Old Post Office, the Wharncliffe Arms etc brought back much of 'the joyful years' 'when you were finding yourselves children'*

Yrs ev
EE

*quotation on title[26]

One day in early August, near the end of *The Fringes* run, Alice Stuart of Wortley entertained the four singers and Elgar to tea in a restaurant at 396 The Strand. When the Coliseum performances finished, Elgar spent the week remaining before Manchester at The Elms.

Stoke
Wedy [8 Aug. 1917]
My dear Windflower:

I was so delighted to get your dear letter & to know you are well.
Business first: here is the 'change'—& thank you again for the gracious entertainment of my crew; they were so delighted as you know.
I have no news: everything just as usual: the country silent [—] no birds sing: but it has been lovely; to-day heavy rain: I am looking out trains to Manchester but they are vague & the posts here worse—days seem to go by & no post in or out. I will let you hear further plans

Love
yrs
EE[27]

Stoke
Augt 11: 1917   Midland Hotel Manchester *tomorrow*
My dear W.

I feared I had said little in my note but there was very vague feelings [*sic*] in the air as to my movements owing to my being away—important Coli[seum] letters took days to reach me & only *yesterday* was the engagement *legally* ratified

So I travel on Sunday: a week (as you know) at M. then a week at Leicester

---

[26] HWRO 705:445:4142.     [27] HWRO 705:445:4206.

& after that quite uncertain. Alice is going to Hereford & may go on to Gloucestershire: but our proceedings after Leicester are uncertain but I think it very doubtful if I return to London until Sep: 8th for the Chiswick week [of *The Fringes*]: we shall see.

No news here, except dreary rain—the Colvins say the same—it is terribly depressing & we *have* wasted our lives.

It was good of you to arrange the little feast for my sailors [—] it seems as though that vision of you will have to last for ~~ever~~  a very long time, alas!

> Bless you
> Yrs ever
> E.E.

It is *not* good here: only do not say so. Madge's heart is all wrong & May is working much too hard etc etc[28]

From Manchester he wrote a longer letter, enclosing a leaflet of doggerel verses about the *Fringes* performances by one of the singers, Frederick Henry. Once the Leicester performances were over, the Elgars were looking forward to inviting Algernon Blackwood to Brinkwells (which they had taken for another fortnight).

Midland Hotel, Manchester.
Thursday [16 Aug. 1917] a m

My dear Windflower:

Your letter is most welcome. I have no news [—] all goes well. Very bad orch. & varying audiences

I find nothing to do & the weather has been awfully uncertain. I have had many people to see about winter (proposed) Concerts etc etc & have found my dear Paul Sandby & his fellows at the Whitworth Gall[er]y—a mile distant. So delighted to know yr dear plans. Blackwood *is* back & we are trying to 'rig up' a picnic party at the Sussex Cottage—we shall see how he is engaged

*[twelve to fifteen words eradicated]*

I am glad you 'feel' Stoke—that is a place where I see & *hear* (yes!) you. A. has not been there since *1888* & does not care to go & no one of my friends has ever been but you[.] No one has seen my fields & my 'common' or my trees [—] only the Windflower and I found her namesakes growing there—aborigines I'm sure—real pure sweet forest folk. Bless you. Nice to hear of dear old Lady C. & the Beresfords—I *wish* people cd. be happier, & it *is* kind of you to think of Carice & poor dear old Claude.

I enclose Mr.*Henry's* verses which are really amusing to us who have worked together—I thought I posted them to you two days or so ago. If you already have them you might, dear, send this copy back.

Poor Madge is, I fear[,] really not well, but I have found port & Dried Milk

& everything I cd. think of. May is really overworked & the trains are horribly inconvenient, alas!

My dear love to you[.] I kiss your hands

Yr affec
EE

Mr.Henry's verses are not published [—] only a private amusement.[29]

The same day found Alice Elgar writing of her holiday—a reminiscent journey to Hereford and then through the scenes of her childhood:

29, Castle Street, Hereford.
16 Augt. 1917.

My dear Alice

I have been so occupied even in this ancient city, I take the first moment to write to you. First I am thankful to tell you I have had excellent accounts from Edward, confirmed by a nice letter from Mr.Henry & E. tells me all goes well—You may think how strange it seems to be here without him & I have been longing for him to be here & see some of the lovely places—He wd. be distressed however to see what looks like a large mining village just below & opposite Plâs Gwyn, all that part wd. now be impossible to live in. Plâs Gwyn looks so charming, I did not go in, I thought I wd. rather keep the picture of the interior in my mind as it was—

I have seen such numbers of old friends & it has been so touching to have such warm welcomes—Today I am to go on to

Hasfield Court
Gloucester

till probably Wednesday, & tomorrow I am to be taken over to Redmarley & it is most thrilling to think of seeing my old home which I love so much.

I do hope you are all well, it has been very stormy & thundery but looks better now.

We motored yesterday to Madley, the most beautiful Church. Edward was constantly going to see it, did we go there when you were with us?

Hereford misses Dr.Sinclair terribly, & meanwhile Mr.Hull [the assistant organist, now interned in Germany] is still in captivity—

Vandals, the 6 great Elms in the [Hereford Cathedral] Close have been cut down—

My love dear Alice

Yr aft.
C. Alice Elgar[30]

Alice Elgar returned to Hampstead on 25 August, and Edward came from Leicester next day. They went to Brinkwells on the 29th, to have as much time there as possible before the next engagements to conduct *The Fringes of the Fleet*—at Chiswick and at

[29] HWRO 705:445:7681.        [30] Elgar Birthplace parcel 584 (xiiL).

Chatham. At Brinkwells they were not able to entertain Blackwood then, but one day they went over to Tillington to visit the Colvins (who had taken E. V. Lucas's house there for a holiday).

Brinkwells
Sep 5: Wedy.

My dear W:

I was so glad to receive your letter & to know you had a nice walk last Tuesday [—] so long, long ago! I have no news of anything. It is lovely here but I am tired of lovely vistas which end in nothing. We return on Saturday night as I must have Sunday to prepare for Chiswick Empire.

We went over to see the Colvins on Monday & I found them well & rejoicing in the weather, which has become good at last[.] They are in a highly civilised (*residential* I shd. think) village, quite lovely for them but I shd. die of it—here we are *quite* wild & free. I *wish* you were here. Your abode, (whether cottage, house, palace or abbey I know not), I hope is a happy one for you. Please enjoy it all you can & come back well.

Love
EE[31]

For she had been suffering from a form of influenza.

After the Elgars' return to London for the week at Chiswick, he began to feel ill from giddiness. The Chiswick audiences were very appreciative, but the week finished on Saturday afternoon with a message for them all to go straight to the Coliseum to give *The Fringes* that night. Meanwhile Rudyard Kipling, the author of the words, was threatening to withdraw permission for any further performances—without giving any clear reason. Elgar wrote during the week intervening between Chiswick and the further engagement at Chatham:

[n.p.]
Tuesday   Sp 18: 1917

My dear W:

Your letter has just come & finds me better & on the pt. of writing—   I have been *very* unwell all the week & sadly worried about *everything*. I 'got thro'' the Chiswick week but had to be taken down & brought back [to Hampstead] every evening—I mean *convoyed* as I was so giddy. This morning I feel better for the first time—   Next week Chatham. I fear the Songs are doomed by R.K. [—] he is perfectly stupid in his attitude. I recd. the Ballads with great joy—but have been unable to read them—or *anything* for a week[:] head gone quite giddy alas!

Yes: everything good & nice & clean & fresh & sweet is far away—never to return.

I feel that [ *a name erased so heavily it has holed the paper*] is really enjoying himself with the Germans—he is found out at last.

[31] HWRO 705:445:7675.

I quite agree with you about the description of the man in the book: you shd. write to the author—he confuses *pianists* with musicians—you see the only *musicians*, artists & lit[erar]y men meet are the wretched piano-mongers who infest Studios.

I cannot get to Stoke this time but am going to Frank at the Hut for two days: the 2 Miss Springs are there & someone unknown who, as he says on the telephone this morng, arrived yesterday—one of his feeblest jokes

Percy A[nderson] & Sidney C[olvin] were here on Sunday—otherwise I have had the dullest time possible. I will *tell* you, too long to write—about our wild expedition—the crew & Alice & me—from Chiswick on Saturday night to the Coliseum—Mrs Pat Campbell suddenly ill & they begged me to go & give the songs

I kiss your hands

Love<br>EE[32]

The Chatham performances were to begin on Monday 24 September. No sooner had the Elgars arrived and gone to the theatre for an afternoon rehearsal, than all the lights went out because of an air raid on the Navy installations there. Next day he wrote:

Chatham
Tuesday [25 Sept. 1917]

My dear W—

I was delighted to have your letter.

Alice & I are here—no performance last night—terrible gun firing—raid etc etc [:] they expect one every night

I am not well as the place is so noisy & I do not sleep—the guns are the quietest things here. I long for the country & Stoke. I think all the time of it—& you—I have been thinking also so much of our lost festivals—no more music

Do not write here—we return on Sunday & then, I trust[,] Stoke.

Love<br>Yrs ever<br>EE[33]

Two days later Alice Elgar wrote:

[32] HWRO 705:445:7679. The pianist enjoying himself with the Germans was probably Eugène d'Albert, born in Glasgow in 1864 of a Franco-German father and an English mother. D'Albert had his earliest training in Britain, but soon went to Vienna and Germany, where he lived for many years—but kept his British passport until the First World War.
[33] HWRO 705:445:7680.

Sun Hotel[,] Chatham
27 Sept. 1917

My dear Alice

I must send a little line to say I hope you have had a nice change & are all well. We are *not* enjoying Chatham, what a place! Last evening however, 'The Fringes' were actually performed & recd. with wild enthusiasm, more than ever, but you may think it has been rather like a nightmare to be here since early Monday & a raid each evening so *no* performance cd take place— utter darkness prevailing. The Monday evening raid lasted longest, E. had gone up to the Theatre *close* by, & well protected—I had a wonderful glimpse of star shells &c, & was very thankful to see him back safe when it was over. The next evg. it did not last so long, & E. came back while firing &c was going on— *Crowds* in the streets not minding at all & on Monday evg. at the picture Palace wh. E. has to pass through on his way, they were sitting there & singing Land of Hope & Glory in all the firing, joining in Chorus—rather fine & touching. We had a very nice day at Canterbury yesterday & thought much of that wonderful day of The Apostles [in June 1914], it was such a delightful escape from this—

> With love
> Yr aft
> C. Alice Elgar[34]

Some performances were possible late in the week, but on Saturday there were air raids on both Chatham and London. The Elgars' journey home was long and difficult, and they arrived back at Hampstead very late at night exhausted.

He agreed to conduct another week of *The Fringes of the Fleet* at the Coliseum. Before that, he wanted Stoke. An air raid prevented his going on 2 October. He went next day, and wrote the day after that:

Stoke
Thursday [4 Oct. 1917]

My dear Windflower:

I am safely here in pouring rain which I don't mind: I had a good rest in the train & wonderful! began smoking a pipe again which is a mercy: so soothing to the nerves. I do hope you are safe & well, I hope this weather will stop the raids

I have just 'signed on' for the Coliseum next week so I [*red smudge*]ˣ hope to return on Sunday night & find you well & gay next week.

Juno is quite well & gave me the warmest welcome.

It is sad to see the tons of fruit wasting, alas!

---

[34] Elgar Birthplace parcel 584 (xxiii).

I was going to save the best apples but now comes the rain.
I see someone amongst the trees & reach out but——nothing

> Bless you
> d.o.m.d.
> Yr
> EE.

<sup>x</sup> I am so sorry for this red mark: it is from my stamp
GLYN & Co.
A/C SIR E. W. ELGAR. !<sup>35</sup>

Alice Stuart of Wortley sent a box of clothes to the family at The Elms. Elgar responded:

Stoke
Saturday [6 Oct. 1917]
My dear Windflower:

Oh! how cd. you send so much: the merest trifles wd. have given these dear children pleasure & now they are *distracted* with joy. The opening of the box reminded me of the 1st Sc. in the *Starlight* [*Express*]: such joy & wonder—you would have loved to have seen it all. I send this with heartfelt thanks—but I may see you before this reaches you & bless you bless you for what you have done—May was in Birmn. & in the middle of the excitement of unpacking the box the lamp burst! I kiss your hands: d o m d.

> Yrs
> EE<sup>36</sup>

He returned to Hampstead on Sunday, to begin the week of Coliseum performances next day. The Windflower probably attended one of the Tuesday performances, for on the day after that he wrote (enclosing an appreciative letter from Stoke):

The Athenaeum
Wedy [10 Oct. 1917] eveng
My dear W.

Yes: it was really good yesterday
I enclose the letter—dear children[.] You *have* given them happiness. Bless you

> Love
> EE<sup>37</sup>

When the latest Coliseum week was over, he went to The Hut for several days. In London one day the two Alices lunched and went to a '*dreadfully* foolish & empty play'. Then Alice Elgar joined her husband for the weekend at The Hut.

<sup>35</sup> HWRO 705:445:4124. In the final paragraph 'one' (in 'someone') and 'nothing' have been eradicated, as have the stops after initials in the closing.
<sup>36</sup> HWRO 705:445:7820.
<sup>37</sup> HWRO 705:445:4110.

At the end of the month the Elgars went to Leeds for the first performances of the completed *Spirit of England*. There is an envelope postmarked from Leeds 30 October and addressed by Alice Elgar to The Lady Stuart of Wortley[38], but its letter is lost. The Leeds performance, including the première of 'The Fourth of August', took place on 31 October despite loss of voice by the tenor soloist, Gervase Elwes. Elgar wrote next day:

Queen's Hotel, Leeds.
Nov 1 1917
My dear W.

It was lovely to have a word in this desert—for so it was, in spite of the warm kindness of our friends[.] The North never is part of me & it is only the sweetest of memories that hold it to me. Your news of [*three or four words erased, holing the paper*] familiar names, made me very homesick [—] or rather longing for the old days.

We live in a nightmare in this hotel—nothing ever comes! meals arrive anyhow—at anytime except the hour for which they are ordered. A *very* fine chorus & *fine* orch.—& then!—dear Elwes cd. not sing—suddenly failed—no time to find a substitute—so after all—he just came on to the platform & *whispered* a few phrases & spoke it: just like praying—

I did not mind, but it is too dreadful for these dear people who have worked so hard. I do not know when I shall come back as I *may* go to Stoke if the trains serve [—] I have nothing to come back to

Love
yrs ev
EE

Miss Barclay's book, for which thanks, is too awful—amazing rubbish. Thanks also for the dear telegram[39]

After a second performance at Huddersfield, the Elgars returned home. Soon the Windflower had the briefest note:

Queens Hotel, Birmingham. Passing through
Wedy [7 Nov. 1917]
My dear W.

I am really on my way to Stoke

Yrs
EE[40]

He stayed ten days at The Elms. During his absence his own Alice attended a Wigmore Hall recital by the young violinist Louis Godowsky, which included the entire Elgar Concerto with piano: she told Alice Stuart of Wortley about it when they lunched next day. The Windflower was not very well.

[38] Elgar Birthplace.          [39] HWRO 705:445:4185.          [40] HWRO 705:445:4186.

Stoke
Friday [16 Nov. 1917]

My dear W.

I was so glad to get your letter & the enclosure, which I now return; but I am sad to think of you having a 'sight' of influenza again: please take care. I shall be home very soon now as I have a silly chorus rehearsal [for the London première of 'The Fourth of August'] on Monday evening—alas!

So glad you are seeing Frank—Alice writes of THE Vn. concerto & said the boy played well.

I have no news but many thoughts. Lovely day here & I hope with you also

Love
EE       P.T.O.

P.S.   Thanks for the Punch. I asked May [Grafton] to send you a little bread—local & amusing I think but you may not like it. Bless you.[41]

He returned on Sunday 18 November. But giddy illness prevented his taking the Monday choral rehearsal; instead 'A.S.of W. to tea & talk to him'. On the 22nd she came again and took him out for a short walk. Next day he was just able to take the orchestral rehearsal for *The Spirit of England* at the Albert Hall with the two Alices in attendance. Both Alice and Charles Stuart of Wortley were in the large party of friends filling two boxes for the performance on Saturday afternoon 24 November.[42] The day after that they came to Sunday tea at Severn House, where the two men talked 'much of topography'.

The last week in November was filled with what would be a final series of *The Fringes of the Fleet*—because Kipling now succeeded in having them stopped.

The Athenaeum, Pall Mall, S.W.1.
Tuesday [27 Nov. 1917] eveng

My dear W.

I am not very well alas! It was lovely to see you on Sunday.

Are you coming to the Fringes—the *funeral* this week. so sad. Perhaps you will have tea—I have *such* a nice sitting room at the Colis: I kiss your hands

Yrs ev
EE[43]

Perhaps she came once more. She did come to Sunday tea on 2 December in very cold weather; but that is the last record of her in Alice Elgar's fragmentary diary for December 1917—a month of air raids by the new German Gotha bombers. Elgar was ill again. Sir Maurice Abbot Anderson prescribed new medicines and ordered rest. Alice Stuart of Wortley wrote from Bowerswell, Perth, where she had gone for the Christmas holidays. He responded:

[41] HWRO 705:445:4199. Alice Stuart of Wortley pencilled the correct date, but Clare made a rare error in changing it to 9 November. The Godowsky concert took place on 14 Nov. and Elgar's choral rehearsal was scheduled for the 19th.
[42] Alice Elgar's diary says only 'A.S. of W.', but Elgar's letter of 25 November to Frank Schuster mentions 'the Wortleys' among the friends who attended (HWRO 705:445:7017).
[43] HWRO 705:445:4187.

[n.p.]
Sunday [23 Dec. 1917]
My dear Windflower:

Your dearest letter arrd. yesterday evening. I cannot tell you how glad I am to know that you are safe. Bless you! It *was* a dreadful evening for you to be out—the damage appears to have been unworthy of the means as usual—I found a heavy piece of shell case & two smaller pieces in our garden, either one enough to end a passenger.

I am just the same alas! But I have stopped *all* medicine & take long walks, *lonely*. I went up to Judge's Walk—& people are skating on the pond—I did not [*word or two heavily eradicated*] down the road—[*perhaps ten words eradicated*]

All good wishes, Keep well & warm [*perhaps five words eradicated*]

Love<br>EE[44]

He continued ill. On the morning of 29 December Sir Maurice brought in a consulting internist, who pronounced: '*no* organic trouble'. Alice Elgar wrote:

Severn House, Hampstead, N.W.3
29 Dec. 1917.

My dear Alice

*How* dear & kind of you to send those splendid looking pheasants, arrived today—  They are so appreciated & will make such a nice change for E—

It was dear & sweet of you to send them[.] Also the Shortbread which is a great feature at aftn. tea—

How lovely the p.cards are—  I hope you are not the worse for the Cold—& am frightened at the idea of your ski-ing, it must be so difficult—  Mind & come home safe. We shall be delighted to see you again—

The Dr. promises improvement. E. is down again this aftn. & I trust will be feeling better very soon—

With much love dear Alice

Yr aft<br>C.A.Elgar

To this Elgar added his own note:

P.S.—The Doctors say nothing the matter: but I am not well.

Love<br>E.[45]

---

[44] HWRO 705:445:4198.          [45] Elgar Birthplace parcel 583(xvi).

The winter was wretched for Elgar. The Windflower came several times to take him out for short walks. But when the Elgars tried to go to Cheyne Walk to Sunday lunch on 20 January, he felt so unwell that they had to turn back. He was able to lunch there on the 30th, but came back feeling 'very unwell again & disappointed'.

In February came the anniversary of the windflower theme.

[n.p.]
Feb:6:1918

My dear W.

I hope posts will be good & bring you this on the 7th. *All good wishes & love*

We may hear of you tomorrow on the telephone but there's much silence

EE[1]

7 February 1918. E. very tired & on sofa all day. A.S. of W. to tea—Lovely mild day & evening. Alice brought a lovely flying butterfly, Japanese—

They tried theatres:

16 February. E. & A. lunched at home & met A.S. of W. at Theatre for Pinero's play, 'The Freaks'[.] Enjoyed it & were interested but it is a *very* poor play—& the 2 worldly characters so farcical & exaggerated.
Raid in Evening. Only 1 Gotha got through but it dropped bomb on house by Chelsea Hospital & buried the poor people in it—horrible— ...

23 February. E. & A. to lunch with Alice S.ofW. at Pall Mall Restaurant & then to Apollo Theatre to see 'Within the Lines'. Most delightful play[.] Most thrilling & amusing. Such English *Gentlemen* in it & a delightful old American[.] We did enjoy ourselves—E. not feeling well—alas ...

27 February. E. not very well. E. & A. to lunch at the Cavour. Met Alice S.ofW. there & then to the Old Vic. School for Scandal a most entrancing play, *very* well given—Ben Greet admirable as Sir Peter—E. delighted—a wonderful play—E. not well all the time alas—

Early in March another consultant said that his tonsils were infected and ought to be removed. He decided it was worth trying. But the Elgars had already planned a Sunday musical afternoon at Severn House on the 10th with W. H. Reed's string quartet. They went through with it, and the Stuarts of Wortley were among the large party of guests. Two days later he wrote:

[1] HWRO 705:445:7125.

Severn House[,] Hampstead, N.W.
March 12 1918

My dear W.

It was nice to see you here on Sunday.

I am going on Thursday, I can't say where, but do not write[x] until you hear please.

I wonder if your nephew cd. do anything for mine.

　　　Signaller Gerald Grafton　　Mess 49　　H.M.S.Actaeon

He joined the R.N.V.R. two years ago & wants a commission which he well deserves: he is bank cashier & asst. manager & of course should be in the *pay* dept

I hope to see you soon again

　　　　　　　　　　　　　　　　　　　　　　　　Yours ever
　　　　　　　　　　　　　　　　　　　　　　　　EE

[x] I mean *after* Thursday[2]

The operation took place three days later in a Dorset Square nursing home. Convalescence was slow and at first very painful. Alice Stuart of Wortley visited twice during his week in the nursing home. He went home to Severn House on 22 March, and three days later began sketching a string quartet in E minor.

26 March. E. felt better early— Tried to go into town with A. but not well enough & returned— A.S.ofW. in aftn & to tea—*Very* hopeful about Gerald getting a commission[:] do hope & trust he may— E. writing music all day—Lovely exciting things. Very anxious days, fearful numbers of Germans— Our men so splendid.

The Windflower went westward for a holiday—to Dorset, with the possibility of Tintagel after. Looking for her return, Edward sent to Cheyne Walk a letter written on the typewriter:

Severn House, 42,Netherhall Gardens, Hampstead, N.W.3.
Wednesday Ap:[3]:1918

My dear W.,

I am hammering away at fearsome business letters on this machine and, for the first time I think, I venture to send you a printed word. We are wondering where you are and how you are, as we heard nothing for, it seems, a long, long time: Sherborne was reported and a lovely little cheese arrived and was sacrificed to the goddess who provided the offering.

The weather has been cold and ungenial but A. and I have been experimenting in luncheons in town to try to acclimatise me: it is weary work

[2] HWRO 705:445:7124. Alice Stuart of Wortley's nephew in the Navy was the future Admiral Sir William James.

but I think I am better on the whole. We lunched at Canuto's (Saturday) at Cavour's (Monday) and at Scott's (Tuesday) and I have borne it moderately well. I have now proposed myself to Frank for a space in pursuance of his very kind plan. But you will be home before I, or we, leave I hope: anyway we shall hear of you soon.                                    Everyours E.Ep[*sic*]

He added in his own hand:

This does not look right, does it — so I add

                                                                   Love,
                                                                   EE[3]

Then came a letter from Tintagel. He answered at once:

Severn House[,] Hampstead, N.W.
Thursday [4 Apr. 1918]
My dear W:

   Your welcome letter came this morning: I was quite wondering what had become of you & sent a (*type!*) letter to Chelsea—which I hope you will get in due course.
   I wish it would be warmer for you but the air must be reviving & the quiet.
   Here all is as usual—I *think* I am a little better but it is not much[.] A. & I go out to lunch everyday to some restaurant for practice.
   Poor dear Lan is ill again—but better today
   Please take care of submarines—those awful spies—they must be English I fear.
   I have offered myself to Frank in pursuance of his kind plan but I don't know *when* he can, or will have me. I wanted to go to Stoke b[ut] it seems to quite upset A. & it is really too far for a first attempt.
   I remember *all* of Tintagel

                                                                   Yrs ever
                                                                   EE[4]

Severn House, Hampstead, N.W.
Friday [5 Apr. 1918]
My dear W

   This is only to say that Gerald was sent for by his captain who told him he had heard from the Admiralty etc[.] He has to send for 'credentials' from the bank so the future depends on himself I suppose.

[3] HWRO 705:445:7123. Elgar's date was 'Ap:4'. Wednesday the 3rd is correct, since the postmark is '3 APR 18'.
[4] HWRO 705:445:7122. In the sixth paragraph, last sentence, Elgar wrote 'by'.

I do not know *how* to thank you for doing all you did—it was too good of you—

I felt the injustice of the position ACUTELY & now that the boy has a *chance* to move (he was buried before) that is all that is wanted

Bless you
Yrs ever
EE[5]

Next day he sent her a new E minor theme in 9/8, written out for piano & inscribed:

'    ?    '

arranged for a special pianist
a thank offering to a good Windflower
from Edward Elgar    March 1918

Severn House, Hampstead, N.W.
Saturday [6 Apr. 1918]

My dear W.

It has been a pleasure to try & write this out for your own, very own, use. I have no nice paper & I write badly but you can make me it out

Love
EE[6]

This music was soon to emerge as the principal first-movement subject of the Cello Concerto.

Then she returned—a difficult journey as it turned out.

Severn House[,] Hampstead, N.W.
Thursday [11 Apr. 1918]

My dear Windflower

I was so distressed to hear of your entanglements with—or rather *without* luggage etc & hope all is well & that you were not worried beyond endurance. Thanks for the telegram also. It was wrong of me to put that inscription on the poor little M.S.—*all* is yours not only that bit. I have written the continuation now—which is strange & *good*—it drove poor dear Claude to tears—I played it to him at Mrs J[oshua]'s yesterday. I have been *very* unwell again but was better yesterday & we went to lunch. Today I am not so well & tomorrow, Friday, Alice & I go to Frank's; A. for the week-end & I, if well enough, stay on.

I hope you are well & that Clare is also.

Forgive a dull note

Yrs ever
EE[7]

[5] HWRO 705:445:7121.    [6] Elgar Birthplace MS 36.    [7] HWRO 705:445:7112.

He spent a fortnight at The Hut, returning to Hampstead on 25 April. Next day Elgar wrote in the diary he kept for himself in 1918:

26 April . . . A.S.W. to tea—played E minor things [—] Sad.

On the last day of April he managed to take himself to Cheyne Walk to tea.

Then it was time to go to Brinkwells—this time for a stay of several months. Elgar wrote in his diary:

2 May 1918. to Brinkwells. A.S.W. angelically met E. at Vic[toria Station]: lunch there. Alice came by car. Carice from office—left comfortably at 1.36. Alice drove from F[ittle]worth sta. to Cottage. Carice & I walked. Lovely but quite cold . . .

Carice had to return to London the following afternoon, and Elgar sent a typewritten letter with her:

Brinkwells
FRIDAY [3 May 1918]

My dear W.,

Forgive this machine but we have no INK! the goods have come from Petworth & the ink is omitted so I feverishly dash off this for Carice to post in London as under the latest regulations this is a two-day post; please remember this. We arrived all safely & I walked up to this really divine country place; I am not well and feel desperate about getting better but we must hope: it was so sweet of you to see me through that luncheon and afterwards: it made our departure a human thing. I will write properly soon. It is dreary for Carice to return to town but she sticks to duty; we had a walk in the heavenly woods and I killed one of your friends, [a snake] length 2 ft 2 in. ! !

> Bless you
> E.E.[8]

He was soon busy at carpentering, making rough footstools and the like. Then Alice Stuart of Wortley's next letter reminded him that he had asked her to shop for a compass, to aid his walks in the woods.

Brinkwells
Tuesday [7 May 1918]

My dear Windflower:

Your letter cheers a very wet day: the woods are too lovely & full of birds (nightingales!) and flowers—many of your namesakes still here but rather too sunburnt to send or you shd have some—the bluebells & primroses all are in gorgeous profusion.

[8] HWRO 705:445:7113.

Thanks: for all your account of [*illegible*] & of yourself: I think over all 3 the nice London places but I try to *be* here for a time in hopes that I may get better—no signs of this yet, alas! Thank you for thinking of the compass but you must not go to any trouble over it. You will be amused to hear that I get Beer here in 'plural quantities' as O.Henry says—it seems strange after the difficulties in London.

We are settling down & I have done some wonderful amounts of work in the carpentering line.

We expect you!

It is really *very* comfortable here & the food plain but excellent, of which I eat hugely.

It is lovely to hear the birds—nightingales abound & their song is really the most lovely thing in nature. Except one other thing which had a lovely tea in the Strand.

Yr<br>EE[9]

Saturday 11 May found Edward cleaning a sundial for installation at Brinkwells. That afternoon Alice went to Fittleworth for the post, and brought back a packet which contained the compass. It helped him place the sundial next day: for a visit from the Windflower was in prospect.

Brinkwells
Sunday [12 May 1918]

My dear Windflower:

The lovely little pocket compass arrived yesterday—or rather was fetched from the post or it wd. not have reached us until Monday 11.30—posts are extraordinary here! I send you thousands of thanks for it but you *must* let me pay—that was the bargain over our little lunch I think—anyhow bless you. I immediately made use of it & fixed the sundial—I found a very nice gnomon here so mounted it — found N. S. E & W. by your compass: it is the neatest & sweetest thing.

Today it is quite cold & raining hard but we have had two or three *lovely* days—on Friday walked to Pulborough & had lunch at the little hotel [The Swan]: *we* must do this. We are settling down & seem to have been away *years*, when I think of you, but when I look round here it seems as though we have only lived in it a moment. There has been much rearrangement of furniture to be done etc etc. I rise about *seven* [—] work till 8.15—then dress[.] Breakfast—pipe (I SMOKE again all day!) work till 12-30[:] lunch (pipe)—rest an hour—work till tea (pipe)—then work till 7.30—change [—] dinner at 8. bed at 10—every day practically goes thus—of course instead of work, which means carpentering of the roughest kind, sawing wood, repairing furniture etc etc *and* weeding, we go lovely walks—the loveliest walks really—The woods are full of flowers, wonderful—some anemones still left but just leaving us for a year, bluebells & primroses etc

It is lovely to know you are coming: I hope the weather will be kind: we will order the pony for you & I shall be at the station of course & it may be that you would like to walk up, at least some of the way. The train we came by is good [—] 1.36 [—] but *earlier* if you like it better. The only thing to remember is that it is difficult to alter the pony arrgts. for conveyance as he—it—is in request—I am looking forward to your coming with acute joy: it really is lovely here—food good & plentiful—*much beer!*—but do *not mention it.*

We have not been able to see the Colvins yet[:] it really is a difficult thing to arrange under the circumstances of travel.

Love
Yr affc
EE[10]

Then she was not well, and the visit was put off to the last week of May. What supplies or provisions could she bring?

Brinkwells
Friday May 17: 1918
My dear W.

Your letter gave great joy & sadness too for I hoped you were quite well as this lovely weather intends you (& all of us) to be: please be quite well & come here & rest. It is divine just now but I fear the flowers will have vanished, the primroses will have gone but the woods are still carpeted with bluebells—but the heavy rain of three days ago tried them severely and they looked rather faded: I have been down the wood & told them YOU are coming & asked them to remain for your loved visit.

No news: it is now very hot but there is shade. I say no more now but will tell you all when we meet. Gerald sent some more fish which arrived rather *tired*—he had still no news of his promotion so it hangs fire.

We get on well with the provisions generally: you need bring *very little* of anything *but* if quite convenient some dry biscuits *might* be a joy— as the stock in these villages (& towns, e.g. Petworth) has run out for days: but the thing is to bring yourself. & rest: there will be a full moon & all lovely & nightingales

Love
EE[11]

That day saw the arrival of their first Brinkwells guest, Lalla Vandervelde: she stayed four days. Next was to be Alice Stuart of Wortley. Alice Elgar wrote:

[10] HWRO 705:445:7694.    [11] HWRO 705:445:7699.

24 May. Very cold early, feared it might be miserably cold for Alice S.of W—
Day improved & grew sunny & warm. E. with Mr. Aylwin [the farmer who
owned the pony and cart] to station & met Alice S.of W.  . . . Alice delighted
with everythng. enjoying herself like a baby child—

25 May. Lovely warm day. A. & A.S.of W. went up to the Farm, view quite
wonderful . . . E. & A.S.of W. for walk in woods, A. to Fittleworth for post &
paper . . .

26 May. Grey & windy—& cool . . . E. A. & A.S.of W. walked to Stopham
[in evening] . . .

27 May . . . Bright & hot again—   E. very busy clearing out opposite gate—
We wished to take down old wire netting. A.S.of W. worked quite hard
helping. E. & she to Bedham, strange trees & Bignor Common after tea & A.
to Fittleworth for post—

28 May. Lovely day again. E. busy opposite gate. After lunch A.S.of W. left
[—] Mr.Aylwin took her in pony carriage,   As she got in she sd. to A. 'You
have an ideal place', at which he said, 'It is we who are blest having so many
titled ladies come (or come to live?) amongst us'! . . .

   During her visit the news had come that Charles Mott had died of wounds in
France. That saddest of topics no doubt found its place in their conversations. But the
life of the country went on, tended by Farmer Aylwin and rustics like Mark Holden.


Brinkwells
Friday [31 May 1918]

My dear Windflower:

   All goes on as usual but you are missed
   The young birds are coming out & eggs hatching: it is very fine, cloudless &
warm, & the flowers blaze themselves out in a day; so soon over alas!
   Mark goes on gardening & we have taken down, this morning, the whole
of the wire to which you objected. The besom is still in working order but I
have not used it, or anything much for it is really hot & I cannot work so well
alone! I fear your journey was tiresome but you will make it all again soon

Love<br>EE[12]


   On 7 June Carice came for a long weekend. Alice Stuart of Wortley had met her at
Victoria and loaded her with choice foods for Brinkwells—lobster, plaice, dates,
chocolate, biscuits, jam, and teas. Next day Alice Elgar wrote:

---

[12] HWRO 705:445:7135.

Brinkwells
8 June 1918
My dear Alice

Carice arrived all safely, but, dear Alice, you really are too good sending such lovely things, thank you very much but you really should not have thought of so much. The jam is hailed with real joy! & will be most valuable, & the delicious dates & Chocolate, & supply of tea & biscts. but those you really are too spoiling to send.

E. so enjoyed some of that gigantic Lobster—says it is the best he ever tasted.

It is a *wonderful* day [—] the views & colours perfectly exquisite[.] I wish I cd. take you through a hayfield C. & I have just been in, it is a glory of colour. Edward has not been so *very* grand just lately but loves it all more than ever—he has made two delightful tables, one of which adorns the guest room & the other the Studio.

Mrs Hewitt [the cook] has been rather ill & I was expecting Grace [a parlour maid from Severn House] back again but today have just had a telegram to say she cannot get through today, it is from Victoria, poor thing[:] I suppose it was impossible to get into the train at all [due to wartime crowding].

Carice is enjoying herself & looking forward to a week again soon—

What a mercy to have better news—  Do write & tell us about yr.self & the outer world, if anything nice may happen in it—  Much love & warmest thanks for all yr. sweet kind thoughts

> Yr.
> C:A:Elgar[13]

At Edward's request the Windflower sent down a carpentering plane—but it was small. There was also talk of fishing tackle.


Brinkwells
Monday [17 June 1918]
My dear Windflower:

We have been having thunder & rain etc & intense heat between but it is still lovely. I miss you & wanted your learned 'instruction' in fishing. I have a permit & on Saturday for the first time went to the pond & landed two trouts! We ate them for dinner—or rather *at* dinner—although one was quite a good sized fish. I did not like to say anything about tackle to you so I have sent to the A[rmy] & N[avy] Stores & I know what they send will be dull!

I fear the plane must stay here—because they will say it's 2nd.hand &

[13] HWRO 705:445:7904.

charge the Windflower too much. So I keep it for the most delicate work. I want you to come & explore (for fish) the *two* rivers for which I hold Permits

Love
Yrs ever
EE.[14]

She asked whether she could send some special fishing flies.

Brinkwells
Sunday [23 June 1918]
My dear W.

Your letter came yesterday & was truly welcome. Do not think of me in connection with '*flies*': there seems to be no fly fishing so I 'dangle' baits & it is a very good slow & sedate occupation. The pool is full of trout—I caught a nice one & came home: I fear it[']s food more than sport.

Alice wants you to come again & SO DO I—as soon as you can: we can then fish. I think I have everything now for this rough fishing but if you saw a cheap Knife *with scissors* (fisherman's) I shd. like it but I *must pay* for it. I wd. not mention it but all my men friends are gone & there is no list to be had to order from, a bit of fine *tying* silk & some *india rubber* float caps wd. be a joy but I have 'substitutes' which do for everything except Windflowers for which no substitutes are to be had.

It is quite full-blown summer now but a cold wind still.

Gerald has been very ill—pneumonia [—] but is getting all right again—I enclose his letter so you will see what he says about the commission—please tear it up.

I will not tell you how lovely it is here—better than ever. Lan wrote about his delight at your luncheon—poor dear, I fear he is very very delicate, he will come here in July but I *dread* his 'delicate' ways & I think our living etc wd. shock him!

Come soon

Love
EE

The plane is too lovely for words but *delicate*. I love it.[15]

Then a box of tools and tackle arrived.

Brinkwells
July 1:
My dear Windflower:

Yes, the nice things came quite safely all too dainty (as usual) & want a lot of getting used to like other things but the knife is really useful. I must please pay for them—silk & float caps

[14] HWRO 705:445:7134.     [15] HWRO 705:445:7132.

I am glad to have your cutting about [Henry] Ainley: I do hope he's settled *quietly* & peacefully this time

Do come again—soon—it need not be a 'week-end' [—] a middle does as well: it is divine here now—high-summer, rich full & perfect—birds gradually silencing & flowers overblown but the trees & woods generally are *fleecy* & soothing: everything requires refreshment including E.E.—the others want rain.

A. & I walked to Petworth *and* back on Saturday & none the worse for it— No not Petworth—Tillington    a mile further I mean—we had tea (& talk) with the Colvins: he is rather a weakling alas! You *must* get over to them when you come next week(?)

> Bless you
> Yr
> EE[16]

But the Windflower was again at Stratford. Lalla Vandervelde returned, weary from war work for Belgian charities. And they hoped for a visit from Algernon Blackwood.

Brinkwells
Sunday [14 July 1918]
My dear Windflower:

I have not written as we hoped you wd. be sending to Alice.

It was thrilling to receive a letter from Stratford, I remember *everything* there so well & feel I like you to be in the dear old place only I shd. like to be there too, & in summer weather, how divine it wd. be.

The fishing tackle is *really* all right & it is a shame to tease you about its being, as usual, too delicate

No fish lately. The poem is really sweet & wonderfully true: the weather is very rainy & we are today in thick mist.

Mad:Vandervelde has been here to rest: she has been very ill indeed & a week at the Hut made her worse if anything. So Alice thought a real rest wd. do her good: it did but she was lying about here all day and rather(!) incommoded us; but A. & I have been feeling that it is selfish of us to have this lovely place all to ourselves & want to be useful in repairing broken nerves. That comes to you: when are *you* going to visit or revisit these haunts of ancient peace? I suppose it is difficult but I hope & hope not impossible.

Blackwood is in England & *may* (very remote chance) come—he is too busy & has a new apptmt offered him: Troyte has really got something (Air Force) at Norwich & has fled thither: we offered the Stoke people [i.e., Pollie Grafton's family] quarters but they want the sea for the poor little one [Madge] so we seem fated to be selfish & have no one: so you see it is an added duty to your coming—that is to prevent us being selfish. I have had a

[16] HWRO 705:445:7695.

long letter from Percy A. who is much better. Poor Frank, you will have heard, had a great shock: his two garden boys accidentally *drowned*[:] they were *'larking'* in the dinghy [—] of course against orders—also his new little car was smashed between a bus & a tram-car! I kiss your hands, dear Windflower, & am yrs ever

EE[17]

Blackwood was able to get down for a single night.

The end of July found Elgar cleaning the garden studio—whitewashing it, building steps to its door, and clearing out its view through the wild garden to see over the Downs to Chanctonbury Ring. The beginning of August saw preparations for Alice Stuart of Wortley's second visit to Brinkwells.

Her journey was fixed for the afternoon of 3 August. But she—wanting to be fresh on arrival—secretly took the 10.10 train from Victoria, lunched and rested at the Swan Hotel, and was at the station at her very best when Farmer Aylwin drove up to meet her at 3.55. Elgar wrote in his diary of the following day:

4 August 1918. Soissons [retaken by the Allies.] Fine in mg then dull & hot[.] A.S.W. & E. walk to Hardman's. River—Brickfield[.] Heavy rain in night

He gave her a tray he had made from Brinkwells wood. Then Alice Elgar wrote:

5 August. Very wet & stormy. E. & A S of W. to river later—

6 August. Stormy & wonderful cloud effects. A.S.of W. left for 3-train— Mr.Aylwin drove her. She told us afterwards good journey to Horsham, there thought she wd. not get into train at all, at last got into a 3rd [class carriage compartment] as 10th passenger. 'Charlie' returning, travelled in Guards Van . . .

In her letter of thanks, the Windflower asked if she might send an adjustable blind for the garden studio with a special spring to control the light over the newly opened view. Also there were further moves in the still unresolved matter of Gerald Grafton's military placement. Elgar answered hurriedly:

Brinkwells
Saturday [10 Aug. 1918]
My dear Windflower:

All thanks for your letter which arrived *last night* too late to do anything. I am rushing this word of grateful thanks for the G. business so as to catch post otherwise you will get nothing till Tuesday: I have copied out the par[agraph]s & sent to Gerald[.] Bless you!

[17] HWRO 705:445:7139.

1. Elgar and Alice Stuart Wortley at the Norwich Festival, 28 October 1911. The caption from *The Norwich Mercury* has them as 'Sir Edward and Lady Elgar'.

II. (*a*) Charles Stuart Wortley and (*b*) Beatrice Trollope (Venice, 1878).

II. (*c*) Wedding photograph (London, 1880). II. (*d*) The young widower with his daughter 'Bice' (*c*.1884)

III. Alice Caroline Stuart Wortley in 1887 (the year after her marriage to Charles Stuart Wortley), by her father Sir John Everett Millais. This was the portrait she bequeathed to the Elgar Museum at Worcester.

IV. Charles Stuart Wortley, *c.*1910. An election photograph. The inscription is typical of his humour, according to his grandson.

v. Alice Stuart Wortley, *c.*1910. As she disliked being photographed, this studio portrait was probably taken in connection with one of her husband's election campaigns. It may be the photograph of which Elgar wrote on 10 February 1910: '. . . it is not *you* — you would never make a good photograph. Gott sei dank.'

VI. Elgar on the day of the *Gerontius* performance at Lincoln, 9 June 1910. Only Alice Stuart Wortley was with him at Lincoln, and she may well have been present in the garden of the Cathedral Organist, G. J. Bennett, where this photograph was taken.

VII. Alice Elgar at Severn House, *c*.1912.

VIII. Clare Stuart Wortley, by John S. Sargent.

IX. Carice Elgar, by Percy Anderson.

x. Bayreuth Festival, 1911 or 1912. Alice Stuart Wortley (centre, half facing camera), with Clare (right), and Charles Stuart Wortley's sister Margaret Talbot (three-quarters back to camera).

XI. (*a*) Beatrice ('Bice')
Stuart Wortley, the Hon.
Mrs James Cecil, with her
daughter Mary Elizabeth
and Larry the bulldog,
*c*.1910.

XI. (*b*) Robert Cecil with
his grandfather Lord Stuart
of Wortley, at Finchcocks,
*c*.1923 (snapshot by Mary
Elizabeth Cecil).

XII. (*a*) Nigger, the Stuart Wortleys' Aberdeen terrier.

XII. (*b*) Elgar with Meg (Aberdeen) and Mina (Cairn) at Napleton Grange, Kempsey, Worcestershire, *c.*1925.

It seems like a wonderful dream—but it was real
The Blind will be gorgeous.
The wheat is cut today
In haste

                                                            with love
                                                            EE

I'll write tomorrow[18]

If he did, the letter is missing. But the next surviving letter, written several days later, seems to take up the story without a break.

Brinkwells
Friday [16 Aug. 1918]
My dear W.

   No news of you & we wonder how you are & if all is well: please write & tell us—   A fortnight tomorrow since you made your wonderfully clever journey *via* the Swan. I have not been feeling well—the heat & dryness [—] & have missed a great deal but have much to think over & love to think over. The harvest has been going on & now all, except the oats, is safely housed & gorgeous crops. It has been too hot to go to the Colvins & for him (she does not travel) to come here: but we expect him tomorrow

   I have made (sketchily) a floor for the new garden room—*your* room—but I sadly needed help—it was a heavy job & the sun hot.

   All goes on as usual & it is very lovely: tell me any news. I returned yr. Captn nephews letter; so kind of him & of you. I wrote to Gerald at once but have had no reply so I feel stranded without any news. I fear you may have left for Cornwall before this reaches you.

                                                            Love
                                                            EE[19]

   The garden room was being made ready as a composing studio detached from the cottage. Elgar ordered the Steinway upright piano given him at Plas Gwyn to be taken out of storage and sent down to Brinkwells. Three days later piano and blind arrived together in Mr Aylwin's waggon.

Brinkwells
Monday [19 Aug. 1918]
My dear Windflower:

   A day of great excitements: first the Blind has arrived & is the greatest success; you are so clever knowing the exactly right thing in every case—it is, of course, too good (refined & delicate) like the plane & all of you, for everyday use, but it makes the garden house yours more than ever. And the

   [18] HWRO 705:445:7138.          [19] HWRO 705:445:7120.

piano arrived in the same waggon & is now in the Studio & I have been playing away: it is the old one we had in Hereford & is quite good still. I am hard at work at music I hope. Then, when the blind & the piano were arriving the postman brought the lovely brass nails; they are lovely & I wish I could add a circle of them to your tray.

No more now but to wish you a lovely time at Tintagel & everything—thoughts & feelings of peace & [*word or two torn out*].

Love<br>EE.

A. is overjoyed with the sight of the blind—& of me with music paper again.[20]

Two days later Alice Elgar wrote:

Brinkwells
21 Augt. 1918
My dear Alice

I hope you both are safely at Tintagel & did not suffer discomfort on the way. It is certainly the moment to be out of London[.] What should we do without the [Bus No.] 2s. & 13s—bringing us such a welcome guest from Chelsea?—   It is such marvellous weather, so wonderful for the Harvest, Mr.Aylwin looks radiant over his splendid crops, safely stored—   He is to go & meet 'Missy' [Carice] tomorrow, & 'my Sarah' [Allen, Alice Elgar's maid almost from her childhood] whom you were so sweet & kind to go & see at Droitwich once, is to arrive with her. She wrote that she was much better so is coming on a visit & I think this wonderful climate may set her up—& then perhaps she may be able to stay—

It is so wonderfully beautiful just now, I must say it over again! & the Garden house quite delightful with its lovely blind—a 1000 thanks[:] it is so complete & perfect, lovely green shade, & pretty acorns &c—

& now I expect E. told you the Piano is in the Studio, I call it the music room now, as E. seems delighted to have it, & has been playing lovely tunes— *Such* a joy to hear again—& to see him reconciled somewhat to thinking of them!—Sidney Colvin brought Mr.E.V.Lucas over to tea on Saturday, & we had a very pleasant time but Brinkwells did not do itself justice as it was grey & a little rainy—

Has it not been a blessing to have good news—I do trust they will continue, surely the German people must begin to *feel* all is not prospering.

The Sea must be lovely now. I hope you are both already much refreshed—

With love<br>Yr. afte.<br>C.Alice Elgar

20 HWRO 705:445:7133.

Forgive ill writing out of doors. E. has been resting in the garden house, thoroughly enjoying it, & with eyes shaded & yet able to see Chanctonbury Ring! thanks to lovely blind—[21]

Day by day the war bulletins brought news of Allied advances, fully aided at last by huge fresh forces from the United States. At Brinkwells it was as if all might return again to pre-war summer, as Alice wrote in her diary:

24 August 1918. Lovely day—sunny & hot. Mr.Aylwin's Clover field finished—lovely scent. E. writing wonderful new music, different from anything else of his. A. calls it wood magic. So elusive & delicate ...

In his own diary that day Elgar noted the arrival of fresh music manuscript paper from Novello. His work in hand was to be of some size—a 'Sonata for Piano and Violin' (as he headed the manuscript). The 'wood magic' was almost certainly the wraith-like opening of the slow movement.

On 26 August they had a telegram to say that Alice Stuart of Wortley had broken her leg very painfully: out walking the Tintagel cliffs after rain, she had slipped sideways on a grassy slope. Lord Stuart had had to summon help to carry her to the little house they had taken.

Seemingly as a direct result of the news, the wraith of the Sonata slow movement turned to long-lined melody—the kind of big-scaled slow melody which had given Elgar's music its most celebrated distinction in the past. It made a strange bedfellow for the 'wood magic'. But now as always Elgar's best music reflected with astonishing directness his own feelings: and at Brinkwells his feelings were almost exactly divided between present and past.

On 6 September Alice Elgar recorded: 'The Sonata was vibrating through his very being— He wrote & offered dedication to Mrs. Joshua.' But his thoughts were also with the Windflower at Tintagel. When Lord Stuart sent an account of her progress, Elgar responded:

Brinkwells   Fittleworth   Sussex
Sep 6 1918

My dear C:

It was good of you to write—we hope the dear patient is progressing well & without pain; I know she is always interested in my music & I have been writing a lot; if you think she is well enough I would write & tell her about it but I hesitate to do so as she may be better without letters even about music.

> Our love to you all
> Yours ever sincy
> Edward Elgar[22]

Then she was able to write for herself. Elgar responded with a letter enclosing his first sketch of the central slow movement Sonata melody:

[21] HWRO 705:445:7901.         [22] HWRO 705:445:7914.

Brinkwells.
Sep 11: 1918
My dear W.

It was the greatest joy to get your letter & to know that in spite of the dreadful things you have been through that [*sic*] you are recovering: we think of you very, very often & hope you are not suffering pain. I wrote to Charlie a few days ago asking if you were able to receive letters as I shd. like to tell you of the music but I hesitated to send as you might be wearied with letter reading. And now a letter comes from you so I send a few words as to our proceedings. All goes on as usual as regards the scene & surroundings. Our local cook, whom you saw, has gone to her returned soldier husband & we have Alice's former maid Sarah whose rheumatism is better & her niece is coming as cook etc. I suddenly took to writing music! & have nearly 'done' a sonata for Violin & piano in E minor[.] Ronald & Reed both like it—what I played to them, a little to Ronald & more to Reed[,] for whose use I copied out a violin part & we played & thought you ought to be here to help generally: a sad little chair with a pencil is beside the piano now. The first movement is bold & vigorous[;] then a fantastic, curious movemt with a very expressive middle section: a melody for the Violin—they say it's as good as or better than anything I have done in the expressive way: this I wrote just after your telegram about the accident came & I send you the pencil notes as first made at that sad moment. You will make nothing of it from this but a better copy shall come as soon as you can play again—I hope this will be very soon. The last movement is very broad & *soothing* like the last movemt of the IInd Symphy[.] I have been sketching other things which are full of old times.

Your last visit was the greatest joy & is remembered very fully.

Tell me if you get this safe & if I may write again.

Love from us both

Yrs ever
EE[23]

Three days later the Elgars learned of the sudden death of Mrs Joshua. She had been overwhelmed with the offer of the dedication (her daughter had written for her a week earlier) but was sick with a chill and would write soon. The chill had turned rapidly worse, and she had expired without ever responding for herself. The sad news reached Brinkwells when Elgar was far on in the Sonata finale: and on learning of her death, he made the finale's music suddenly turn back to the central slow movement melody first associated with the Windflower.

It was akin to his use of other personalities to vary and develop his own music in the *'Enigma' Variations* twenty years earlier. Only now there was no development toward some concluding self-portrait. In this Sonata of past and present, two entirely separate personalities had suddenly become one. Elgar the composer instinctively recognized this: for he had already cast the Sonata finale in a binary shape—

[23] Elgar Birthplace parcel 583 (iii), (transcript: HWRO 705:445:7696).

exposition followed almost directly by recapitulation, with no intervening development to mark any further gathering of experience.

Yet the synthesis was not complete. Before the Sonata was finished, he began a piano quintet. Thus once again—and almost for the first time in Elgar's creative life—the instrument associated chiefly with the Windflower was taking a central place in large-scaled writing, though now it was chamber music.

In the fabric of all this music was the wooded country round Brinkwells. As if to increase his possession of it, Elgar asked the Stopham Estate if he could buy the wood below the garden studio—not the ground, but the wooded growth upon it. Alice Elgar wrote:

16 September 1918. Fine—Wonderful sunrise[,] trees shining ruddily—   The woodreeve came to see E. & E. bought the Underwood below garden house. Very excited & pleased & took chopper & worked hard clearing path. A. helped—E. wrote more of the wonderful Quintet—Flexham Park—sad 'dispossessed' trees & their dance & unstilled regret . . .

On that day Elgar also marked his possession by sending lavender from the edge of the wood to the Windflower.

Through the latter half of September he was making the most of the time at Brinkwells, soon to be interrupted by engagements in London. (One was to conduct a special performance of *The Fringes of the Fleet* for one of Lord Beresford's naval charities; the other to play cymbals in a celebrity performance of Richard Blagrove's *Toy Symphony*.) The Windflower had written her thanks in mid-September; at the end of the month she wrote again, and then he replied:

Brinkwells
Oct 1: 1918

My dear W.

Yes. I had your letter of a fortnight or so ago with great joy but I have been not quite so well & am now better. It is good to know that you progress really well although so slowly[.] Please be very patient—I know you are—

We had a very sad shock—after all our mild pleasantries—over the sudden loss of poor dear Mrs.Joshua—a real, true friend[.] The sonata has gone to the printer! but it may be weary months before it is published—it seems strange—oh! so strange that you—the Windflower—have not heard a note of it—& yet you must have heard it all in some other sphere: you *will* like it I know & I have *struggled* hard to make *my* piano passages fit other fingers—& I wanted help in this direction

The weather is lovely now but cold—early for autumn—but the local people promise us much fine weather & *no* winter. I am supposed to be going to Frank on the 14th so as to be near for the Palace (Fringes) Charity affair (C. Beresford) & a *recording* at the Gramophone & a 'comic' concert that L.Ronald is getting up—but I have had—at the thought of town life—a recurrence of the old feelings & have been just as limp as before the nursing home episode.

I told you I have bought 1½ acres of the wood—the *crop* not the land [—] & between times I cut it down[.] Here again I desire help.

Love from us both.

Yrs
EE

I am really all right again now but cannot endure the thought of moving[24]

The final ten days before London he filled with work on the Piano Quintet and the String Quartet begun after the nursing home episode in the spring.

On 11 October the Elgars went to London. Since Novello's editor had queried some of the piano writing in the Sonata, the Elgars used the opportunity to reopen Severn House so that Edward could try the new music before a large group of friends in the music-room. The Windflower was not yet able to manage stairs. He wrote:

Severn House[,] Hampstead, N.W.
Oct 16 1918

My dear W.

We came up hurriedly on Saty and—as the printers were clamorous for the M.S.—we had an impromptu 'party' & Reed & I played the Sonata twice—before tea & after. Frank came & the Colvins & the Fortescues, Lan. Ronald[,] Muriel F[oster] & one or two others: we *missed* you dreadfully & were saying it did not seem right to do it without you. It was liked.

Now, we do hope you are really getting well & strong: if you have Clare give her my love. I am going to the Hut today & come up for C.Beresford's affair (Naval charity) at the Palace Theatre next week. We go back to Brinkwells in a fortnight's time & I am wondering if you will be home before then & if you wd. be equal to hearing the Sonata if Mr.Reed wd. come with me & play it to you? This is my *idea* but it may be unrealisable for many reasons; do let me hear soon.

The air does not agree with me & I long to get back to my quiet woods. I have placed the piano in the Studio on the left as you enter next the egregious mantlepiece so that the light is good.

Lan gave a good acct. of you from your letter to him of which he was justly proud!

Our love & all good wishes

Yrs ever
EE[25]

That day both Elgar and Charles Stuart of Wortley attended St Paul's Cathedral for the funeral of Hubert Parry, a very old friend of them both.

Another reason for the Elgars' presence in London was a wen which had appeared on Alice Elgar's forehead. On 29 October Sir Maurice with two other doctors removed the wen. It would depend on her recovery when they could return to Brinkwells. Elgar wrote in his diary:

31 October 1918 ... News report re Austria [preparing to sign an armistice.] to Cheyne Walk with Reed to play to Alice Wortley ...

It was probably then that Elgar gave her the short score manuscript of the Second Symphony[26] and proofs of the first two Sonata movements fresh from the printer. But the visit gave small scope for intimate conversation.

Severn House[,] Hampstead, N.W.
Thursday [7 Nov. 1918]

My dear Windflower:

It was so sad that I could not get one word with you & you were so sad too. Alice's operation was much more of an event than we anticipated & than she knows even now—there is a large wound. The doctors refused to let us go & all plans had to be altered by telegraph etc etc & endless confusion of course. *Now* they say Monday—after promising Friday or Saturday—I do hope I shall see you before we leave. Which wd. be best, tea or lunch any day. The music is yours as always but the pubrs sent only one proof & printing is difficult. My writing new stuff has been held up by the confusion & I am in despair at ever overtaking it— our coming away—which was necessary— has been a *tragedy* for my music, alas! It is lovely to see you so well &, despite grave difficulties, able to get about: I hope you will soon walk as ever.

A. & I went to the Court Theatre [*Twelfth Night*, but not under Granville Barker's management]—a very dreary performance and the music truly a disgrace[.] We have no plans & only wait doctors' orders.

Love
yrs ever
EE

PS. I hope the 2nd.Sym M.S. interested you & I am sorry I gave you poor Gerdes' letter—do not trouble about it.[27]

Two days later he lunched with Alice Stuart of Wortley. And two days after that came the return to Brinkwells. Alice Elgar chronicled it:

11 November 1918. E. & A. heard Armistice was signed. Muriel telephoned. E. put up our Flag, it looked gorgeous— Crowds out & all rejoicing. D[eo] G[ratias] for preservation & Victory.
E. & A. to Brinkwells—Lalla came to train at Victoria[.] C[arice] tried too but just missed & went to Coliseum where 'Land of Hope & Glory' was sung twice[:] the 2nd time the words of refrain were thrown on the screen & people stood & joined in—Very exciting & moving—

---

[26] Now at the Elgar Birthplace.     [27] HWRO 705:445:7127.

Brinkwells, Fittleworth, Sussex
Thursday [14 Nov. 1918]

My dear Windflower:

We arrived all safely & found everything ready. It is cold but *vividly* bright weather & the woods divine: there are still leaves & the colours ravishing[.] Music does not go on yet: my poor dear A. has a cold & keeps her room—I doubt if she will be able to stay here but we shall see.

We have had the threshing machine & the drone of the humming 'sorts well with my humour'. I have been cutting down some more of the wood but I spare one spot! I hope your progress is still good & when we return I trust we shall find you walking as well as ever.

It was sad to miss the great day in town. I thought of you so much at the station—six months ago when I was a poor thing you lunched with me & saw me off. Bless you!

The *third* movemt [of the Sonata proofs] has not reached me yet—but you shall have it as soon as possible. I kiss your hands

Love<br>EE[28]

The cottage was cold, and Alice Elgar spent nearly a week in bed with persistent cough. Edward gradually found his way back to the chamber works.

[n.p.]
Sunday [24 Nov. 1918]

My dear Windflower

The pen—music pen—is busy again & the weather divine. Alice is better but I fear does not enjoy life here as I do.

Will you let me have Gerald's letter back sometime? I *am* truly sorry for the poor boy & feel he has been treated badly but do not trouble to do any more—you have been more than kind over it all.

There are still some leaves & the sun & colour are gorgeous on most days: today quite warm & still. I *wish* you were here: the studio is not too cold in the early morn. How I remember it all.

I have the last movemt of the Sonata now & hope to send it [in a revised proof] but the printers are slow

Love<br>EE[29]

Early in December came another trip to London. Alice's cough had been with her so long that she had to see the doctor again. And Edward felt he should be present on 5 December when Landon Ronald was to conduct *Falstaff*—its first London hearing for a long time. They went up on 4 December and settled at the Langham Hotel rather

---

[28] HWRO 705:445:7116.        [29] HWRO 705:445:7114.

than opening Severn House again. Alice went to Sir Maurice Abbot Anderson, who took X-rays.

Next day brought the rehearsal and performance of *Falstaff*. In the audience both morning and evening were the Stuarts of Wortley—she on crutches. Edward brought for her proofs of a new full score of *Falstaff*: although a miniature had been available since 1913, the full score engraving in Germany had been overtaken by the war, and it was only now to appear. The performance registered a triumph for this music at last.

The following morning Sir Maurice called to say he found nothing the matter with Alice's lungs: they might return to Brinkwells. Edward paid a quick visit to his dentist. The surgery was almost next door to the hotel at which (the Stuarts of Wortley had told him) Paderewski had just arrived. Edward looked in and left a friendly card, before he and Alice went to Victoria Station for an early lunch before the 1.36 train to Sussex. He wrote:

waiting for train
Victoria Stn
Friday [6 Dec. 1918] 1 o'c
My dear W.

No writing room available, so I buy 2d. of paper & envelops at the Book stall & sit on a deserted bench. Forgive pencil—this is to say that I found my dentist was [—] is—a few doors from Paderewski's Hotel so I left a card saying *'welcome'* & *'just off to the country'* so you will understand if he shd. say he has heard. I *do* want *Polonia* [booked for recording but again postponed in hopes of Paderewski's attendance] cleared up.

It was lovely to see you last night & I remember this train & a more human-feeling-Station last May    Bless you

Yrs
EE[30]

Brinkwells
Saturday [7 Dec. 1918] morng
My dear W.

We arrived all safely but tired & A. has seen the doctor & is all right on the way to convalescence.

It is a heavenly *brilliant* morng & the view.

I am writing to say that if you do not want the *Falstaff* score wd you post it to

W.H.Reed, esq.
Froom
Chatsworth Road
E.Croydon

[30] HWRO 705:445:7128.

It is yours *of course* if you want it.
The room is full of music & memories

Yrs ever
EE[31]

He worked now at the Quartet finale.
She read and returned a letter from her nephew, Capt. William James, about the failed attempt to place Gerald Grafton.

Brinkwells, Fittleworth, Sussex.
Monday [9 Dec. 1918]
My dear W.

*Many* thanks for reading Capt James's letter: I am so sorry the thing has been a trouble. Gerald would have done *anything*, as I explained to you—submarine or destroyer but was asphyxiated in the lower deck & the so called regulations did not permit a R.V.N.R. (or whatever the cursed thing of Churchill's is) to get any *chance* of a rise or even change. It seemed logical for him to go into the pay dept only because he is a trained & skilled accountant.

Many thanks for the 10/- note which I will return if you send the Sc[ore] to Reed! we will be strictly honest in these severe commercial transactions
I think much of you & it is lovely here but the mornings are cold & dark—and *lonely*.

Love
EE[32]

As he was finishing the Quartet, there came news of a burglary at the long-closed Severn House. Alice Elgar struggled up to London to deal with it on 17 December. At Brinkwells Edward still waited for a proof of the Sonata finale which he might send to Cheyne Walk for the Windflower to try with W. H. Reed.

Brinkwells
Tuesday [17 Dec. 1918]
My dear Windflower:

Our letters concerning Gerald[,] Paderewski & the Falstaff Score *crossed* so much that I waited for a day—& then have had a most disastrous chill. I am just creeping about (*not* outside my room) & today am alone as poor dear A. has had to fly to London as burglars have ravaged Severn House—I know no particulars & of course cd. not possibly go out.
I am so very much obliged to you about Paderewski: needless to say I have *not* heard & also, needless to say, I never shall! such are great artists.
The music is of course stopped—the weather is brilliant but cold wind & A.

---

[31] HWRO 705:445:7137.        [32] HWRO 705:445:7136.

does not get well—it is disastrous her going to-day but she *would* & so there we are.

I loved your letter & all the news but I am deeply concerned about the effect (on your arms) of the crutches; I do hope it is all settling down properly: I am so selfish;—who will play the piano to me if you do not? so please have your hands in great playing order when I return to London.

The wretched printing of the Sonata drags on—I have corrected some proofs but I have nothing more to send to you yet. I live in hopes of seeing it in print someday—but when I cannot foresee. I suppose we shall return to Hampstead early in January—the coal expert has only just awoke to the fact that our 'ration' business has not yet been settled & no letters answered!

I hope everything goes happily with you & long for a talk—*we* seem to have fallen on evil worrying times what with burglars & the attempt to pass a forged cheque for £75 in Alice's name! Stirring times—but we have caught no one yet.

I am hoping to finish the Quartet this week but it has been cruelly hindered.

There are still sprigs of *lavender* on the bushes & I think of you every time I pass them: the blind is taken down & stored away for next year—we are to be here D. V. & you *will come* won't you.

Love<br>EE[33]

Then at last he was able to send her a proof of the Sonata finale. Meanwhile an apology arrived from Padereswki for lateness in responding.

Brinkwells, Fittleworth, Sussex.
Saturday [21 Dec. 1918]
My dear W.

This is only to say that I have now received a most charming & *sufficient* letter from P. [—] he gives no address & I forget the Hotel so I shall take the liberty of sending it to Cheyne Walk to save time.

In haste

I hope you have the IIIrd movemt.

Love<br>EE[34]

He finished the Quartet on Christmas Eve, and they planned to return for the winter to Hampstead.

---

[33] HWRO 705:445:7129.          [34] HWRO 705:445:7130.

Brinkwells

Friday [27 Dec. 1918]

Dearest Windflower

All thanks for the lovely Q.Conct book which I am *delighted* to have for my own. We had only a *liby* vol before.

Haste! Things have rapidly altered—Carice takes me to London today—I go to Ridgehurst for the weekend & Alice & the servants get to Hampstead on Tuesday or Wedy & we shall be at home again *indefinitely* [—] it is too cold here for the servants & for Alice—I enjoy it.

I do hope you will like playing the sonata—& shall think of you & Reed. I kiss your hands

Love<br>EE[35]

So again, despite her recent illness, it fell to Alice Elgar to clear up and close one house, and to open another for the arrival of her husband from spending the interval with friends.

## 1919

The beginning of January found the Elgars back at Severn House with insufficient staff. Alice struggled to unpack in the dusty house closed for so long—all the while finding more and more things missing after the burglary. Edward could manage to work at the Quintet only against some more or less immediate prospect of performance. So, despite every difficulty, there must be another trial hearing before friends in the big music-room.

4 January 1919. E. settled that the 4tet shd. come on Tuesday—A. seemed always to be having to do impossibilities[:] she said so on telephone to Frank—he said 'but you always achieve them' . . .

7 January. A. arranging for afternoon. Mr.Reed came early. E. & he to Stewart's to lunch. The nice old Harrod waiter came [to cater food]. Quartet came first & rehearsed[.] Then Colvins, Alice S.ofW.[,] Fortescues, Evelyn Horridge, Lan & his brother, Frank. Wonderful music[:] 4tet—1st movement beautiful especially—the Piacevole [second movement] like captured sunshine— Sonata so fine & beautiful with the wonderful 2nd movement. E. played it so wonderfully [—] Everyone delighted & astonished. Then crowning all, the 1st movement of Quintet, so marvellous— A most thoroughly enjoyable aftn. & everything went so smoothly & comfortably. D.G. for such wonderful gifts given to E.

[35] HWRO 705:445:7131.

To bring forth the Quintet second movement, another private performance was scheduled at the Beresfords' London house in twelve days' time.

14 January.   E. writing all day & beginning to look very tired . . .

15 January.   E. very absorbed & not out. Alice S.ofW. to tea . . .

16 January.   E. rather poorly—not out . . . E. went on saying 'this is no home for me'! but worked & helped much— Maids settling down, many things to arrange & moving of furniture . . .

On Sunday 19 January Alice Stuart of Wortley and Frank Schuster were among the Beresfords' guests invited to hear the Quartet, and after tea the Sonata and two movements of the Quintet. Elgar found a bad piano, but the warmth of host and hostess more than compensated, and the enthusiasm of faithful friends was an encouragement towards the Quintet finale. Yet inspiration amid the grandeurs of Severn House was fitful.

Hampstead
Sunday [26 Jan. 1919]

My dear W.

Oh! it is so difficult to keep up with London. No music & interruptions by the thousand—I think of the holy peace at Brinkwells in the early morn.

The 'passionate pilgrim' typewriter came quite safely & the author was quite pleased with the sight of it.

I return, with *all* thanks for all you did, your nephews letter.

I am very sad about everything & see no light & no refreshment

Love
EE

We meet at Frank's on Tuesday[1]

At tea in Old Queen Street on the Tuesday, Alice Stuart of Wortley made the most of arrangements for another performance of *Polonia* at the Albert Hall the following Sunday. But when the day came, the audience was small and the sound disappointing. He wrote:

Severn House
Feb 3 1919

My dear W.

I cannot thank you enough for all the trouble you took for Sunday—it was a miserable sound I thought & I went away quite ashamed & depressed & felt I wd. drop the divine art altogether—it is too degrading to hear one's things done in the Albert Hall—but this is to thank you not to complain.

[1] HWRO 705:445:4079.

It is still all ice & snow here & very cold. I am worried to death by applications for performance of the new things, a sort of announcement was made of them in the Musical Times & the D[aily] T[elegraph] & so letters are arriving—my Hat!

I long for Brinkwells even in this weather & shall shut myself up here hermetically I think. London is a desert, alas! and where are you

Bless you & again thank you

Yrs ever<br>
EE[2]

He worked at the Quintet finale in depressive bad health. When the Windflower came to tea on 11 February, they discussed plans for two Elgar concerts at Bath with Muriel Foster as soloist. Muriel Foster went down with Frank Schuster in advance of the Elgars, and experienced symptoms of what was to prove serious illness. After the concerts Edward wrote:

Empire Hotel, Bath.
Sunday [16 Feb. 1919]
My dear W.

All is over & went well. Poor dear Frank has had shocks as Muriel F. has had a heart attack at dinner on Thursday!!! However she sang all right[.] I missed you—it was really rather nice & *friendly*, but—! we return this evening

I am better

Love<br>
EE[3]

Back in London, there was a luncheon to meet Alice Stuart of Wortley's youngest brother, the bird painter John Guille Millais (1865–1931), who had an exhibition in Bond Street just then, and their youngest sister with her husband, General Sir Neville Lyttleton (1845–1931), Governor of the Royal Hospital, Chelsea.

20 February ... E. & A. to lunch at 7,Cheyne Walk ... John Millais & his wife & Genl.Lyttelton *dear* old man, Col. [John] Buchan there, A. sat between Millais & Buchan & enjoyed it much. E. rather dull neighbour—

Alice showed us cast of Chopin's hand, so strangely like E.'s. Millais said identical. ...

A hearing of the Quintet complete with its finale at last was planned at Severn House for 7 March. Elgar wrote the day before:

² HWRO 705:445:4094.          ³ HWRO 705:445:4088.

[n.p.]
Thursday [6 Mar. 1919]
My dear Windflower

I have been working night & day to get the last movement fairly ready for tomorrow & I hope you will like it. I look forward to seeing you but there will be a lot of people I *fear*. Frank wishes to bring Whittemore!

After this I shall be free from the pen & we must meet next week or on Sunday, but I want to see some pictures with you & we will fix a nice plan

The weather is lovely to-day but *yesterday*!! I did not move but wrote & thought.

Now the Quintet is done I feel I am done

Love<br>EE

I hope Claude is coming & *if no trouble* please bring your proof of the Sonata[4]

The performance next day marked the end of Elgar's chamber music composition: there remained only some revision of the Quintet.

The middle of March found the Elgars on a weekend visit to Liverpool for him to conduct *Gerontius*. Carice was taken in by the Stuarts of Wortley, and Edward wrote:

Midland Adelphi Hotel, Liverpool.
Friday [14 Mar. 1919]
My dear W.

It was so good & sweet of you to think of such a nice plan for Carice. It is *awful* here—all dreadful *U.S.* Americans—the lowest of the human race—& a jazz band. I am dreadfully unhappy at everything. We return as soon as we can. I remember buying notepaper here with an unnecessary E on it which I kept for you till it was all gone.

Do ring up on Monday morng & we will try for Tuesday & make a nice plan.

Love<br>Ed

Frankie's music was suddenly cut off by his sister's death.[5]

Schuster had planned a private performance of the Elgar chamber music at Old Queen Street: that was postponed. The sister who died was not Adela, whom the Elgars knew (and who lived until 1940). The next days in Alice Elgar's diary are blank.

[4] HWRO 705:445:4057.          [5] HWRO 705:445:4096.

Severn House, Hampstead, N.W.
Monday [24 Mar. 1919]

My dear W.

I rang up on Saty & we are wondering—as we have heard nothing of you—how you are & hope you are well.

I enclose the little piece of nonsense which I hope will amuse you—let me have it back sometime.

I have not been out for days—chill [—] but A & I are starting to Ridgehurst for the night—but I am far from well

*Please* let me hear

Love
E[6]

The second day at Ridgehurst brought a visit from Alice Stuart of Wortley and the discussion of a poem (not identified) for setting to music. Back at home Elgar wrote:

Hampstead
March 27: 1919

My dear W.

I wish I could give a better report of the poem—'it will not do'.

It was good to see you yesterday & I hope for this afternoon

Yrs ever
EE[7]

At Lord Beresford's house on 1 April Elgar dined with guests including Melba, Lady Maud Warrender, and Landon Ronald—but not the Stuarts of Wortley. He wrote a week later:

The Athenaeum, Pall Mall, S.W.1.
Tuesday [8 Apr. 1919]

My dear Windflower:

I have been much occupied with silly businesses—the dinner was odd & amusing. Mina wants me to go to Brighton this week end.

At Foster's in Pall Mall is to be sold on Thursday next some original Plaster statuettes by Boehm—there is one of your father—19 in. high—a poor thing but you might like to see it[.] Ring me up if you can go to see it

Love
E[8]

He went to Brighton, accompanied by Frank Schuster, for four days. He returned on the 14th, and wrote next day to enclose some windflowers:

[6] HWRO 705:445:4061.          [7] HWRO 705:445:4089.          [8] HWRO 705:445:4083.

Severn House, 42,Netherhall Gardens, Hampstead, N.W.3
Tuesday [15 Apr. 1919]

My dear Windflower:

Here are the first of your namesakes—I fear they are very tired after their long journey. (My sister sent them on *Sunday*)

Frank & I returned from B. yesterday—it was not unamusing but I will tell you of it all—I am *fearfully* busy getting the M.S. of the Quintet clear & ready for Frank's music *on Saturday week*—you will get a card from him in due course

> Love
> EE[9]

Side by side with Quintet revisions, Elgar was sketching music for a possible new engagement at the Coliseum (which did not in the end come to anything). He took a new butler-valet on trial—a war veteran whose wounds made his work difficult despite an attractive personality. Then on 20 March the Elgars spent Sunday afternoon at the zoo: they saw the former aviary now occupied by monkeys (one of the few subjects about which Edward Elgar and Alice Stuart of Wortley entirely disagreed). All these topics found places in Elgar's next letter, written two days before the chamber music performance at Schuster's house. But Alice Stuart of Wortley was now away.

[n.p.]
Thursday [24 Apr. 1919]

My dear Windflower:

It seems so sad amongst all the rehearsing that you are not here & will not be, alas! at the performance. It does not seem *right* somehow & I lose my pleasure in it all in consequence.

However I am hoping that the change will do you good & that you will come back very well indeed. I am going to the Hut *soon*, Frank says[,] & I expect to be working at the *'Air'* (Benson) turn if the Coliseum take it on. I have much *sketched* & playable & wanted you to hear it—however that will come.

It was too bad of me to mention monkeys—but it really is something *extraordin[ar]y* to see *60* playing about in the open air—I went again yesterday alone—they are enlivening & it's quite different from that old monkey-house with its *perturbed* atmosphere, we will go & see them when you return. I wanted to tell you of Brighton, which was *variegated* but amusing, Mina priceless.

Send me a line saying how you are improving—I wish the weather *could* be warmer: we are in domestic troubles—*very* nice servants but ill health abounds & my nice new military man, who promised so kindly & well, has old trouble recurring from his wound—Sarah is in hospital & last night the housemaid sprained her ankle! etc. etc.

   Dear love & wishes

Yr
EE[10]

After further revision, the Quintet was being prepared for the printer. The first public performance took place in a concert at the Wigmore Hall. Alice Elgar wrote:

21 May 1919 ... Hall very nice & full—   The 'faithful band' much in evidence ... The players were *wonderful* [—] Sammons exquisite in Sonata. The last movement of 4tet most exciting & brilliant, A.S.of W. said 'miraculous'. Then the *wonderful* 5tet beautifully given—   Interesting to watch the *delight* creeping over faces—   A most tremendous reception of each work & at the end an overwhelming ovation & when E. appeared more than ever. *Shouts & roars.* A lovely afternoon.

   A Cello Concerto was shaping in his mind. On the last day of May he went with the two Alices to hear the Portuguese cellist Suggia:

... Wonderfully picturesque looking in bright green & vivid claret silks— Disappointed with her playing. To tea at Langham, E. & A.[,] A.S.of W. & Mr.&Mrs.F.Salmond ...

Felix Salmond was another cellist on whom Elgar had his eye: and it was he who would ultimately give the Concerto its première.
   Soon the music was far enough advanced for a private trial:

10 June. E. working very hard not out at all. F.Salmond came & played the Concerto with *great* delight, Alice S.of W. came & was allowed to turn over ...

Home
Thursday [12 June 1919]
My dear Windflower:

   Many many thanks for the cigars which are lovely. I was so glad you heard the Concerto sketch & that it 'will do'—I am beginning to like it.
   We are off [to Brinkwells] tomorrow early & I wonder how we shall fare. I have had a busy day rehearsing the Quintet (for Saturday) and the Quartet all the morng.

<hr>

[10] HWRO 705:445:7701.

I have a few necessary things to put together—I cant call it *packing*—for tomorrow

So I kiss your hands

                                                    adieu
                                                    Yrs ever
                                                    EE[11]

During nearly three weeks at Brinkwells, the Concerto was brought to a state in which it could be played before invited friends in the Severn House music room on 5 July. Afterwards Elgar spent a week with the Edward Speyers in Hertfordshire.

Ridgehurst, Shenley, Herts.
Sunday [13 July 1919]
My dear W.

I am still here—M.Maurice Kufferath, my hostesses' [*sic*] brother & director of the Brussels Opera[,] is here—a delightful man—& talking of many musical doings in B. He wants to do 'the Apostles' on *the stage* etc etc which we are discussing—

I am so very sorry your delightful plan for the theatre with A[lgernon] B[lackwood] could not come into being [—] we hope for another time[.] I hope you will have a nice summer-country-time soon

I go to Brinkwells on Tuesday *or* Wedy early & shall only return for the 'command' affair at the Coliseum on the 28th.

                                                    Love
                                                    E[12]

That was a performance involving *Land of Hope and Glory* and the *Imperial March*. At Brinkwells in the latter half of July Elgar worked at the Concerto orchestration.

Brinkwells
Wedy [23 July 1919]
My dear Windflower:

Your lavender bush is flourishing but the weather is frightful.

I send the enclosed photograph of two of your friends [monkeys] admiring the gramophone

We want news of you & what you are going to do: we have some concern in arranging servants but A. wants you to come [—] *so do I* sometime but I fear you may be gone on your travels. I *may* go to Brussels with Frank S. in Augt for a week but poor dear Mr.Kufferath was taken ill at Ridgehurst & has not yet returned to B.—   I do not think the music plans will be of much good—but I must try

[11] HWRO 705:445:4097.          [12] HWRO 705:445:4095.

I am arranging the acc[om]p[animen]t of the Violon*cello* Concerto for piano & writing it out fair—which I detest

No fish & no luck anywhere

Love
EE[13]

The plan for Brussels came to nothing then.

In London Elgar conducted the Coliseum performance on 28 July. Later the next afternoon he played the Concerto for Alice Stuart of Wortley in the Severn House music-room. Then back to Brinkwells.


Brinkwells, Fittleworth, Sussex.
Sunday [3 Aug. 1919]
My dear Windflower:

Here is everything the same & the weather divine. Felix Salmond has been & we have polished the Cello concerto: Carice is here until Monday night. Poor dear A. has had a bad cold, better now. No news—the great events are such things as taking a large wasps' nest which reminded me of Walls, Ravenglass etc [—] all so remote & far away.

I want to finish or rather commence the Piano Concerto which *must* be windflowerish so I hope you will come but somehow I know you will not. Your lavender blooms apace.

Love
EE[14]

Five days later the Cello Concerto score was sent to the printer. There was no progress on the piano concerto. Alice Elgar wrote to invite the Windflower:


Brinkwells, Fittleworth, Sussex.
14 Augt. 1919.
My dear Alice

How are you standing this intense heat? We are finding it rather exhausting & cannot attempt walks or fishing— Our plans seem to be clearing up somewhat & all being well, we should leave this about 28th for some visits. We thought we wd. let you hear in case you should be able to fit in a little visit before then— We have asked Lan to come as he is just returning from Cornwall but have not heard yet— We should be so pleased to see you. I am sorry to say we have no parlour maid here, all the holidays are being

[13] HWRO 705:445:7702.          [14] HWRO 705:445:7703.

fitted in, & fear it wd. not be as comfortable as I could *wish* but will do our best towards it— I hope we shall be here for the autumn months & tints.

> With love
> Yr afte.
> C.Alice Elgar

The Music room is so silent without the Concerto, gone to be printed.[15]

20 August. Very rainy. Alice S.of W. arrived about 3 in pony cart, rather wet drive— Pony cart to Fittleworth later & a wheel came off, problem how soon it wd. be mend. A. to P.O—pleasant after the rain— E. played most beautifully after dinner—2nd Symphony & other wonderful things ...

21 August ... Most lovely day, brilliant sunshine & wonderful views—Alice seemed to enjoy it & being here again ...

22 August. Still fine & lovely, a little cloudy. A.S.of W. left about 12 in mended pony cart. E. & A. felt very tired & lay in summer houses more or less all the afternoon—later went up into field above springs, perfectly beautiful there ...

A week later the Elgars returned to London. But he went almost immediately to The Hut, and a few days later his own Alice joined him.

The Hut, Bray, Berks.
Sunday [7 Sept. 1919]
My dear W.

We are here & have had Salmond on Friday & the Quartet (Reed) yesterday. I hope you are well & having nice weather.

I send the enclosed—which will not interest you—because you gave me the books & I wd like to let you know how much I loved having them

> Ever
> E[16]

That day came news that Lord Beresford had died at the age of seventy-three. The Elgars attended a memorial service at St Paul's Cathedral on 13 September, before returning to Brinkwells three days later.

---

[15] HWRO 705:445:7915.          [16] HWRO 705:445:4086.

Brinkwells
Monday [22 Sept. 1919]

My dear Windflower:

Many thanks for your letter & for the sight of Mary Crawshay's: it is too sad: we were at the funeral service (St Paul's) that was all I could do. I feel very much depressed by it all.

Here we are, very cold & I want to get away—strange: but the Studio is sad sad & I feel I have destroyed the best thing I ever wrote & that it had to be so. I am not well & worried in many ways. Perhaps we shall meet over the Concerto [première] on the 27th [Oct.]? I hope you will find old, dear feelings at Bowerswell[.] The world is a changed place & I am awfully tired of it

Love
EE[17]

The Elgars stayed nearly a month at Brinkwells. But no new music came. After the Concerto proofs were corrected, and bonfires of rubbish made and burnt, they prepared to return.

Brinkwells
Sunday [12 Oct. 1919]

My dear W

Thank you for your letter which came on Saturday[.] I hope you are safely through all the exciting times at Sheffield & the long long journeys: that one from Perth to Edinburgh must have been sadly trying.

We are busy, more than busy, packing up & leave tomorrow (Monday) for home. Poor dear A. has been much worried by the cook turning ill—& everything had to be done for her & she is a most *un*human creature which makes it hard.

There is no news & I dread the winter: alas! there is nothing fine, or great or noble to look forward to & I feel grey & distressed. A very old puppy! The weather has been too wonderful & much work has been done in the wood: we shall hear of you, & you of us by telephone, as soon as we arrive.

Love
Yrs ever
E[18]

The Concerto première on 27 October registered only a *succès d'estime*, because of insufficient rehearsal. Then Elgar went to participate in functions at Dudley and Worcester. Between them he spent two nights with his sister.

[17] HWRO 705:445:4085. Elgar's statement about having destroyed the best thing he ever wrote and its having to be so may refer to the 9/8 E minor theme of 1918, and its incorporation into the Cello Concerto.

[18] HWRO 705:445:4092. The Elgars left Brinkwells on 13 Oct. Clare Stuart Wortley mistakenly gave the date as 19 October, citing a postmark of 20 October. Such a postmark would only pertain to another letter now lost.

The Elms
Monday [3 Nov. 1919]

My dear Windflower

such an odd pen!

I have come on here where you only, of all my friends, have been. Very cold & not able to go out but the boys are home & they are very happy in their own quiet way. Juno, bless her, has six babies four days old, but when she heard my voice (after two whole years) she left her family (for the first time) & came & laid down at my feet—too, too touching.

I miss you. We had a civic affair at Dudley & I go to one at Worcester tonight & then home as it seems cold—but if it shd. be warmer, I shall go to S-on-Avon for the last time & look once more on that sweet old place—where you once were.

Love
EE

The girls are well & are still very proud of their lovely clothes![19]

After that, Alice Stuart of Wortley sent a further shipment.

At Hampstead, Alice Elgar was ill again with cold and cough which doctors could not remedy. So Edward journeyed alone (with the faithful Norwich valet John Cousins) to fulfil conducting engagements in Brussels and Amsterdam.

Amstel Hotel, Amsterdam.
Thursday [20 Nov. 1919]

My dear Windflower

I wish you were here! such a wonderful orch: & everything played so well.

I want to thank you over & over again for your great kindness to those poor dears [at The Elms]—they are delirious with joy & gratitude & tell me they cannot really write to you what they feel. Bless you!

The journeys are *awful* & the expense here unbelievable & everyone trying to cheat one[:] 12s/- for ½ mile cab this morning! dinner 15s/- lunch 7s/- etc everything double what it wd be in London

I long to be home & shall come soon

Love
E[20]

He reached Hampstead a week later. His own Alice was not well enough to join him at Felix Salmond's musical party to play a Fauré piano quartet on 30 November: Alice Stuart of Wortley was there. Another Salmond party a fortnight later was devoted to Elgar. Again his wife did not go, but she preserved Edward's report of it:

[19] HWRO 705:445:7704.          [20] HWRO 705:445:4063.

14 December 1919. Always grey & misty but mercifully not cold—Mr.Reed to dine & went with E. to the Salmonds. A. *could not* go— rapturous reception of E.'s music, especially the 5tet [—] people were wildly excited & mad over it— A.S.of W. & Charlie, Frank, Robert Nichols especially enraptured, [the Ernest] Newmans, &c&c—[William] Murdoch played splendidly E. said— Little supper together when E. reached home—

The holidays that year were quiet, with Carice gone to Switzerland for a long holiday alone.

25 December. E. & A. all by themselves, very quiet happy day—E. hardly out at all. Fine rather grey[,] not cold—

26 December. E. to lunch with A.S.of W. & to play 'The Choice'. Very poor play even with Gerald duMaurier's help— Troyte arrived & E. & A.S.of W. came for tea ...

27 December ... Rather wet— E. & Troyte to lunch with A.S.of W. & then to M[erchant] of Venice ...

Severn House, Hampstead, N.W.
Monday [29 Dec. 1919]

My dear Windflower:

All thanks for giving dear old Troyte luncheon on Saturday—it *was most* kind. He enjoyed the Shylock [Moscovitch] very thoroughly indeed & wanted to go again but he has had to depart this morning to Malvern & has left a blank.

Alice is better & I hope, now she is in better spirits, will improve rapidly & get out of doors

Love
Yrs ever
E[21]

# 1920

Alice Elgar's diary had seldom referred to her own moods. The opening of this year tells much:

1 January 1920. Very quiet day— Thankful to be still together. The year opens with many heavy clouds ...

[21] HWRO 705:445:4060.

Severn House, Hampstead, N.W.3
Jan 6

My dear W

Thank you much for your letter & the Christmas roses: my sister sent some
to Alice—the latter does not get on much but comes down to Breakfast
I am tied & unhappy—the world for me is ended indeed.
Everything goes wrong & everything looks bad all round: I am tied to
gramophones & all sorts of oddities for a few days—then I will write

Love
E[1]

On 10 January the Windflower came to tea. Two days after that Alice Elgar took
her first short walk outside the house in two months. But she was not able to go with
her husband a week later when he met Alice Stuart of Wortley for lunch with the plan
of attending a Felix Salmond concert afterwards. In fact Elgar found himself with a
headache after the lunch and escaped to the zoo and then a cinema. Soon he began a
cold.

Lord Stuart invited Elgar to join them on a visit to the Cowley piano factory in
Watford, and Lady Stuart also wrote.

Severn House[,] Hampstead, N.W.
Thursday [22 Jan. 1920]

My dear W.

Many thanks for your letter. I return Frank's with thanks also: he *is*
making the best of things.
My cold mends & cracks again. I am so very sorry to miss our afternoon.
It is most kind of C. to think of me in the Watford expedn.—I fear it will be
difficult to find a day which I can manage but I shall be glad to hear all about
it—you—and hope the pianos will be worthy of the means taken to run them
to earth.
Alice has, I fear, a fresh cold & is a notably poor thing—it is wearing[.]
Carice is having good weather [in Switzerland] now & her visit is a success.
I fear (*private*) the Cenotaph affair will not include me—the *present*
proposals are vulgar & commonplace to the *last degree*. I really cannot
appear in it!

Love
EE[2]

For the dedication of the Cenotaph in Whitehall, planned for November 1920, Elgar
was asked to make an abridged version of *For the Fallen*. (He ultimately did the work,
published as *With Proud Thanksgiving*, but it was not performed at the Cenotaph
dedication.)
Soon he went down with a bad sore throat. The two invalids at Severn House had a

[1] HWRO 705:445:4098.     [2] HWRO 705:445:7687.

visit from Alice Stuart of Wortley with books and grapes for them on 29 January. A week later Muriel Foster brought a car to take Alice Elgar to the dentist. Edward, immersed in letters about investments disrupted by the war, responded to an invitation from the Windflower to lunch on Monday 9 February and see a statue of *Leda and the Swan*, said to be by Michelangelo: it was at the house of her uncle, Sir Albert Gray.

Severn House, 42,Netherhall Gardens, Hampstead, N.W.3.
Thursday [5 Feb. 1920]
My dear W.

Forgive *business* paper. I am so busy writing foolish business letters. Muriel has mercifully called with a car & taken poor dear A. out: she continues to cough badly: it *is* so very distressing.

I shall be only too delighted to lunch with you[,] Bless you! on Monday. I fear there's no chance of meeting before. If you should by any chance be free on Sunday afternoon *do* come to tea—    Some people are coming & Felix may bring his cello

Love<br>Yr<br>Ed[3]

Alice Elgar felt she was up to having a small tea party, and Alice Stuart of Wortley was invited to be one of half a dozen guests.

In her reply, the Windflower enclosed a note written by her father, Sir John Everett Millais, on the subject of the statue they were to see. This fired Elgar to some research, and his reply enclosed a note of his own on the subject:

[n.p.]
Feb 6 1920
My dear Windflower:

Many thanks for sending your father's 'note' about the 'Leda'—it is most interesting.

I am sorry it's not possible to do anything to-day and tomorrow: Monday I look forward to very much indeed. I suppose 1.30[:] if not perhaps you will cause a telephone message to be sent.

Felix *is* coming on Sunday & we shall 'do' the Concerto—so *if* you & Ch. wd. care to come *please* do. Muriel took A. out yesterday & I think she is better

Love<br>EE

P.S. On p.2. I can't make out the name 'S_____ of B' is it Sansovino? but why '*B*'? I enclose a note thereon. P T O

3 HWRO 705:445:4084.

P.S. Please shew my note to Claude on Monday—I do not care if says [*sic*] I am an idiot therefor![4]

### LEDA.

Your father writes 'Sansovino of B.'

If 'B.' means Bologna I do not understand it.

The name SANSOVINO was adopted by several artists: — Andrea CONTUCCI, (the best known), Jacopo Tatti, Niccolo Soggi and Stefano Vetroni.

The last-named is, I think, the only one who had any connection with Bologna and he was a painter: Soggi was also a painter. If the work is not by Michael Angelo and if a Sansovino is indicated in any way, I should suggest Tatti (b.Florence 1479, — d.1570). He was a pupil of Andrea Contucci.

There is in the Bargello (No.132) a 'Leda with the Swan' by Bart. Ammanati *after Michael Angelo*; what is this like?

(Is the picture formerly attributed to M.A. still in the possession of the Natl. Gallery?)

I do not see where Vincenzo Danti comes in.

E.E[5]


Sunday 8 February brought the tea party at Severn House. The hostess's cough seemed easier, and the host played his Concerto with Salmond for Alice Stuart of Wortley and the other guests. He had no new project on his desk. Next day came the lunch at Cheyne Walk with Claude Phillips and Sidney Colvin, and the viewing of the statue: it was immediately declared to be not by Michelangelo.

Severn House, Hampstead, N.W.
Thursday [12 Feb. 1920]

My dear W.

I hope you are all well: I am so sorry about the Statue & fear you must be sadly disappointed—alas! I had a penitent note from Claude—quite unnecy but very pleasant & 'good'—he is very much worried—poor old dear—over that law case.

I have been very busy with all sorts of nothings—but yesterday aftern. crept into The Crimson Alibi—RUBBISH[.] I then went to tea at 396 [Strand] & it was overcrowded to the eye but quite empty to the soul. so long ago!

I *may* get to Stoke but my days fill up I don't know how.

Love
E[6]


During the next ten days Alice Elgar was able to get out and about for short journeys with Edward.

[4] HWRO 705:445:4082.        [5] HWRO 705:445:4081.        [6] HWRO 705:445:4078.

Severn House, Hampstead, N.W.
Monday [23 Feb. 1920]

My dear W.

It seems weary ages since I saw or heard of you: things are very dull & my poor dear Alice does not really improve in strength. So after all I did not go away to Stoke; it seemed too lonely for her [to be left alone at Severn House]. Carice will be back [from Switzerland] in about a fortnight & we shall see what can be done.

I have just been down to the club a few times & tried a lonely theatre as occasion offered but everything seemed dreadfully commonplace & awful! I go to the Gramophone tomorrow & have several silly meetings etc—it is a brainlesss soulless existence & I wonder very often what it is all worth & why it is so—but so it is.

Do ring up some time—I want to go to *Pygmalion* one day—wd. that do for you?

Felix was here yesterday eveng & delighted at the prospect of going to you [to play the Concerto with piano accompaniment].

Have you played the Sonata with Reed yet or again?

Love
Yr
EE.[7]

Next day Alice Elgar was able to go with Edward to Hayes for his recording session. It included a selection of music from *The Sanguine Fan*.

On 2 March came a letter from Pollie Grafton at Stoke to say that The Elms, where they had lived so long and where Edward had so enjoyed coming, was to be sold over their heads. In his distress he telephoned to the Windflower, and then wrote:

Royal Societies Club, St.James's Street, S.W.
March 2: 1920

My dear W.

I am so sorry I told you the depressing news about Stoke—but I was full of it & very melancholy[.] Everything I have ever loved & wanted has been denied me[:] but I hate to think of my sister, after 37 years, being turned out. I will see what can be done.

Adieu till Thursday & forgive my being so *futile* over this affair

Love
Yrs
E[8]

That afternoon the 'Art and Film' Company came to Severn House to make moving pictures of Edward. Three days later his Alice was well enough to join him and Alice Stuart of Wortley to lunch and the matinée of *Pygmalion*. The following day found the Elgars out again—to see the results of the filming at Severn House, then

[7] HWRO 705:445:4090.          [8] HWRO 705:445:4093.

to lunch with Muriel Foster (who was also not very well) and go with her to see Shaw's *Candida*. Edward wrote to the Windflower:

Severn House, Hampstead, N.W.
March 6 1920

My dear W.

I hope you were not tired after our theatre. It really was splendidly done on the whole—yesterday. *Candida* is a finer play but is *not* at all well acted—the actors are not adequate except the vulgar old man who was very good—but that part is not so important as the △.

Alice was tired (rather) & our hostess not at all well & I was rather on edge but, of course, enjoyed it.

I went down to a cinema [afterwards] & got thoroughly wet on my walk home at eight o'clock,

I saw myself(?) on the film yesterday & you shd see it some day—it is going to be 'edited' a little.

Love
E[9]

Two nights later he 'sat with Alice Wortley in the old seat' at Queen's Hall for a concert in which Albert Coates conducted a bad performance of the *Introduction and Allegro*.

42, Netherhall Gardens, Hampstead, N.W.3.
March 10 1920

My dear W.

I have scarcely recovered from that awful scratch! And now have a sort of slight cold & cough—nothing I think & it will go away—with this I have a dentist—several visits—also nothing—only a general look round.

I enclose the remnant of your ticket—I think it is 'spent' but you may want it. I was sorry the time was so short & only wish the occasion had been more—well—pleasant

Love
Ed[10]

Carice arrived home three days later. On 16 March Alice Stuart of Wortley came to Severn House to lunch with the younger composer John Ireland. Then Elgar went to Leeds to conduct *Gerontius* and *The Apostles*. He returned on the 25th to find his Alice 'very unwell in bed'.

[9] HWRO 705:445:4091. Both Elgar and his wife kept diaries in early 1920. Alice Elgar's account differs by one day and reverses hostesses for the two plays (she was ill, often made up her diary in arrears, and this diary shows signs of occasional confusion). Elgar's letters of 2 and 6 March to Alice Stuart of Wortley show that his diary provides the correct sequence.
[10] HWRO 705:445:4069.

Severn House[,] Hampstead, N.W.
Friday [26 Mar. 1920]

My dear W.

I returned yesterday[:] all was most successful at Leeds & the Chorus better than ever.

Carice & I are in much trouble of mind about poor dear Alice who seems really very ill & weak & does not improve. I hope you will have a nice rest

Love
Yrs ever
Ed[11]

Before leaving London for her holiday at Tintagel, the Windflower came to tea on 29 March and again on 1 April. These visits were mainly to try to cheer Alice Elgar and her much worried family. Edward managed to tell the Windflower about a scheme for bringing performances from Rutland Boughton's Glastonbury Festival to the Old Vic in London: he himself had accepted the chairmanship of the scheme's London committee. Next day he sent a note enclosing a printed broadside which concluded: '*Your support as a Subscriber or as a Guarantor is requested*'. He marked this line with 'x' at either end.

Severn House[,] Hampstead, N.W.
Ap 2 1920

My dear W.

Here is the scheme: I don't dare ask Charlie to be a guarantor but if let [*sic*] you are not overwhelmed (*we all are*) with such things you might think of the Old Vic.

Yrs ever
EE

It was lovely to see you yesterday & for my poor dear A[12]

Alice Elgar slipped rapidly downhill. The doctors could do nothing. On 6 April she was incoherent. A specialist who was called in gave a 'bad report'. By the next day it was clear that she was dying, and that evening just after six she expired in Edward's arms. His grief drove him far within himself.

The funeral was fixed to take place three days later at St. Wulstan's Catholic Church in Little Malvern, above the cemetery Alice herself had chosen years before. Frank Schuster arranged that Albert Sammons, W. H. Reed, Lionel Tertis, and Felix Salmond should go down and play the *Piacevole* from the String Quartet—a movement Alice had loved. Afterwards Schuster wrote to Alice Stuart of Wortley:

---

[11] HWRO 705:445:7100.          [12] HWRO 705:445:7102.

The Hut, Bray, Berks.
15 April—
Dear Carrie.

I wired you 'no memorial Service probable' and I think it is dropped—it would have been very unwise I think. Oh how I wish you could have been at the funeral & heard the sweet & simple serenity of that exquisite movement, rising from some hidden part of the *lovely* little chapel—    Mind you, there was *no* other music—no organ—no singing & a very simple ritual. You can imagine I hope,—the impression left on one's ears & heart! it is *ineffaceable*.    The church & cemetery were exquisitely placed on a hill overlooking a wide panorama—all blossom & brightness—the house Edward & Carice were to stay in overlooked the same scene (it was the priests' house & is now a *charming* private hotel)—they were the only occupants & we had tea in a room flooded with sunshine & full of flowers—just what she would have *loved*—everything so *neat & dainty*. I could leave them there with a light heart!

I will let you know later what the expense of the quartet comes to, & you shall take what share of it you like.

*Do* come back soon!

> Your affecate.
> Frank[13]

Next day Alice Stuart of Wortley wrote:

Tintagel[,] N Cornwall
April 16 1920
My dear Carice,

I have thought much of you all these days, but I have not written you before this, because I knew you would be so preoccupied & busy & your sorrow & loss so fresh I felt I had better wait—but now I want to tell you how much I sympathise with you & feel for you—    You have been ever such a dear good daughter, & now you will have much to think of and do—    I am so glad you have your dear kind Sarah, She must have been such a comfort to yr. dear Mother & to you & she will grieve I fear much[.] I sympathise so much with her and she had been with yr. Mother so many years—& loved her—    Dear Carice how little I thought when I said Goodbye to you that last afternoon, how soon this great change would come, how merciful it is we do not know what is before us—    I hear you & yr. dear Father are wonderfully brave & I hope this means that you & he are well notwithstanding all you have been through this last week. Do not trouble to answer this now—    Some day let me hear from you—    I do not know whether you are

[13] Elgar Birthplace parcel 584(vi).

back at Severn House—I hope not for it will be so sad for you yet awhile—
but I send this *there* to be forwarded—    I want you to know you are much in
my thoughts & I am always

> Yrs affectionate [*sic*]
> Alice Stuart of Wortley—[14]

From Little Malvern Carice took her father to Pollie Grafton's house at Stoke
Prior, and after a few days she returned to Severn House to begin the heavy task of
dealing with affairs there. Edward remained at Stoke through a cold and rainy
fortnight. Then he went to Kent to wander round the haunts of his Elgar ancestors.
On the last day of April he returned to Severn House, and next day the Windflower
(now back from Tintagel) came to tea. She wrote to him, and he responded:

[*mourning stationery*]
Monday May 3. 1920
My dear W.

It was a great refreshment to see you: thank you for your letter.    alas!
there is nothing to be done—only lawyers & money to be found.

Do arrange to come up the day after Heifetz' Concert—I don't know the
day but will look out for it

> Love
> EE.[15]

The nineteen-year-old Jascha Heifetz was to make his Queen's Hall debut on 5 May,
and Alice Stuart of Wortley went to hear him.

The day after the concert she came to Severn House, where the Bohemian Quartet
were rehearsing the Elgar String Quartet for performances in London and elsewhere.
All were given tea. Elgar had hoped the afternoon might 'break the awfulness of the
change', as he wrote to Ernest Newman: 'but—without the hostess, My God.' Six
days later when the Bohemians played the Quartet in London, Elgar sent a note with
Carice, while he spent the afternoon at Severn House with the Windflower.

She came again a week later, and possibly after that as well (the diary Edward tried
to carry on was beginning to show many blank pages). Then it was time to fulfil a
conducting engagement booked long ago for South Wales.

[*mourning stationery*]
Hampstead
Tuesday [25 May 1920]
My dear W:

It was good of you to come up: I have made a great effort to go with Carice
to S.Wales this afternoon.

Tremendous muddle—Frank is going & wants tickets & hotel reserved—I
have no moment at Cardiff [changing from train to car for the final journey

to Mountain Ash]—& telegram asking us to alter our journey; all arriving too late to permit any change. I hope you like the hot weather—it kills me.

It was good of you to write to C. this mg.

> Good bye
> Yrs ever
> EE

I am so sorry I have no proper envelope [—] all packed[16]

After the concert he went to stay a few days with Troyte Griffith, near Little Malvern. But when he tried to leave to go to The Hut on 29 May, he fell ill with giddiness. Three days later, awaiting a car ordered to take him to Stoke, he was giddy again. Carice got him into a little hotel, fetched a local doctor, and informed Alice Stuart of Wortley. Next day—her father's birthday—she wrote:

The Grove Private Hotel, Great Malvern.
June 2nd

My dear Lady Stuart,

It was most kind of you to send me a telegram— I think Father is getting better— It was all arranged that he should go to his sister yesterday, but he had another giddy attack in the morning, so it all had to be put off, & I fled for a Dr. (who has turned out most understanding) & we found these rooms, where he is really comfortable I think & has a lovely view, & *nice* light food— it is really a very nice place. The Dr. says he *is* better today, but wants to keep him quite quiet a little longer—only quite sees that that depresses him so much & worries him, so I daresay will allow him to do more tomorrow—I do not yet know about returning or any future plans yet [*sic*]—its all very trying & difficult. It is so distressing this giddiness again—& depresses him so—& everything seems useless & hopeless.

I will let you hear how he goes on & when we return.

Very much love & *many* thanks for your telegram.

> Your loving
> Carice

Of course Father's love & *many* thanks—I forgot—[17]

The Grove Private Hotel, Great Malvern.
June 6th, 1920.

My dear Lady Stuart,

How good of you to find time to write such a lovely long letter full of news, when you have so many things to do—I did appreciate it. I did not answer at once as there was not much to add to what I had already told you—Father has been in bed all the week, except yesterday when he got up for tea & we

---

[16] HWRO 705:445:4080.        [17] HWRO 705:445:7905.

had a short stroll along the Wells Road. He is very limp & tired & not well as I hoped—but better I think. He was to go for a quiet drive today, but I do not know yet (11.30 a.m.) if he feels so inclined— He is naturally very depressed [—] & now about himself & disappointed at being so unwell, & it is very difficult to find things to take his mind off. We read a lot of silly novels— I have been reading aloud a lot— Troyte comes in when he can which is good, but he is very busy—& the only other person we see is the *very* nice Dr.— He has suffered from the same thing himself, so is full of understanding & sympathy—& Father likes him— When we shall get back I do not know— He is tired of being here, yet it is a great risk to try a railway journey until he really feels he can cope with it— The Dr. is here now so I will finish after he is gone & tell you what he says.

Later— The Dr. is quite pleased with Father & thinks he *might* be able to go home on Tuesday—of course we do not *know* but are thinking about it— Troyte has just come in for a visit—& is going to take him for his walk later in the afternoon.

Such lovely weather—except for a cold east wind, but it is very sunny & everything looks lovely.

No more news— Father's love & thanks for all your letters—We *were* so surprised about Lady Bagot—

> Very much love,
> Your loving
> Carice.[18]

Two days later they managed the journey home by train.

There was some thought of his going to Brussels and Prague for concerts: Lalla Vandervelde urged him to make the effort, and passport applications were begun. Then he decided he could not go.

[*mourning stationery*]
Hampstead.
June 16. 1920

My dear W.

I have been ill & am not well yet—all this you will have heard. It is well that I decided against the long journey. I can, at present, do very little, but rest as much as possible but I am improving: thanks so much for enquiring.

I cannot tell anything of the future: I do not *like* the outlook & cannot *control* events any longer—I must follow arrangements which have to be made from lack of gold—or paper [—] & stronger forces than I are at work! This sounds mysterious—but I only mean that we are drifting & at the mercy of the waves—and human beings.

---

[18] HWRO 705:445:7902.

We are *trying* for [a new lease at] Brinkwells, but it is very, very difficult for my dear C. to get a servant etc. etc.

I hope you are well & that this hot & depressing weather is not affecting you.

> Yours ever sincy
> E.E.[19]

They got the lease and went to Brinkwells on 22 June. Three days later Carice wrote:

[*mourning stationery*]
Brinkwells, Fittleworth, Sussex.
June 25th, 1920.

My dear Lady Stuart,

I intended to write to you earlier in the week to say how we were getting on here—but there has been so much to do getting it all straight. Now at last it is in fair running order, & we are loving it. Of course it was dreadful just the first day—but I think the air, & the quantity of lovely milk butter eggs & fruit all are doing Father good—& he seems better. It is all so sweet & the memories here are happy & peaceful that I think he is better here. In fact we do nothing but long for it to be our own. The weather has been lovely—today looks cloudy but may pass off— He is quite busy with his wood & little repairs— I have some one to help & now the house is settled, it will all work quite easily I think. I have my bicycle & so can go off & get things. What really is overwhelming is the amount of fruit & getting anything done with it! I want to weed & do everything at once!

I *am* so glad we came. I dreaded it— but now we *are* here, I am sure it is so much better for him. He is resting or would send his love. I do hope you are not feeling too hot & tired—

> Much love,
> Your loving
> Carice.[20]

Their only visitor at Brinkwells then was Lalla Vandervelde. One of the few contacts with London came from Frank Schuster, acting in his capacity as trustee for part of Alice's money (a duty taken on at the time Severn House was purchased). Then in the latter half of July they planned to leave Brinkwells for a fortnight to give Carice a rest: she was to go to stay with her friend Catherine Petre at Ingatestone Hall in Essex. On their last full day at Brinkwells Edward wrote:

[19] HWRO 705:445:7142.    [20] HWRO 705:445:7906.

Brinkwells
Sunday July 18 1920

My dear W.

A divine day.

All thanks for your letter—I saw the one to Carice & thank you many many times for sending the things. I have no good account to give: I have had *three* more slight attacks & do not like the outlook at all: I take no notice of the conditions only I have to lie down for a day or two. I only hibernate—& do not walk or anything: music I loathe—I did get out some paper—but its all dead. Our affairs are not yet settled & there is a man looking, or rather has looked at Severn House. If I am able to travel C. & I go home tomorrow; & I go to Frank for the week & then to Ridgehurst—but I was ill yesterday & not up.

The old life is over & everything seems blotted out: we are quite happy—that's not the word—serene I suppose, over our financial affairs because they are definitely settled—or rather visible. & are bad. It seems odd that Stoke was advertised last Saturday week (the sale)—the *same* day Birchwood Lodge (the old Worcester cottage) advertised & *sold*—I wanted it; & then in Country Life *same day*!! all the Wye fishing where I used to lie & fish & write & dream & where you & I walked once. Does it not seem strange that the *three* only havens of rest, to which in my busy life I have always fled for comfort & rest, should all be sold in the same week? Strange such a clean sweep of my old life.

We have no servant but a good woman comes in & Carice cooks the breakfast & other things & does housekeeping wonderfully. We had Madame V. here for a few days who did help C. but fled. & we cannot cope with visitors.

All goes on the same: Mark and the routine of the farm. The weather has been terribly depressing but we have not really felt it—I am 'numb'[.] I could not have borne the many memories but they have cut down the woods so much & made a road etc which alters the look of the place but of course dear A. *made* it & it is full of remembrances—too too sad for words. One odd thing I must tell you: in the shelter which Mark built for her & which I do not allow anyone to use, touch or look at, a Wren has built a nest just where A's head used to touch the roof-twigs; Muriel always called her the Little Wren. So it seems pitifully curious. Now, my dear W., do not think we are gloomy—far from it; but everything in life has changed,—I, to all intents and purposes, am an invalid—you see the stronger I get (& I am fairly well) the worse my *ear* is—if I am low in health & unable to get about, my ear is less troublesome: so there it is—in a vicious circle.

I hope you are well. I cannot hope that you have enjoyed the London Season because I see little in the musical world which wd. be pleasing to you—it all seems 'gone ugly'.

Frank gives a rosy acct of our finance—as he had to sign some papers being a trustee—but (as I told him) he knows *nothing* of the affairs (money left to dear A for life) outside the one trust he is in: I fear he is unwittingly making out things much better than they are. My friends always remind me of the gillie who said to Dr.Johnson (when he was nearly dead riding over the moors) by way of encouraging & amusing him: 'Oh! such pretty goats!' Thats about all they say!

> Bless you
> Yr affte
> EE

I wonder where you & your family are going for the holiday time?[21]

At The Hut and Ridgehurst now he met the Brave New World. There were the de Meyers of shadowy background. She was said to be an illegitimate daughter of Edward VII—who had certainly asked his cousin of Saxony to create a Baron's title for her husband-of-convenience, a photographer of genius who had taken the best pictures of the dancer Nijinsky. Having fled to New York for the war, the de Meyers were suddenly back and pursuing the bright young things from one European capital to another.

Then there was a handsome young New Zealand officer who had lost a leg at Gallipoli—and awoke in hospital to find Frank Schuster bending over him. Now 'Anzy' Wylde and his fiancée—a chic artist who had already attracted the elderly attentions of Walter Sickert—were calling Schuster 'Nunkie'. He talked of making The Hut over to them.[22]

Back at Brinkwells in early August, Edward Elgar reflected on the world into which he had survived. He planned to attend a revived Three Choirs Festival at Worcester where he had engaged his late Uncle Henry's rooms facing the east end of the Cathedral. Now he answered a letter from the Windflower which said she had picked some of 'the roses'.

Brinkwells
Friday Aug 6 1920

My dear W.

Carice & I returned here, on Tuesday[,] after a fortnight's visits—she wanted a change badly (but I did not)—but we are both glad to be back. We have no servant—C. gets breakfast & a woman (very capable) comes in—the rest is wonderful & the absence of servants an extraordinary calm.   C. was with Lady Petre, but came with me to Ridgehurst—I cannot say that I appreciate the influx of *Germans*—the de Meyers (now Americans) came over & Frank—*also* some extraordin[ar]y females, friends of the youth whom F. introduces as his '*Nephew*'—are we all mad?

---

[21] HWRO 705:445:7686.

[22] Information from an introductory note by Michael Parkin (based on material from the Wylde family) to an exhibition catalogue of pictures by Wendela Boreel, 1–18 Oct. 1980, at the Parkin Gallery, London SW1. The spelling of 'Anzy' is taken from her notes: elsewhere, as in Frank Schuster's letters and Siegfried Sassoon's *Diaries*, it is 'Anzie'.

After this, *what*? then at Ridgehurst we had a German lady & her daughter—who sang to the Germans in Brussels!!!

I am not well but try to rest & get ready for Worcester where we *hope* to be—but I am not at all sure: we have my uncle's old rooms & shall see no one & be quite quiet. I must do what I can. Frank talks of going but I have not heard definitely

Alas! about Stoke—I have asked a millionaire friend—I descended so low—& begged he wd. save it: he sympathised & sent an agent who reported it wd. only *pay four percent*—so my friend cd. not entertain it!!!

That is the end: the public have all my best work for nothing & I have not one single friend who cares—except you! My whole past is wiped out & I am quite alone.

I wonder where you picked roses—not here alas! I wish we cd. ask you— but it is too primitive[.] Carice loves it & is such an excellent cook.

I am glad you played the Cello Concerto [with Salmond]—I have forgotten it.

Poland [being overrun by Russian Bolsheviks] is too dreadful to think of— I cannot bear it: in fact there is absolutely nothing left in the world for me. We are trying to sell the house [in Hampstead] but hesitate every now & then as our tenure of this is uncertain

I *wish* I could send some cheerful news—but it is useless to pretend to a real friend—In the midst of it all I am not really depressed—only I see the inevitable.

[*sentence of perhaps four or five words cut away*]
Have you heard anything of Mina B.?

I hear nothing of anyone[.] I do not write, at all—in fact I have 'gone out'—& like it.

The nice woodmen are all at work & during the gleams of sun it is divine

I wish you cd. come! there is no train service allowing for a day visit I fear & it is really too far for such a journey alas!

I kiss your hands

ever<br>E

Let me hear that you get this
This envp has been directed two days & then your letter came![23]

The roses, she said, had been picked on 26 June on the way to Ludlow, where she now was. Elgar was mystified.

---

[23] HWRO 705:445:7705. In the closing, 'I kiss' and 'hands' have been eradicated.

Brinkwells
Aug 15 1920
My dear W.

All thanks for your letter. Your former letter was so vague—we thought
you were in London & shd. have been overjoyed to have seen you.

I do not in the least understand about June 26th & roses (you might tell
me)—we received none—did you send some? or what ?

We are hoping to go to Worcester & have my uncle's old 'lodgings'—but I
am not well & do not look forward to what will be a very trying ordeal. [At
the beginning of 1920 he had made plans to go to the Festival with his Alice.]
Things feel worse everyday [sic] & I feel I am[,] perforce, sacrificing Carice &
there is no friend left in the world—alas!

I am so glad you are in that lovely country—Milton['s *Comus*] at Ludlow
Castle & all the rest of the assocns. were so sweet. Let us know if you are
going to Worcr. after all. We *let* this house for a fortnight to our landlord! It
is lovely here now & harvest just over so the fields are as bare as my mind &
soul.

Yours in dejection
EE.[24]

Frank Schuster also wrote to her about Worcester. He had been over to Brinkwells,
found out Edward's plans, and provisionally engaged rooms next door for the rest of
them—including Anzy.[25] Alice Stuart of Wortley decided to come to Worcester, but
she resolved to make her own arrangements.

Then she explained to Edward that the roses had been picked from the hedge of the
cottage of his birth, 'The Firs' at Broadheath, beyond Worcester. An undated note
from him without salutation (except for 'Windflower' on the outside) was perhaps the
reply. It contains one of Elgar's most memorable self-revelations.

So you have been to B.—   I fear you did not find the cottage—it is nearer
the clump of Scotch firs—I can smell them now—in the hot sun. Oh! how
cruel that I was not there—there's *nothing between* that infancy & *now* and I
*want* to see it. The flowers are lovely—I knew you wd like the heath—I could
have shewn you such lovely lanes.

The church is new but it is more than a mile from the cott: so we must go
again. Let me know when you return but please make the most of the lovely
sights, sounds & scents.

I rose at 3—cd. not sleep & worked hard for hours before breakfast [*word
or two removed*] Monday [*word or two removed*]

Love
EE[26]

Then it was time to go up for London rehearsals before the Festival.

[24] HWRO 705:445:4216.
[25] HWRO 705:445:7908,7909.
[26] HWRO 705:445:7683. Some dried wild roses are preserved at the Elgar Birthplace in an
envelope inscribed by Alice Stuart of Wortley, with the place and date they were picked, 26 June
1920 (parcel 584(xxxiii)).

Brinkwells                    (*Stationery exhausted*)
Tuesday [24 Aug. 1920]

My dear W.

Posts are so long & vague that I inflict an[othe]r letter on you. We leave on Monday for the *Langham* as our house is shut up.

Worcester: 9 College Precincts on Friday afternn [3 Sept.] That is the plan—if I am up to it: if you *should* have any tickets you do not want my Stoke Children would I am sure be only too glad of them—but do not think of me if you have any use for any odd ones.

Frank has not been again as the weather has been too dreadful—It *is* depressing but I hope you & yours are better off for weather if for nothing else

Love<br>EE[27]

Six days later found him and Carice at the Langham Hotel. There were some spare Festival tickets sent by Alice Stuart of Wortley.

Langham Hotel, London.
Monday [30 Aug. 1920] eveng

My dear W.

All thanks for your letter & the tickets—every one will be joyously used.

We have just arrived & so much to do. I look forward to seeing you so much

9 *College Precincts   touching* the Cathedral

All thanks,   Love<br>EE[28]

During the Festival the Windflower came to see him in his rooms, and he gave her a vocal score of *The Music Makers*. Few other friends called on him, and he was very quiet between performances. Afterwards he and Carice went to the Berkeleys at Spetchley Park near by.

Spetchley Park, Worcester.
Sunday [12 Sept. 1920]

My dear W:

I was so sorry not to see you again: I hope you were not overtired. I think the [St Matthew] Passion went very well, on the whole, (you were much too close) except that afflicting young man.

---

[27] HWRO 705:445:7141. Elgar headed this letter with the words 'Stationery exhausted' in square brackets.
[28] HWRO 705:445:4215.

It is wonderful here—tell Charlie I think of his ancestor Sir F.—as the Harts are beginning to Bell (A lovely sound). I fish but catch nothing.

Our plans are quite unsettled—the servant question at Brinkwells, as some wretch has bought our cook's cottage & turned her out—she has a husband & family or we wd. take her in—*oh! my Hat!*

I hope Scotland will be lovely for you—you can make it so for other people

Love
Yrs
EE

I send this to Chelsea as you will have left Forde [near Ludlow][29]

The last half of Elgar's September diary is blank: he spent some of the time at The Hut. His next known letter to Alice Stuart of Wortley was a note of sympathy on the death of her nephew Sir John Everett Millais (3rd Baronet) from tuberculosis. Edward himself was on the eve of a three weeks' conducting visit to Amsterdam and Brussels:

Langham Hotel, London.
Friday [1 Oct. 1920]

My dear W

Just passing thro & get your letter—it is so sad, sad—your news[:] but you were prepared somewhat.

C. & I are just resting a moment & cross tonight [—] Harwich & Rotterdam.

Love
EE[30]

Near the end of his continental engagements, he wrote on the day of dining with the Belgian Prime Minister:

Ministère de la Justice: Cabinet    Bruxelles
Friday [22 Oct. 1920]

My dear W.

I was so delighted to receive your letter & to know that you are well, amongst all the sad times. I thought much of you & wondered how you were bearing it all.

Amsterdam was all right—but I find I take no interest in things except for the moment—  *It won't do.*

Carice & I came on here from Holland—she went on to S.House to try to

---

[29] HWRO 705:445:4087. The 'afflicting young man' in the *St Matthew Passion* might have been either Steuart Wilson or Herbert Heyner. Ironically both were soloists in the *Gerontius* performance which Elgar conducted in Feb. 1927, and which was partially recorded.

[30] HWRO 705:445:4217.

get it hospitable & I return on Sunday: —*how* we shall get on remains to be seen but I shall ring you up very soon & tell you.

I have been fairly well but have an awful cold now—I am hoping to get it mended for the journey.

I had a quiet time with Frank at the Hut: garden etc very much *tidied* up & more like the old well kept garden. There still remain *traces* of D. o. m. D. etc. but the summer house has been acutely washed & *tidied* up.

I feel very dull & stupid—I like to think of the Worcester days & you & the flowers & the fruit & the warm sun & my cathedral & the music: but it *is* lonely.

My dear love
Yrs
EE[31]

Returning to Severn House at last two days later, Elgar decided to hire a car for three months.

Hampstead
Tuesday [26 Oct. 1920] eveng
My dear W.

So many thanks for your letter. I lunched with Frank to-day &, as I had 'our'!!!!!!! car[,] went on to Claude. I want him to see *Linda Condon*—I shd. have come on to you but I had to rest—  I think 'my'!!!!!!! car will be useful. Do let me know when you will be in & I can easily come to you or fetch you here! It seems incredible

Excuse a mad note[.] I have had so much writing to do—please ring up at once

Love
EE[32]

She came to visit, and proposed further plans.

[*mourning stationery*]
Saturday [30 Oct. 1920] morning
My dear W.

It was 'nice' to see you here again.

I am so sorry about next week. Monday *night* I am engaged so no L.S.O. possible.

As to the theatre—on Thursday we could manage the Dennis Eadie matinée if you like. On Friday we go to Brinkwells for the night to clear up a

---

[31] HWRO 705:445:7707.        [32] HWRO 705:445:7140.

few things etc. Will you let me know about Thursday. We cd. use the car of course

Love
E[33]

Could he join her to an exhibition preview?

[*mourning stationery*]
Hampstead
Sunday [31 Oct. 1920]
My dear W.

Alas! I have no invitation for the private view, so it seems impossible to meet 'over' it.

I wrote last night about the Theatres, etc. I want you to come to *our* little theatre [The Everyman at Hampstead] some day but we must talk of this as we *must* get to Brinkwells this week for necy things

Love
EE[34]

After the next weekend spent at Brinkwells to close the cottage for the winter, Edward and Carice went to Birmingham for him to conduct a concert, and then for some days to Stoke (where the Graftons were able to remain a few more months). On 25 November he attended a Philharmonic concert conducted by Albert Coates, in which the young Heifetz played the Violin Concerto. The Windflower was also there—apparently elsewhere in the audience, as she wrote a note of congratulation.

Severn House[,] Hampstead, N.W.
Nov 27 1920
My dear W.

Thank you: yes, it was a tremendous display—not exactly our own Concerto: as to the noise afterwards—none of it was for me or my music— the people simply wanted Heifetz to play some of his small things with piano—the latter instrument being dextrously provided by the agent. I shd not have 'gone up' but I was called—and went, much against my will.

I have not forgotten the days at H'ford when 'it' was made—but there is nothing in it all somehow & I am sad.

Ever sincy
EE.

Be sure to let me have the enclosed priceless gem some time[35]

---

[33] HWRO 705:445:4068.
[34] HWRO 705:445:4070.
[35] HWRO 705:445:7858. The enclosure is missing.

Elgar's increasingly fragmentary diary records a few engagements in the next weeks—none with the Wildflower. But then they made a plan to see *The Knight of the Burning Pestle.*

[*mourning stationery*]
Thursday [16 Dec. 1920]
My dear W.

Many thanks: unless I hear from you I will be at the Kingsway Theatre on Saturday in good time.

I *hope* you may be able to lunch somewhere but we shall see. I can take you home in the car or bring you here for tea & send you to Chelsea. What weather!

Love<br>EE[36]

Afterwards she sent him a Christmas present of cigars. They reached him on the eve of starting with Carice to Stoke for a last Christmas there.

[*mourning stationery*]
Dec 21: 1920 evening
My dear Windflower.

Your lovely present has just come: thank you a thousand times—I am very very busy as we are just finishing packing ready for an early start[.] We intend to go in the car after all.

Best love: I will let you know how we fare. I was at the Colvins' yesterday—they are very *frail* I fear

Send me a word to Stoke.

Yr ever affec<br>EE[37]

But the Christmas journey itself produced painful evidence of post-war change.

Stoke Prior
Thursday [23 Dec. 1920]
My dear W.

We arrived all safely yesterday & find all well. The cigars are *too* lovely.

Our journey was quite successful, BUT another shock!!—we stayed for lunch at Stratford. Alas, alas! we can never go again: it seems unbelievable— the dear old [Shakespeare] Hotel is in new hands & much enlarged;—*smart*(!) waitresses with *very short skirts*, — the dining room *very* large (The next house has been taken in & a covered 'awning' put up to the Town Hall)—(a piano in it) partly used for DANCING, — they were jangling rag-time at two

[36] HWRO 705:445:4225.        [37] HWRO 705:445:4035.

o'c:, a three-weeks' carnival (sort of thing) dances every night for three weeks & a JAZZ BAND specially imported—    Do tell C.

The dear old porter is still there [—] very sad but trying to be very loyal to the new chief. Every room booked for this venture—*Birmingham* etc fast people. Thus goes another (I think the last) of my peaceful, poetic old haunts. I know well that this sort of thing has always been but *not* at S-on-A.

It is cold—but not too cold. Carice is out with the pony & I am writing by the fire & by the dog.

Love
EE

Forgive odd paper. I find it in my old writing case[38]

That letter could stand as an epigraph over much of his life in the decade to come.


# 1921

---

Back at Severn House for the New Year, Elgar had a diary which he hardly kept. Experience now was written on water—time spent, as for most men and women, with little to show where he had moved. His daughter Carice kept her own diary, and for much of 1921 it offers some help to the chronicler. Father and daughter waited in the big house for a purchaser who did not emerge. He suffered from intermittent giddiness.

On 6 January Alice Stuart of Wortley came to tea. Ten days later Elgar lunched at Cheyne Walk. Near the end of the month they made plans to share a play—*The Great Lover* with Moskovitch (which he had already seen and enjoyed).

The Athenaeum, Pall Mall, S.W.1.
Friday [28 Jan. 1921]

My dear Windflower:

This is only to say that I understand lunch at the Pall Mall restaurant at one o'clock tomorrow (Saturday) unless, of course, you alter this in the meantime.

I am frightfully *sad*—I always used to write foolish little notes from here to amuse my dear A.

Alas! I can amuse no one now! So Prospero must break the Wand—(of Youth)!

My love
Yours
EE.[1]

---

[38] HWRO 705:445:7706.          [1] HWRO 705:445:7189.

Both liked the play well enough to plan a return visit.

He alternated plays and cinemas with microscopes and slides at home—diatoms, plants and water creatures gathered from the garden or nearby ponds. When Alice Stuart of Wortley came to tea on 1 February, she was shown these wonders. During the next two months Carice's diary records only two further visits to tea—and on 30 March another performance of *The Great Lover*, which they shared with Carice herself and Frank Schuster.

During these days, however, Lady Stuart of Wortley formed a private project which was to reach far into the future. She wrote a note to accompany her will:

7 Cheyne Walk, Chelsea, S.W.
March 27. 1921

In the event of my death I wish the whole of these bound works[,] signed gift copies & MS[S] of Edward Elgar's [,] to be offered to the town of Worcester. Failing a suitable convoyance of them[,] to be offered to the British Museum for the nation—they are NOT to be sold[;] but I trust Worcester will see their way to accepting them & that later on a national fund may be started to acquire the house at Broadheath where Edward Elgar was born & that these valued possessions of mine given me by him should be placed there permanently—I bequeath also my portrait by my Father—the head & shoulders one in the *front* drawing room here done in 1887 to go with the above books, MS[S] etc to the town of WORCESTER.

I trust that these wishes of mine will be carried out by those to whom I leave it & who have the power to do it as a SACRED request

Alice Stuart of Wortley

Everything is carefully put together in the years from 1905 until the present as given to me.

A S of W.[2]

It is not clear whether Edward or Carice knew of these plans at the time, or whether Edward ever knew of them. But here was a first shadowing of a plan which Carice was to carry out fifteen years later, after her father's death—to persuade the Worcester City Corporation to buy 'The Firs' to make an Elgar museum. Carice said it was her father's wish: and under that rubric it has provided a centre for Elgar study and interest to this day. But it may well be that its first visionary was the woman whose inspiration had lighted much of his later creative life.

When she came to Severn House again on 14 April 1921, she found him sad. It had been the anniversary week of his own Alice's death; and it had just become clear that he could not buy Brinkwells, nor have it beyond the present summer: the owners of the lease, the artist Rex Vicat Cole and his wife, wished to go back to it. The day of the Windflower's visit was further clouded by the threat of a general strike. When she got back to Chelsea safely she wired, and he replied instantly:

[2] Elgar Birthplace parcel 584(li).

[*mourning stationery*]
Severn House[,] Hampstead, N.W.
April 14 1921

My dear W.

I am glad you are safely back at home—the times are disquieting indeed &
no one can tell what is going to happen.

I have been very very sad during the anniversary time & we are planning—
as well as we can—for the future. Brinkwells alas! is definitely *not* to be
ours—the Coles intend to keep it after all; naturally we cannot blame them
only it seems rather hard after we were led to believe we could have it.

Love
EE.[3]

The general strike did not materialize, and she came to tea a week later.
Carice had met a man she wanted to marry. Samuel Blake proposed, she accepted
subject to her father's consent. Edward agreed unhesitatingly, though her departure
would mean his leaving Severn House whether sold or not. They had just acquired
another Aberdeen terrier, called Meg: she would go with Carice when the time of
separation came. Then the cellist Beatrice Harrison (who had recently made records
of the Concerto) offered another Aberdeen, Laddie. He was at Severn House one
night, and Meg liked him. Edward found himself sorely tempted, but decided ruefully
it would be wholly impractical.

Severn House[,] Hampstead, N.W.
Tuesday [26 Apr. 1921]

My dear W.

It seems ages since you were here.

The dog came—beautiful & perfect manners & so gentle & *alive*;—I kept
him one night & on Friday took him, REGRETFULLY back. Our plans are so
vague & I shall soon have no home—& a dog in lodgings—I do not like the
idea. He *was* a perfect dog.

The enclosed (torn) note came from Mina

—I have told her I am going away & will telephone on my return—  I
have heard nothing of Kreisler yet & Lan, who was here on Sunday[,] knew
nothing of his time of arrival etc.

Love
EE

I am going to Bournemouth for a concert.[4]

He went down on 28 April to conduct the Second Symphony, and stayed several days.
He returned to conduct the première of *With Proud Thanksgiving* with a new
orchestration (the accompaniment had first been scored for band) on 7 May in the

---

[3] HWRO 705:445:7761.      [4] HWRO 705:445:7202.

Albert Hall before the King and Queen: Alice Stuart of Wortley and Carice shared a box. That evening the Windflower went to a performance of *The Apostles* (which the Elgars also attended).

Fritz Kreisler made his post-war reappearance at Queen's Hall on 4 May. He and his wife stayed in London some weeks. They sat with Edward and Carice for the London première of Kreisler's String Quartet on 9 May. Six days later Kreislers and Elgars came to a party given by Landon Ronald, at which Felix Salmond played the Elgar Cello Concerto. On 19 May Salmond was to give a chamber music party (Fauré, Brahms, and Beethoven) to which Kreislers and Elgars came again. Edward wrote to the Windflower, now on her spring holiday:

Severn House[,] Hampstead, N.W.3
May 18 1921
My dear W.

I hope you have had a nice country time in this weather—divine. I had hoped to have seen you either at Felix Salmond[']s or at the Ronalds—but you were away. I will tell you of the music. I returned from the Hut on Saturday,—I was very dull & *sad* there: it is so different & so *odd*. I will not write about it—but the curious sight of Frank *walking* to Maidenhead Station to catch a train when the young man was off in the car early is too puzzling—& F. will not pay for a cab!! I wanted to shriek for enlightenment.

We are planning to leave on Sunday for Brinkwells—I wonder what you thought of *The Apostles*? That & Kreisler gave a glimpse of the grand old artistic past life of me: gone!

> My love to you
> Yrs ever
> EE[5]

Before Brinkwells, the Windflower returned and came to Severn House to tea on 20 May. She found Edward making a fair copy of an orchestral arrangement he had just finished of Bach's organ Fugue in C minor. She asked him to join her the following evening for a rare performance of *The Black Knight* at Queen's Hall: he wanted to go with her but did not feel well. His next letter was from Brinkwells—where the chaffinches seemed to be singing 'Three cheers!' as they had three years ago in that spring of recovery and resurgence.[6]

Brinkwells
Thursday [26 May 1921]
My dear W.

We came down by car—it is divine but sad beyond words & empty. I was not well on Saturday evening & was so sorry to have missed the pure white lady—not the Black Knight.

[5] HWRO 705:445:7214.
[6] Elgar's diary for late May 1918 contains a note: 'All this time chaffinches (many) singing *"Three cheers!"*'.

I have finished my score of the fugue & have sent it away—I think it is *brilliant*—a word I wanted in connection with Bach, who, in arrangements, is made 'pretty' etc etc.

'*Three cheers*'—(alas for memories) I hear from all parts of the garden: there is a nest on the lawn with six(!) larks—sweetest things & there are many other things—I do not know how long we shall, or *can* rather, stay: our domestic is calm up to the present. Meg is wild with delight—everything is a thrill—very naughty but a dear.

Love
EE[7]

Brinkwells
Saturday [4 June 1921]
My dear W.

So many thanks for the book—which is a wonderful piece of work.

It is lovely here but very sad: we return to Hampstead on Wednesday—I have to be up for several things but we shall return here, I think, very soon. I do not write now as I shall hope to see you

Love
EE[8]

They went up four days later. On 11 June Alice Stuart of Wortley came to tea. Three days after that she went with Edward to an exhibition of Max Beerbohm caricatures, lunched, and they went to see *If*—which was condemned. Edward spent ten days away—at The Hut (where appearances were no better) and Stoke (where his sister was now preparing to move). He returned before the end of the month, and entertained the Windflower to tea and a walk on 30 June.

Then Edward and Carice began the long process of sorting the family effects of thirty years before Severn House was closed. Carice wrote:

2 July 1921 ... Father went through all his sketches, M.S.S. etc.[—] sad work. Destroyed much & got all in order. At it all day...

3 July ... Finished sorting M.S.S. ... Father to lunch at Stuart of Wortleys—Lan there & Mrs.Perugini (Dickens' daughter).

Three days later he was off to Herefordshire, to rehearse the chorus for the Three Choirs Festival.

[7] HWRO 705:445:7708.      [8] HWRO 705:445:7207.

Brockhampton Court, Hereford.
July 7 1921
My dear W.

I did like my lunch—I mean you & the people more particularly—but you will know this.

I came down to this heavenly place yesterday to rehearse the chorus today—after that my proceedings are unknown—I can't tell *what* to do.

Love
EE[9]

Music did not tempt him. After his return he wrote a long letter to *The Times Literary Supplement* drawing together many references to Shakespeare's works in the novels of Sir Walter Scott. And he prepared a speech to open a new Gramophone Company showroom in Oxford Street on 20 July. He said:

The days when the Gramophone was held to be nothing more than a scientific toy have gone by; now it takes its rightful position, and a very important position, in the world of music. ... The gramophone can lead listeners to appreciate music from a point of view embracing structure and effect apart from any responsibility of execution; it can bring into being a new public which shall understand music by hearing great compositions adequately recorded.[10]

Now that these prophecies have been more than fulfilled, their truths seem obvious: but they were far-sighted indeed in 1921.

Next day he and Carice went to Brinkwells for what was to be their last stay.

Brinkwells[,] Fittleworth[,] Sussex
Wedy [27 July 1921]
My dear W.—

I have let the days go by to see if it is possible to say anything not melancholy about this dear place—but it is too sad. I do not sleep & can do nothing all day but wonder what it is all for, what it means & what the end will be. One person is really enjoying herself—Meg:—every moment has a new thrill & discoveries are made with the greatest joy—I refrain from sending you a list of Meg's toys, or rather things she has brought into the house or, at least, garden: you know well the puppy's 'mind':—but two dead snakes are a little beyond what we wished for in our wildest dreams:

I do not know how long we shall stay—it depends on so many things. I think of going over to Crowborough to see Landon Ronald next week for a day or two but that depends on the hotel—it is of course full.

---

9  HWRO 705:445:7179.
10  Quoted in *Elgar on Record*, p. 38: taken from a transcript edited after the event by Elgar himself and published in the Gramophone Company's house magazine *The Voice*, Aug. 1921.

*Living* here is difficult,—worse than in wartime—milk & eggs very scarce so we can ask no one here;—Carice manages wonderfully & our little London maid likes it—for the time. Mark just as usual, but the garden is burnt up & not many flowers. Our farm crops are wonderfully good considering the drought. I have heard no news of anyone.

My speech at the Gramophone opening was shockingly reported—it was quite long & *important*—the reporters only seem to have noted a few stupid things which they turned inside out. I sent a little letter to the *Times Lity Supplement*—which you will not have seen—but everything is remote & worthless.

I have countless absurd letters to answer—only one new phrase *pleases* us—a German writes, *in his best English*, 'the celestial, unearthly Quintet that to hear I had the occasion only one *meal*.'—meaning of course, *einmal*.

I think you will soon be going north—Scotland will be divine & it has had some rain so you may see some *green* amongst the purple & greys.

Love<br>EE.

I hope your sister is now on the way to recovery.

My little invalid is really no better—but they are settling down to the new life quietly.[11]

The invalid was his niece Madge, who had now moved with the Graftons from Stoke Prior to a new house called Perryfield, a few miles away at Bromsgrove.

Alice Stuart of Wortley wrote a letter of news, and asked about coming to the Hereford Festival with Frank Schuster. Elgar's reply showed again how unhappy he was with the changed conditions in his old friend's life.

Brinkwells
Tuesday [2 Aug. 1921]

My dear W:

Your very welcome letter came (in the *rain*) this morning & everything begins to look cool & refreshed: only one person does not like the weather; I need not say it is our darling Meg: she is now curled up on *the couch* in the studio.

I go to Crowborough tomorrow—I shd. like to see Lady N[orthcliffe]—but do not know her well enough to find her. N. is making a terrible fool of himself [in his private life] alas!

I am delighted to hear all your news & that the dear pictures [of Millais] are safe for all time— I seem so out of everything now that a gleam of 'art' is refreshing. Did you see my letter in the *Times* Lity Supplement on July 14th. [*sic*]—I meant you to read it, being about Scott, etc:—not worth sending—however.

I have given Frank up! he is hopeless & so an end [The rift did not last

[11] HWRO 705:445:7208.

long.] I fear you will not get to Hereford & I wonder very much if I shall! I am glad to hear of Mina & Claude:

I have really nothing to say—we are sorrowfully putting things on one side here for the final departure & marking things to be given to the villagers—the piano will go to Carice's new home—it is all very depressing but necessary & must be faced & is being faced.

Harvest is finished here—last year it did not begin until Augt. 6th. I should like to do some wood cutting & such things—but of course it is of no use to touch anything. I have not put up the blind in the summer house this year & all the ferns we planted round about are withered dry. The place is not the same as it was in the lonely war years—there are so many men at work in the woods now & in the quarries—quite a dozen men in one—& the vast loneliness of it, which was it's [sic] charm, is (, *in a measure* only) gone.

The wild things are still here—nightjars very much to be heard.

I hear that the Stoke People are settling down in their new home: they were very sad at dismantling the old home & the home of the windflowers is desolate for evermore. What a blight has come over my life in the last eighteen months. Stoke, Worcester, Birchwood[,] Brinkwells [—] all gone!

Love
EE[12]

He went for three days to Crowborough and returned for a final fortnight at the beloved cottage.

Brinkwells
Augt 17: 1921

My dear W.

This is the last note from this dearest little place—nearly everything is cleared up—I leave on Sunday & Carice remains for a day or two longer.

Meg progresses—has discovered a rats' nest & has destroyed *five*: marvellous for an infant.

If you want a book get *Tahiti* by Geo. Calderon [—] it is ravishing.

Love
EE[13]

The beginning of September found Edward and Carice at London rehearsals for the Hereford Festival.

Langham Hotel, London.
Friday [2 Sept. 1921] a m

My dear W.

Your letter very welcome, just come[.] C & I are starting for Brockhampton Court[,] Hereford[,] where we shall be during the week.

[12] HWRO 705:445:7169.          [13] HWRO 705:445:7709.

I shall *strive* to see you—do not get too tired—it seems an awful journey: rehearsals have been good.

I was so glad to hear that the hotel at S-on-A was not so bad as I found it

Love
EE[14]

For the Hereford Festival week, she stayed at The Green Dragon Hotel, close to the Cathedral. There Edward could visit her between concerts. On the Wednesday evening, after conducting *The Apostles* earlier in the day, he was at the Hotel office handing in a note—when Schuster's friend the poet Siegfried Sassoon walked in. Sassoon wrote in his dairy:

... I could think only of the magnificence of *The Apostles* this morning. Could this possibly be the man who composed that glorious work—this smartly dressed 'military'-looking grey-haired man, with the carefully-trimmed moustache and curved nose?

And the great man actually seemed pleased to see me! Was amiable, and even modest in his manner. I wanted only to tell him of the delight I'd got from his music. And, of course, I did so. He admitted that the final climax in *The Apostles* had been 'pretty good'. I suppose he is very 'English'—always pretending and disguising his feelings. ...

Lady Stuart of Wortley (a daughter of Millais the painter) is in this hotel—an old friend of Schuster's. She told me that she remembers, as a child, hearing old Trelawny tell about his burning Shelley's body. What a link with glory![15]

After the Festival, Edward returned to Severn House to help Carice sort through furniture. As the house had still found no purchaser, they had decided to auction it in November.

Severn House[,] Hampstead, N.W.
Oct 5 1921

My dear W.

Thank you for your note: I have not written anything since Hereford: I asked C. to ring up your house & learnt that you are to return next week.

It is a fearful wrench this moving & clearing up things

Love
EE.[16]

By then he had seen a flat he liked in St James's Place, a quiet West End backwater close to his clubs and Green Park.

---

[14] HWRO 705:445:7093.          [15] *Diaries 1920–1922*, p. 80.          [16] HWRO 704:445:7079.

Severn House[,] Hampstead, N.W.
Oct 13 1921

My dear W:

I am so glad you will be back in London soon—perhaps today: the postmark of your letter *Bromsgrove* sounded very Worcestershirish & near home.

I think this will be the very last note you will receive from this address— Carice will remain a little longer: I go away one day soon (not fixed yet)—I *may* go to Frank at the Hut for a few days before starting housekeeping on my own acct. I will not write more now as you may ring up.

Love
EE.[17]

Next day Carice noted: 'Lady Stuart to tea—awful fuss over round table . . .'. It was the table he had bought in 1912 for the Severn House music room. Edward had decided not to have it in his flat. Alice Stuart of Wortley may have felt that its continued proximity might yet stimulate further music. His next letter, written on new stationery, gave his answer in more general terms:

37, St.James's Place, S.W.1. [*really from* Severn House]
Oct 15 1921

My dear Windflower:

Of course you will know I am not yet at the address named above! But the paper has just come & so I use the very first sheet to you—   You know I bought some with E on it in Liverpool long ago—so long ago.

I feel reconciled to the change—things here seemed to become more sad & hopeless—   I could not help feeling, until about, really I think, a few weeks ago that my dear A. wd. be sure to come back & take charge of things—   I cannot explain, but I never touched anything without feeling—   I cannot say *thinking*, one doesn't think—that I was responsible to Her for every movement. Now I feel the desolation & hopelessness of it all &, curiously, feel more satisfied—not happy but *calmer* over the situation. It must be. With all my artistic stupidity I have always been, in other people's troubles[,] the strong man—but I failed for myself & no one did anything to help. Salah! The end of Severn House was more *radiant* than the beginning.

I am sorry about the table—what can be done?

Love
Yrs ever
EE.[18]

Ultimately the Windflower herself gave the table a home at Cheyne Walk, until Carice was able to take it into the large farmhouse to which she moved in 1924. (It is now at the Elgar Birthplace.)

[17] HWRO 705:445:7062.        [18] HWRO 705:445:7688.

Elgar went to stay at The Hut while Carice supervised the moving of his furniture and books into the flat. It was the office her mother had done in so many moves of the past. When he returned on 20 October, he could walk in to find everything prepared for his new life.

37, St.James's Place, S.W.1.
Oct 22 1921

My dear W.

You will understand that C. & I have been more than busy—I returned from the Hut & found all ready here—things not quite settled yet as we sent down too many things but you may be quite happy about me so far—the sitting room is in bright sunshine now & looks *lovely*: all other arrangements perfect & all the servants—so far—charming.

I enclose a detailed account of the telephone arrgts—my own number I shall not put in the book.

I can give you any meal,—lunch, tea or dinner—all very simple.

I have, as waitress, a nice French young lady, or Belgian & a dear old valet who turns out to be the br. in law of a valued parlour-maid formerly at Severn House!

Love
EE

P.S. I am writing to Charlie about admission to the H[ouse] of C[ommons] etc[19]

Two nights later the Stuarts of Wortley and Clare went to Queen's Hall for a performance of the Violin Concerto by Albert Sammons with Coates conducting. Elgar was there separately, and he wrote afterwards:

The Athenaeum, Pall Mall, S.W.1.
Oct 26 1921

My dear W.

Thank you for your letter—yes, it was good to hear the reception & Sammons played splendidly

I was at the Chamber Concert at Chelsea Town Hall—excellent—why don't you go to them?

I shall *see* you on Thursday but I have two tickets sent to me for C[arice] &

Yr aff
EE[20]

It was a concert conducted by Eugène Goossens, to include the first performance of the Bach Fugue arrangement. It was a great success, and was encored.

[19] HWRO 705:445:7176.          [20] HWRO 705:445:7191.

Then the Stuarts of Wortley invited him to dine the following Monday evening before attending the first night of a new Diaghilev ballet season, opening with a new complete production of Tchaikovsky's *The Sleeping Beauty* — choreography completed by Nijinska and costumes by Bakst. He replied the morning after the concert:

37, St.James's Place, S.W.1.
Friday [28 Oct. 1921]
My dear W.

Many thanks. I will gladly come on Monday night;—I suppose rather early; will you let me hear the hour?

Do see the Daily Mail about the fugue [—] and the D.Telegraph.

I have no car now so I cannot help to convey my guests as on one former occasion.

Goossens is a great conductor.

Love
EE[21]

In the event their evening was postponed two nights.

Royal Societies Club, St.James's Street, S.W.1.
Sunday [30 Oct. 1921]
My dear W.

Many thanks for your telegram: I shall be delighted to come on Wedy.— tell me the time of your dinner—or do I meet you at the Theatre?

In great haste [—] just back from A. Boult[']s concert at the People's Palace

Love
EE[22]

They dined at Cheyne Walk, and enjoyed the postponed ballet evening—despite the fact that some London critics likened Tchaikovsky's score to circus music.

Yet Elgar felt the current ballet mania was extreme. He wrote two months later to Frank Schuster: 'The Russian Ballet enthusiasts keep well on shouting to each other that the present is the finest production altho. they know its the worst; they are so 'committed' to it that they get angry—   I brought the house down the other day by saying (paraphrasing the old proverb) 'It seems if you scratch the Russian Ballet you get the Tartar emetic!' The which is a hard saying.[23]'

The next night Albert Coates was conducting the *'Enigma' Variations* at a Philharmonic Concert, but Elgar had a dinner engagement. Then he had news that his sister Pollie Grafton was suddenly and seriously ill at her new home in Bromsgrove.

[21] HWRO 705:445:7166.          [22] HWRO 705:445:7078.          [23] 6 January 1922.

Royal Societies Club, St.James's Street, S.W.1.
Nov 4 1921

My dear W,

Thank you for a very delightful eveng on Wedy—it did not matter about the music at all.

I could not get to Q's Hall last night—I hear very varying reports but I suppose the climax must have been very great.

I am sorry to tell you that I hear very bad accounts of my dearest sister—she has been sleeping now & we hope may be better: of course the cruel break-up of the old home—more to her than we can tell—must have affected her extremely—she is very ill—I have given up the weekend visit [to Ridgehurst] as I may be wanted
    Alas!

> My love
> Yrs ever
> EE[24]

Carice was still clearing Severn House, for its auction on 8 November. On the 7th she sent the round table to Lady Stuart, had a car to take a quantity of Elgar manuscript scores to the publisher Novello for safe keeping, and joined her father in the evening for the first part of a Queen's Hall concert at which Albert Coates conducted the Bach Fugue arrangement. The Stuarts of Wortley were there. Next day Elgar answered a letter from the Windflower:

37, St.James's Place, S.W.1.
Tuesd[a]y Nov 8 1921

My dear W.

Thank you for your letter: I had hoped to have said this in person but I have a sort of inward chill & do not creep far afield.

The news from Perryfield is more reassuring—& all will go well if no accident interferes—  She eats a little & sleeps well but of course there *may* be a recurrence of the first symptoms—I trust not.

I just looked in for the fugue last night but the conductor sat a little heavily on it—no champagne.

> Love
> Yr
> EE

Christies are beginning their sales. I go in every Monday or Tuesday at 3. or Willis' rooms or both.[25]

---

[24] HWRO 705:445:7169.
[25] HWRO 705:445:7690, with Clare Stuart Wortley's note (HWRO 705:445:7204).

At the estate agents' auction that day, Severn House failed to attract a fair bid. The dispersal of its contents continued. On 14 November Elgar went to Sotheby's to see his own suite of Louis XV furniture—the gift of Frank Schuster for Severn House—in the rooms awaiting sale. (It too failed to sell.) That afternoon, however, he met the Windflower at Christie's to visit another sale.

Eugène Goossens was to repeat the Bach Fugue arrangement on 23 November. The day before it Elgar attended a rehearsal, but on the night of the concert he had a dinner engagement. The Stuarts of Wortley were going, and she telegraphed to him to join them. He answered:

37, St.James's Place, S.W.1.
Wedy [23 Nov. 1921] eveng. *6 o'c*

My dear W.

Your kind telegram has just come: thank you very much but I have my own ticket & cannot go!

I heard G. do the fugue yesterday, & he makes it really *go*. I was at the galleries yesterday and Monday but found nothing very interesting to look at.

I hope you are well: you see Kreisler *is* giving the Concerto

Yrs ever
EE.[26]

There had been speculation as to whether Fritz Kreisler would include the very difficult Elgar Concerto in his post-war repertoire. But it was placed in an afternoon concert to be conducted by Landon Ronald on 6 December. Alice Stuart of Wortley, Clare, and Bice (Lord Stuart's elder daughter) came into a very crowded Queen's Hall. By the time Carice arrived, Edward had to ask for an extra chair to be placed for her in the gangway next his own. The performance was a triumph, the composer was called to the platform to share applause with the artists, and afterwards he went across to the Langham for tea with the Windflower.

His next letter referred to a later concert (not recorded in his fragmentary diary or in Carice's: since the clearance of Severn House she had been staying with cousins in south London and not seeing her father every day). Elgar also had news of his brother Frank's illness.

37, St.James's Place, S.W.1.
Dec.14.1921

My dear W:

It is most kind of you to let me see your very Windflowerish speech. beautiful. I return it as you will want the copy.

I did not stay many minutes at the Concert.

My two invalids are (to-day) reported better. my sister will probably get all right again but my brother's improvement can only be temporary I fear. I am

[26] HWRO 705:445:7174.

not sure about going away:—it depends upon Carice's arrgts which are not settled till Thursday.

Mr. Embleton (who has just succeeded to his brother's vast fortune) was here yesterday with plans for Canterbury etc.   otherwise I see no one

Love
EE[27]

Four days later he and the Windflower went to another concert conducted by young Adrian Boult at the People's Palace in the East End of London. On Christmas Day Edward lunched at Cheyne Walk—and lunched again with the Windflower on Boxing Day before they went to a matinée. Besides her present to Edward, she had sent a ham to the Graftons at Bromsgrove, and that elicited the first of several surviving letters from Edward's favourite sister:

Perryfield, Bromsgrove.
28th Dec 1921

Dear Lady Stuart

I am writing to thank you for your kind remembrance & good wishes for Christmas and the New Year—   The lovely Ham came quite safely yesterday[.] It was so sweet of you to think of us, and we all appreciate so much your kind thought.

So many changes since this time last year, but everything happens for the best, and we love our new little nest and have no wish to be back at 'The Elms' now we are really away—   This place is very small but compact, and every convenience—

My illness has been a weary time but I am soon to be on my feet again & the D$^r$ says better than I have been for a long time, so that is hopeful & something to look forward to—   I am thinking so much of dear Edward, he loves his new home he says, but I fear he will be very lonely when Carice is married—   I think of him very much and hope he will keep well and bright.

I hope you are very well—   With every good wish for the coming year— Again thanking you so much from all here

Yours very sincerely
S.M.Grafton

This letter is as clear a speaking likeness as any of her brother's—and her thoughts, even amid her own troubles, were with him.

[27] HWRO 705:445:7181.

Alone in his London flat, Elgar settled to the life of a non-composer. If he kept regular diaries henceforth, only a few fragments seem to survive. Carice was married on 16 January 1922: with her departure, her diaries offer only occasional help in chronicling her father's life. And now, as Elgar's life found few new patterns, his letters to the Windflower declined into repetition. 1922 was perhaps a low point, and for that reason some letters henceforth are summarised. The majority of those omitted are notes to make, break, or acknowledge engagements to meet. Nothing has been omitted whose essence is not already well represented, and the footnotes give manuscript references to everything the compiler has seen.

In January 1922 Richard Strauss came to London for the first time since the war. On the day after Carice's wedding, Elgar dined with the Stuarts of Wortley before they all went to the first Strauss concert. Six days later he gave a lunch to introduce Strauss to younger British musicians—John Ireland, Eugène Goossens, Arthur Bliss, Rutland Boughton, Adrian Boult, Arnold Bax, and Norman O'Neill. He also invited George Bernard Shaw, and two old friends who could help with translation—the singing teacher Victor Beigel and the violinist Max Mossel.

Two days later Elgar wrote on the stationery of Brooks's Club, to which he had just been elected: 'real XVIII centy & full of memories of Fox etc. etc. which I love'.[1]

Brooks's[,] St James's St[,] S W 1
Jany 25 1922
My dear W.

This is the first time I use this address, which I have a right to do, but I am not there because I am in my room with a cold—only a cold so do not think of influenza.

The Strauss-Shaw lunch was a great success; I, with more wiles than any serpent—(EVE—in he of paradise)—got Mossel & Beigel—who cd. both interpret & so all was understood.

I remember our eveng & how glorious the music was after the empty rot we have now. I am quite upset about Nikisch—quite unexpected.

Love
EE[2]

The great Hungarian conductor, a notable protagonist for Elgar's music on the continent before the war, had died very suddenly on 21 January.

In February Elgar and Alice Stuart of Wortley dined with the formidable hostess Sibyl Colefax,[3] and lunched with Mina Beresford before sharing a concert at the People's Palace at which Adrian Boult conducted the *Variations*.[4] Elgar himself was

---

[1] 27 January 1922 (HWRO 705:445:7691).
[2] HWRO 705:445:7787.
[3] Monday [6 Feb. 1922] (HWRO 705:445:7213); Sunday [12 Feb.] (HWRO 705:445:7188).
[4] Saturday [18 Feb.] (HWRO 705:445:7159); Sunday night [19 Feb.] (HWRO 705:445:7080).

shortly to conduct a programme of his own music with the Hallé Orchestra in Manchester.[5]

Charles Stuart of Wortley was meanwhile taking up his pen to address the editor of *The Musical Times*. It was a long letter on a topic close to his heart, showing sound judgment and giving fascinating sidelights of personal history:

7, Cheyne Walk, Chelsea.
February 15, 1922.
Sir,—

In the *Musical Times* for January, 1922 (pages 25–27), Archdeacon Gardner enters a timely protest against (among other things) 'the undue hurrying of familiar choruses [of oratorios] in order that they may sound fresh and exciting.' May I be allowed to give my humble support to this protest, and even to show that there is need for it in respect of many other performances than those of oratorio choruses?

Having sat next to Hubert Parry in a back row of second basses in the Bach Choir for the first ten years (1875–85) of its history, I may be allowed to call to mind that though our then conductor's (Otto Goldschmidt's) *tempi* may by some have been thought too slow, he did nevertheless get such tone from his instruments and such vocal quality from his singers that on three occasions he actually won encores from St.James's Hall audiences: twice (1876 and 1879) for the *Cum Sancto Spiritu* in the Mass in B minor, and again for the *Fecit Potentiam* in the Magnificat of Bach.

But in subsequent years it has been my fate to hear *Cum Sancto Spiritu* taken so fast, even under very distinguished conductorship, that all the force of the great ascending and descending sequential ladders of phrases was completely lost. Owing to forced speed, there was no breath in the singers and no tone in the strings; and all that a first hearer could get was a succession of crude patches of orchestral colour with small suggestion in them of either line or shape.

I remember too, how, when I wished to repeat the pleasing experience of a performance of *Phoebus and Pan* under Mr.Julius Harrison, I went again to Covent Garden, to find enthroned another conductor who thought he could get more vivacity into Momus's song *Patron, Patron*, and more boisterous fun into Midas's *Pan ist Meister*, by taking both at much faster *tempi*. The only result of the higher speed was that both songs became long and tedious instead of crisp and short as before.

Let me try and show why there is no paradox here, and why the performance that takes the shorter time seems longer in effect. Surely all undue accelerations are achieved at the expense of instrumental tone and timbre, of the clarity of decorative figures, and of the breaths and voices of singers. Composers must be supposed to choose their instruments and write their choral parts so as to get the best tone to be had at the given pace. In

[5] Friday [24 Feb.] (HWRO 705:445:7160).

other words, speed, tone, and clarity all act and react upon each other. At forced speeds graceful or brilliant string passages may well degenerate into mere unmusical scratchings. In such cases your gay movement, losing the effect of its humorous or exhilarating figures, becomes not more 'jolly' but less so, and may indeed become ineffective to the point of tedium.   ...

Music, most jealous of mistresses, brooks neither competitors nor distractions.   ... Conductors who aim at excessive speeds are doing the very thing that must deprive music of its ascendancy over our attention. How can you listen with attention to music of which its chief executant makes it seem his one desire to get to the end? ... So it is that conductors who force speeds beyond what the character of the music will bear are in truth defeating their own chief objects.

> Yours, &c.,
> Stuart of Wortley.[6]

When this letter appeared in *The Musical Times* on 1 March, Lord Stuart sent the cutting to Elgar—who returned it with approval.

7, Cheyne Walk, Chelsea, London, SW.3.
March 6/22

My dear Edward,

Many thanks for returning the cuttings about the Forced Direction.

I was glad you approved of my views in the Musical Times. I was afraid you would condemn them as those of a presumptuous amateur.

I suspect you are having a strenuous time with Landon's provincial engagements.

I have been ill, or I would have written sooner.

> Sincerely yrs
> Stuart of W.[7]

Lord Stuart's persistent cough then caused him to go with his wife to the sea air at Folkestone. Elgar was conducting five concerts in northern cities for Landon Ronald, who was ill.

Then he was asked for still another, as he wrote afterwards:

Brooks's, St.James's Street, S.W.I
Sunday [19 Mar. 1922]

My dear Windflower.

I was telegraphed for to go to Leicester to take Landon Ronald's Concert—his mother (a very old lady) died—so I fled up to L. & came back on Saturday.

---

[6] *The Musical Times*, 1 Mar. 1922, p. 199. The Bach Choir conductorship passed from Goldschmidt to Stanford in 1885—the year Stuart Wortley left the Choir. The later conductor of *Phoebus and Pan* at Covent Garden was probably Sir Thomas Beecham.

[7] HWRO 705:445:6177.

I have had a slight cold—but I desire news of you & the family & hope that you are all permanently well & refreshed by the sea air.

I saw Frank this morning—he is well & seems very flourishing—I dine with him tonight: on Tuesday we go to the first night of Arnold Bennett's play [*The Love Match*]—

I have much to tell you—but my adventures in the north have not been exciting but I have been interested & loved conducting the Liszt [*Hungarian Fantasia*] with Katherine Goodson.

Let me hear soon.

My invalids are not very satisfactory I fear

Love
E[8]

At the end of March he went to Leeds to conduct the Choral Union in *The Apostles*.[9] It was at the urging of Henry Embleton, who was planning further performances in London and Canterbury in hopes of tempting Edward to complete the trilogy. But at Leeds Edward caught a chill—in circumstances described in a letter written a week later from his sister's home:

Perryfield House, Bromsgrove
Wedy [5 Apr. 1922]

My dear W.

Your letter to St J[ame]s's & the second one addressed here—(with the dinner card etc) have reached me this a.m.

I am better & *should* return tomorrow.

I have not been in London since last *Monday week*. I left for Leeds on that day: VERY well. The Apostles was on Wedy night: I was, of course, very hot [after conducting] & some one took my (ordered) taxi—   So I had to walk thro that awful E.wind to the hotel: I came on here (my sister can *creep* about a very little) *stiff*—I hoped it wd. pass but I got a chill and could not travel on Monday. My friend at Leeds was too busy looking after *five young soldiers* to pay any attention to me! It does seem rather odd & shews what adulation is worth that the composer & conductor should be left *alone* to find his way on foot thro' dark streets on foot [*sic*]!! What an odd world it is. I rather like the complete isolation, but it seems odd.

Thank you for your news of the dinner to Ronald. I hope it all went well

Love
EE

Of course I was not at a concert in London last Thursday—I was here—
*stiff*[10]

Next day he returned to London.

[8] HWRO 705:445:7162.
[9] Friday [24 Mar.] (HWRO 705:445:7693).
[10] HWRO 705:445:7835.

37, St.James's Place, S.W.1.
Friday [7 Apr. 1922] early

My dear W.

Many thanks for your letter, I am back & *really* all right again only I feel somewhat bored with life & want to be lonely—it suits me best & it is evidently intended by the fates that I am to be so—so, with all thanks, I will not come on Sunday.

Bless you.
Yrs ever
EE

No. on Saturday I cannot face the 'arranged' rubbish that these choirs always sing[11]

The Stuarts of Wortley had sent two invitations. One was to join them next day for a Queen's Hall concert by the Glasgow Orpheus Choir. The other was to Sunday lunch at Cheyne Walk: the guests included Mina Beresford, Lady Colefax, Frank Schuster—and Elgar himself, who came after all.[12] On 3 May he joined the Windflower for *Parsifal* at Covent Garden, as Lord Stuart had another cold.[13]

They were all ageing. Mina Beresford fell seriously ill in mid-May, went quickly downhill, and died on the 26th. The funeral was to be at All Saints' Church, Margaret Street. It was a question whether Alice Stuart of Wortley could attend, as she had badly scalded herself with a drawing-room tea kettle. Elgar went to consult about the funeral music, and wrote:

Brooks's, St.James's Street, S.W.1
Monday [29 May 1922] m[ornin]g

My dear W.

I have been to the church & the Vicar forbids any hymns referring to the Saints in connectn with funerals—or something of the sort.

I am so grateful for the sight of the book & will return it soon.

I do hope you are well again after the boiling water shock: it sounded too dreadful

Love
Yrs
EE

There will be no hymn at all—All Saints' *plan*[.] The choir will sg. *Angel's farewell*[14]

---

[11] HWRO 705:445:7156.

[12] Monday [10 Apr.] (HWRO 705:445:7155).

[13] Tuesday morng [2 May] (HWRO 705:445:7164), with Clare Stuart Wortley's note (HWRO 705:445:7165-2).

[14] HWRO 705:445:7144.

Alice Stuart of Wortley was able to go with her husband and Edward to the funeral next morning. Lord Stuart had to go on to business, but she drove with Edward to the Putney Vale Crematorium and back to lunch.[15]

He went to The Hut, but found no more pleasure there than on recent visits.

Brooks's, St.James's Street, S.W.1
Wedy [7 June 1922]

My dear W.

I arrd. last night from the Hut.

I missed you: Claude, Glyn Philpot, R. Nicholls, S. Sassoon & myself were the party &, of course, the N.Zealander—reminds me of Macaulay's N.Zealander sitting on the ruins not of London Bridge but of the Hut, and the Host!

Maud Warrender came to tea on Sunday & some 'odd' people *tea*ed on other days

Franks dog is a sweet lamb

I hope you are now well again: it was dreadful to think of you suffering.

I shall look for you in the artists' room after the Concert tomorrow

Love
EE[16]

The following afternoon he conducted the Leeds Choral Union in *The Apostles* to a half-empty Queen's Hall. The day after that the performance was repeated at Canterbury.[17] Lord and Lady Stuart went down for it, had tea with Elgar after, and she returned with him to London, Lord Stuart going on to visit Bice. Her letter of appreciation afterwards drew a bitter reply:

37, St.James's Place, S.W.1.
June 14 1922

My dear W:

It is strange to look back to last week: I suppose that *I* really did something towards the Canterbury affair! but Mary Crawshay sent a note (after Q's Hall) & today I receive your dear letter about Canterbury—that's all: I have *seen* no one, *no one* has written or taken the *slightest* notice & I have read nothing & seen no papers: truly I *am* a lonely person if I liked to think so;—but my *'friends'*!!! where, oh, where! are they? Silence profound. I was talking to Claude last week & he said 'Don't be a Timon.' I am not—but do these horrible frauds expect me to continuously 'attend' them when they happen to want me?

I cannot stand Galsworthy so that knocks out Lady Tree's[.] Barrie I

[15] May 31 (HWRO 705:445:7153).
[16] HWRO 705:445:7157. For another account of this visit to The Hut, see Siegfried Sassoon, *Diaries 1920–1922*, pp. 168–9.
[17] Monday evng [8 May] (HWRO 705:445:7171).

tried[:] 'The Dover road'—farce; but it is a disgrace to the English stage to put on an entirely incapable & stupid young woman for the principal part—I came out after the II act—it is an insult—Ainley, Aynesworth & Hannen & the other man superb: and the runaway man is supposed to be wildly in-love with this awful girl!—it's incredibly dreadful! *Do* come to the Theatrical Garden Party on the 23rd.—I have never been to one. I am very uncertain about plans—rehearsal for Suggia on Friday.

Love<br>EE[18]

The Portuguese cellist was playing the Concerto in a Henry Wood concert on 22 June.[19] Elgar did not attend the concert, but he did go with the Windflower to the Theatrical Garden Party next day.

July found him with time on his hands.[20] He went again to stay with the Graftons.

Perryfield[,] Bromsgrove
Thursday [13 July 1922]

My dear W.

I am here & shall stay on for a little time: I will let you know of my return—not this week. I have seen in the hay & picked mushrooms & heard larks singing; dear Juno went through the exciting ritual of dancing round me—she is now old & fat alas! but a darling doggie & *very* wise. My sister is a little better & can creep round the house.

A lovely day yesterday but quite hot—today heavy rain again.

You see the £10,000 000 widow did not hold me to London!!

I hope you are well

Love<br>EE[21]

He half enjoyed being the object of feminine pursuit, but the ladies came and went without a serious attraction on his part for nearly another decade.

Back in London, he relapsed into theatres.[22] In August he went to Crowborough again to visit Landon Ronald on holiday with friends.[23] Later in the month he rehearsed choruses at Gloucester and Worcester for the Three Choirs Festival—at which both *The Apostles* and *The Kingdom* were to be given, as well as the Bach C minor Fugue orchestration now prefaced by his new orchestration of the Fantasia.[24] But the Windflower was unable to attend.[25]

[18] HWRO 705:445:7843, with Clare Stuart Wortley's note (HWRO 705:445:7170).
[19] 17 June 1922 (HWRO 705:445:7158); Thursday [22 June] (HWRO 705:445:7154).
[20] Friday eveng [7 July] (HWRO 705:445:7771).
[21] HWRO 705:445:7774.
[22] Wedy [19 July] (HWRO 705:445:7770); Friday 1 o'c [21 July] (HWRO 705:445:7197). The plays mentioned were *Pot Luck* and *A to Z*.
[23] Wedy [9 Aug.] (HWRO 705:445:7149).
[24] Sunday [27 Aug.] (HWRO 705:445:7692).
[25] Saturday [2 Sept.] (HWRO 705:445:7150).

After the Festival he went back to Perryfield. The Windflower was at Stratford, and she noted in her diary:

Friday Sept.22nd. 1922.   E.Elgar arrived for the day—lunched with me— Drove with him to Bromsgrove to see Mrs.Grafton[,] leaving him there. Returned in motor to Stratford.[26]

He wrote afterwards:

. . . it gives a different feeling to the new little place that you have been to it.[27]

In October he vacated his London flat for a week to enable electricians to install a new heating system.[28] It was not finished on time:

37, St.James's Place, S.W.1.
Oct 11 1922
My dear W.

How are you? I am back but the electric work is not complete yet. I went to the Hut—of whilk mair anon—& went to look at Cottages—then I went to Ridgehurst until Monday—since then overwhelmed with rubbishy work.
Do tell me how you have fared since the lovely S-on-A time.
I long for the country—Carice writes radiantly happy.
They [Carice and her husband] motored over to Brinkwells on Sunday— (shut up) but she saw all the sweet old villagers & said it was lovely, peaceful & sad. The thought of it has made me ill—so I have to lie down.
I have been *thinking* of music but—

Love
EE[29]

Four nights later he dined at Cheyne Walk, and afterwards played on one of the schoolroom pianos.[30] But when he returned to The Hut to try to compose again, it came to nothing.

St Js's
Friday [27 Oct. 1922]
My dear W.

I came back from the Hut a week ago: you cd. not say the one word to F[rank] as usual—so consistent. the Miss Springs were there & I tried to write but the effect has been that all idea of composition is 'choked off'[.] So we will forget my little delusion about taking up music again: that is over.

---

[26] Copied by Clare Stuart Wortley for her note to HWRO 705:445:7201.
[27] Tuesday [26 Sept.] (HWRO 705:445:7201), with note by Clare (HWRO 705:445:7146).
[28] Monday mg [2 Oct.] (HWRO 705:445:7190).
[29] HWRO 705:445:7086.
[30] Clare Stuart Wortley's copy of her mother's diary, 15 Oct. 1922 (HWRO 705:445:7167).

I have no news & I am sure you are devastated with politics [the Government had resigned on 19 October]—I am asked to write letters & must do so for some local elections—but I am tired of politics & music & particularly of

E.E.
Love
with sun[31]

When Carice came up to visit him on 1 November, he played her sketches for a third oratorio and the piano concerto. Still there was no result. There were more theatres.[32] He shared a concert with the Windflower on 20 November,[33] and there was a dinner party at Cheyne Walk on 6 December.[34] They are the surviving records of their meetings before he went to the Graftons at Bromsgrove for Christmas.[35]

# 1923

37, St.James's Place, S.W.1.
Jany 5, 1923
My dear Windflower.

All thanks for the lovely calendar—I fear it will not record anything pleasant.

I hope you are well; you do not say.

I returned on Wedy to find an overwhelming mass of rubbish to contend with: at Perryfield we had a quiet time & much enjoyed your good present [to the Grafton family]. The weather was mostly *vile* & I got only one real walk. I do want the country so much.

Our dear old farmer [Aylwin] at Brinkwells—he drove you in the old ponycart—is dead; so another link with all that was sweet, peaceful & lovely is gone.

I enclose two 'pictures'—send them back please as the two animals (who look so naughtily humorous) amuse me: my mother was a gorgeous old

---

[31] HWRO 705:445:7839.

[32] Monday [30 Oct. 1922] (HWRO 705:445:7172); Monday night [30 Oct.] (HWRO 705:445:7081); Friday [3 Nov.] (HWRO 705:445:7837) and Clare Stuart Wortley's note (HWRO 705:445:7089); Nov 16 1922 (HWRO 705:445:7173). The plays included Conrad's *The Secret Agent*, which Elgar pronounced 'rubbish'.

[33] Friday morning [17 Nov.] (HWRO 705:445:7161).

[34] Wedy [6 Dec.] (HWRO 705:445:7151). Clare Stuart Wortley's note on the dinner is HWRO 705:445:7065.

[35] Sunday [17 Dec.] (HWRO 705:445:7187); Wedy [20 Dec.] (HWRO 705:445:7082) and Clare Stuart Wortley's note (HWRO 705:445:7145).

dame—it is only one of my (then) little niece [May Grafton]'s snapshots & the noble face is rather screwed up: you will like it, please.

I have no news—only dullness & family troubles (& expense!)

Love
EE[1]

Two short letters written later in the month discussed meetings, but seemed to dismiss all idea of music.[2]

None the less Elgar had resolved to try to write incidental music for Laurence Binyon's play *Arthur*, due for production at The Old Vic in March. His creative resort was again the country—this time the farmhouse of Carice and Samuel Blake at Chilworth, near Guildford. He went down on 1 February, and was greeted also by Meg.

Chilworth, Surrey.
Friday [2 Feb. 1923]
My dear W.

Your letter reached me here (Carice's) this morning—I am so sorry; I am to be away for a little time & am *thinking* of the music: I will let you know what happens about it.

Meg is a darling & quite one of the prettiest Aberdeens—such a love

Yours ever
EE[3]

He stayed ten days, struggling hard. At last he began to sketch and write. He went on to Worcester and Perryfield, and then to Brighton—working all the while at *Arthur*.

Old Ship Hotel, Brighton.
Monday [19 Feb. 1923]
My dear W.

I have been away a long time—a very long time & had 'nothing to report' as the old war telegrams used to say. I have worked at the Binyon music & have nearly finished it—one or two Windflowerish bits — but it is short. I am down here for Ainley's production *Cromwell*—& return tomorrow—

I went to Carice & then to Worcr. where they have hung Phil's portrait (alas!) in the Guildhall.

Love
EE[4]

[1] Elgar Birthplace parcel 583(xxiv).
[2] Thursday [18 Jan. 1923] (HWRO 705:445:4045); Tuesday mg [23 Jan.] (HWRO 705:445:4025).
[3] HWRO 705:445:4040.
[4] Elgar Birthplace parcel 583(xxix).

37, St.James's Place, S.W.1.
Friday [23 Feb. 1923] eveng

My dear W.

Your dear second letter: I am ashamed that I have not written but I am overwhelmed with this little music.

I could be free tomorrow afternoon from 2 o'c—if you wd like to arrange a theatre (Vaudeville?) or anything you like I will meet you—please telephone—failing this I *cd.* come to tea—but I am rather tired of music & then Suggia is playing the Concerto Q's Hall.

Perhaps you cd. telephone early?

> Yr
> EE[5]

By the beginning of March the *Arthur* music was scored and the parts copied, and the tiny pit orchestra (including piano) began to rehearse under Elgar's baton.

Brooks's, St.James's Street, S.W.1.
Sunday [4 Mar. 1923]

My dear W.

There is a rehearsal (orch.) at the Old Vic at *one* o'clock on Tuesday;—if you could possibly come at such an odd hour I shd. be only too delighted but I foresee that it is an impossible time

We tried the entr'actes on Friday eveng—a curious sound I think from such a small but very good-hearted seven!

I shall have to decide on Tuesday whether or no I conduct on the first night—a weighty judgment

I am not at all well & am depressed

> Love
> EE[6]

S.Jas's
Monday [5 Mar. 1923] eveng

My dear W:

I am so glad you can come; Carice is coming—food *is* difficult but we will arrange anything. I go to *Waterloo Station* for a meal, quite large, clean & good & near.

> In haste
> Yrs ever
> E[7]

[5] HWRO 705:445:4037.          [6] HWRO 705:445:4041.          [7] HWRO 705:445:4028.

Brooks's, St.James's Street, S.W.1.
Tuesday [6 Mar. 1923] night
My dear W.

Only to thank you for coming & to say how glad I am that *you* liked it

Love<br>Yrs ever

a quill![8]
EE


37, St.James's Place, S.W.1.
Thursday [8 Mar. 1923]
My dear W.

All thanks for your note. I will gladly join you at supper [after the opening performance on 12 March].

There is a rehearsal (stage) all day tomorrow Friday & *orch* at five o'c. Come if you can—

Ever yrs<br>EE.[9]

The production opened four days later. Lord Stuart wrote in his diary:

Monday. March 12th 1923: Early dinner & went with A.S.W. to Old Vic to see 1st production of 'Arthur' (Binyon & Elgar). Sir G.Arthur & Lady Arthur joined us in a box. Supper aft[erwar]ds at Savoy. Selves, G.Arthurs, L.Binyon, E.Elgar, F.Schuster.[10]

On 15 March Carice came up to see it, and joined Lady Stuart in the stalls. But few other friends where there. Next day he wrote:

Brooks's, St.James's Street, S.W.1.
March 16 1923
My dear Windflower.

I am so glad we saw the play together—

In these solemn (& sympathetic) halls I have destroyed my letter & am going on the dull round—detesting everything but going to endure to the end. My barren honours are dust. Not a single friend has shewn any sign of life, except your house, for years.

---

[8] HWRO 705:445:4039.

[9] HWRO 705:445:4042.

[10] Transcript by Clare Stuart Wortley, appended to Elgar's letter of thanks for the supper, dated Wedy [14 Mar.] (HWRO 705:445:7066). Sir George Arthur was a courtier; he had been private secretary to Kitchener, whose biography he wrote.

I forgot,—Blackwood sent a telegram—that's all.

Poor dearest Mina was an odd woman but she had more heart really than all the rest of the freaks put together. How odd life is.

—I only feel with the D. of Wellington that I only hope that they do not think I am, (or rather *was*) such a d——d fool as to believe them.

I waver betwn. going & staying in town in such disastrous weather

Love<br>EE[11]

Despite this bitterness, he had decided to try another rural retreat. His choice had fallen upon Napleton Grange, a rambling black and white property set in fields near the village of Kempsey, a few miles south of Worcester. It was to be let furnished, and he signed a six-month lease. During the run of *Arthur*, he prepared what he would need for a summer away from the flat: a significant portion of his cellar was earmarked for transporting to Worcestershire.

Brooks's, St.James's Street, S.W.1
Tuesday [27 Mar. 1923]
My dear W.

I am still in town but overwhelmed with 'packing' up a few books & things to send on to Napleton Grange[,] Kempsey nr. Worcester.

I am not sure about conducting at the Old Vic: on Saty [the final day] but I *may* do both performances if they can get the extra instrumentalists. Carice is coming

What heavenly weather

[illegible]<br>EE[12]

Before that came a small catastrophe in Surrey.

37, St.James's Place, S.W.1.
Wedy [28 Mar. 1923]
My dear Windflower.

I do not know why I should tell you sad news—but I must.

Meg (my darling) is killed—motor—: Carice writes, as she always does, in a measured & calm way, but she is really TERRIBLY *upset* & Blake also—the sweet thing was the life & soul of the house[,] farm & village

Oh, God!

Love<br>EE

I cannot keep back my tears & am not ashamed of them[13]

---

[11] HWRO 705:445:7836.          [12] HWRO 705:445:7840.          [13] HWRO 705:445:7848.

Saturday 31 March saw the final performances of *Arthur*. Carice came up for the matinée, and lunched with her father, Alice Stuart of Wortley, and W. H. Reed before the performance. Edward conducted, but the afternoon ended in a scramble, as he wrote a week later:

37, St.James's Place, S.W.1.
Ap 6 1923
My dear W.

Thank you for your letter. I could not get away down to you at the interval as I was held up: after the performance I had to rush off with C.—Mr.Reed had to leave early and all was confusion.

I am back from B[ourne]mouth & find that the *perfect arrgts I made* about packing & forwarding my things have been completely upset by mistakes on the part of the [Army & Navy] Stores. I arrd late on Wedy night & found my sitting-room full of *bottles* (of all things) which shd. have been in Worcester long ago. I can't pack bottles, oh! dear what fools people are.

I start tomorrow & have bought some cocks & hens for Madge to play with.

Love
E.E.[14]

Madge Grafton was now well enough to join her uncle at Napleton for the first ten days as his hostess. It was an arrangement (as she told me forty years later) that hugely pleased them both and was often repeated by herself, either of her sisters, or their mother. Among the chickens at Napleton a favourite hen emerged—to be named Roxelana.

Napleton Grange[,] Kempsey[,] Worcs.
Ap 19
My dear W.

Madge & I 'settled in' ten days ago: it is very comfortable & all goes smoothly: very cold with some sun occasionally—today we change about & my sister comes.

The common, five minutes away, is lovely & I walk about a great deal—lonely & thinking things out: no music yet. There is a fair Bechstein grand in the hall & we have huge peat fires etc[.] We are thinking if it will be possible to have visitors or whether they wd. find it too dull—I fear they would. The plum blossom is nearly over & the apple coming on—a cuckoo appeared this morning. I hope you are well—this seems far away—far away

Love
EE[15]

[14] HWRO 705:445:7092.      [15] HWRO 705:445:7085.

The first product of his return to Worcestershire was literary. It was a letter about windflowers, sent to *The Times* and published on 28 April under the title 'THE VERNAL ANEMONES: A Beautiful Native (From a Correspondent.)'

The pleasant legend which couples the tears of Venus with the anemone is not one that need try the receptive imagination very high, for in its simple, graceful beauty the flower may well have had a celestial origin.

The little group of anemones commonly called windflowers are happily named, too, for when the east wind rasps over the ground in March and April they merely turn their backs and bow before the squall. They are buffeted and blown, as one may think almost to destruction; but their anchors hold, and the slender-looking stems bend but do not break. And when the rain clouds drive up the petals shut tight into a tiny tent, as country folk tell one, to shelter the little person inside.

Our native windflower, *Anemone nemorosa*, is often overlooked by gardeners, who think of it, perhaps, as always white, as in many places it is. But there are wild colonies of it where it 'sports' through French grey into pink and lavender, and then to blue. Though the wood-anemone does not challenge the liquid blue of the infant's eye like its cousin of the Apennines sometimes, since there is a tell-tale leavening of pink in the flower, there are some fine colour forms of it. Who that has read it can forget Farrer's story of his finding the blue wood-anemone, which, like many another, he had pursued all his life as a will-o'-the-wisp? It was in Cornwall, and doubtingly he had plunged into the wood at twilight in search of the phantom flower.   ...[16]

He sent the cutting with this note:

Kempsey, Worcester.
Ap 30 1923
My dear W.

Here are some Windflowers from the garden: a different kind from the Stoke sort—they grow wild in the shrubbery here
I hope you will have a nice time away

Yrs ever
EE[17]

In May he arranged Handel's Overture for the Second Chandos Anthem for a modern orchestra, and orchestrated an anthem by Battishill and another by Samuel Sebastian Wesley for the Worcester Festival that year. The following months were to bring two partsongs and a keyboard fugue.

Back among the Three Choirs, Elgar asked the Stuarts of Wortley to help in a project to obtain a knighthood for the Gloucester Cathedral organist Herbert

[16] Elgar Birthplace parcel 584(vi).        [17] Elgar Birthplace parcel 583(ix).

Brewer.[18] (The venture was finally successful, and Brewer's name appeared in the New Year's Honours of 1926.)

To the list of Elgar's London clubs had been added the Garrick, the haunt of actors and artists.

Garrick Club, W.C.2.
Wedy [20 June 1923]

My dear W.

I am only passing thro town to Wales—a rehearsal for the Aberystwyth festival: & under the shadow of your father's portrait I write to ask you to give all messages of love[,] admiration & devotion to Paderewski—you will be sure to see him: I remember him as one of the great gentlemen in the art I have now given up.

By the way you may make exactly the same messages to yourself

Love
EE[19]

The Stuarts were to see much of the Paderewskis during their London visit over the next ten days.

In early July Elgar was back in town but looking forward to his return to Napleton—there to remain until the London orchestral rehearsals at the end of August for the Worcester Festival.[20] Late August found the Stuarts of Wortley visiting Stratford. On the 25th Elgar went over to lunch accompanied by another Grafton niece, Clare. Next day the Stuarts returned the visit by motoring over to Napleton to tea. It was this visit which Clare Stuart Wortley later associated with the manuscript of Elgar's recent Fugue (dated 'Napleton, June 29. 1923') discovered later among her mother's effects:

No envelope or covering letter was found with this MS.; it was loose among a lot of ordinary sheet music by various other composers, which Lady Stuart was accustomed to play.

It may have been given by Sir Edward in person to her, or to Lord Stuart, who was (of the two) the more inclined to play fugues. They visited him together at Napleton Grange, on Sunday, August 26th, 1923, and had tea with him and his niece Miss Clare Grafton.

The Worcester (Three Choir) Festival opened the following Sunday, and Lord & Lady Stuart attended parts of it, from a hotel at Shelsley Beauchamp; but went to Napleton from Stratford-on-Avon, where they had been awaiting the Festival.[21]

[18] June 5 1923 (HWRO 705:445:7849); 11 June 1923 (HWRO 705:445:7068).
[19] HWRO 705:445:7841. Clare Stuart Wortley's note on this letter is HWRO 705:445:7076.
[20] July 3: 1923 (HWRO 705:445:7084).
[21] Elgar Birthplace.

Kempsey, Worcester.
Sep 12 1923
My dear W.

Many thanks for your letter after the festival—the only word I have received. I am so delighted you were there & liked the dear old things—they sounded well in the cathedral but I cannot see the future—where *are* the new soloists? Both [Florence] Austral & [Leila] Megane had to give up because they cannot keep a bar of time & can read (or learn) nothing except by hammering one note at a time—all right for opera but not for concert works, alas!

I am quite alone here & very lonely—Madge comes on Saturday. I have no news & have no plans. I send this to Chelsea, but I hope you are still living in this heavenly weather in the country. I heard nothing of Frank & do not know if he came to Worcr.—I saw Adrian Boult for a moment & one or two ghosts which, who wd have been better 'laid'.

My invalids are still very TRYING: & do not improve much—certainly not in temper—a lively time for me.

Love
EE

The Kingdom, Gerontius & For the Fallen are not bad: I think I deserve *my peerage* now, when these are compared with the new works!!![22]

This broadest of hints revealed to the Stuarts an idea which had been in his thoughts for some time. In March he had written to Madge Grafton from Brooks's that he had just been summoned with the words: 'Dinner is waiting, my lord.' He added for Madge's benefit: 'Oh! lord—the latter is a mistake—for the present—but still.'[23] It could suggest how keenly he was missing the constant reassurance his own Alice had given him.

Alice Stuart of Wortley answered from Tintagel. Frank Schuster had indeed been at the Festival. But his life at The Hut was beginning to take its final turn: Anzy Wylde was hoping to marry his Wendela, and as a result Schuster was to build an annexe for them.

Elgar's lease at Napleton was to run out at the end of September.[24]

Kempsey, Worcester.
Sep 20 1923
My dear W.

Many thanks for your letter: I really *did* read the last one which told me you were going to Tintagel—but I knew not for how long.

I am delighted beyond words that you have such a lovely sea & the hotel,

[22] Elgar Birthplace parcel 583(xxxv).
[23] Sunday [11 March 1923] HWRO 705:445:BA.
[24] Sep. 15, 1923 (HWRO 705:445:4053).

in spite of its gorgeosity, must be more comfortable than the old house you were in for so long & which I remember so well.

I am leaving this next week—there were several difficulties—(which I did not care to overcome—I might have done) & I shall return to London for a few days, & then on into the inane.

I am sending a word to poor dear old Frank: the whole thing is very odd indeed: shall you go to the Hut? I will, if he asks me, but I do not *want* to—it all seems so dead. However I am glad he liked the things at Worcester. & that you did also.

Thank you for asking: my invalids do not really improve, but my brother *walks* much better (pro tem).—the others are stationary both bodily & physically

Love<br>EE[25]

A further disaster had overtaken the Frank Elgar household. His daughter Mary, still in her twenties, was attacked by tuberculosis—the disease which had already killed her elder brother.

Edward left all this, and Perryfield too, when he returned to London at the end of September. Then from Perryfield came the news that 'his' old dog Juno, who had lived out her life with the Graftons because no place could be found at Severn House or later—had died.

St Js's Pl. S.W.1
Oct 10 1923
My dear W.

I have been 'home' or shall have been home a fortnight tomorrow. I detested leaving it all but will tell you when we meet. Thanks for your letter just recd.—I nearly called up 313 [the Stuarts' telephone number] to ask but was too busy: I have found—as you have done—such an absurd accumulation of odd things. And the SADDEST saddest days have come—darling *Juno* is no more & the whole family is in deep distress—I say no more but it is really a tragedy. Poor dear old Sarah [Allen] (Alice's maid) mercifully died a week ago. The invalids do not improve alas!

I went to the Hut—but cd. not enjoy it—Cobb & the Misses Springs were there but—poor dear old Frank.

I have been to *12* theatres since I retd: I am so desperately lonely & turn in to see anything.

It is interesting to hear of Hardy but I never by any chance think of music now—entirely gone. I hope I may see you because I may shortly be away for ever—or at least a very long time—but do not say so. I shall go away without a word eventually

[25] HWRO 705:445:7072.

I have really no news. Roxelana my own hen went to Perryfield but we are a sad folk.

I hope C. is well & you are I know

Love<br>EE[26]

It was in his mind to go far away. He fixed on a voyage to South American waters and a thousand miles up the Amazon to Manaos. The *Hildebrand* would depart from Liverpool on 15 November: there were comfortable quarters for some passengers but it was primarily a cargo ship, so no firm date could be given for returning.[27]

Brooks's, St.James's Street, S.W.1
Nov 14. 1923
My dear W.

This is just to say good-bye, & bless you. I had hoped to have seen you but I took a bad chill at Eastbourne last Friday & have been shut up

better now & leaving early tomorrow for the unknown

Yrs ever<br>EE[28]

If messages reached Cheyne Walk during the rest of 1923, they seem not to have survived. The ship sailed up to the interior port of Manaos, where Brazilian rubber barons had built an imposing opera house, magnificently equipped. Then the ship returned to Liverpool on 30 December—in time for Elgar to see the old year out at Perryfield. There another Christmas present had arrived from Lady Stuart of Wortley.

# 1924

Brooks's, St.James's Street, S.W.1
Jany 4 1924
My dear W.

I arrd. in town last night—I went to Perryfield & found them very delighted at your most kind thought.

I *must* go back to the tropics as soon as I can clear up things.

I wish you all good things for 1924—too late for Christmas

Yrs ever sny<br>E.E.

---

[26] HWRO 705:445:7838.
[27] Monday [22 Oct. 1923] (HWRO 705:445:7077).
[28] HWRO 705:445:7090.

I have no news & have not seen a newspaper since early in November & I do not [know] who is alive—or anything![1]

One engagement offered was to write a series of songs to poems by Alfred Noyes for a 'Pageant of Empire' to open at the Wembley Stadium in April. There was a song each about England (*Shakespeare's Kingdom*), Canada, Australia, and New Zealand, as well as a sailing song, one of history, one of war memorial. Elgar did them quickly, sketching several over a weekend at The Hut. He reported to the Windflower (who was still on holiday):

Brooks's, St.James's Street, S.W.1.
Jan 10 1924
My dear W.

Thank you for your letter. I hope your retreat is worthy of you & that you find it restful etc etc[.] Since my return I have been trying to help this Wembley affair—an awful muddle—& I have had no moment. I have 'composed'! *five* things this week—one about 'Shakespeare' you will love when I shew it you — slight & silly
My love to you
I went to the Hut on Friday till Monday—Frank does not think or talk of anything but this wedding! Sickert was there etc

Yrs ever
EE[2]

The wedding of Anzy Wylde and Wendela Boreel was to take place in July—with Schuster and Sickert in a sense its godparents.
Then Elgar was asked for an 'Empire March' for Wembley. His creative recourse this time was his sister's house.

Perryfield, Bromsgrove.
Jany 21:
My dear W.

I have to write *the* March for the Wembley affair so have come here

I begin thus—without any prelude &, with a great Military Band, should rouse people up—I *could* rouse Brazilians but not English.

[1] HWRO 705:445:7182.          [2] HWRO 705:445:7842.

Beatrice Harrison has given me a new little Juno who* brought me here on Saturday: it is a sweet thing.

*the dog I mean. I was supposed to bring the dog but I soon found out who was the superior person.

The weather is terrible & I hope you are well. I remain here for a little time

Love
EE

I *suppose* the strike is on as we have no newspaper but no word from the outside world yet—[3]

He remained at Perryfield a fortnight, returning in early February. Then came an invitation to dine with the Stuarts and go with them to the first night of Shaw's *Back to Methuselah*.

St James's
Thursday [7 Feb. 1924] 9.30 a m
My dear W.

Many many thanks. I am so sorry for the delay & fear it may be too late. I wd. gladly dine with you on the 18th & go to the Shaw at the Court. I recd. your letter only a minute ago. I retd on Monday night & have been occupied ever since—publishers—Wembley—gramophone etc etc: do not give yourself the slightest trouble over the tickets because it is my fault!

I have brought the 'frame' of the March back & am working very hard at it—but there is great *chaos*—I am bored with life

I was delighted to have a long conversation at the [Garrick] Club amongst old members who were enthusiastically remembering your father with the greatest admiration & touching affection.

My plans are vague but I must be here for a short time

Love
EE[4]

Brooks's, St.James's Street, S.W.1
Feb 12 1924
My dear W.

Very many thanks[.] I will gladly come at seven next Monday. Shaw sent me the play (or plays) long ago & I am most anxious to see it, them, *you* or rather *you* them it

Love
EE[5]

[3] Elgar Birthplace MS 51. Later he gave her a manuscript version of the March for piano.
[4] HWRO 705:445:7069.
[5] HWRO 705:445:7064.

They all dined early and attended the first night on the 18th. Nine days later she and Edward saw a play that was popular then and later, Sutton Vane's *Outward Bound*.[6]

In mid-March his brother's daughter Mary died in Worcester of tuberculosis—'a merciful release'.[7] Another death later in the month exerted influence of a different kind. Old Sir Walter Parratt had been Master of the King's Music—an office that went back to the days of the Royal Household Band. Now the elimination of the office seemed to some an advisable economy. Elgar saw things differently as he prepared to conduct the opening of the Empire Exhibition at Wembley.

On 30 March he rehearsed massed choirs in the huge stadium. *The Daily Telegraph* reported:

> The choir cheered the veteran conductor as he mounted the steps. The National Anthem was the first thing Sir Edward desired to test. He wanted the singers to shorten and sharpen their words, so that each word would be carried distinct and ennobling to the microphone, and thence by cable to the amplifiers, whence it is conveyed by another cable to the great sound projectors massed on a high platform and transmitted into the Stadium like an invisible sea of sound.
>
> To the musicians Elgar called out 'Hit it! Hit it!' Lieutenant Adkins, Director of Kneller Hall, added with a younger, louder voice 'Attack with the beat!' and again the massed choir and band filled the Stadium . . .[8]

Elgar called Alice Stuart of Wortley's attention to the article,[9] and a fortnight later sent a full account of his adventures and frustrations. The musical programme, undergoing constant changes, he described as 'short & lurid'.[10]

St Js's
Wedy [16 Apr. 1924] night
My dear W.

Your letter comes as a refreshment: I have been at Wembley & am overwhelmed with etiquette & red tape. My March will not be done as there are difficulties in the way of the Brigade Bands co-operating etc etc—so the Military Bands will play the old Imperial March. We rehearse the whole thing in St Paul's Cathedral on Tuesday: Stadium on Saturday. I enclose some rubbish *which please return*—the 'youthful voice' was a man speaking thro' a six foot megaphone! No wonder it sounded more vigorous than my unaided pipe.

I wrote to Stamfordham [the King's Private Secretary] urging that the Master of the King's Music shd. be retained—its suppression wd. have a very bad effect abroad—where the effacement of the last shred of connection of the Court with the Art wd. not be understood. It is not S's dept so it was turned over to F.Ponsonby [Keeper of the Privy Purse]. He wrote to me that it was one of the offices which it was (long ago) proposed (scheduled) to cease. I wrote again offering myself (honorary)—*anything* rather than that it

6 Tuesday [26 Feb.] (HWRO 705:445:7183).
7 Sunday [16 Mar.] (HWRO 705:445:7088).
8 31 March 1924.
9 1 April 1924 (HWRO 705:445:7148).
10 Sunday [9 Mar.] (HWRO 705:445:7075).

shd be publicly announced that the old office was abolished. No reply.
Colebrooke [Permanent Lord-in-Waiting to the King] wrote to the Ld.
Chamberlain — but as far as I can make out the three(?) depts. simply
quarrel over these things: no grit, no imagination—no *music*. no nothing
except boxing, football & racing[:] so it is—I have had no further reply & I
believe the matter is to drop tacitly—no public announcement

The Wembley affair will be a mixture: the K. insists on Land of Hope &
there were some ludicrous suggestions of which I will tell you—if we ever
meet. But everything seems so hopelessly & irredeemably *vulgar* at Court. I
was at the processional rehearsal all the morning—quite simple but it takes
time. If you like to write to Vi[s]c[oun]t FitzAlan [formerly Lord Edmund
Talbot] do—but I fear the matter of the 'Master' is dead. As to any peerage I
fear it is hopeless but it wd. please me.

Frank called one day—he is at the Hut—Bankrupt he says & very vague:
this afternoon he was sitting in the back of a smart car—the young man was
driving with an *odd looking*—I hate to say it—'*bit of fluff*'!! in flamboyant
PINK on the front seat, all laughing loudly; they did not see me & I was glad
for I shd. have been thoroughly ashamed.

I was standing alone (criticising) in the middle of the enormous stadium in
the sun: all the ridiculous Court programme, soldiers, awnings etc: 17,000
men hammering [—] loud speakers, amplifiers—four aeroplanes circling over
etc etc—all mechanical & horrible—no soul & no romance & no imagination. Here had been played the great football match—even the turf, which is
good, was not there as turf but for football—but at my feet I saw a group of
real *daisies*. Something wet rolled down my cheek—& I am not ashamed of it:
I had recovered my equanimity when the *aides* came to learn my views—
Damn everything except the daisy—I was back in something sane, whole-
some & GENTLEMANLY — but only for two minutes.

I do not think there will be any orchl. concerts next season—or only by
popular visiting Conductors—Broadcasting is killing all the concert room.

My brother is in a bad way of nerves—I went down a fortnight ago—
Worcester—Gloucester—Perryfield—Leeds etc. etc. Tell me what you do
about the Peerage! It wd be interesting to find how the idea wd. be received.

My love
ever
EE

It has been so dreadfully cold that windflowers had not appeared—at least
there were none in the old places where I looked for them in Worcs.[11]

The Wembley Empire Exhibition was opened a week later, on St. George's Day.
Then Elgar went back to Worcestershire for a few days.

---

[11] Elgar Birthplace parcel 583(xxvii).

Perryfield, Bromsgrove.
April 28.1924

My dear W.

I came down here on Friday & it has mercilessly *poured* with rain all day &
every day—I cannot even get into the garden. Many thanks for your letter:
the full account of Wembley was in the D[aily] T[elegraph]—I wd. send it but
I have it not—*do* get it. I mean the *day after* the opening. Do go to the
Concert on the 2nd.May—Central Hall[, Westminster, from which he was
conducting his first broadcast].

PRIVATE

I had a letter from Windsor this morning offering me the *Mastership of the
K's Musick*[:] this I have accepted—so that's settled. I know *you* will be
pleased.

It is good to know that you had a refreshing time at Brighton—my days
were very full & it was uncommonly *hot* on two days.

Love<br>EE

P.S. I have found the D T.—let me have it back sometime. I return on
Wednesday—so you will understand I cd. not meet anywhere before.[12]

The new appointment was announced on 5 May. Among the first congratulators
were the Stuarts.

37, St.James's Place, S.W.1.
Monday [5 May 1924] morng

My dear W:                          IN HASTE

Thank you for your letter: I will come gladly on *Thursday* [to *Tristan und
Isolde* at Covent Garden] but please let the *meal* question stand over for a
little.
There is a really nice paragraph in the Times this morning and also in the
Daily Telegraph. I am so glad they seem pleased with the apptmt.
The Central Hall is very bad acoustically & I fear we made an appalling
*noise* sometimes.
I *am* going to Paris as Mr.E[mbleton]—who was here yesterday—has
engaged the L.S.O.

In haste<br>Love<br>EE[13]

---

[12] HWRO 705:445:7067.
[13] HWRO 705:445:7096. A note of Wedy eveng [7 May] says that he cannot dine but will meet
at Covent Garden (HWRO 705:445:7211).

The expedition to Paris was the latest project of the faithful Embleton to aid Elgar's music.[14] Elgar went to Leeds to rehearse the Choral Union in *Gerontius*, and returned to rehearse the Second Symphony (also in the Paris programme). He invited his actor friend from the Garrick Club, Norman Forbes, as well as the Windflower.

Brooks's, St.James's Street, S.W.1
Tuesday [10 June 1924]

My dear W:

I am just back & find your note. I am so very sorry but I did say *Thursday* the 12th for rehearsal

I shall, D.V., be there from 10 – 1

If you see dear old Norman Forbes at Q's Hall (he promised to come) *do* tell him what we are playing—he has such a vague notion of what *I* have done. We rehearse *solidly* the Slow movemt & the Rondo for the 2nd Sym

Love
EE[15]

The French concerts took place at the weekend. Bilingual banquets were a strain, and Elgar was glad to get back to London.[16]

In early July he spent a weekend at The Hut. Alice Stuart of Wortley was not there; but Siegfried Sassoon, who was, drew a sketch in his diary that tells everything about Elgar at this time:

5 July 1924 ... Elgar led me to the music-room and played the piano for nearly an hour. It was delightful. He played snatches (from/of) my piano-music, Mozart A major Concerto, Bach Organ Fugues, Chaconne, etc. Afterwards I got him going on his own choral stuff, and he played through 'Death on the Hills', 'Te Deum', and 'Light of Life', making it sound superb. Quite sketchy unpianistic playing, but the rhythmic sense of course wonderful.

He also played some of Schubert's Rondo Brillante (for piano and violin)—lovely melodies: 'the best *natural* music ever written' he said (of Schubert as a whole) and 'I could listen to it for ever'.

It was splendid to see him glowing with delight in the music, and made me forget (and makes me regret now) the 'other Elgar' who is just a type of 'club bore'. At lunch, regaling us with long-winded anecdotes (about himself), he was a different man. The real Elgar was left in the music-room.[17]

The only other guests were Anzy Wylde and his Wendela, to be married on 16 July, and Sickert.

[14] Wedy [?14 May] (HWRO 705:445:7203); June 4 1924 (HWRO 705:445:7168).
[15] HWRO 705:445:7091.
[16] Thursday [19 June] (HWRO 705:445:7194).
[17] *Diaries 1923–1925* (Faber, 1985), pp. 151–2.

That summer, without Napleton, Elgar wandered. He went to see Claude Phillips and Frances Colvin, both old and mortally ill. Then he went to Scotland. This was a private reminiscence—going over the ground he had trod forty summers earlier (before he had met his own Alice) in the wake of the broken engagement.

The Great Western Hotel, Oban, N.B.    Passing through
Augt 3 1924
My dear W.

Your letter reached me here where I am just resting a moment. I rushed off quite alone without premeditation & the incessant rain, mist & cold seem to suit my lonely meditative end of life. I am glad you have a 'desirable' weekend house [at Worthing]—it must be a change from the toil of London. I have no news—& am just starting (shall I?) to the Shetland Isles, & may go to S.Kilda.

I don't know why—but this desolation suits me now. I came here forty years ago, alone. I have had my career & ——. Well there's a difference—I was of course quite unknown then: now, I went into the Bk of Scotland & asked for money—they *cashed my cheque* at *once*—that's fame in *Scotland*!!!

There is a great change in travelling—40 years ago there were many ladies & gentlemen. Now all U.S.A. & utterly unspeakable people. I thought of writing an article on it—but it wd. be rather condemnatory & therefore old fashioned—a thing I am determined never to be. I am only old fashioned in loving you. I am not sure—as I sd. about my movements but I shall call at the Station Hotel Inverness during the next month.

Love
EE[18]

The Station Hotel at Inverness was where, in the summer of 1884, he had met a girl whose initials were also E. E.: the meeting had produced one of the loveliest of his early melodies, *Idylle*. Clearly he had confided the story to the Windflower.

Letters from her told him of the death of Lady Colvin at the beginning of August, and of Claude Phillips ten days later. Elgar answered from the London flat, where he had returned for orchestral rehearsals before the Hereford Festival.[19]

37, St.James's Place, S.W.1.
Sep 4 1924
My dear W.

Thank you. I am so glad you have a peaceful time and place. I am in the midst of rehearsals. I did 'pass' all the places & had all letters I believe: but the weather was desperation & I came back. No it did not depress me—I spent the afternoon with Claude just before &, as he told his friends, I

[18] HWRO 705:445:7846. See *Edward Elgar: A Creative Life*, p. 107.
[19] Augt. 29 (HWRO 705:445:7184).

soothed his later moments—then I went on to Sidney—& stayed with him—
dear Frances was dying. So I did my duty—& fled!

I have no news—I go to Brockhampton [Court for the Hereford Festival]
tomorrow.

You will be amused [—] *do not tell anyone at all* [—] that I am driving a car
& am buying one to career wildly in! Only I do not want it spoken of until I
appear in the Row or wherever motorists exhibit themselves.

Yrs ever
EE[20]

The Festival did not yield him great pleasure that year, and it was a relief to go on
to his sister's house.

Perryfield, Bromsgrove.
Monday [15 Sept. 1924]
My dear W:

Many thanks. Yes it was wonderful to see. I hated it all—a strange house
party—very very luxurious of course but only one *soul*—really. Everybody
kind—but I am desperately *lonely*. I came here & Juno much much delight at
seeing me—that's all.

I am going to Gloucester—& shall not return to London for sometime.
They send love from here—or at least such of them as dare.

I hope it is still very pleasant at Worthing

Love
Yrs ever
EE

I did not see anyone among the crowd [at the Festival.] I was told F[rank]
was there etc.[21]

Both Edward and his daughter were moving—he back to Napleton Grange with a
new lease, Carice and her husband (after many months in temporary accommoda-
tions) to a large farmhouse at Hoes, near Petworth, Sussex. Carice asked if the round
table from Severn House might now come there—when Lady Stuart should return to
Cheyne Walk.[22] Her father echoed the request:

37, St.James's Place, S.W.1.
Oct 5 1924
My dear W.

I was delighted to get your letter & to know that you are safely back in
town[.] As to the table, *please* let Carice have it, as she has room & will take
care of it. I really have no room for it here as you know, nor at Kempsey

---

[20] HWRO 705:445:7175.
[21] HWRO 705:445:7196.
[22] 2 Oct 1924 (Elgar Birthplace).

either. I go down there for the winter—that is I am going to try it—as I have some work to do—  Heaven knows if I shall do it!

It is too good of you to have treasured my beloved table[.] But I did not *hire* a table at Kempsey. I bought a 30/- *kitchen* table & it is still there & it is of course *quite* small.

Carice is making her house—just getting in—very nice. I have given them electric light & a 'listening in' set of the best type so she will not be so lonely.

I have my own car now & they have a car at Perryfield: Madge comes to me first. But they are in *very sad* minds as Gerald has been so ill—a little better now but it is disquieting these more frequent & sudden 'turns'—& Roland, the giant, is not well. Oh! the terrible legacy of that war. However my sister writes at last more cheerfully & hopefully so I must hope too.

I have no news. I went to Lan's Party last Sunday. But I am entirely lonely & left. I went for the first time for years to the Promenade Concert. I thought it dreadful—Wood managed to make the grand old Eroica sound commonplace & stupid. I cannot think how it is done! Richter & Nikisch made a noble thing of it.

Love<br>EE[23]

The table duly went to Sussex.


37, St.James's Place, S.W.1.
Oct 16 1924

My dear W.

I was so glad to get your letter: it is too good of you to have taken care of 'the' table. It was a most disconcerting set of circumstances to contend with. Carice's moving from her old house—where I wrote 'Arthur'—then her nearly two years' 'holiday' and now, at last, getting into her new home—so at last the table will be where I can use it sometimes.

I go to Kempsey on Monday to see if the winter will be kind.

I was at Qn's Hall for the Berlioz [*Symphonie Fantastique*] & left immediately after—the *March* in the Sinfonie is *tremendous*—the rest is rather dated.

I am so sorry to hear of the illness of Lady Lovelace.

Cortot & Thibaud play the Sonata next Sunday—shall you be able to go?

I was at Oxford on Wedy where they had (Reeds IVtet) all my chamber music. I wish you had been there.

Do ring me up—I have to go to the Palace once or twice to clear some matters up connected with the Kg's Musick.

[23] HWRO 705:445:7178.

I am to have Juno's *sister* & a spaniel [Marco] & I drive my own car now—
it is the lambiest lamb you ever saw!

Love
EE[24]

At the Cortot–Thibaud concert, Elgar was called up to share the applause after his
Sonata. The Windflower was in the audience. That evening he wrote:

37, St.James's Place, S.W.I.
Sunday [19 Oct. 1924]
My dear W.

I was sorry I had to 'bow' & go to see the two great artists after
I *do* like the Sonata 'written in dejection'—but what tunes!
I am beginning to like my own music.

Love
EE

Napleton Grange[,] Kempsey nr. Worcester
I am going here tomorrow & want to write oh! such a lot[25]

Yet engagements in London and elsewhere were to interrupt the time at Napleton.
One was a request to attend Bruno Walter's rehearsal and performance of the First
Symphony.

Napleton Grange, Kempsey, Worcester.
Nov 27 1924
My dear Windflower:

Many thanks but I am here again—I rushed down to Eastbourne & back
on Tuesday. My time in London was overcrowded with silly business.

I shall be up for the *rehearsal* on the morning of the 4th.—Walter asks me
to be there—I *think* he is splendid but I do not know if he will understand *me*
& if he *cannot* I shall avoid the concert—   However I hope to sit with you;
thank you for the ticket

I have had nearly three weeks of lovely autumn weather & have had two
nieces two nephews & Troyte off & on & have driven my own car 600 miles[.]
I wd. like to drive you but you wd. be too nervous!

I have one of Beatrice Harrison's Aberdeens whom I named *Brenda*—she
sleeps in my room & rides in the car.

I saw Frank at Eastbourne—quite alone: he has taken a furnished house at
Brighton—I thought of course he was driving from B—but he says he has no

[24] HWRO 705:445:7206. For an account of Elgar at the Berlioz performance, see Compton
Mackenzie, *My Record of Music* (Hutchinson, 1955), pp. 84–6.
[25] HWRO 705:445:7844.

car! I suppose the Hut & all that is therein is annexed by the newcomers. I felt very sad.

> Love
> EE[26]

At Walter's rehearsal on 4 December he was joined by Alice Stuart of Wortley, and Norman Forbes and his brother, the great actor-manager Johnston Forbes-Robertson.[27] And he did attend the performance.[28]

His next letter from Napleton mixed rural realities with aspirations in the capital. It was written on printed stationery of the Master of the King's Music office in St. James's Palace.

Kempsey
Dec 6 1924
My dear W.

I arrived here yesterday & find one of my dogs very ill & I am distracted— poor dear lamb!

How nice it was on Thursday—the luncheon & the concert.—I felt I liked some of the Symphony & really deserve *some* recognition (Your *peer*less idea—not mine. However I like it) for having written it!—this is vanity. Thank you for giving me a seat & making everything so happy.

Now I must drive my little dog to the Vet.

> Yrs ever
> EE

I use my first official envelope for you![29]

She sent him a diary for the new year.

Kempsey, Worcester.
Dec 17 1924
My dear W.

Many many thanks for the diary: I fear there will be nothing pleasant to enter in it. Troyte will, I think, spend Christmas with me—we shall be alone—two old men & a dog. I shall go over to Perryfield for the day—

—They have been in great trouble over their old Clara [a servant]—who has been ill a long time & they have been having stop gaps of various disqualifications & consequently unable to come here much, altho' they have a car.

My brother gets about with me & I have driven 1300 miles lately!

The dogs have both been ill! etc. etc. Marco is the loveliest Spaniel I have

[26] HWRO 705:445:7199.
[27] Wedy [3 Dec.] (HWRO 705:445:7186).
[28] Tuesday [2 Dec.] (HWRO 705:445:7083).
[29] HWRO 705:445:7834.

ever seen—quite a silly baby & cries for nothing; He loves riding in the car. Mina—the little cairn—is a love & so sharp.

Madge has been here but has had to go home as I said pro tem.

I have heard nothing of Frank or Muriel [Foster].

Love<br>EE

I have had dear Claude's piano (which came to me [at the executor's suggestion]) sent down to Worcestershire where it will end its days with respect & affection.[30]

For Christmas she sent some pâté.

Kempsey, Worcester.
Dec 29 1924
My dear Windflower:

All thanks for the paté which Troyte & I have enjoyed hugely. I am to say that *he* is 'extremely indebted to you' etc—

Thanks also for the book, Music & Letters but I never read anything about Music! bless you.

I have not been well & Marco sympathises[.] Perryfield has been here & we have been to Perryfield; the little cars make this sort of thing possible

All good wishes for the New Year. I heard from Frank who had the audacity to suggest my going to him with those awful people—in Mina's old house.

Love<br>EE

I cd. not write about the Symphy—I was so distressed over it[31]

# 1925

This was to be Elgar's first full year of living at Napleton Grange. Conducting engagements in London and elsewhere appeared as interruptions. After a brief note on the death of her aged uncle,[1] his first real letter of the year to the Windflower was written on the Master of the King's Music stationery:

---

[30] HWRO 705:445:7063.
[31] HWRO 705:445:7094.
[1] 8 Jan 1925 (HWRO 705:445:7185). The uncle was her mother's brother George Gray (aged 93), owner of Bowerswell, Perth.

Napleton Grange
Jany 24th 1925
My dear W.

I am so glad you approved of the st[at]ionery! I chose it!

I fear there is no chance of my being in London again for a long, long time, it is so good of you to think of my going to Paderewski's concert—but I have forgotten *all* my music & do nothing but dogs & cars! It is dreadful to hear of the fogs you have had & suffered from—truly a desperate adventure getting home after the concerto[.] I am bathed in glorious sunshine many days & to-day birds are singing wildly, & carrying feathers to build nests with—poor deluded things.

Love
EE[2]

In February he asked her to support a small concert given by a violinist down on his luck.[3] On 7 March he sent some windflowers.[4] Later in the month he wrote: '. . . this lovely land is full of departed spirits—Oh! for the gracious days gone by'.[5] He came to London to conduct another broadcast concert from BBC studios on 31 March, but stayed only two nights:

37, St.James's Place, S.W.1.
Ap 1st
My dear W.

My beloved Marco is ill—& I am flying back with everything undone. He is now the only thing left in the world to me—& he's ill & looking for me everywhere.

Love
EE[6]

She learned of his resignation from The Athenaeum. He answered on 9 April:

What you say about the Athm. is ancient;—I took my name off *last year*— the instant I knew that R[amsay] M[acdonald, the first Labour Party Prime Minister] had been passed into the club—not really elected in the ord[inar]y sense of the word.[7]

The Athenaeum's custom had long been to invite the incumbent Prime Minister to ex-officio membership.

[2] HWRO 705:445:7200.
[3] Thomas Fussell had written to Elgar on 25 January (HWRO 705:445:7115). Elgar sent the letter to Lady Stuart with his covering note on 1 February (HWRO 705:445:7180). On 12 February he sent his thanks for attending Fussell's concert (HWRO 705:445:7198).
[4] HWRO 705:445:7209.
[5] 24 Mar 1925 (HWRO 705:445:7098).
[6] HWRO 705:445:7847.
[7] HWRO 705:445:7210.

The Stuarts went to Paris for a spring holiday, but proposed to come to Stratford-upon-Avon after that. Elgar answered on 4 May: '*please* let me know your days at S.on Avon. Marco & I wd. drive over.'[8] The day chosen was a Sunday, when Edward regularly took his invalid brother Frank for an outing: so the two brothers motored over to lunch with the Stuarts.[9]

Edward's letter of thanks mentioned several London engagements—a dinner to Sir Frederic Cowen on 14 May and two concerts—discussed at Stratford. One was a concert of chamber music organized by Frank Schuster as a memorial to his friend Fauré, who had died the previous November. The other was a twenty-first anniversary concert for the London Symphony Orchestra; they were to replay the programme of the Orchestra's very first concert in June 1904—with Edward himself conducting the *'Enigma' Variations* now. This letter was written from Carice's house in Sussex, where Edward had driven with a valet he had engaged—a Kempsey man named Richard Mountford.

Hoes, Petworth, Sussex.
Tuesday [19 May 1925]

My dear W.

I drove the little car down here with Marco (& Dick!) to see Carice—154 miles

It was so delightful to see you & C. again & I thank you both for your great kindness to my poor invalid—

I am to conduct the Variations at the L.S.O. 25th [*sic*] Annivy Concert on June (I think) 9th—but you will see the date—I shall try to get a day or two free.

Frank spoke to me, at the Cowen dinner, about how necessary it was for me to back the Fauré Concert—but I do not know the date or anything about it. I suppose he only wants a pound for a ticket! & I am tired of the world which never notices my existence except to ask for a pound.

The country here is lovely & Marco hunts hares all day in comp[an]y with Carice's dog & they have found a long stretch of private river—a paradise for dogs.

My love to you
Yrs ever
EE[10]

Unfortunately the Fauré concert was scheduled the same day as the London Symphony Orchestra concert. The Stuarts invited Edward to dine and go to the theatre the following night.

---

[8] HWRO 705:445:7205.

[9] HWRO 705:445:7177.

[10] HWRO 705:445:7845. Clare Stuart Wortley wrongly dated it a week earlier, which would have placed it before the Cowen dinner.

37, St.James's Place, S.W.1.
Monday [8 June 1925]

My dear W.

Very many thanks[.] I shall be delighted to come on *Wednesday* at seven
o'clock—It will be lovely to see you all again.

I arrd. last eveng & had a long rehearsal: it is a pity the Fauré people
managed to blight the L.S.O. Concert

However—

Love
EE[11]

His letter of thanks, written the following week from Napleton, showed how the
Windflower's presence could still inspire a flickering light:

I *am* doing the Piano Concerto but do not tell anyone as I may switch off at
any moment—as is usual[12]

It proved a true warning. Out of all Elgar's dreams of creative work at Napleton, 1925
was to produce only two small partsongs.

July brought more illness to the Graftons at Perryfield. Pollie's eldest son Gerald
had to undergo surgery for an ulcer.[13] Edward suggested that if the Windflower could
send 'a *short* note to my sister it wd. be angelic'.[14] Lady Stuart did write to Pollie
Grafton. Pollie's reply survives:

Perryfield, Bromsgrove.
[29 July 1925]

Dear Lady Stuart,

I cannot tell you how touched I was to receive your sweet letter full of love
and sympathy, also the beautiful box of good things. I am deeply grateful, for
we could not get such luxuries—for the dear boy—    It has been a very trying
time for us all, especially the invalid himself, and when he had to leave us, it
was a bit too much for the poor old Mother but—we are round the corner
and the operation a success as far as they can tell so far—

[*There follows a long account of illness and progress since the operation.*]

. . . I need not say what a consolation and help the frequent visits of that *dear
big brother of mine* have been, coming so bright and doing all he can to cheer
us up with his bright happy smile, and consoling words [—] for we were a sad
little circle for some days till *it* was over—

[11] HWRO 705:445:7095.
[12] 15 June 1925 (HWRO 705:445:7851).
[13] 10 July 1925 (HWRO 705:445:7070).
[14] HWRO 705:445:7163. Elgar's date of 'June 20th 1925' was a mistake for 'July'.

ELGAR: THE WINDFLOWER LETTERS

I am afraid you will be tired of all this, but I feel I am writing to a very sympathetic, may I say friend . . .

> Believe me
> Yours most Sincerely
> S.M Grafton

The Stuarts had been planning to attend the Gloucester Festival but were not able.[15] They sent their tickets to Edward for the Graftons.[16] At the Festival Edward conducted both *The Apostles* and *The Kingdom*, but he was not well. A severe late summer cold turned to bronchitis during an October visit to Carice. He was hardly back on his feet at Napleton before his eldest sister Lucy Pipe, who had lived her entire life in Worcester and had been latterly very deaf, fell ill and died at the age of seventy-three.

Napleton Grange, Kempsey, Worcester.
Oct. 28th 1925
My dear W.

I hope you are all well [—] it seems ages since I have heard anything of anyone. I saw no one at the festival except *locals*.

You will be interested about my poor old sister: I was with her till the end—she died on Friday—funeral yesterday: it was rather *fine* (or something which I cannot quite find a word for) but she sat up (with a most becoming light blue cap on) till the end & *refused* to use her ear trumpet at all: so she never heard one word for *many* days & declined to let us think she was wanting to hear or rather missing hearing. You have heard so much about her odd & angular (*fashionable*!) oddities that I must tell you the last; she was most carefully 'arranged' to see me the day before she died—blue cap & all—she said 'Edward, there should be a bottle of perfume behind the medicine—give it me'. I did & almost wept at the unswerving character.

I went down to Carice close on two months ago: was taken very ill—Bronchitis very sharp attack[.] I have been moved here but am only just allowed out & am ordered away for the winter—so I ought not to have gone to the funeral but I decline to obey doctors, [*four words eradicated*]!

Love to you all

> Yours ever
> Edward Elgar

My nephew is now better & about as usual.[17]

In November he himself seemed well enough to return to professional engagements. At the centre of them was an all-Elgar concert on 19 November, at which Henry Wood presented him with the Gold Medal of the Philharmonic Society, with a

---

[15] Tuesday [18 Aug.] (HWRO 705:445:7097).
[16] 2 Sept. 1925 (HWRO 705:445:7212).
[17] HWRO 705:445:7074.

formal supper to follow. The Stuarts attended the concert, but were unable to come to the supper as Lord Stuart's health was giving concern.[18] Carice came up for the events, and wrote in her diary:

19 November 1925 ... Wonderful concert—good audience. Sir H.Wood gave Father the gold medal of the Phil.Society near the end—great enthusiasm. Wortleys, J[essie] Snow, Landon Ronalds, Forbes Robertson & Norman Forbes there— Supper at Verneys after[.] Sat next Lan & Sir H.Wood[;] all Harrisons there & Mr.Schuster [—] back at 1. Wonderful evening.

20 November ... Sir Maurice came to see Father at 11. Thought him well [—] no need to go abroad if he did not want to. Father left by 12.45 for Worcester ...

Napleton Grange, Kempsey, Worcester.
Nov 21st 1925
My dear W.

Thank you very much for your note—it seemed to me a *dreadful* evening— such a sparse audience. I *was* glad when it was over. Then we had a supper[.] B.Walter was there & made an excellent speech. I came back yesterday & found two wildly delirious dogs! who will not leave me. I could not help looking round at you at some of the windflower passages! A fine orch.— I hope all your people are well, I am so sorry not to have seen more of you. Frank was at the supper & was leaving for Rome yesterday—he has taken an apartment in the *lower* parts which seems oddly rash. I cd. not help thinking of your scheme of aggrandisement of the undersigned when some of the big, brilliant passages resounded. However I have the medal!

Love
EE[19]

So there it was again—the theme which was to make an embarrassing obbligato in his letters over the next year and more. It was beneath the surface of a note responding to Lord Stuart's separate thanks for the concert.

Napleton Grange[,] Worcr.
Nov 24th 1925
My dear Charles:

It was very kind indeed of you to write about the concert—I only wish that others thought as you do of my essays in the Art! The orchestra was fine.

---

18   12 Nov. 1925 (HWRO 705:445:7099); Sunday [15 Nov.] (HWRO 705:445:7071).
19   HWRO 705:445:7073.

I am so sorry I did not see you; I quite hoped that you wd. have found your way to the artists' room

> Best regards
> Yours very sincly
> Edward Elgar[20]

Next day he replied to an invitation from the Windflower to come up for a revival of Granville Barker's play *The Madras House*:

Kempsey, Worcs:
Novr. 25th 1925

My dear W.

Many, many thanks but I shall be held here this next weekend—my brother is (alas!) really ill again. So all Madras House etc must be relinquished. If you *do* see Barker please be an angel & give him warm messages from me—tell him I was at the *1st* of this play (& all the others) & know every syllable of it

It is *very very* cold & dogs do not like it—I almost envy poor old Frank even in THAT company

> Love
> EE[21]

Just before Christmas he had to have an operation for haemorrhoids. It meant a stay in a Worcester nursing home of three weeks. Before going in he wrote:

Napleton Grange, Kempsey, Worcester.
Tuesday [22 Dec. 1925]

My dear W.

This is only to wish you all every good thing for Christmas & the New Year.

My plans are altered & Troyte will not be with me & I am leaving this tomorrow till after the holidays.

Carice is here—such weather

> Love
> EE[22]

[20] Elgar Birthplace parcel 583(vi).
[21] HWRO 705:445:7195.
[22] HWRO 705:445:7193.

Napleton Grange, Kempsey, Worcester.
Jany 12th 1926
My dear W.

This is only to thank you for the lovely calendar & to say that I am in less pain (which has been more than I can bear to think of) & that I come here in the day & go back to prison for the night

All good wishes for the New Year. I do hope all your people are better & everything good for you

Love<br>EE[1]

Two days later he went home finally to Napleton, and two days after that Carice (who had been with her father since 22 December) returned to Sussex. At the end of the month Pollie Grafton sent a report:

Perryfield, Bromsgrove.
Jan 31st 1926.
Dear Lady Stuart,

I hope you will not think I am taking a liberty in writing to you, but I thought it may be a comfort to you to hear from me of our dearest Edward[.] No doubt you hear frequently but I thought I would send this in case you may like it—

Carice went home when dear E. left the Nursing Home & my Clare went and took complete care of him for 10 days or so

I am so glad to be able to tell you she said the Doctor was quite satisfied [—] everything going on all right—   Gerald took me over to see him and we had quite a merry time, He reading aloud some Comic things that amused him & all of us and he laughed & laughed[.] Clare said it did him good—   I was so delighted to see him looking so well, and bright, and clear and full of fun—   He walks all about the fields and often goes into Worcester in the car—   He was coming here to lunch yesterday as the car was coming for Madge—who is there for this weekend—but it turned out so wet, he did not come—   I expect May will go to him for next weekend[.] He does so look forward to one of my Trio [of daughters] being with him, they are so bright and lively—   Things have been a little difficult here as our trustworthy old maid who really did everything seems to have quite broken down and in the Hospital here the last three months. She is hoping to come back but I fear, and in the mean time we are managing without side help, partly to please her

[1] HWRO 705:445:7790.

as she is longing to be back with us. I should like you to know I conveyed your message *quite privately* to E when in the Home, I felt you would like it so.

With kindest remembrances & love from

Yours very Sincerely
M. Grafton—

Please forgive my writing but this is quite to ourselves—

By mid-February Edward found himself longing to get out and prevented by severe weather.[2] On the 27th he went to London for a Press Club dinner, and responded to the toast of 'Music' with a depressed speech: 'It had been his wish that something lively and vital to music should pass through this country, but his wish had not been realised.'[3] He proposed a meeting with the Windflower,[4] but Lord Stuart was ill. She sent Edward a newspaper account of the Press Club speech, and asked if he had done anything further about the peerage.

Brooks's, St.James's Street, S.W.1.
March 2nd 1926

My dear W.

Thank you for the cutting. I hope your invalid is better & that your anxieties are subsiding: it is a most trying *time of year*—this east wind;—& to me, it makes everything difficult to bear.

You are kindness itself & of course I shd love to have the *offer*—but it is impossible for me to suggest in the remotest way that I want it: this sort of thing I have never done & although I know well that it *is* done and is held to be in no way blameworthy I cannot think of it: so adieu! to all my greatness.

I go down to Kempsey in a few minutes

Love
EE[5]

Another letter a month later covered all the same ground.[6]

He came to London for a visit beginning 23 April to conduct a London Symphony Orchestra concert and record for the gramophone.[7] But at Cheyne Walk Lord Stuart took a sudden turn for the worse, and he died on Saturday afternoon 24 April.

37, St.James's Place, S.W.1.
[Sunday 25 Apr.] night

My dear W.—

I can say nothing in this dreadfully sad time except that my thoughts are with you always & my good wishes

[2] 16 Feb 1926 (HWRO 705:445:7762).
[3] *The Times*, 1 Mar. 1926.
[4] Sunday [28 Feb.] (HWRO 705:445:7779).
[5] HWRO 705:445:7721.
[6] 1 April 1926 (HWRO 705:445:7769).
[7] 15 April 1926 (HWRO 705:445:7777).

Sir George Arthur said you had gone to Stratford so I did not announce my coming—& then last night the news came—a sad sad blow

Bless you & keep you now & always

Yrs most sincerely
EE.[8]

There is no record of his having attended the funeral, and it is likely that his closely following engagements prevented it. His next letter was written three weeks later.

Napleton Grange, Kempsey, Worcester.
May 17th 1926

My dear W.

I have been very anxious to hear something—after the Concert on the 26th I was laid up with cold. I got through the evening very well musically I am told but it was a great ordeal & I missed something too great to express—I looked at the familiar seats & my eyes filled—however, I *had* to go through with the programme—I wanted to give it up but my do[in]g wd. have dislocated so many plans for other people so I made what was really a sacrifice.

Please let me hear how you are & what the future will be. I have thought incessantly & wished you all the best things possible in this dreadfully sad time.

Yours ever
EE.[9]

She answered that she was going to Switzerland for a long rest when she was able.

Napleton Grange, Kempsey, Worcester.
June 29th 1926

My dear Windflower:

It was good of you to write: I did not send again because I know, from sad experience, the endless worries you must have been enduring. I hope Switzerland will be kind—I remember every minute & the book I made when you were there 13 years (is it possible?) ago. Carice, who has been with me for two weeks, left this morning but my two dogs make every possible fuss of me & seem to know I am lonely—bless them! I was reading of you—in Lehmann's Reminiscences of half a century—there is your father's very amusing 'poem' on your being 'returned'—all so alive & brilliant—& all past. What have we now? nothing that I see.

It is so good of you also to think of the plan you have spoken of so sweetly & which seems beyond a dream for its slightness—may yet come!

[8] HWRO 705:445:7778: dated by Elgar 'Saturday night', but Clare Stuart Wortley pointed out that the text requires Sunday.
[9] HWRO 705:445:7780.

My brother will not come out again & my niece Madge has been *very very ill*—[*about five words heavily eradicated*] serious—but she is able to sit up again: my sister was overcome & she too has been really laid up: so you see I have much to think of here. I fear poor old F. was the stranger, not you—his world is different now.

As to myself. I am getting 'fat & scant of breath'—Hamlet [—] I fear & I take no interest in anything now—however I have my memories—chief of which is you.

Bless you: write to me sometimes.

Love<br>EE[10]

The rest of the summer seems to have passed without surviving letters. On her return in September she told of an injury in Switzerland, and of hearing Margaret Fairless play the Violin Concerto.

Napleton Grange, Kempsey, Worcester.
Monday [?13 Sept. 1926]

My dear W.

This is only a very hurried line to thank you for your letter: I was so dreadfully sorry to hear of your Swiss accident & the great discomfort of moving etc etc. I do hope you feel nothing of it now. I have lost all interest in Music—it seems to have taken an odd turning—everything has to be hurried & vulgarised.

I am so glad you heard the Concerto: the young lady does it remarkably well.

Love<br>EE[11]

A letter of 17 September told her of a projected performance of the Concerto with Albert Sammons in November.[12] A month later he reminded her again.[13] Elgar conducted the performance on 25 November, it was broadcast, and the Windflower came—perhaps his first sight of her in many months.

Brooks's, St.James's Street, S.W.1.
Novr. 26th 1926

My dear W.

It was delightful to have a glimpse of you & again the Concerto was good to hear. Frank was there & came round to the artists' room—very radiant & rushing to his Brighton train.

I wanted to ask you about the subject which you had (very much) in mind long ago; the last time we spoke of it you said I was to do something. Can you

---

[10] HWRO 705:445:7765.

[11] HWRO 705:445:7755.

[12] HWRO 705:445:7775.

[13] Thursday mg [14 Oct] (HWRO 705:445:7723).

tell me *who* knows or has known anything of the idea? Do not worry or trouble at all about it but I should like to know if 'it' is entirely dead—my birthday (70) next June is to be 'recognised' by concerts in the musical world & I do not want this or these & shall *squash* them unless the other thing turns up. Forgive me for mentioning it even when you have so much to think of otherwise—but time is short & I wd. like to know where it is.

Once more I say how happy I was to see you & to see you at the Concert

Yours ever sny
EE[14]

This attempt to force the issue did not succeed.

Napleton Grange, Kempsey, Worcester.
Novr. 30th 1926
My dear W.

Thank you very, very much for your dear letter this morning; please *please* understand that I do not want to worry (you least of all) anyone. It wd. be good to know—that is what I meant when I wrote a day or two back—if the thing is done with or not. Of course I shd. be delighted if anything could be done now—i.e. for the New Year [Honours]; the state of affairs, as you suggest, seems to warrant it *now*. As to friends, dear old Ld.C[oventry] is impossible now. I never see him as he is generally unwell & only appears at the door sort of thing. Perhaps after you have seen F. you wd. let me know anything—what he thinks, etc. Of course for myself I can do nothing—I never have asked except that the Office of Master of the Music shd. be retained & it was given to me. I really do not know the P[rime] M[inister, Stanley Baldwin]; I have only met him once. Lord Beauchamp & Ld.Shaftesbury wd. be the people, I think but, of course, I had no idea that they had been spoken to.

Do take care in this weather: at last the sun shines (—your letter made it— I think!) but the wind is bitter & I have a neighbour's funeral to go to.

I cannot forget the Concert—a breath of the old fresh air. I have letters from all parts: I cannot *realise* that Brodksy in Manchester & Carice in Sussex both heard perfectly—amazing.

My love
Yrs ever
EE

Of course Stamfordham shd. be seen & the (musical) position explained to him: but he is rather severe & dry in art matters I fear.[15]

But another holiday season approached.[16] The Windflower sent a diary to Edward,[17] and a hamper to Perryfield.

[14] HWRO 705:445:7760.                [16] 7 Dec 1926 (HWRO 705:445:7757).
[15] HWRO 705:445:7759.                [17] Monday [20 Dec. 1926] (HWRO 705:445:7776).

In his first letter of the new year, thanking the Windflower for the Perryfield hamper, Elgar wrote: ' . . . there is nothing in my art that calls me to London'.[1] But 1927 was his seventieth birthday year, and soon his concert schedule was as full as ever. On 14 February he was to conduct the London Symphony Orchestra in a concert of his works at Queen's Hall. That morning he wrote:

Brooks's, St.James's Street, S.W.1.
Monday [14 Feb. 1927]
My dear W.

I should have written but the fog—which was in the Midlands when not in London—made travelling so uncertain that I thought I shd. never get here.

Thank you for your letter & I *do* hope you will come round to the artist's room—Norman [Forbes], etc. will come. Carice is coming to me to-day but I must rush off tomorrow: *next* week I shall be in town from Monday till the following Monday & shd dearly love to see you

haste just going to rehearsal

Yrs ever
EE[2]


The Windflower came to the concert with Clare.

The following Monday afternoon saw him in London again. On the Saturday afternoon, 26 February, he was to conduct the Royal Choral Society in *Gerontius*. On his way to an evening rehearsal he sent a note to ask about lunch and a theatre one day.[3] But she had a chill. He visited Cheyne Walk, and there got into a discussion of linguistics, at one point referring Clare to H. W. Fowler's *Modern English Usage*. Afterwards he wrote:

37 St James's Place
Feb 25th 1927
My dear Clare:

I have sent on the book: do not be angry with your old friend for wishing you well.

My love
Yr affect
E.E.[4]

[1]  3 Jan 1927 (HWRO 705:445:7764).
[2]  HWRO 705:445:7773.
[3]  Monday evg [21 Feb. 1927] (HWRO 705:445:7800).
[4]  HWRO 705:445:7903.

The next afternoon brought *Gerontius*. Despite pouring wet weather, the Albert Hall was filled with a huge audience that included Alice Stuart of Wortley and Frank Schuster. The novel feature was that half the performance was recorded by 'His Master's Voice'. (Four of the 78 r.p.m. sides were issued commercially during the birthday year: all but one of the rest survived in Elgar's own test copies, and they were issued together more than half a century later.)

A note of 9 March rejoices in spring sunshine at Kempsey.[5] Then he was in London again.

Brooks's, St.James's Street, S.W.1.
Weds [16 Mar. 1927] morng

My dear W.

I had to fly up on business & am just starting back. I just managed to see a *very nice* little play with dear Norman F[orbes] otherwise no free minute: the play is 'No Gentleman' quite fresh, clean & amusing, do go.

I really began to write this to enquire if the Hereford people have sent you the usual circulars about the festival—mine are here. I do hope they have sent and that you will be able to be there.

I am so glad Clare (& you) are amused at the Modern English Usage.

> Your
> EE

I have now heard from Frank.[6]

She made her plans to attend the Three Choirs Festival at Hereford in September.

At the beginning of April he was in London again to conduct a new recording of the Second Symphony, which was to be issued for his birthday in June. A week later he was looking forward to broadcasting *Gerontius*—having just conducted a concert at Hastings, another in London, and that evening attended a supper given by Schuster for Wagner's son Siegfried during his visit.

37, St.James's Place, S.W.1.
Friday [8 Apr. 1927]

My dear W.

I am just off home but shall be back on Tuesday till Saturday; I have rehearsals Wedy & Thursday mornings, & a performance (B.B.C.) of Gerontius on Friday evening: do let me know if you are to be in London: this week I *rushed* to choral rehearsal all Wedy morng—then to Hastings: yesterday rehearsal in the morng & concert in afternoon: then back here & to Frank's supper for Siegfried Wagner: I fully hoped you would have been there—quite in old Frankies grand (iose) manner.

My invalids are fairly—quiet.

> Love
> Yrs ever
> EE[7]

[5] 9 Mar 1927 (HWRO 705:445:7772).    [6] HWRO 705:445:7756.    [7] HWRO 705:445:7758.

The end of April found him in London once more, and they met on the afternoon of the 30th. A week later he wrote from Worcestershire:

Kempsey
May 6th 1927

My dear W.

Your namesakes are flourishing but as they are *garden* production & not 'nemorosa' (of the wood) I do not send them.

I arrived here yesterday & was nearly devoured by dogs. I was so sorry not to see you again—it was a lovely afternoon on Saturday; but I was overwhelmed with engagements after that including a day on the bench (next the judge) at Old Bailey! I hope to be back in town directly. As to your little aggrandisement plan, I have definitely ruled it off the map!

Love and thanks

Yrs ever
EE

P.S. I went down to Frank on Sunday (luncheon) & was delighted with his improvements[8]

Schuster was living largely at Hove now, having more or less given over The Hut to Anzy and Wendela Wylde.

Later in the month came the death of the old Countess of Wharncliffe, Lord Stuart's cousin by marriage. Edward wrote:

Brooks's, St.James's Street, S.W.1.
May 20th 1927

My dear W.

I am just leaving for Worcester (really only passing through): I could not help feeling that you wd. have old memories stirred by the death of your aged kinswoman; I may be wrong but I am always thinking.

I shall have to be up for B.B.C. June 2nd. & I have an official dinner on the 3rd.—I shall write on the chance of finding you free for a theatre

Yrs ever
EE[9]

On 2 June, the night of his seventieth birthday, he conducted a broadcast concert of his works. The following evening he dined at St. James's Place. But the most personal tribute was devised by Frank Schuster. He borrowed back The Hut (now renamed by Anzy 'The Long White Cloud') to give a Sunday afternoon concert of Elgar's chamber music for a large gathering of friends on 26 June. Edward hoped that the Windflower could be there.[10] But she was not well enough to come.[11]

---

[8] HWRO 705:445:7740.
[9] HWRO 705:445:4031.

[10] Monday [29 May 1927] (HWRO 705:445:7793).
[11] Thursday [23 June 1927] (HWRO 705:445:7741).

Napleton Grange, Kempsey, Worcester.
July 4th 1927

My dear W.

I hope your improvement has continued well & that you are quite strong again.

I need not say that you were sadly missed last Sunday at the Hut—or rather at the new place as the Hut atmosphere has gone never to return. Dear old Frank was radiant &, as usual, a perfect host. The music was well played—the Quintet *quite* satisfactorily. Murdoch has improved wonderfully: the rest you know. The house-party *seemed* to consist of S.Sassoon, who only appeared once,—a mercuric lady Mrs.C.Beddington & a Robert Schuster & his wife—I *hope* I behaved as becomes an old visitor but I wandered round the garden alone & found D.o.m.D.etc still legible. I *wish* you could have heard the things which seem to me to be of my best & the Quintet is not of this world; but you know more of this than I do.

I wish also you cd. hear the gramophone records of the IInd Sym.—the new H.M.V. machine [with electric reproduction] is marvellous & you really shd. have one!

Mary Anderson came over to tea—a voice from the past! with messages from Maud White who, as far as I cd. make out, is not well & at Broadway. I am sorry to say *my* invalids are troublesome. Please tell me you are better.

Love
EE[12]

Later in the month he wrote to Clare Stuart Wortley (who had had a fall[13]). *Modern English Usage* had provided food for thought.

Napleton Grange, Kempsey, Worcester.
July 20th 1927

My dear Clare: first, I hope you are really not any the worse for your fall; I should have been uplifted had you been at *The Long White Cloud* (formerly The Hut) but your very, very trying experience wd. not help in listening to alleged music. 'They' played extremely well. I do not know how far your questions as to 'Welsh rabbit' are rhetorical, but, at the risk of being more ridiculous than usual, I will say that 'it' is '*toasted cheese*',—a humorous & allusive (e.g. Merry Wives, V. 5.) name for the Welsh product—which the principality is supposed to devour in large quantities. It began life as a merely comic expression, like Norfolk capon = red herring, or Essex lion = calf, & some fastidious person suggested that rabbit was a vulgarisation of 'rarebit'. I am glad you find amusement in the book & am overwhelmed with shame

[12] HWRO 705:445:7781.
[13] A note from Elgar to Clare, dated 16 June (did that mean July?) 1927, mentions her possession of a cane (HWRO 705:445:7797).

when you tell me that the reference is wanting. I live here generally but hope to be in London before the end of the month & shall hope to call.

I really do not 'mind' the use of 'one' in the proper place—as you use it in your letter; but it must not be used to implicate the reader in the doings (*or opinions*), right or wrong, of the writer; e.g. 'one condemns these poems' or anything you like: I *feel* this to mean, 'I want to condemn them, but as I dare not make a definite condemnation, I gather you, my readers, in & suggest that you are to share in damning' whatever is in question.

My love to you & good wishes

Yr affect friend<br>Edward Elgar[14]

In September the Windflower came to the Hereford Festival—which saw the novelty of 'His Master's Voice' vans beside the Cathedral, experimenting further with actual-performance recording: Elgar was heavily involved. But after the Festival, back at Kempsey, the three-year lease of Napleton Grange was coming to an end with no news of the renewal he wanted. He wrote:

37, St.James's Place, S.W.1. passing thro'—(only one hour) to Margate!
Sunday [11 Sept. 1927]
My dear W.

I was so very sorry to be so useless in Hereford, but you will understand that I had much more to see to than appeared on the surface. It was lovely to know you were there amongst the music once more: the things went fairly well &, I hope, made some effect.

I am not at all sure about my future—which is vague as the lease of Kempsey is in such a *mixed* condition;— so my darling dogs are in a weary state of uncertainty

Carice travelled with me [from Worcestershire to London] today & has gone home [to Sussex]—I go on to Margate of all awful places [to conduct a concert].

I shall hope to find you in town soon. I was delighted to see you looking so much less 'tried' than I feared might be the case.

Love<br>EE[15]

The lease of Napleton was not renewed, and so October brought another move. He was able to rent Battenhall Manor, an old black and white house on the outskirts of Worcester, for the winter: it too was furnished.

---

14 HWRO 705:445:7792.     15 HWRO 705:445:7763.

Napleton Grange, Kempsey, Worcester,
Oct 24th 1926[*sic*]

My dear W.

Excuse odd stationery but I am moving: Carice is here &, of course, there is not really much in the way of *quantity* but an accumulation of books papers (*& dogs*) needs some looking after.

I hope you are well, it seems ages since Hereford & I have only been in London for one day since. Lan gave your own Symphony last week & I am told it went very well.

I have the Manor House only for the winter—after that I cannot tell. I shall be glad to hear all about everything

Frank goes to Brighton, or near, for the winter.

Troyte has just left, after a week-end

> Love
> Yrs ever
> EE.[16]

The Windflower herself was looking for another house. No. 7 Cheyne Walk was too large now, and Clare had her own flat elsewhere. Lady Stuart heard of a large property near the eastern end of Cheyne Walk which was announced to be rebuilt as smaller houses. Her choice fell here, even though reconstruction was to take some time.[17]

Elgar continued to conduct concerts. On Armistice day he broadcast *The Spirit of England*.[18] Then 1927 drew toward its close.

Battenhall Manor, Worcester.
Dec 10th 1927

My dear W:

Do you know what a *wonderful* thing the gramophone is? I mean the latest *H.M.V.*—I have just been playing over your Symphony & most of it sounds divine. I wish you would get such an instrument—the tone is superb. I have also a supreme record of Brahms 4th Sym. in E minor.

I have been quite laid up with a persistent cough: I hope you have escaped & that you are well & happy.

Carice & her husband & Troyte are coming to me for Christmas—I wish you were.

You wd. like the Manor House—

My love & all good wishes

> Yr affec
> EE

[16]  HWRO 705:445:7742.
[17]  17 Nov 1927 (HWRO 705:445:7734).
[18]  10 Nov 1927 (HWRO 705:445:7802).

I wrote to Frank a week ago, but I imagine he is far away.

I hope this bit of real old Italian paper will please you[.] Hold it up to the light & rejoice in a real Florentine watermark[19]

Schuster was not far away. Two days later he and Alice Stuart of Wortley attended the conducting debut of young John Barbirolli—who substituted at the last moment for Sir Thomas Beecham with a fine performance of the Elgar Second Symphony.[20]

That season saw the posthumous publication of Charles Stuart of Wortley's book, *The First Lady Wharncliffe and Her Family (1779–1856)*. The two volumes were in fact an annotated edition of the letters of his grandmother. Clare Stuart Wortley wrote:

> ... For many years past he had been reading, editing, causing copies to be made, & generally preparing [the letters] for publication—a very considerable work to carry out in his scanty spare time. He died before it was completed, and his sister Mrs. Grosvenor finished the putting together of what he had assembled, & published it ...
>
> Lord Stuart (my father) often read bits of the letters to us of his family, or intimate friends likely to be interested in them.[21]

Now the Windflower offered to send a copy to Edward.

Battenhall Manor, Worcester.
Dec 14th 1927
My dear W:

Thank you for the Wharncliffe book. I had seen it & was greatly interested & a good deal *emotioned* when I remembered the old days & hearing a scrap or two of the letters. I am glad you liked the [Barbirolli] concert—I knew nothing of it!

Do go to H.M.V. 363 Oxford St. & hear a new gramophone, (*Buy* one) & get them to play you a little of the Brahms Sym E min or your own No.2 in E flat! You ought to have one & about 100 records.

Your maid wd. manipulate it for you

I wish I could have given you a Christmas here—it is a real Yule-loggy house & you wd. have met, in spirit, Oliver Cromwell, Charles I & II & a lot of agreeable restoration ghosts.

Love
EE[22]

[19] HWRO 705:445:7783. The recording of the Brahms Fourth Symphony was that played by the London Symphony Orchestra conducted by Hermann Abendroth. (See *Elgar on Record*, p. 234.)

[20] Schuster wrote about this performance on 17 Dec. (HWRO 705:445:6901). It was to be his last surviving letter to Elgar.

[21] Note on HWRO 705:445:7720.

[22] Elgar Birthplace.

A week later she sent word that Frank Schuster had suddenly been taken ill at his house in Hove. Clare Stuart Wortley recalled:

He had lunched with Lady Stuart and gone with her to the Messiah at the Albert Hall as recently as Sunday December 18th, & seemed fairly well. She had first heard of his illness on Dec.21st, & noted in her diary 'Dear Frank seriously ill,' & there follow similar entries each day ... [23]

Battenhall
Dec 24th 1927
My dear W.

Thank you for your news of dear old Frank: I have wired & have reply that he is progressing: it was an awful shock as we had been exchanging notes about dates etc. Poor dear I hope he is in 'no pain'

All good wishes & 1000 thanks for the volumes which have just arrived—I remember C. reading extracts from the letters long ago.

I am very sorry to tell you that H.M. has offered me the wretched *K.C.V.O.*(!!!) which awful thing I must accept!

Alas!

Love<br>EE

My guests are here. [24]

This end of the effort to secure a peerage was not allowed to dampen holiday cheer at Battenhall. It snowed for much of Christmas Day, and by evening drifts were deep.

Battenhall Manor, Worcester.
Decr 26th 1927
My dear W.

I had your p.c. & I have written to Hove: I do not expect a reply to my general messages: thank you many times for letting me hear; I do hope all goes well with dear old Frank. My house party is moved in & we cannot get the car out as the roads are impracticable—however your chocolates have arrived; Carice is delighted with the house etc.

We were all going to the Theatre this afternoon but how to get there is the problem.

I hope you are not minding the cold;—it is blowing a freezing blast & the ground is thick with snow & ice.

Love<br>EE. [25]

They managed to get into Worcester that afternoon for the pantomime *Bo Peep*.

[23] Note on HWRO 705:445:7791.      [24] HWRO 705:445:7720.      [25] HWRO 705:445:7791.

Next morning came a telegram to say that Frank Schuster had died.

Battenhall
Tuesday [27th Dec. 1927]
My dear W.

I know you will be in deep sorrow—a telegram has just come—it is too sad & I had hoped, from the last news I had received, that all was going well. Alas!

Love<br>EE[26]

Clare Stuart Wortley wrote:

His funeral was at Putney Vale on Friday Dec 30th at 2.30. Owing to snow, neither Lady Stuart nor Sir Edward could attend it. The unexpectedness of it all, and the snow, made it all so strange and sudden and tragic. I was with her and I remember. We could only sit quietly through the funeral hour, at home.[27]

Battenhall Manor, Worcester.
Dec 27th [*sic*: *postmarked* 30 December, the day of the funeral] 1927
My dear Windflower:

The roads are impossible so I cannot get to the funeral. I had hoped that I might have driven from here. So I am sitting here in thought—mostly very pleasant & happy ones of dear old Frank. It is a dispensation of Whoever controls us, that in remembering childish holidays we recollect always the *fine* days—the bad ones do not come back so easily; in the passing of friends it is somewhat the same; the radiant happy & sunny Frank I have before me as I write & the small temporary little irritations, which worried one at the time, are gone & forgotten forever.

I wrote to his sister [—] just a note = the rest of the family are unknown to me.

And *you*: I left you till the last because in music you found such a 'world' & in Frank such a friend of music. Your loss in this way is naturally not to be filled—how could it be? So I can only say I *know* & sympathise as *you* know.

Dear love to you Windflower.

Your affecte<br>EE[28]

[26] HWRO 705:445:7801.

[27] Note to HWRO 705:445:7801.

[28] HWRO 705:445:7782. Elgar's letter of sympathy to Adela Schuster was also dated 27 December (HWRO 705:445:6847).

Battenhall Manor, Worcester.
31 DEC. 1927

My dear W.

Our letters cross—    Yes; I am puzzled about it all: I fully expected to see a real notice in the leading papers but only the *Times* has what you sent me & the wretched D. Mail had a line or two. It seems too late now to do anything. F.Toye would be the man. I should *not* like to write (much as I long to do so) because I only knew the last 30 years of dear F's musical life & *really* only so far as that period closely concerns me personally; then I know *nothing* of his family except his sister & it wd. be affronting to them to omit references—

Of course I have met Sir Felix [Schuster] & one or two others casually but I do not know them, even by sight. As to any item 'In memoriam' at an orchl Concert I do not know. F. was not really a *commercial* supporter of the L.S.O. I think & I suppose the authorities of that corporation & others wd. consider that. That dreadful person Albert Coates is to conduct the next concert & he, of course, is hopeless.

It all seems so *wrong* & dismally *inefficient*; but I do not see what can be done.

I thought it was proper to have a memorial service in a London church??

In haste
Love
EE[29]

# 1928

---

An exchange of letters with Anzy Wylde found common ground at last in Frank Schuster's memory. Edward wrote to the Windflower:

Battenhall Manor, Worcester.
Jany 6th 1928

My dear W.

Thank you for your letter: I have had a good letter from Captn Wylde. I wrote to him & thanked him for making happiness for dear old Frank in his later years when we older men with older & fading interests could not possibly fill his mind as they might have done years ago.

And now all is over: I feel a sad want of something in the background—it is as if a support had gone. F. was all the time *there* if wanted,—but I never troubled him in any way. He was a trustee for Carice but I do not think anything need happen over that.

[29] HWRO 705:445:7753.

I should have loved to have had some little memento of him—but it is perhaps better not—

I hope you are well again now that the weather is more reasonable—too warm to-day to be able to move!

This is a very dull note but then it is from a dull person.

I forget if I sent you a picture of this sweet ancient place: here is one, if I did send one you can let me have this back anytime

> Love
> EE.[1]

He enclosed a snapshot taken at Battenhall, of dogs running from the car toward Madge.

At the end of February a weekly magazine published the hope that Sir Edward Elgar, OM, and now KCVO, would return to large composition. Clare Stuart Wortley echoed that hope.

Battenhall Manor, Worcester.
March 1st 1928

My dear Clare:

Thank you for your letter & the fine words; I fear, however, that I have no time for anything so pleasant as composition; I like to hug to myself the knowledge that *you* thought of me in connexion with anything so high. I wish your literary maid wd. find & tell me of the numbers of '*John o'London's Weekly*' containing such flattering things.

> My love to you
> Yr affectate friend
> Edward Elgar[2]

Next day he went to London for this year's performance of *Gerontius* with the Royal Choral Society.

Brooks's, St.James's Street, S.W.1.
Friday [2 Mar. 1928]

My dear W.

I hope you are well: I have to be at the Albert Hall tomorrow, Saturday: I shall of course be tired & dull in the evening but if it happened that you are free I should love to have a quiet meal—but I fear that's impossible for you.

Brewer's death was terribly sudden & I may be telegraphed for.

> Love
> EE

Anemones are thinking of blossoming[3]

---

[1] HWRO 705:445:7766.          [2] HWRO 705:445:4027.          [3] HWRO 705:445:7789.

(Sir Herbert Brewer, organist of Gloucester Cathedral and a conductor at the Three Choirs Festivals for thirty years, had died the previous evening.) The Windflower came to the afternoon performance of *Gerontius* and brought Edward back to Cheyne Walk for a quiet dinner.

Later in the month he was in London again. As Master of the King's Music, he attended the King and Queen when they came to Sir Thomas Beecham's performance of Handel's *Solomon* at a Philharmonic concert on 22 March. But Elgar also arranged something for the ordinary concert-goer: at his suggestion, the King's manuscript score of *Solomon* was exhibited at Queen's Hall throughout the evening, guarded by a plain-clothes policeman. At the end of the concert various presentations took place, and Beecham was given the Philharmonic Society's Gold Medal. Next morning Edward wrote:

37, St.James's Place, S.W.1.
March 23rd 1928—7.30 a.m.

My dear Windflower.

I found your letter & present last night—thank you so much only, my dear, I was to *fetch it*—& intended to do so but you have cut off one reason (as if I wanted any) for calling! Bless you. All went well last night: of course the Times had it all wrong. Beecham had nothing to do with it—& the K. & Q. did not go to the artists' room. Shaftesbury made those presentations; I made the others etc. Nothing of moment of course: I was responsible for dear Billy [Reed]'s presentation & nice Mr.Winterbottom [principal double bass player in the Philharmonic Orchestra for many years and a founder of the London Symphony Orchestra]: I have tried to get a sort of human feeling into it all & 'out of the rut' of mere formulas.

I am going to live at S.-on-A! *near*, on the river: I will tell you all about it when it is settled—it is in the incipient stages

> Love
> Yr affect
> EE

I am so sorry I have no moment—I am at *H.M.V.* (recording [the Cello Concerto with Beatrice Harrison]) *all* day & dine with H.M. tonight & go home early tomorrow to arrange about moving to Stratford (near)[4]

With his time at Battenhall nearly over, he was taking Tiddington House, on the Avon near Stratford, on a two year lease. But he was soon in London again: on 30 March he conducted a concert of his music at the People's Palace in the East End of London, and the Windflower came to it.

Then Frank Schuster's will was published. Schuster had left £7000 'to my friend, Sir Edward Elgar O.M., who has saved my country from the reproach of having produced no composer worthy to rank with the great masters'. Edward wrote from his sister's house:

[4] HWRO 705:445:7751.

Bromsgrove
Easter Monday [9 Apr. 1928]
My dear W.

Thanks to you for your letter, it was the one ray of light your being at the People's palace.

I came here on Saturday & am resting with Marco: I go to Stratford on the 20th.

You will have seen Frankie's will in the papers & everyone else has to my great annoyance (by every post!) but I have heard *nothing*: so that's how it stands

I hope Brighton was good. If I come to town I shall ring you up.

Love<br>EE

There were no Windflowers at Battenhall![5]

Five days later he was in London once more—taking up time before he could get into the new home. He clearly felt the strain of moving about with indefinite arrangements, as he shared a meal with the Windflower before they went to a play at the Haymarket called *The Fourth Wall*.

Brooke's, St.James's Street, S.W.1.
Monday [16 Apr. 1928]
My dear W.

I am so sorry everything on Saturday was *not* quite so smooth as I wished it for you: the play is not really good & droops badly. We must try again, You are very good indeed to overlook my manifold shortcomings:

Bless you<br>Ever yrs<br>EE.[6]

At last his move was made to Stratford. His niece Clare Grafton came to live with him by his invitation: she had severe diabetes, and her doctor had said that she should have more quiet than she could get in the midst of her own family at Perryfield. All in all, it took some time to settle in. They had hardly done so before Edward's brother, Frank Elgar, died in Worcester after his illness of so many years.

Yet the season also yielded happiness. On 4 June Edward wrote to the Windflower: 'our dear Reed has to-day *M.V.O.* [in the Birthday Honours.] I am so delighted: Do, if you can, send him congratulations'.[7] She did so, and Reed responded: 'I never was so surprised in my life, but I have a shrewd suspicion (& I expect you have) that the hand of the "Master of the King's Musick" is in this somewhere.'[8]

That summer No. 7 Cheyne Walk was sold. But the smaller house was nowhere near ready.

---

[5] HWRO 705:445:7752.      [6] HWRO 705:445:7786.
[7] HWRO 705:445:7711.      [8] Elgar Birthplace parcel 584(viii).

Tiddington House near Stratford-upon-Avon.
3rd August 1928

My dear Windflower:

I am so grieved to think of the desolation & wish I could do something [—] anything [—] to ease the parting for you. It gives me a wrench to hear that the dear piano is being removed from the spot so dear *so dear* in many ways. Yes, we (Clare [Grafton] is living with me) go to the theatre [at Stratford] but it is not good except for a few of the actors.

I am to go to Berlin to make records of the Violin Concerto with Kreisler—but it is not quite settled,—you shall hear.

All good wishes and love

Yours affcty<br>Edward[9]

Recording the Violin Concerto with its dedicatee had long been hoped for and projected, but Kreisler was difficult to pin down.

Tiddington House near Stratford-upon-Avon.
16th August 1928

My dear W.

I am so glad to hear; I wondered if you wd. be coming to S-on-A for a play or so: it is too dull to ask you here but the garden is large & lovely.

I do hope the new house will be everything lovely for you: let me know when you are to be visible therein.

All good wishes

Yours ever<br>EE

I suppose you will not be at Gloucester.[10]

In fact she had gone to Cornwall. The day after the Gloucester Festival ended he wrote:

Tiddington House near Stratford-upon-Avon.
Saturday [8 Sept. 1928]

My dear W.

All thanks for your letter: I hope Tintagel is lovely for you—I remember *much* there. You were missed at Gloucester

Love<br>EE[11]

[9] HWRO 705:445:7718.      [10] HWRO 705:445:7767.      [11] HWRO 705:445:7726.

He had had a visit from the actor-manager Gerald Lawrence. Lawrence was producing a play about Beau Brummel, showing the hero ready to sacrifice everything—even life itself—to save a lady's honour. Would Sir Edward write incidental music? Sir Edward agreed to try, and Lawrence spent a day and night at Tiddington in late September discussing the score.

St James's
Oct 19th 1928
My dear W.

Your welcome letter finds me here very busy as I am writing some (trifling) music for a play—costume play—which shd. be produced in Birmingham on the 5th.

I shall be glad to hear that you are settled in your new home, I am sure it will be charming.

We have had a wonderful summer but my dear little niece is *very* ill: we managed to get her home & she is better—so they say—I hope it is more than a momentary flicker—Clare is the one—diabetes

I was greatly shocked at dear F Dicksee's death—and the horrors proposed to succeed him [as President of the Royal Academy] make it so much harder to bear.

Love
EE[12]

St Jss
Tuesday [23 Oct. 1928] night
My dear W.

Your letter has just come: I am sorry your house is not ready.

I am so very sorry not to see you but my plans are no plans—I come to rehearsal only—went to S-on.A. on Saturday—back here yesterday & am off home early tomorrow.

I will not attempt to tell you about the play—we will talk of it

Clare is shewing the smallest improvement

Love
E[13]

The music was finished, and *Beau Brummel* was produced in Birmingham on 5 November. Elgar himself conducted the tiny pit orchestra on the first night. But such a play on such a theme struck no chord in the late 1920s, and a London production was in doubt.

The Windflower found a temporary home, as her daughter wrote:

[12] HWRO 705:445:7745.    [13] HWRO 705:445:7749.

Lady Stuart was staying with her husband's sister Katherine, Lady Lyttelton, wife of Sir Neville Lyttelton, Governor of the Royal Hospital, Chelsea. While there she met Archbishop Randall Davidson, who had recently resigned from the See of Canterbury; he came to dinner one night.[14]

Tiddington House near Stratford-upon-Avon.

6th Decr 1928

My dear W.

Thank you for your letter; I am so very glad to know that you are with real friends;—it sounded so dismal,—the prospect of hotel life I mean.

I have been through very much anxiety over my niece & untellable other worries—not my own really but which I have to suffer vicariously—

The dogs are very well but bored by the bad weather.

I have the greatest reverence & a sort of affection for the (late) Archbishop—you might tell him so—but he knows it already

It is very grave about H.M. but we still hope.

> Love
> EE.[15]

The King was ill for many months with a lung complaint which affected his heart. He did in the end make a partial recovery.

Then another Christmas was upon them.

Tiddington House near Stratford-upon-Avon.

Dec 24th 1928

My dear W.

This is only to bring you all good wishes from Marco Mina & Meg: they also send their love as I do mine

> Yrs ever affectly
> EE

P S.—Your letter just come so I open this to thank you for the lovely diary[.] Troyte is here but Carice & her husband cd. not come—they will be here later.

I had already addressed this to the Governor's House

Yes: it is dreadful to have to miss old Frankie so much—it is just a year.

> Love
> E[16]

[14]  Note on HWRO 705:445:7750.
[15]  HWRO 705:445:7750. A letter of 22 February 1927 from Elgar to the Archbishop is printed in Percy Young, *Elgar, O.M.* (2nd edn., White Lion, 1973), p. 230.
[16]  HWRO 705:445:7725.

On 20 January Pollie Grafton sent the news of Perryfield to Lady Stuart. Clare Grafton was better.

It was so thoughtful and kind of you to send her the jelly & soup, and they are perfectly safe and just what she is allowed—

Edward is wonderful, his health I mean[.] He *never* will come away on Christmas Day, always stays at home, but we went down to tea to cheer things up. He often comes over here, loves it, last Thursday he came over to lunch and spent the day, and is so full of fun and easy [—] just like a boy, it does us good to have him—

One of the girls go over each weekend, and he so looks for them. Clare has not been yet of course since her illness—Madge is there this week[.] Gerald took her yesterday, and Edward is coming back with her in the morning—

Last Wednesday we had great fun. E took us all but Clare, to the Worcester Pantomime[.] We met at the Theatre [—] then afterwards went to the Star Hotel for coffee & sandwiches, then parted company[.] We came home and he & Madge went back to Stratford. So you see we are with him as much as possible, he seems to live to have one of the young ones there— It is a pity Carice is so far away.

I do hope you will come to Stratford this Summer, there I may see you again and so thank you personally for all your kindnesses to us at Perryfield . . . I think you would simply love Tiddington House and garden, and the river running just at the end of the garden down a few steps to the boat . . . My daughters send their love to you with mine—

With kindest regards
Yours very Sincerely
S.M.Grafton

It was the picture of a man settling among his own people in the country; and it was increasingly true in these years. As London saw him less, he saw less of the Windflower. And so their correspondence thinned, though never their affection. His first surviving letter written to her in 1929 says all this between its lines:

Tiddington House, Stratford-upon-Avon.
5 FEB 1929

My dear W:

I am so glad to hear of you again & quite hoped that you were happy & settled in your new house. I fear Brummel is not a success & may not come to London: When anything is printed or performed I will send it also the very small cards—but you will not want these things until you are safely 'housed': I know what a nuisance odd things are.

I fear I may not be in town for some long time—the weather is & has been atrocious—the dullest winter I have ever known—not sharp enough to skate, but one long cold-wind-sleety season[.] My dogs are *bored stiff* with it all. But it is lovely by the river at the end of my garden—wild geese, herons & all sorts of weird creatures—you wd. love it & must come sometime. I think I ansd. all your beautiful notes—so if anything has gone wrong it's mine!

Rest assured that you know all about my music

The windflowers will soon bloom

Love
EE[1]

A month later he was in London to conduct an afternoon performance of *The Kingdom* at the Albert Hall, and the Windflower was there. But he was suffering from a sore throat, and Carice got him to the 6.10 evening train for Warwickshire.

Tiddington House near Stratford-upon-Avon.
13th March 1929

My dear W.

Thank you for your letter: it was delightful to see you last week. I am sorry I was such a dreary person—but I had a cough & fled home: much finer weather lately as you know but trying changes of temperature.

I have no flowers to send you yet—only snowdrops which may not be sent on account of superstitions I am told.

I hope you will now be able to command the new house to be ready at once—at these times how lovely it is to fly back to the Arabian Nights & order a genie to do things.

My dogs are well & I am better but take much care.

Love
Yrs ever
E.E.[2]

Tiddington House near Stratford-upon-Avon.
29th April 1929

My dear W.

All thanks for your letter: I have had a poor time with a throat—but practically all right again now. I am *hoping* to get to the [Royal Academy] Private View & dinner but am not yet sure if I can stand it: if the weather is kind I shall make the plunge & will let you know.

I do hope you have escaped.

Love
EE[3]

[1] HWRO 705:445:7784.      [2] HWRO 705:445:7747.      [3] HWRO 705:445:7731.

Tiddington House near Stratford-upon-Avon.
8th May 1929

My dear W.

Thank you for the book & for your letter: I did not get to London after all—although my name appeared as being at the R.A. dinner

I am *not* well & do not get on—quite *private*—it is my *ear* which has failed (& is painful) after threatening for years!

I hope to get away soon & may come to London & hope to see you

Love
E.E.

P.S. Will the enclosed (1887) amuse you? I wrote an 'article' [on a Brahms String Quartet with which he had then recently become familiar] for the Malvern paper: they made it into a letter by adding 'Yours truly' and prefixing 'Sir'—to avoid paying for it! Let me have it back—I found it turning out some old papers. I feel that I really was something apart from the ordinary country Violin teacher even then![4]

He was in London fleetingly at the beginning of June, and thanked her for congratulations on his birthday.[5]

His next surviving letter to her was written during London rehearsals for the Worcester Festival.

37, St.James's Place, S.W.1.
2nd Septr. 1929

My dear W.

Do let me know how & where you are. I have had no address from you for ages & wished to tell you of the festival & other things.

Shall you be going to Worcester.

I shall be at Marl Bank[,] Rainbow Hill—Worcr for the week.

Love
EE[6]

It was a house standing high above the city, with views over the Cathedral to the Malvern Hills beyond. He had known it from boyhood. Now it was for sale: he had taken it for the Festival week with the thought of buying it and returning to live in Worcester. The Windflower did come to the Festival. On the Tuesday morning she attended the first performance of Edward's orchestration of Purcell's *Jehovah quam multi sunt hostes mei*, and afterwards she lunched at Marl Bank.

In October she told him of attending a Delius concert. He answered during a day visit to London: 'I am glad you went to the Delius'.[7]

---

[4] HWRO 705:445:7717.
[5] 5 June 1929 (HWRO 705:445:7735).
[6] HWRO 705:445:7738.
[7] Monday [14 Oct. 1929] (HWRO 705:445:7736).

Tiddington House near Stratford-upon-Avon.
1st Novr 1929

My dear W.

Thank you for your letter: I am glad you are with sympathetic friends &
only wish your own house was ready for you.

I have bought the cottage you did me the honour to lunch in: a poor little
place but a fitting end for a disastrous career—alas!

I hope you do not mind the cold—it is rather sudden & acute

> Love
> EE[8]

Marl Bank was not a cottage but a spacious old house with two acres of garden.
Carice came up in late November to move him in. It was a huge task this time, for
the house had to be completely furnished for her father, his domestic staff, and
possible guests. She arranged for furniture to be disinterred from nearly a decade of
storage since the closure of Severn House, co-ordinated deliveries, purchased a
thousand and one necessities. Edward moved in on 5 December. Rains were incessant
and flooding widespread.

Marl Bank, Rainbow Hill, Worcester.
11th Decr 1929

My dear W.

I quite hoped that you were happily settled in your new house—I am here
in much tribulation of wind & weather.

Thank you for that glorious cartoon—I have sent for more. The situation
is really serious & one more blow to poor English music

> Love
> Yrs
> EE

Carice sends love.[9]

David Low had published a newspaper cartoon about the proposed new copyright
bill, under which a composer would be allowed to charge only two pence for the right
of performance. The cartoon showed Elgar playing a Salvation Army harmonium
with *Gerontius* on its desk, and Bernard Shaw standing beside him—outraged as an
overfed 'Labour Concert Favourite' chucks tuppence at them while beaming at a
'Cheap Music for the Caledonian Choral Society' gillie who asks: 'For why did ye no
mak' it a penny?' The well publicised opposition of Elgar and Shaw, among many
others, ultimately helped to defeat the bill.

The approaching holidays found Elgar settling into his own house with his dogs.

---

[8] HWRO 705:445:7733. A note of 17 November sends further wishes for her house (HWRO
705:445:7734).

[9] HWRO 705:445:7722.

Marl Bank, Rainbow Hill, Worcester.
21st Decr 1929

My dear W.

Here I am with the 3 lambs: it is very quiet between business noises & I hope the garden will be worth seeing next year. I will make you laugh when I see you & tell you how *everything* went wrong—although, as usual, I took infinite pains two months ago to have everything written down & agreed upon. How the London movers took the stored furniture & my own things from the flat to STRATFORD on the pouringest wet day: how another local van broke into an old well 60 ft deep etc etc.

I do hope you will have a peaceful and happy time during this awful Christmas dismality.

Troyte is coming for the week

I send a card which you will probably *not* like, but it brings my love—or rather a remembrance of it since 1897—thirty-two years accumulation.

Ever
E.E.[10]

The card was probably a recently unearthed survivor of what he had had printed for Christmas 1897 (five years before their acquaintance began), with his carol setting of traditional verses beginning 'Grete Malverne on a rocke, Thou standest surelie . . .'.

# 1930

Marl Bank, Rainbow Hill, Worcester.
6th Jany 1930

My dear W.

I hope you have survived the severities of the holiday season & are quite well.

On the 24th Harty is giving the 2nd Symp. & I am conducting the 1st Sym. at the Phil. on the 30th. —   I wonder if you will go? I have given up the flat & shall be either at the club or Langham.

We have had a fine day at last.

The garden here is 'yielding to treatment' but I have been very quiet. I wish you cd. hear the new Gramophone—it is marvellous & wd be such a joy to you if you wd. only make the plunge

Marco sends love & so does

E

I was thrilled to hear of your *speech*
Forgive funny stationery—I have no time to see to anything[1]

[10] HWRO 705:445:7716.
[1] HWRO 705:445:7704. A note of 13 January 1930 sends thanks for a new diary (HWRO 705:445:7730).

When Edward came up for his Philharmonic concert, she gave him dinner one evening. The programme on 30 January was vigorous: *In the South*, the Violin Concerto with Sammons, and the First Symphony. After conducting the entire concert, he took Carice to a merry supper with Arthur Bliss and his wife. Afterwards Edward wrote to the Windflower:

Worcester
3rd Feb 1930
My dear W.

I am so sorry you did not come to the artists' room: there were some nice folk there including G.B.S.

Thank you for your nice dinner: I am only sorry time was so short—I hope you were happy over your Concerto? It brought back dear old artistic times. I hope to be up again soon & shall report.

Love<br>E.E.[2]

Marl Bank, Rainbow Hill, Worcester.
12th Feby. 1930
My dear W.

Thank you for your letter: I am so glad to hear of you & to know that the house is progressing: when may I see it?

I am in solid trouble—walls (miles) falling down owing to the abnormal quantity of rain etc. & I am (monetarily) a ruined man. The expense is frightful & unlooked for.

However things in the garden are beginning to bud.

Love<br>E[3]

The fallen wall had stood at the top of a steep bank of garden above the main road. It was only finally put right two years later when Edward bought balustrades from the old Worcester bridge (then being replaced) and had them set up. Meanwhile the Windflower tried to make light of it.

Marl Bank, Rainbow Hill, Worcester.
13th March 1930
My dear W.

It was a delight to see your letter. I fear you little understand the overwhelming disasters which have overtaken me & they are not amusing!

---

[2] Elgar Birthplace parcel 583(x).       [3] HWRO 705:445:7739.

I hope to be in London next week & shall try to see you—in your new house??

Love

E.[4]

On 21 March he shared a BBC broadcast with Sir Thomas Beecham, and the Windflower was there. She was at last ready to move into Little Cheyne House, round the corner from her old home in Cheyne Walk.

Marl Bank, Rainbow Hill, Worcester.
3rd April 1930
My dear W:

Your namesakes are a little late this year but never forgotten: it was a little ray of sunshine & the most welcome possible to see you in that unsympathetic hall & you looked lovely! It was so good of you.

I hope your house is really inhabited now & that the Spring is with you & making everything divine again

Love

EE[5]

Still worried over money, he thought of selling the manuscript full scores of his major works—and actually had them all sent down from his old publisher Novello, who had kept them in store ever since Severn House was closed.

Marl Bank, Rainbow Hill, Worcester.
14th May 1930
My dear Windflower:

Your letter of *19th March* sent to the Langham Hotel arrived here *this* morng; I stay at the Club [Brooks's] when they can take me in. I am so sorry you have no acknowledgement before this. You will be really in your new house by this time and I shall call in state soon

I want to 'sell' my original full scores: do you think Molly (Northcliffe) Hudson would have one?

If you will tell me where you are I shall be proud indeed to send some flowers from '*my own*' garden. I have a bed of 2000 red tulips out now etc etc. I am a gardener.

Love

EE

*P.S. Last year for instance the copyright of *The Dream* had to be renewed in U.S.A., & it was seriously questioned if it was worth while to pay the fee— two dollars—; I said I suppose *Gerontius* is merely wastepaper & the official

[4] HWRO 705:445:7746.     [5] HWRO 705:445:7743.

answer was *'yes'*;—but I risked the two dollars which I [*illegible*] my heirs will ever see again. Such things are really humourous.[6]

Relations with his old publisher Novello were loosening. He was now in fact writing a little music again for other firms, including two new ones. During the spring of 1930 a *Severn Suite* appeared for brass band, and a new *Pomp and Circumstance March*. But the surviving Windflower correspondence touches none of this revival (which was to culminate in 1932–3 in projects for a third symphony and an opera).

The beginning of August found him recently returned from a holiday in the north, and the Windflower just going to one.

Worcester
6th August 1930
My dear W.

Thank you for your letter, I *do* hope you will have a good rest in Yorks—& that the weather will be kind.

I 'called' at Perth a week ago & thought of you: I went in the car to Inverness just with my manservant [Richard Mountford]—Scotland is lovely—& so are you

Ever
EE[7]

That autumn he had repeated attacks of what was diagnosed as sciatica or lumbago. On 2 October he was just able to conduct the Second Symphony at Queen's Hall. The Windflower and her daughter were there, but he did not realize it.

Marl Bank, Rainbow Hill, Worcester.
7th Oct 1930
My dear W.

My lumbago has been a great trial: I just managed to crawl to London & 'did' the Symphy: back here on Friday & now again laid low. I do not suppose you got to the Q's Hall: the Sym: went well but I saw no one except *G.B.S.*

My love & good wishes

Yrs ever
EE.[8]

From this point onward for many months the surviving correspondence thins almost to a vanishing point.

[6] HWRO 705:445:7719. The *Gerontius* copyright for the United States had been renewed in the winter of 1928–9 (see *Elgar and his Publishers*, p. 859). The P.S. is on a separate sheet (HWRO 705:445:7714), from which something appears to have been cut away at the top. The recipient has noted on the verso: '14th May.1930.' A note of Friday [30 May] regrets not meeting in London (HWRO 705:445:7729).

[7] HWRO 705:445:7768.

[8] HWRO 705:445:7795.

In early spring he received a letter addressed to him at Judge's Walk, Hampstead. That was the place-name set at the end of *The Music Makers* almost twenty years earlier. The winter of 1930–1 had seen further small composition: but this envelope took his mind back to the days of big works with the Windflower's inspiration at their centre.

Marl Bank, Rainbow Hill, Worcester.
2nd April 1931
My dear Windflower:

I cannot help sending you this envelope:—you remember Judge's Walk?— I put it on one of my compositions & the writer of the (unimportant) letter took it to be my home—well, it was my 'spiritual home' for some years was it not?

There are no flowers to send—it is so bitterly cold. however anemones shall come soon. I hope you are well. I have only a bad report of myself & have a broken tendon so I send no particulars.

> Love
> EE.[1]

A note to Clare Stuart Wortley some weeks later cast further light on his experience in the fourth decade of the twentieth century.

Worcester
18th May 1931
My dear Clare:

Thank you for your letter: there is nothing to be done; human, or shd it be *humane*, feeling in art is dead. In music everything is taken too fast or too slow at the present time: there are psychological reasons (and physiological too) for this—too much to write but worth talking over when we meet

> Yours very sincerely
> Edward Elgar[2]

In the Birthday Honours he was given a baronetcy. Among the flood of telegrams on 3 June came: 'Many warm congratulations    W'.[3] But for much of the summer he was ill: to the sciatica had been added urticaria and food poisoning.[4] He was sufficiently recovered to conduct the BBC Orchestra in the Second Symphony at a Promenade Concert on 1 October. The Windflower was there and sent her thanks.

[1] HWRO 705:445:7732.
[2] Elgar Birthplace.
[3] HWRO 705:445:4890.
[4] 6 July 1931 (HWRO 705:445:7748); 15 July 1931 (HWRO 705:445:7727).

Marl Bank, Rainbow Hill, Worcester.
5th Oct 1931

My dear W.

I was so delighted to receive your letter & glad to know you were at the Concert. I was hoping to call but had an afflicting *cold* & had to fly home on Friday. It is a good orch. & that lot of twelve 'cellos made the thing something like I intended[.] I hope to be up again soon & fit to see—if not people—*you*

I cannot say how happy I am that you liked the performance—the Sym: scarcely sounded 20 years old—oh, that awful first performance.

My love to you both

Ever
Edward[5]

In December he sent holiday greetings.[6] Early in the new year 1932 he thought of her when a prospectus arrived for the Worcester Festival.

Marl Bank, Rainbow Hill, Worcester.
7th January 1932

My dear Windflower:

I hope you are well in all these violent changes of temperature & that Little Cheyne House is treating you well.

Here is the Worcester scheme—Do come—sign this & let us have a nice quiet 'music' once more.

All good wishes, I need not say, for the aging year:

Love
EE.[7]

But she was not well enough to come to the Festival again.

His latest gramophone recording was *Falstaff*. Its publication that spring turned his thoughts again toward her.

Marl Bank, Rainbow Hill, Worcester.
31st May 1932

My dear W.

I shd. have sent some windflowers but they were all washed away except *one*—too ragged (as I am) to send.

Here is the 'notice' of Falstaff. I do wish you had a gramophone—but then I have said this for years & you will not hear one—the real one is my one joy

Ever yours
EE[8]

[5] HWRO 705:445:7715.                    [7] HWRO 705:445:7744.
[6] 21 December 1931 (HWRO 705:445:7724).    [8] HWRO 705:445:7728.

That summer he recorded the Violin Concerto at last—not with Kreisler (who had proved hopeless), but with the sixteen-year-old Yehudi Menuhin. It was the beginning of an association with the Concerto which has lasted to this day. Menuhin's first concert performance of the Concerto, with Elgar conducting the new London Philharmonic Orchestra, took place at the Albert Hall on Sunday afternoon 20 November.[9] Back at Marl Bank Edward sent a card to the Windflower:

Marl Bank, Rainbow Hill, Worcester.
23 NOV 1932

I hope you were at the A. Hall on Sunday: do get a good Gramophone for the winter: the records of the Concerto are wonderful

Yrs ever<br>E.E.[10]

## 1933–1934

The gramophone was now his theme, for he knew the pleasure it could bring to the most sedentary old age.

Marl Bank, Rainbow Hill, Worcester.
6th January 1933
My dear W.

Thank you for the diary which came as a reminder of old days—  I wonder what I shall have to enter in it: a new symphony is promised.

I do sincerely hope you have a gramophone—go to H.M.V. & get the style I have. The records of the Violin Concerto are really satisfying & you wd. find endless 'comfort' & musical joy in the instrument: I have all Brahms Symphonies: all Schumann's, my own two—Mozart & Haydn beside numberless things 'Siegfried Idyll' etc., etc.

The weather has been unseasonable but *divine*—I have still rosebuds in the garden & my dogs revel in the warmth: yesterday the sun was really too hot!

My love to Clare & to you with all good wishes to you both

Ever yrs sncly<br>Edward[1]

[9] Saturday [19 Nov. 1932] (HWRO 705:445:7712).
[10] HWRO 705:445:7737.
[1] HWRO 705:445:7788.

Marl Bank, Worcester.
17th January 1933
My dear W.

Your letter finds me in snow & the rosebuds gone at last.

The serious thing in my mind is your Gramophone: please go to the *H.M.V.* place in Oxford-st. I am writing to the Manager who wd. arrange to shew you everything: you ought to have the *electrically driven* instrument—if you go they wd play you some of the Violin Concerto, 'In the South'—the two Syms: & anything else: the expense will not alarm you—the money will be amply repaid by hours & days of delight. I have just heard the 'Siegfried Idyll'—in the distance most moving & beautiful.

> Love
> EE[2]

And he wrote that day to Fred Gaisberg, who supervised his recordings, asking whether special arrangements might be made at the showroom if she could be persuaded to visit: 'Lady Stuart is an old friend; an elderly lady & does not understand the gramophone: I am anxious that she shall be "converted" by hearing the instrument under the best conditions'.[3] Gaisberg responded with the suggestion that it might even be possible to arrange a demonstration at Little Cheyne House. But no news of any result reached Marl Bank.

On 25 April Edward had terrible sciatic pain, and the doctor was sent for three times in the evening. By midnight he was easier, but was too shaken to go to London for a Musicians' Company dinner with Bruno Walter the following night.

Marl Bank, Worcester.
27th April 1933
My dear W.

I hope you are well & have enjoyed the marvellous Spring weather—there has never been anything quite so sunny & wonderful. I have been rather a trial for a few days & could not travel to London for Bruno Walter's dinner; this was a great deprivation. I also must miss the R.A. annual dinner. I do not 'live' much in London during my very short visits since dearest Norman [Forbes]'s death [in 1932].

I wonder if you ever heard the gramophone?—it is my one joy: to-day I have a wonderful record of Handel's 'Ombra mai fu' sung by Gigli.

I could not get out to gather Windflowers and now they are over—I believe my sister sent some: she can grow them in her garden & I cannot, alas!

Let me hear that you are well

> Yours ever sincly
> Edward Elgar[4]

---

[2] HWRO 705:445:7713. The recording of the *Siegfried Idyll* was conducted by Siegfried Wagner, whose birth in 1869 it celebrated.

[3] See *Elgar on Record*, pp. 189–91.

[4] HWRO 705:445:7785.

That is the last known letter to survive from this rich correspondence over three decades which saw Elgar's greatest triumphs and his greatest griefs. He was well enough to fly to Paris to conduct the Concerto again for Yehudi Menuhin at the end of May; to conduct the Second Symphony once more at a Promenade Concert on 17 August; to conduct *Gerontius* and *The Kingdom* at the Hereford Festival in September.

A month later the 'sciatica' forced him to re-enter the nursing home where he had stayed for the operation in the winter of 1925–6. But the diagnosis now was cancer, and the most that could be done was a small easing operation. His heart was strong, and the ups and downs of illness were reported to Lady Stuart by Carice and Pollie Grafton:

[Carice, 6 Dec. 1933.] He still suffers from his sciatica but it is not so acute—& he is dictating letters & being read to & even reading a little again—& is more nearly sitting up than he has ever been—   They even talk of getting him home later—provided of course he goes on as he is now & has no further attack.

It has been & is a frightful time . . . He has no idea how ill he was those days—or really anything about the nature of the illness & I do not mean him ever to know—[5]

[Pollie Grafton, 7 Dec.] His two dogs had a peep at him yesterday, so things sound better, if it only continues—I went to see him for a few minutes on Saturday—The girls go most days . . .

[Pollie Grafton, 28 Dec.] Thank you so much for the lovely ham which came quite safely. It is a beauty and was most delicious and useful for our Christmas. . . .

Dear Edwards illness casts quite a gloom over us all, he does not seem to improve much, but is no worse which is a great comfort. They go to see him often for a few minutes—He has such a lot of visitors just to go in and out . . .

[Carice, 1 Jan. 1934.] Thank you so much for your letter & the diary arrived safely. I have not given it to him yet. I must find a way of doing it because he is so alert mentally & wants to know everything & see all letters which are by no means always possible to show him—& he would ask how it came & why didn't I show your letter etc! But I will manage it.

He is wonderfully better—still has the sciatica (so called) but is able to move much better & his mental vigour is astounding—   We are moving him home all being well on Wed. & I hope he will be much happier—we shall have to keep the 2 nurses of course, but . . . I should never have dared to hope a few weeks ago that he would be coming home—

[Carice, 8 Feb.] I am sorry to say Father has been going downhill the last 3 weeks very much—& last night he had another attack—he is rallying slightly again, but each time it means he is on a lower plane of vitality . . . He has your diary—but I do not think he has ever realised it . . .

[Pollie Grafton, 8 Feb.] I am writing to you, for my heart is broken. Our dearest Edward is oh so ill . . . He sleeps most of the time, then wakes up a bit quite clear for a short time[,] then off to sleep again[.] Some times he knows them and some

---

[5] Elgar Birthplace parcel 572.

times not. I went on Sunday evening to see him and struck a good moment. I sat by the bed quietly, then he woke up and saw me & said 'Well Beak it is nice to see you again' He always called me beak I don't know why; I sat and talked a bit and *held*, and *stroked* his lovely hands, and he was quite sensible who it was . . . I cannot say much more now[.] I am broken down and I am sure you will be. I wish you could see him lying there, for I know you love him.

At last on the morning of 23 February he died. Alice Stuart of Wortley wrote a letter of sympathy to Carice, with perhaps the best of all the hundreds of tributes that came then:

He is our Shakespeare of music, born and died on the soil in the heart and soul of England with his love of his country, its music, and its meaning in his own heart and soul.

# CODA

Elgar's Windflower survived him by less than two years. She died, the last survivor of the circle of friends, on 1 January 1936. Later in that year Pollie Grafton died. In March 1937 Severn House in Hampstead was pulled down to make way for a series of brick villas. Clare Stuart Wortley wrote:

I was there to the last. I went to buy the panelling for Carice. I *saw* his, Elgar's, studio being demolished. Alas!

After her mother's death Clare moved to Windsor, where she lived until her own early death in January 1945.

Carice and the Grafton nieces and nephews were her contemporaries. Clare Grafton died in 1942, and the others lived varied quiet lives until May died in 1963, Carice in 1970, and Madge in 1972. These three I knew well, and was privileged to listen to their vivid accounts of some events here chronicled.

# Index

(A page-number in brackets indicates an implied reference)